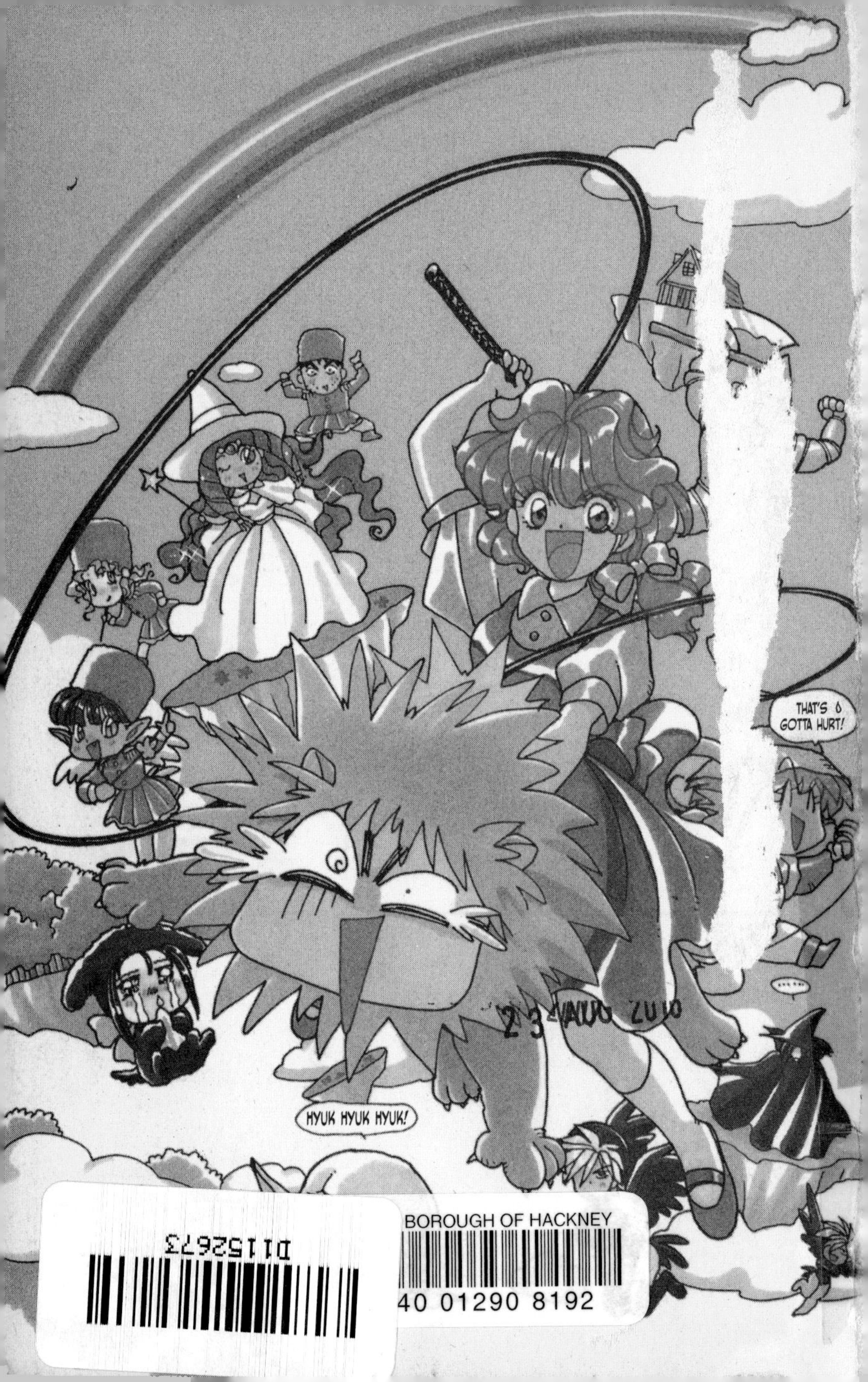
THAT'S 0 GOTTA HURT!
...
HYUK HYUK HYUK!

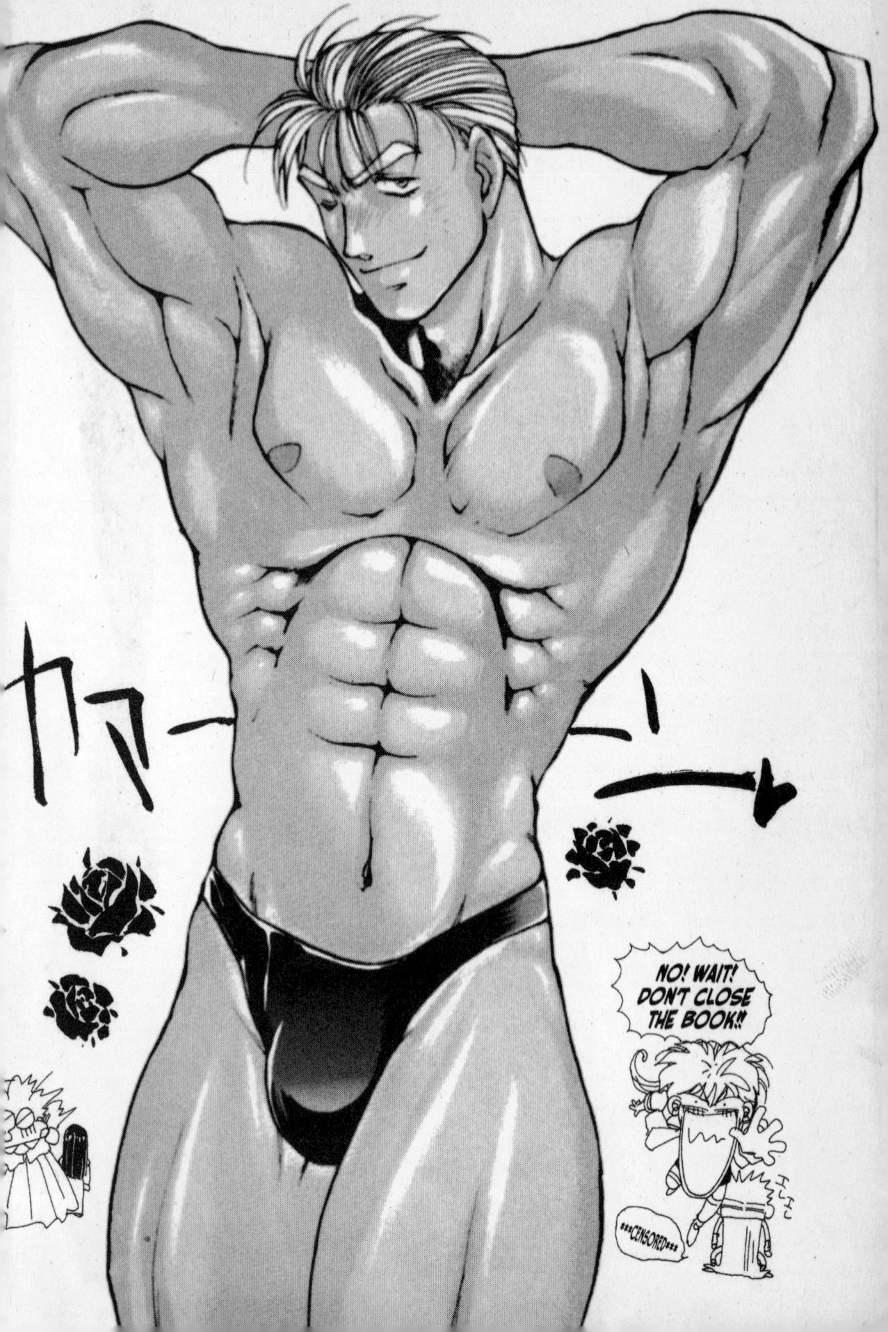
カァー
NO! WAIT! DON'T CLOSE THE BOOK!!
CENSORED

SORCERER HUNTERS™

BOOK 4

BY SATORU AKAHORI
& RAY OMISHI

HAMBURG // LONDON // LOS ANGELES // TOKYO

Sorcerer Hunters Vol. 4
Story by Satoru Akahori
Art by Ray Omishi

Translation - Anita Sengupta
Copy Editor - Peter Ahlstrom
Retouch and Lettering - Rafael Najarian
Production Artist - Jason Milligan
Cover Design - Jorge Negrete

Editor - Troy Lewter
Digital Imaging Manager - Chris Buford
Production Managers - Jennifer Miller and Mutsumi Miyazaki
Managing Editor - Lindsey Johnston
VP of Production - Ron Klamert
Publisher and E.I.C. - Mike Kiley
President and C.O.O. - John Parker
C.E.O. - Stuart Levy

A  Manga

TOKYOPOP Inc.
5900 Wilshire Blvd. Suite 2000
Los Angeles, CA 90036

E-mail: info@TOKYOPOP.com
Come visit us online at www.TOKYOPOP.com

ISBN: 1-59532-497-6

First TOKYOPOP® printing: October 2005
10 9 8 7 6 5 4 3 2 1
Printed in the USA

OUR STORY SO FAR:

Far, far away in the land of Spoolner, terrible, cruel Sorcerers enslave defenseless Parsoners with their evil enchantments, and only one man can end the darkness! Well, actually, there are three men and two women. And those five are kinda helped by a goddess, her magical knights, and past generations of warriors. But still, you get the point--the odds are against justice in this wicked wizard world, where spirit-stealing spellcasters and nefarious necromancers are out to oppress the innocent.

In our previous installment, the Sorcerer Hunters defeated the evil Necromancer thanks to Carrot's "animal magnetism" (in short, he went all snarling beastie on 'im). The Hunters then met a girl that was the spitting image of Carrot (sans the boobs, of course) and foiled the plans of her magic mirror-wielding stalker and his lapdog spawn of hell. The hunters also shut down a corrupt casino and their deadly death matches, as well as solved the mystery of the Snow Queen with the help of that rascally rich kid, Count Potato Chip! It all culminated in a wacky series of bedroom misadventures that placed the Hunters in the bed of the person they least suspected...

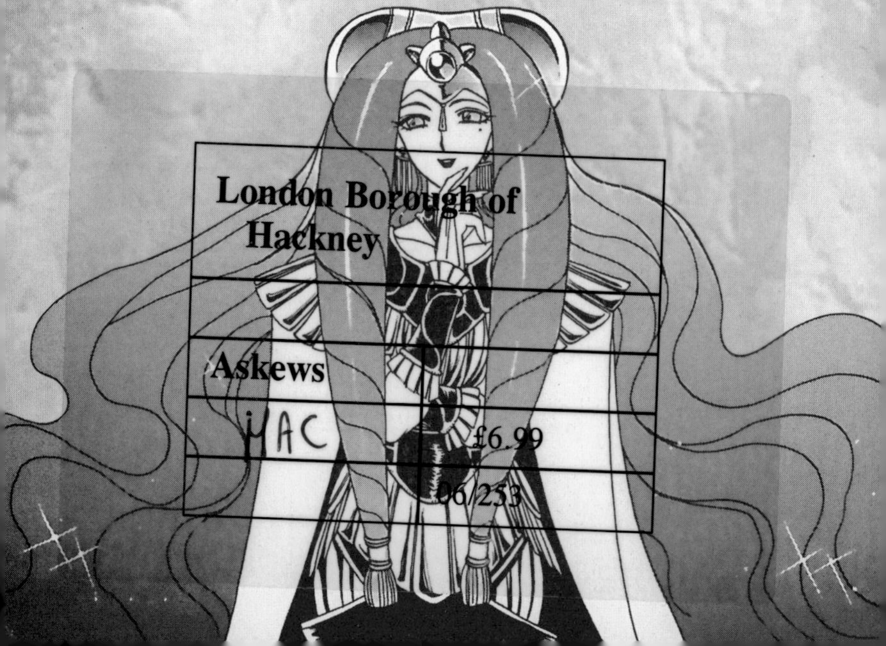

CONTENTS

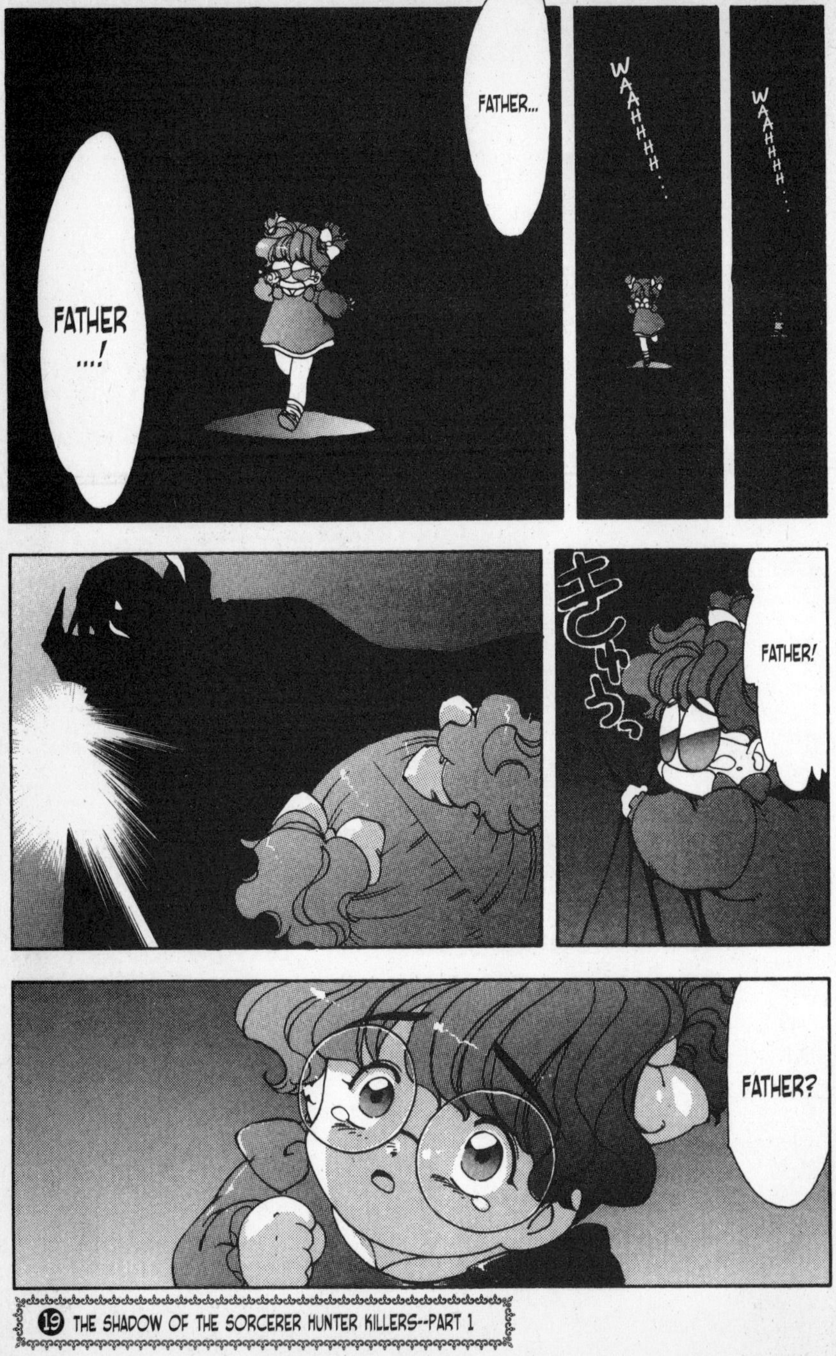
WAAHHHH...
WAAHHHH...
FATHER...
FATHER ...!
きゅっ
FATHER!
FATHER?

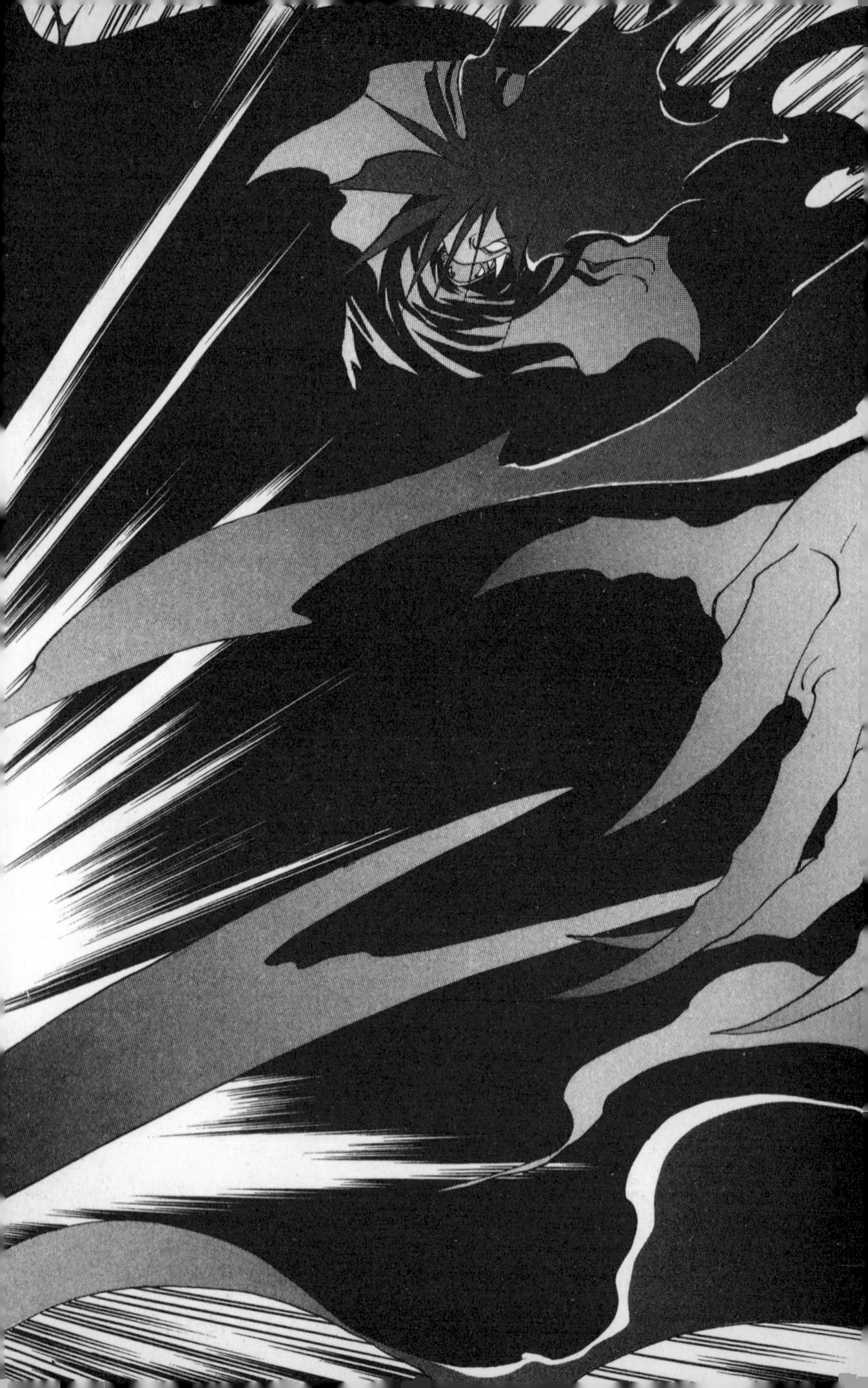

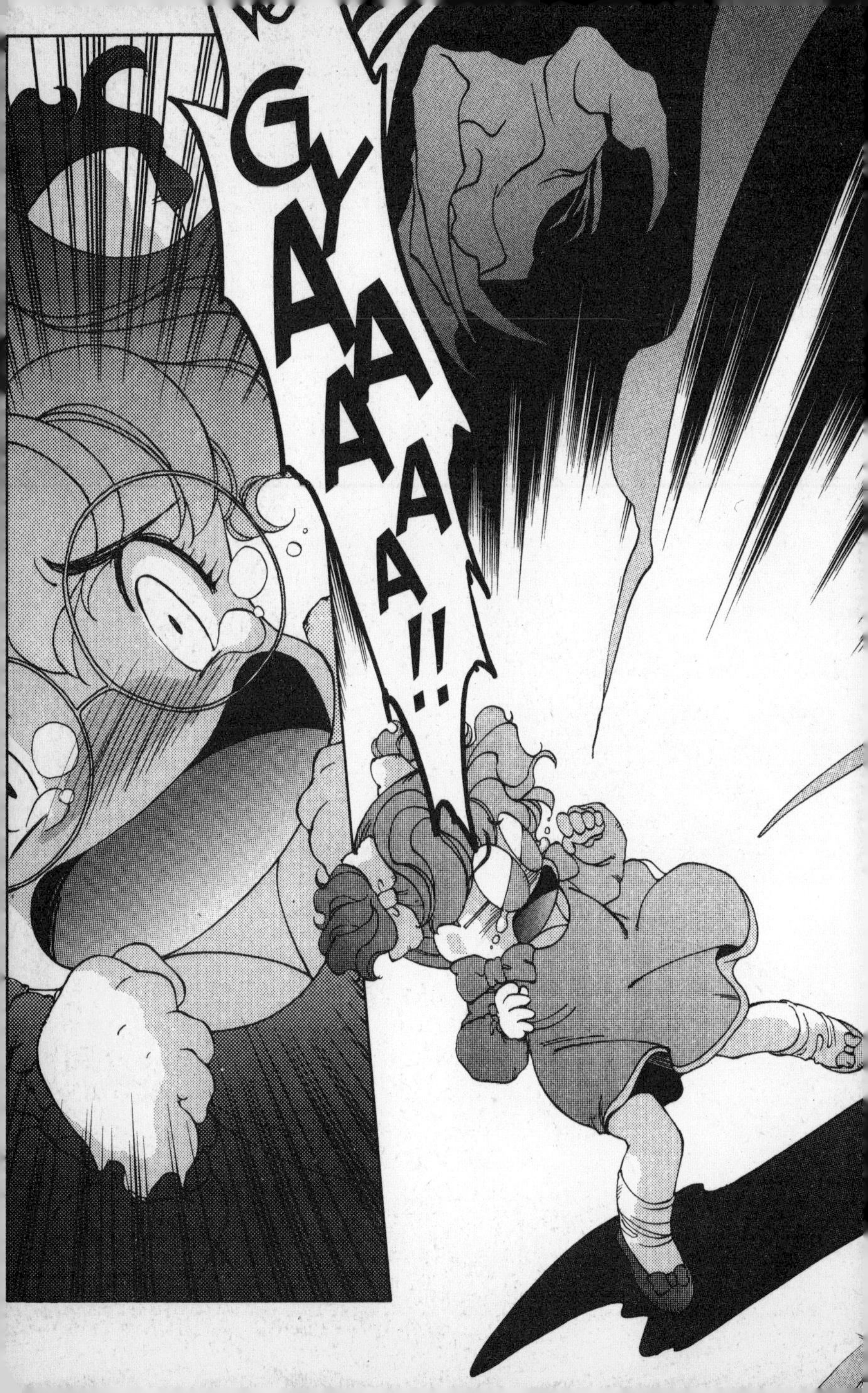
GYAAAAAA!!

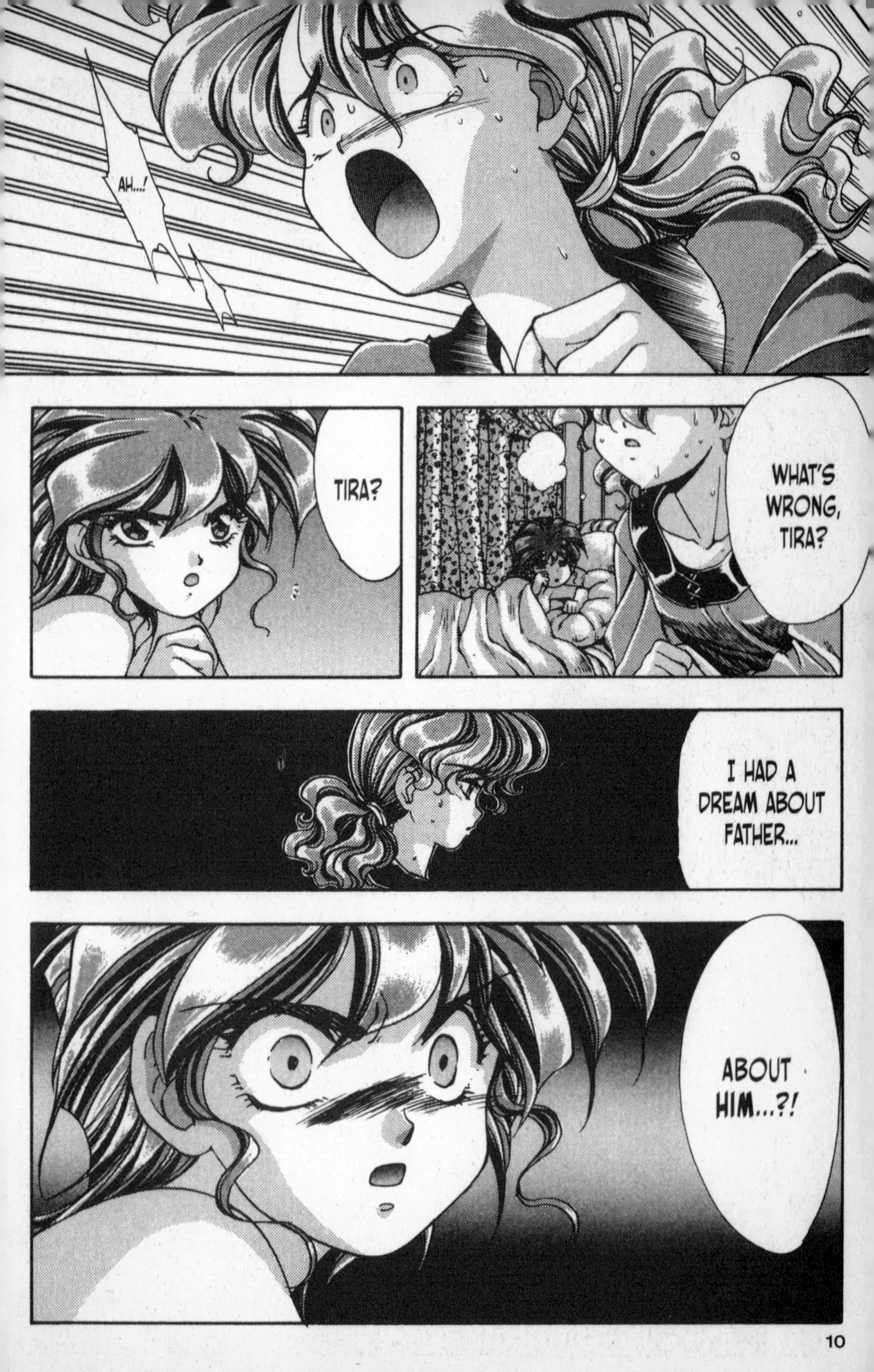
AH...!
WHAT'S WRONG, TIRA?
TIRA?
I HAD A DREAM ABOUT FATHER...
ABOUT HIM...?!

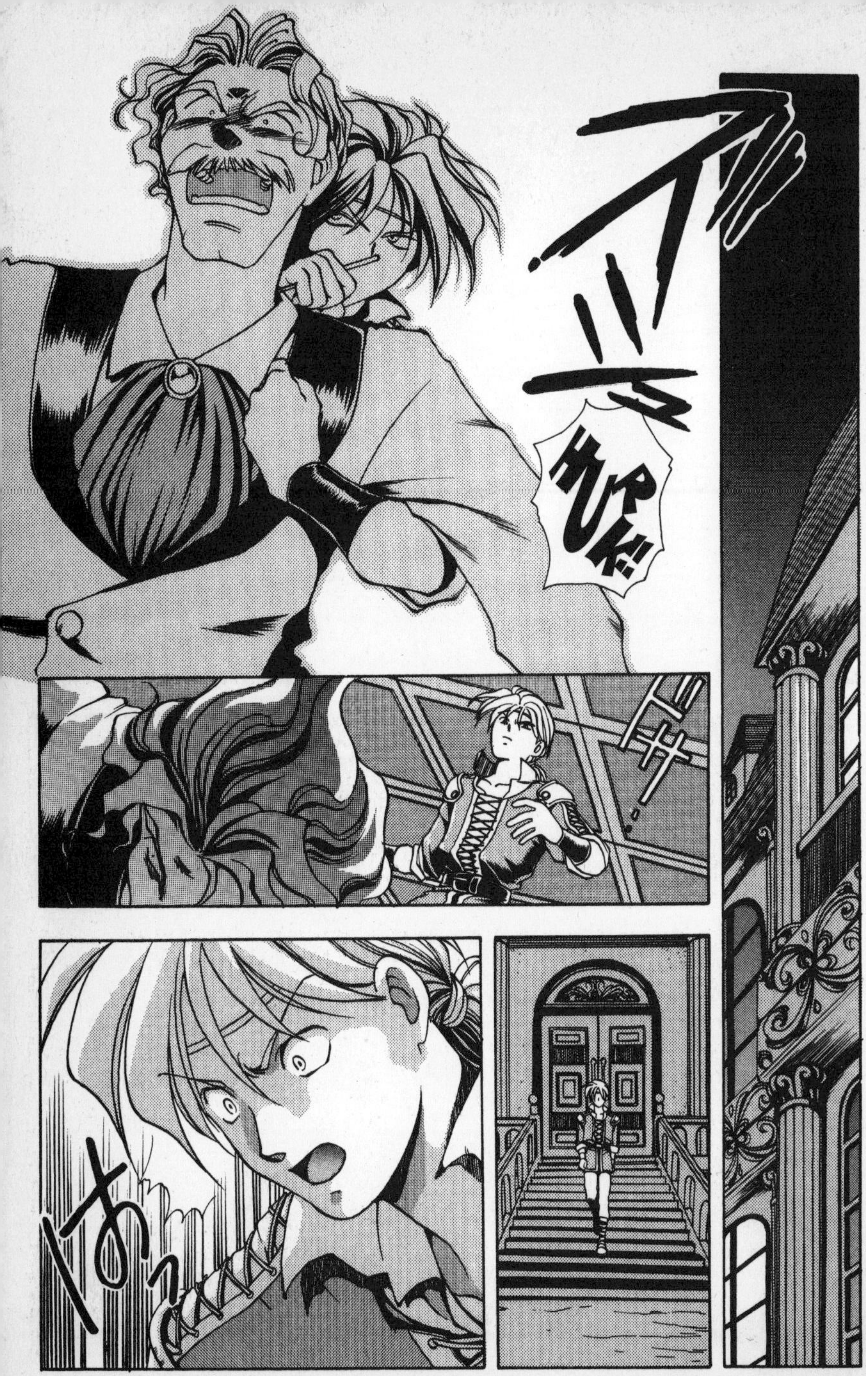
HURK!!

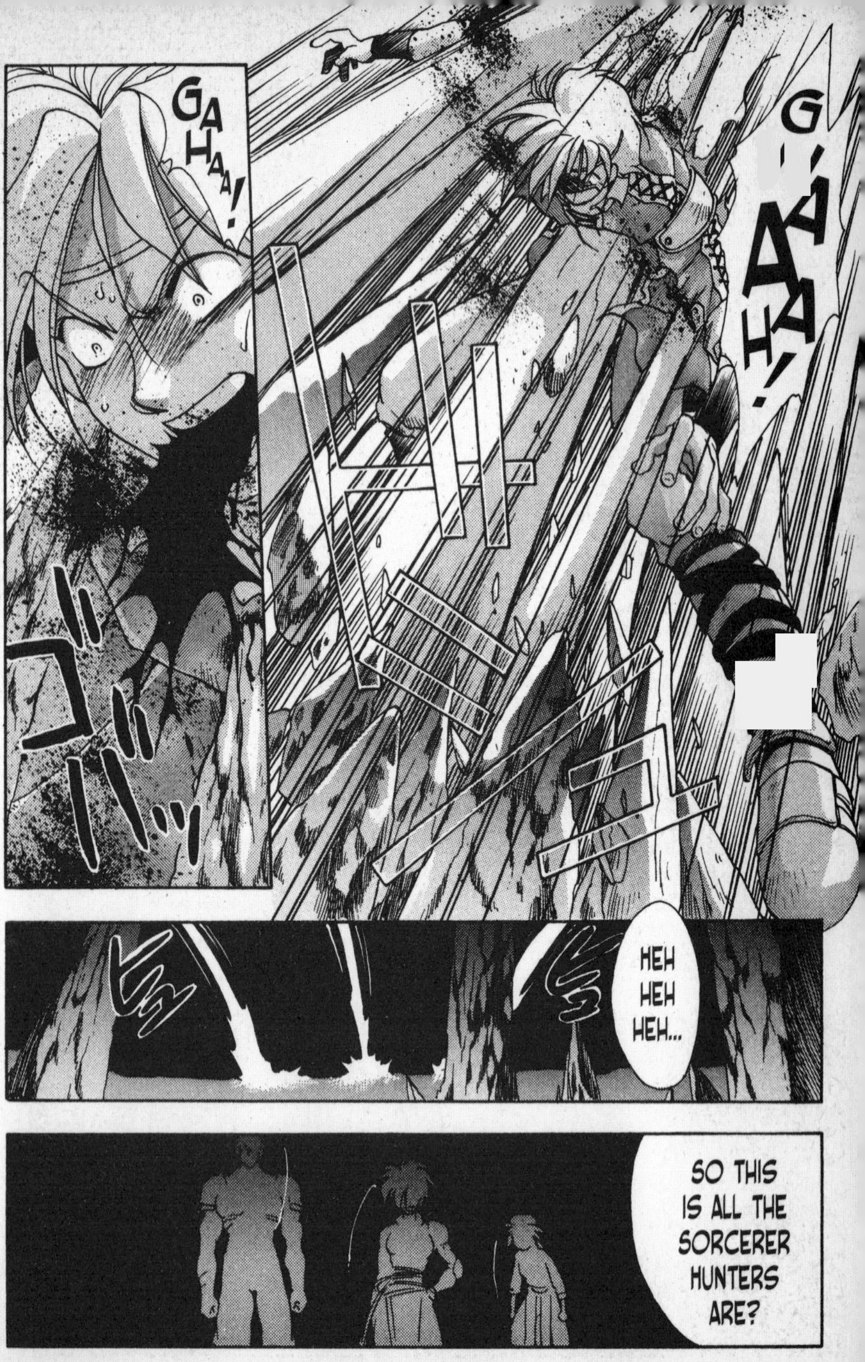
GAAAH!
GA HAA!
HEH HEH HEH...
SO THIS IS ALL THE SORCERER HUNTERS ARE?

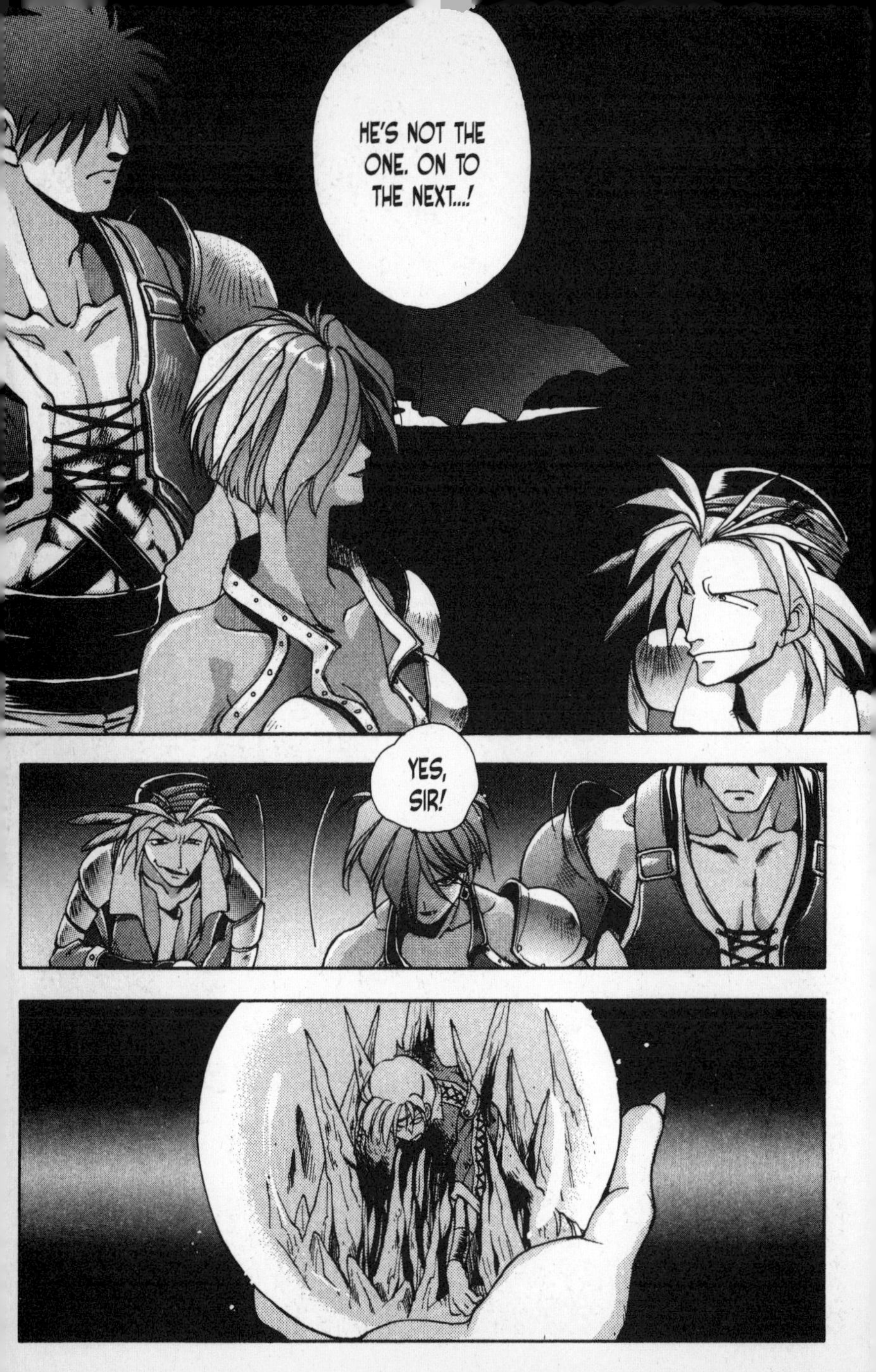
HE'S NOT THE ONE. ON TO THE NEXT...!
YES, SIR!

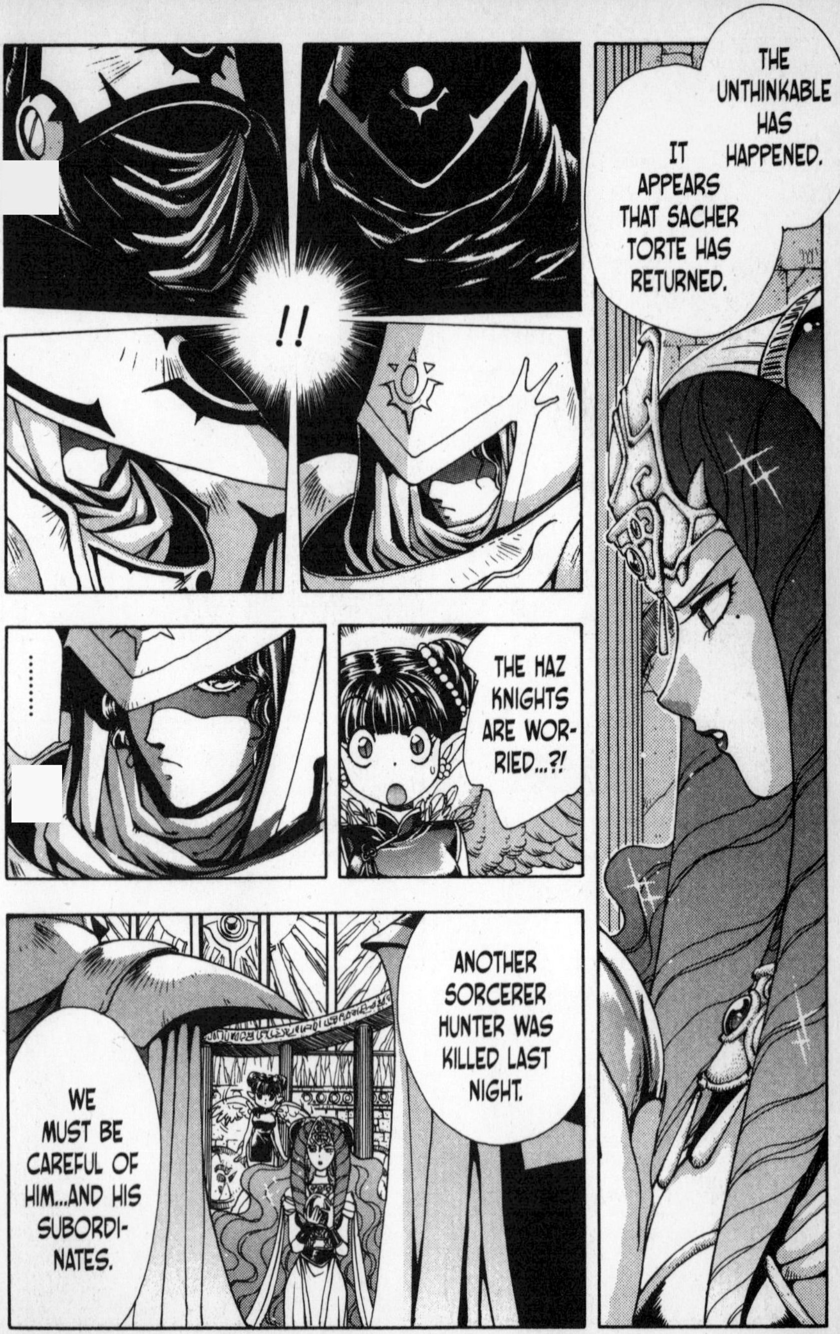
THE UNTHINKABLE HAS HAPPENED.
IT APPEARS THAT SACHER TORTE HAS RETURNED.
!!
THE HAZ KNIGHTS ARE WOR-RIED...?!
......
ANOTHER SORCERER HUNTER WAS KILLED LAST NIGHT.
WE MUST BE CAREFUL OF HIM...AND HIS SUBORDI-NATES.

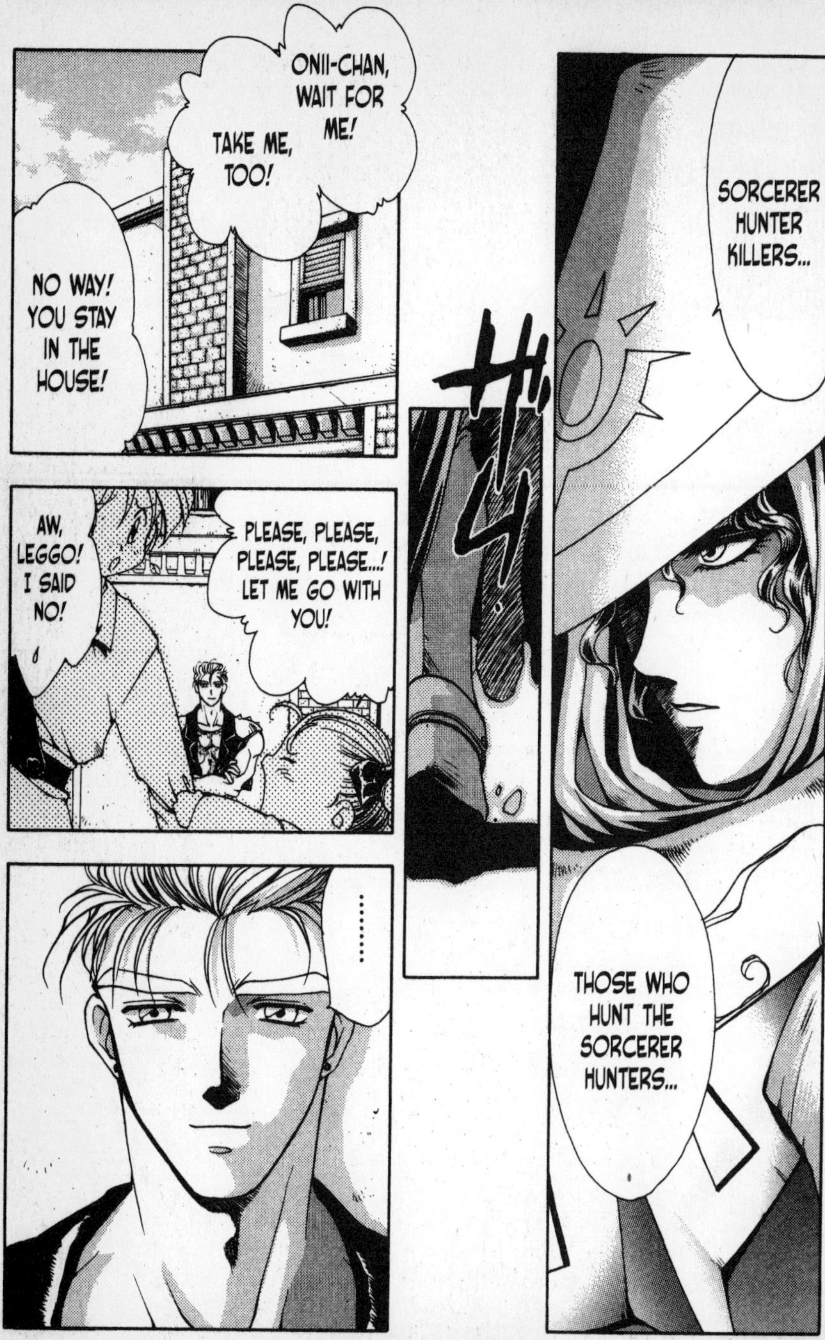
SORCERER HUNTER KILLERS...
THOSE WHO HUNT THE SORCERER HUNTERS...
ザッ
ONII-CHAN, WAIT FOR ME!
TAKE ME, TOO!
NO WAY! YOU STAY IN THE HOUSE!
PLEASE, PLEASE, PLEASE, PLEASE...! LET ME GO WITH YOU!
AW, LEGGO! I SAID NO!
......

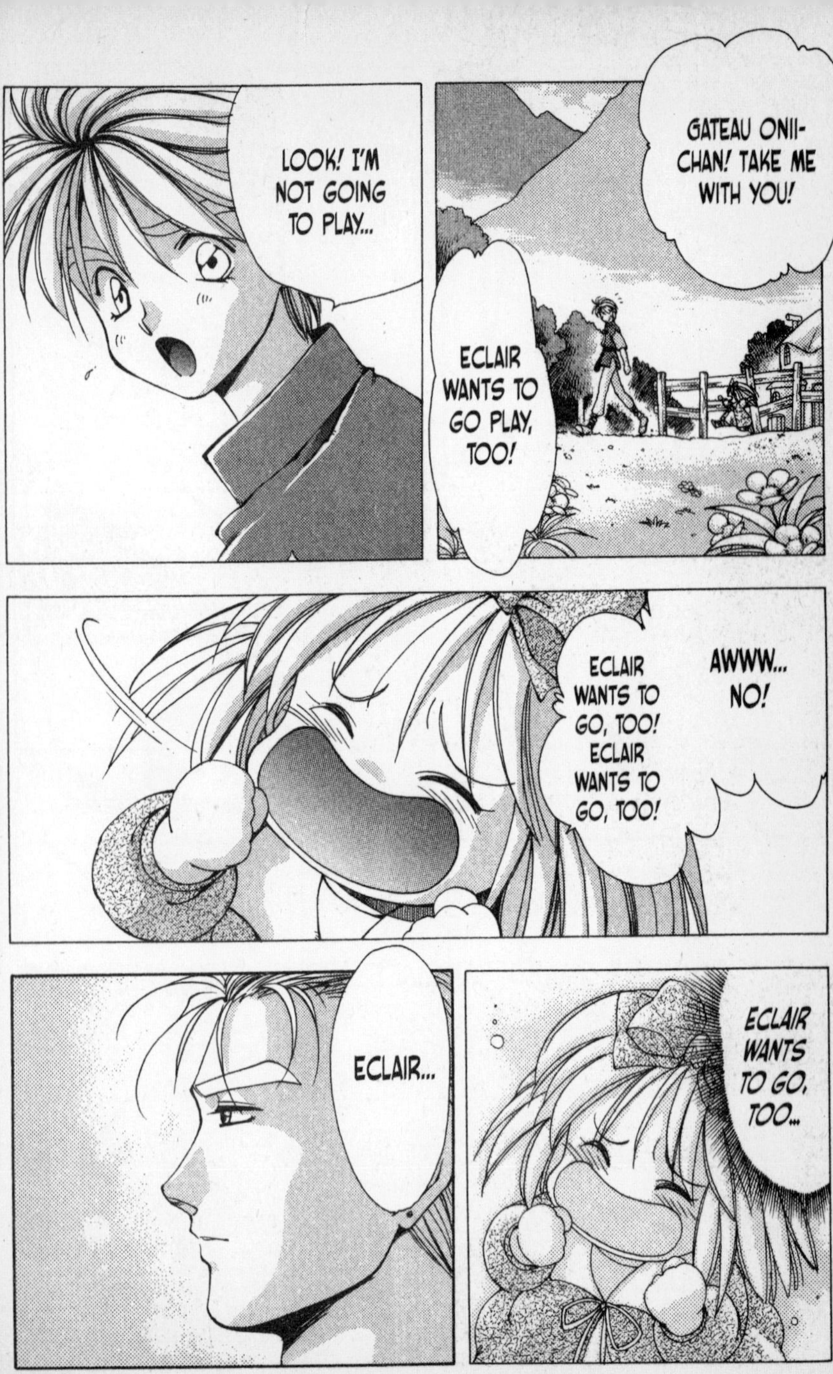
GATEAU ONII-CHAN! TAKE ME WITH YOU!
ECLAIR WANTS TO GO PLAY, TOO!
LOOK! I'M NOT GOING TO PLAY...
AWWW... NO!
ECLAIR WANTS TO GO, TOO! ECLAIR WANTS TO GO, TOO!
ECLAIR WANTS TO GO, TOO...
ECLAIR...

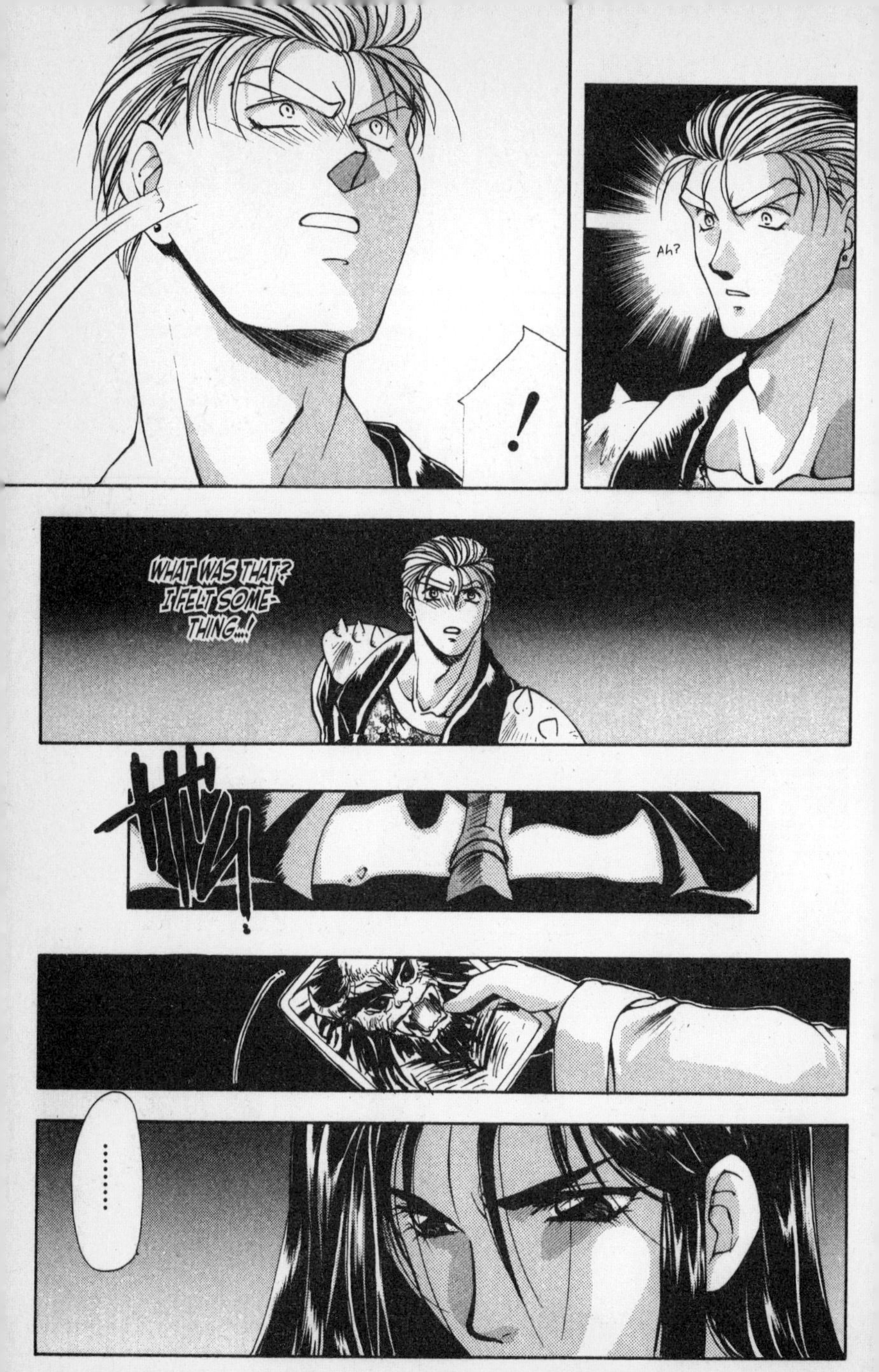
Ah?
!
WHAT WAS THAT? I FELT SOME-THING...!
....

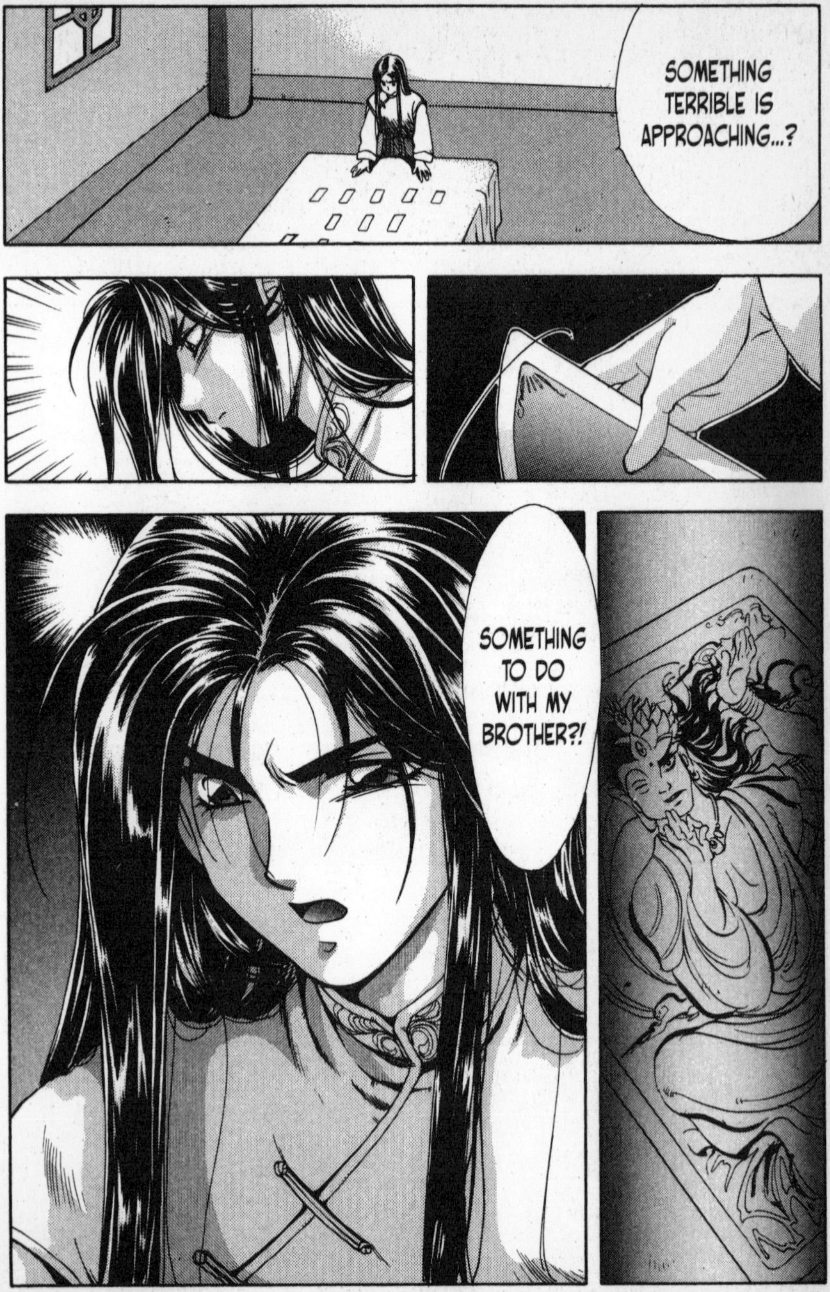
SOMETHING TERRIBLE IS APPROACHING...?
SOMETHING TO DO WITH MY BROTHER?!

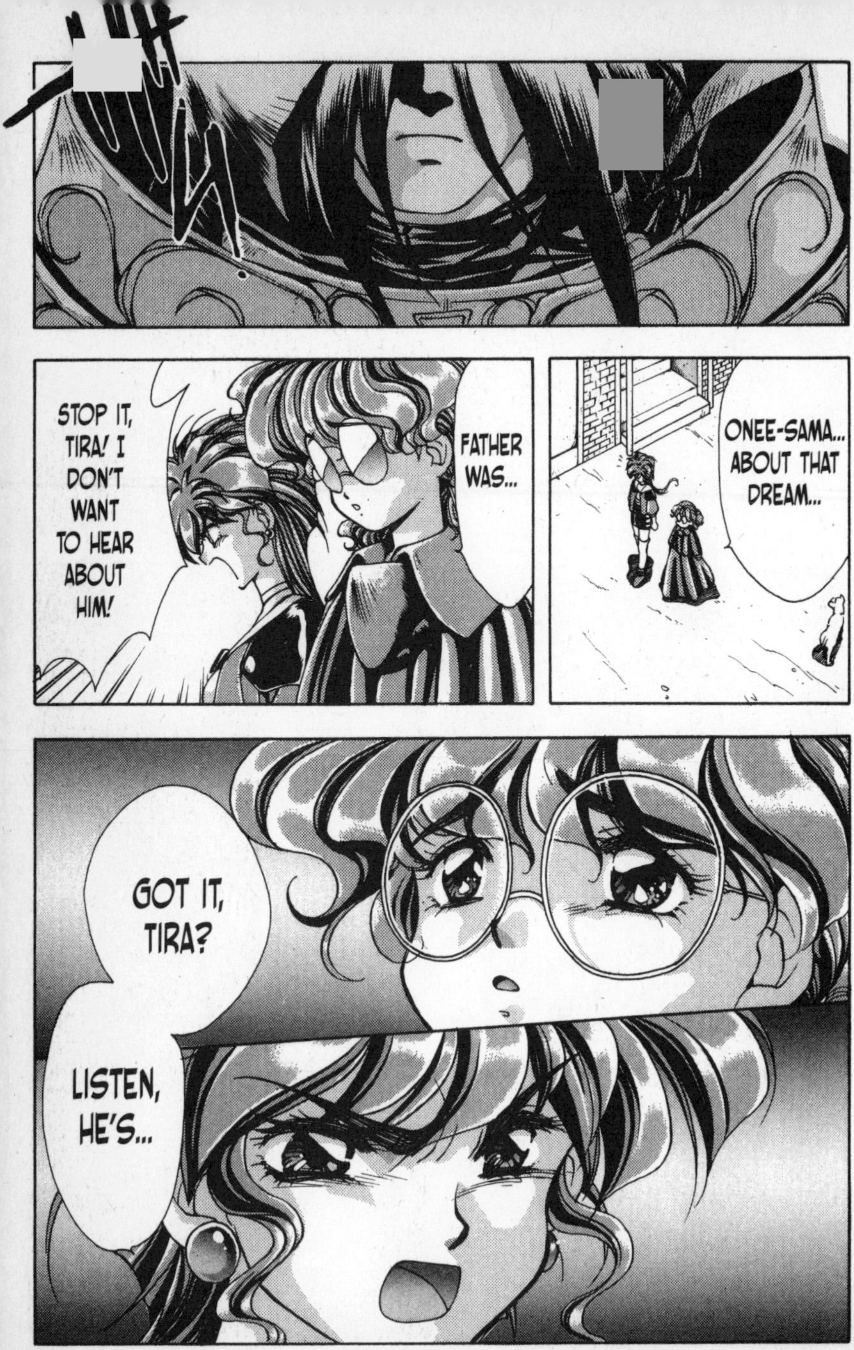
ONEE-SAMA... ABOUT THAT DREAM...
FATHER WAS...
STOP IT, TIRA! I DON'T WANT TO HEAR ABOUT HIM!
GOT IT, TIRA?
LISTEN, HE'S...

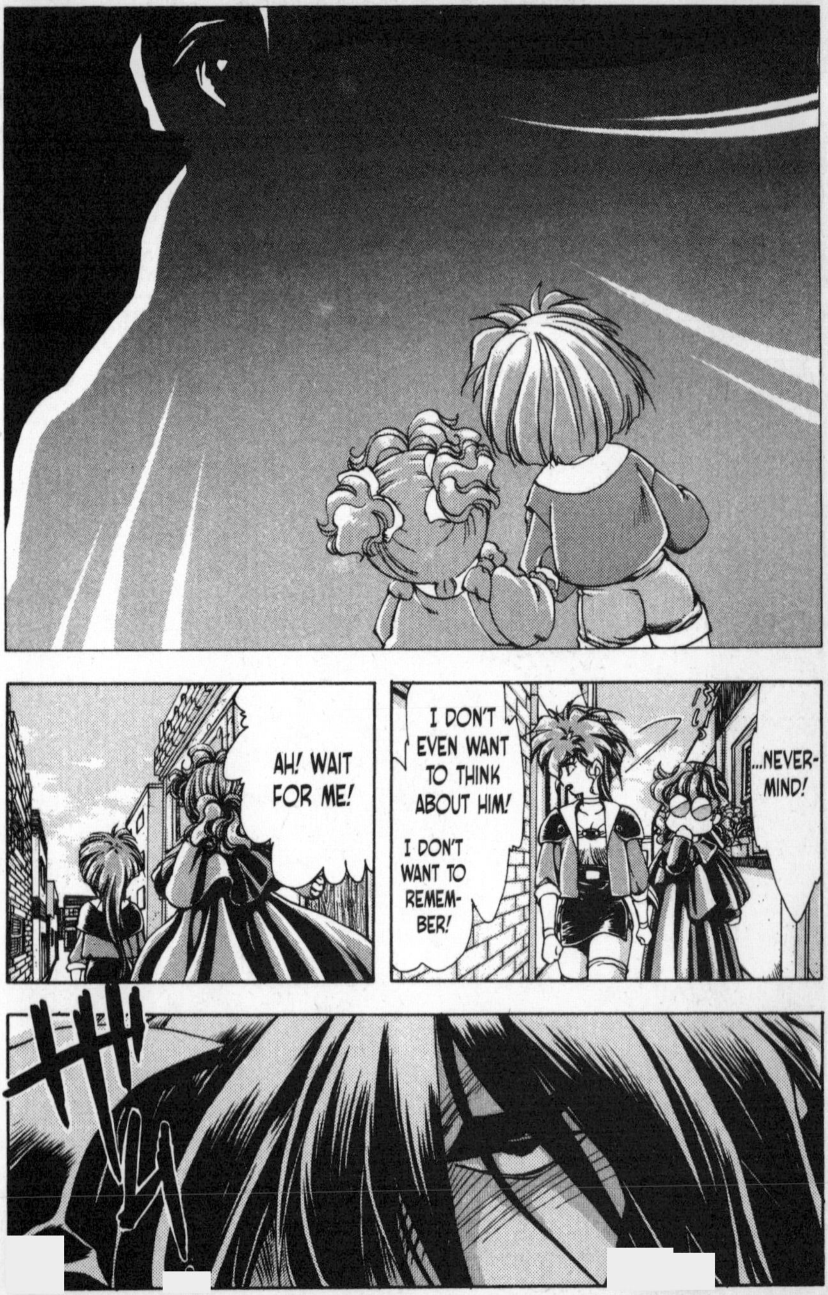
...NEVER-MIND!
I DON'T EVEN WANT TO THINK ABOUT HIM!
I DON'T WANT TO REMEMBER!
AH! WAIT FOR ME!

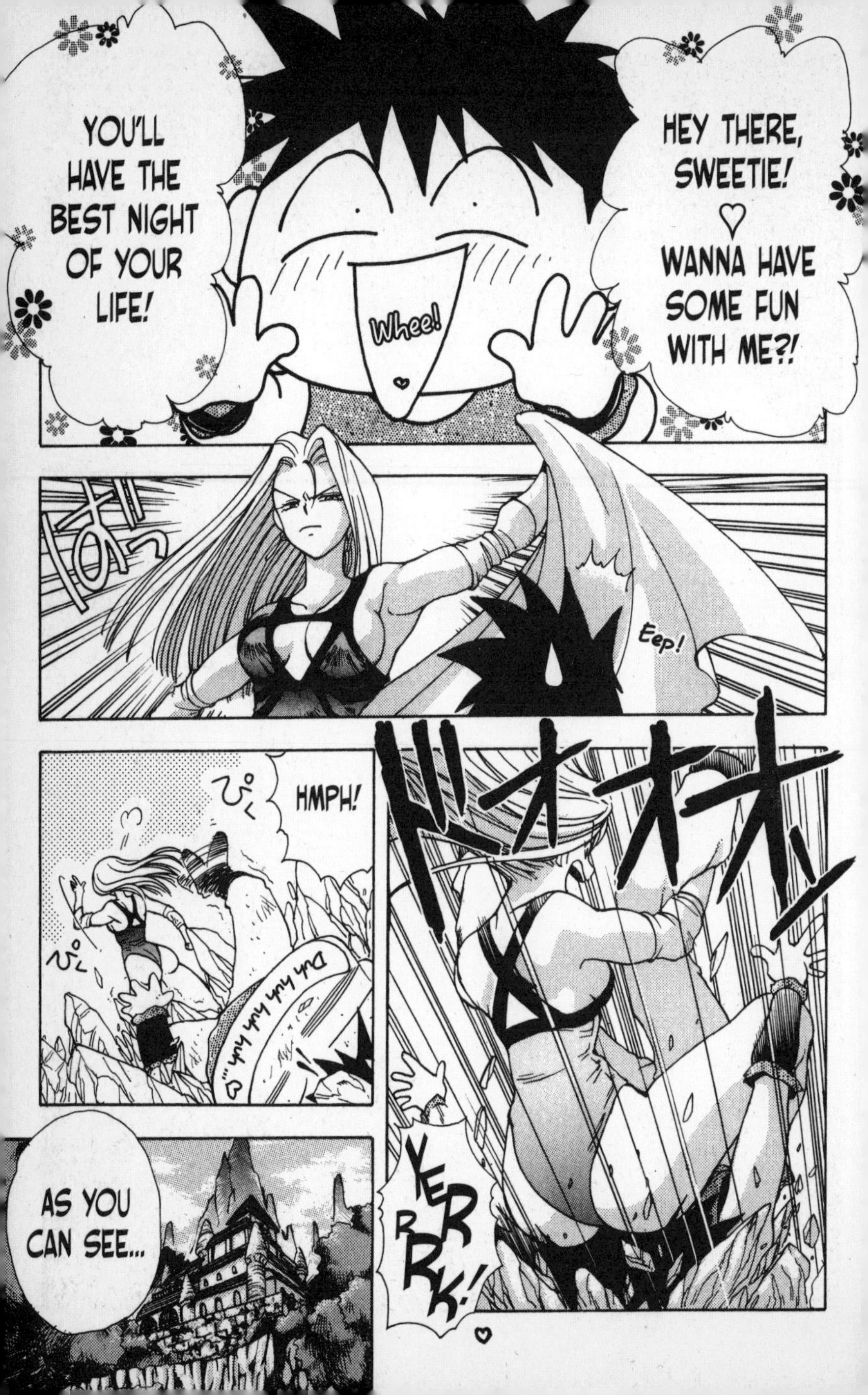
HEY THERE, SWEETIE! ♡ WANNA HAVE SOME FUN WITH ME?!
Whee!
YOU'LL HAVE THE BEST NIGHT OF YOUR LIFE!
Eep!
ドオオオ
YERRRK!
HMPH!
ぴく
ぴく
Duh huh huh huh...♡
AS YOU CAN SEE...

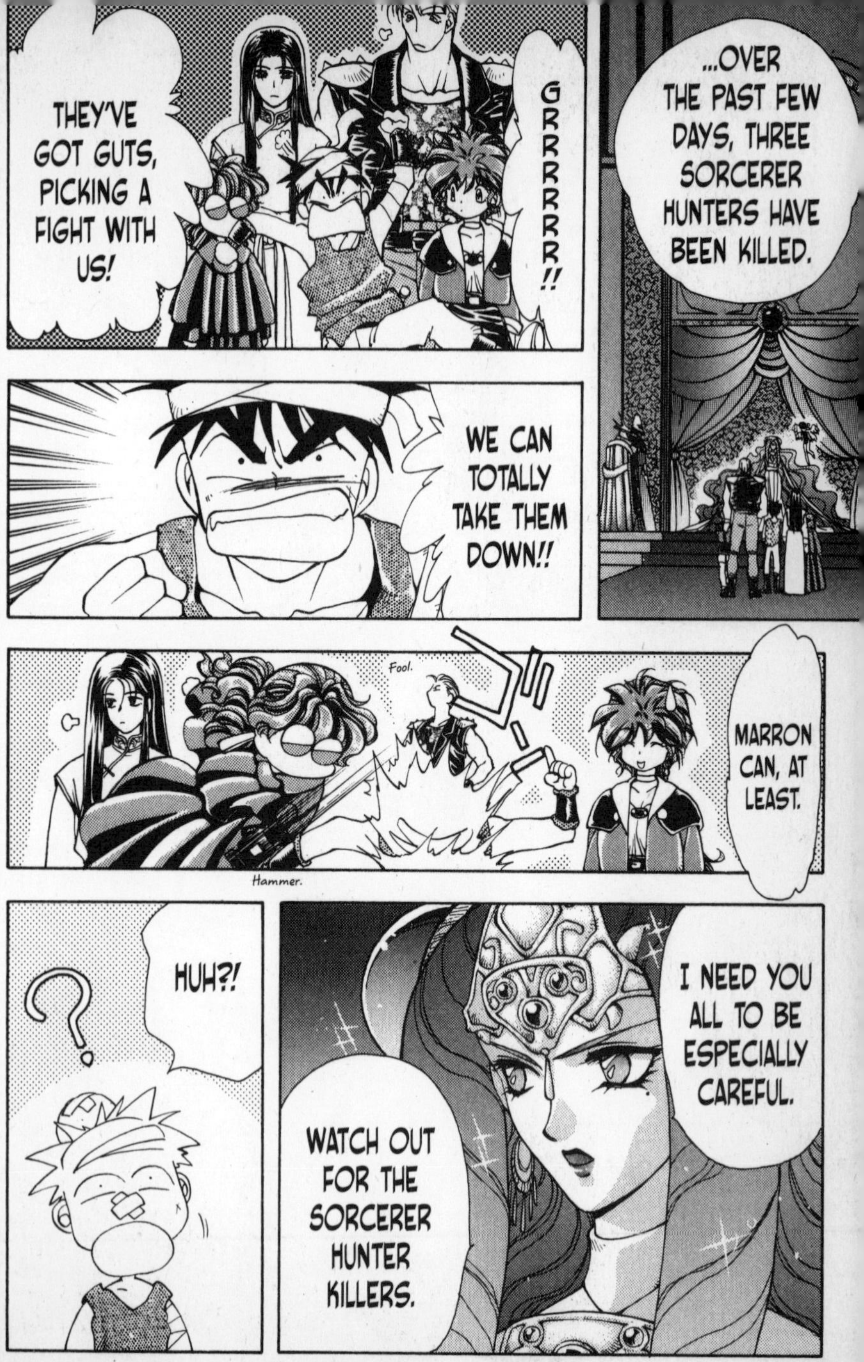
...OVER THE PAST FEW DAYS, THREE SORCERER HUNTERS HAVE BEEN KILLED.
GRRRRRR!!
THEY'VE GOT GUTS, PICKING A FIGHT WITH US!
WE CAN TOTALLY TAKE THEM DOWN!!
MARRON CAN, AT LEAST.
Fool.
Hammer.
I NEED YOU ALL TO BE ESPECIALLY CAREFUL.
WATCH OUT FOR THE SORCERER HUNTER KILLERS.
HUH?!

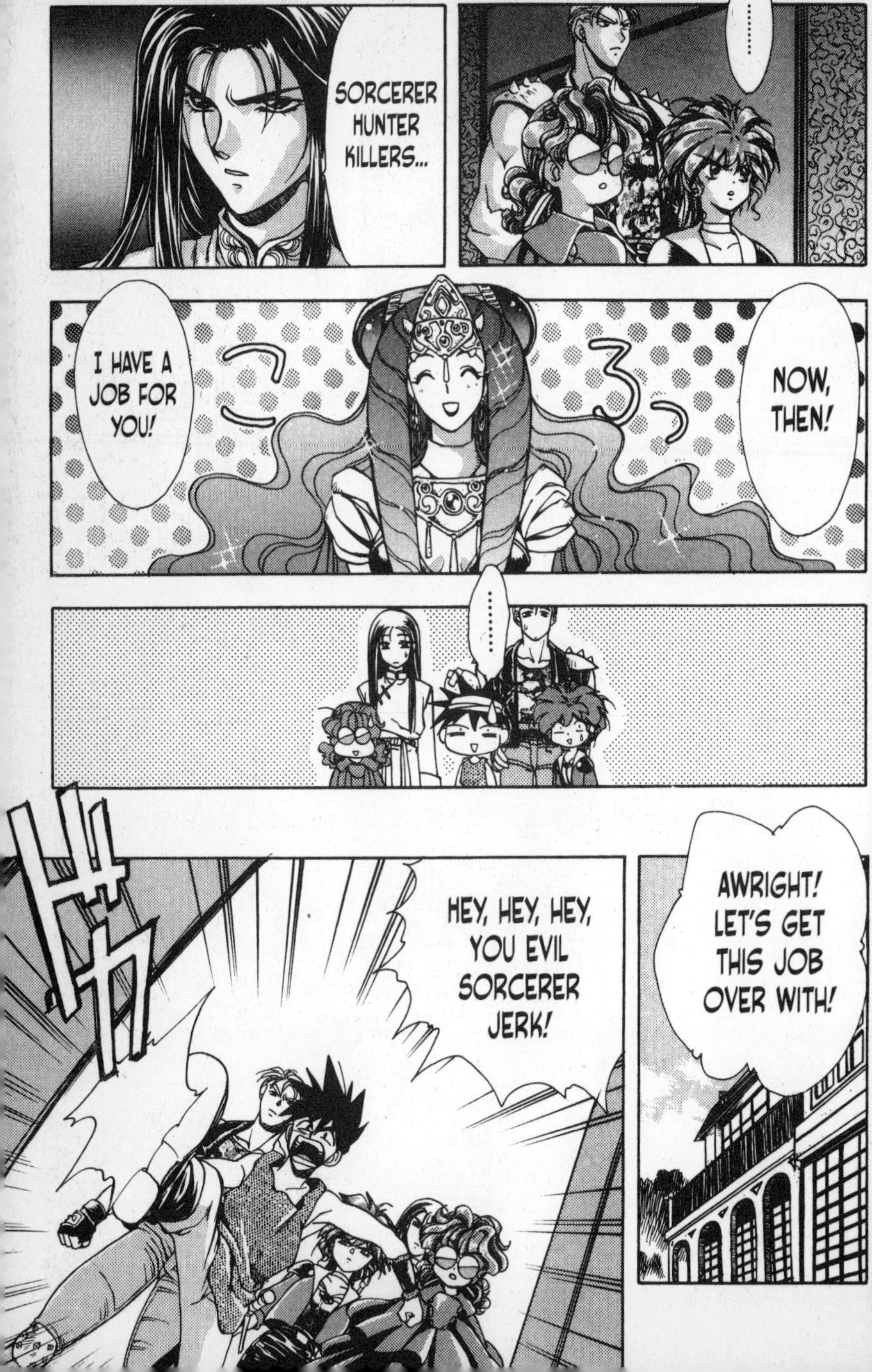
......
SORCERER HUNTER KILLERS...
NOW, THEN!
I HAVE A JOB FOR YOU!
......
AWRIGHT! LET'S GET THIS JOB OVER WITH!
HEY, HEY, HEY, YOU EVIL SORCERER JERK!

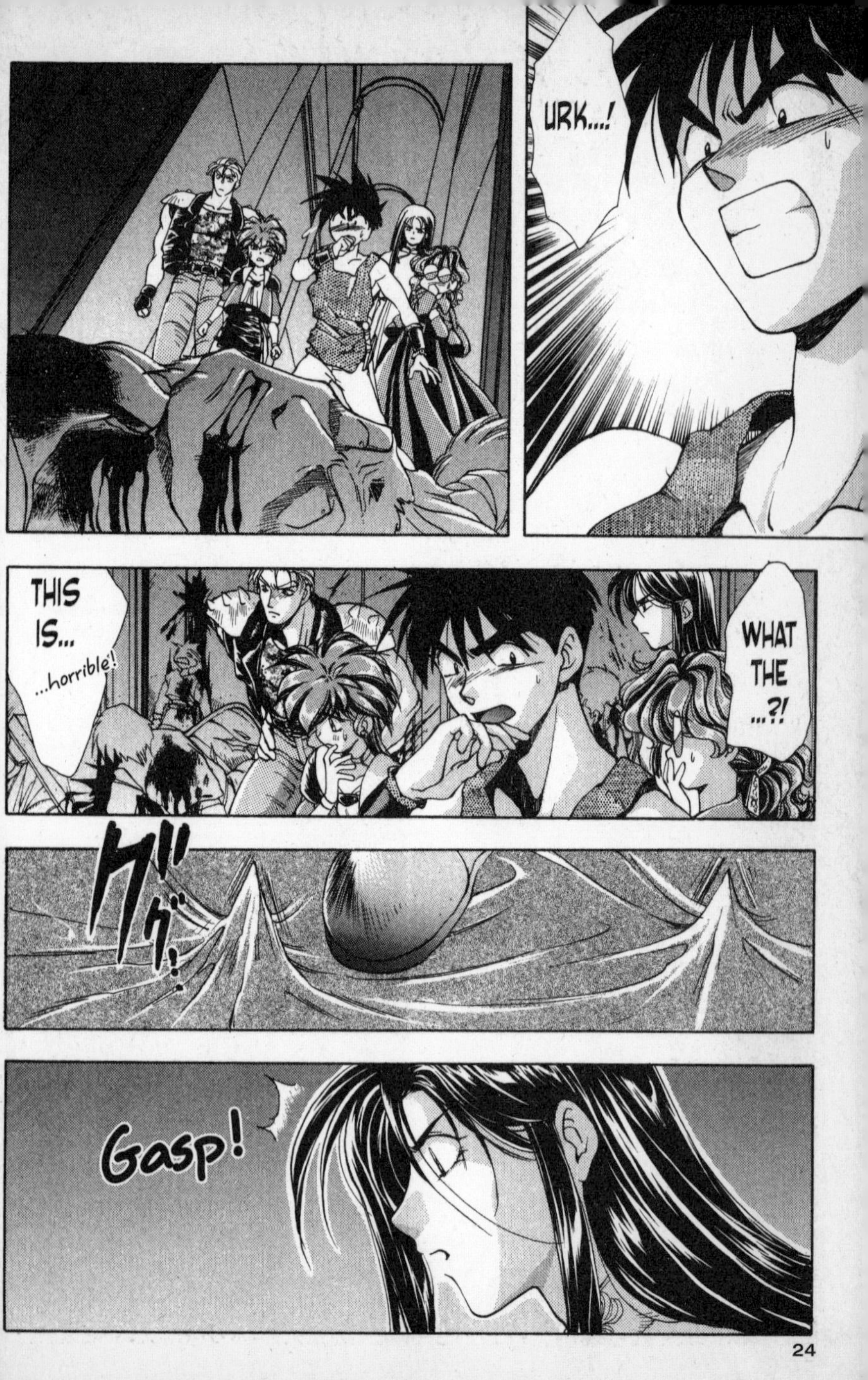
URK...!
WHAT THE ...?!
THIS IS... ...horrible!
ググ!
Gasp!

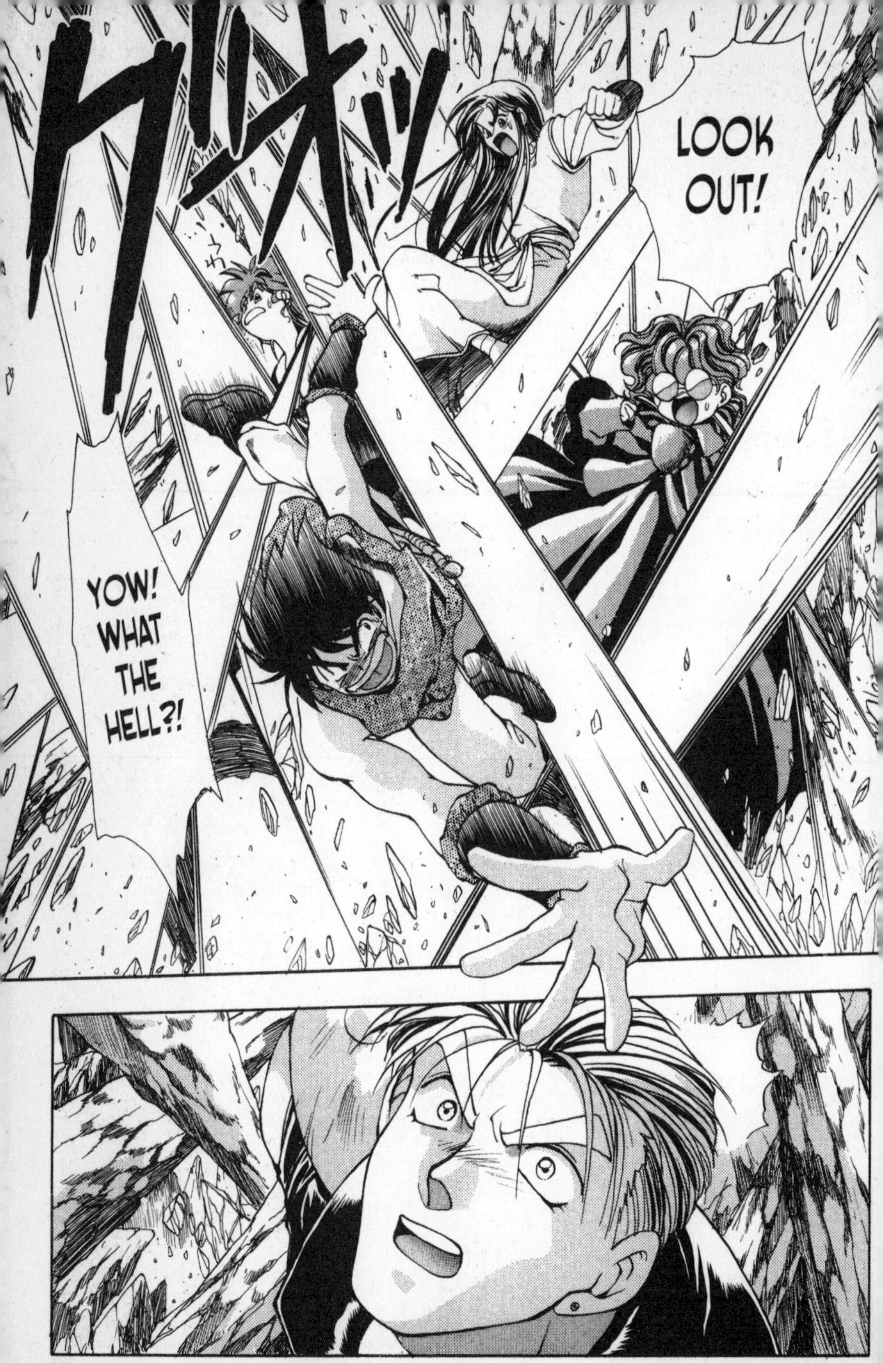
LOOK OUT!
YOW! WHAT THE HELL?!

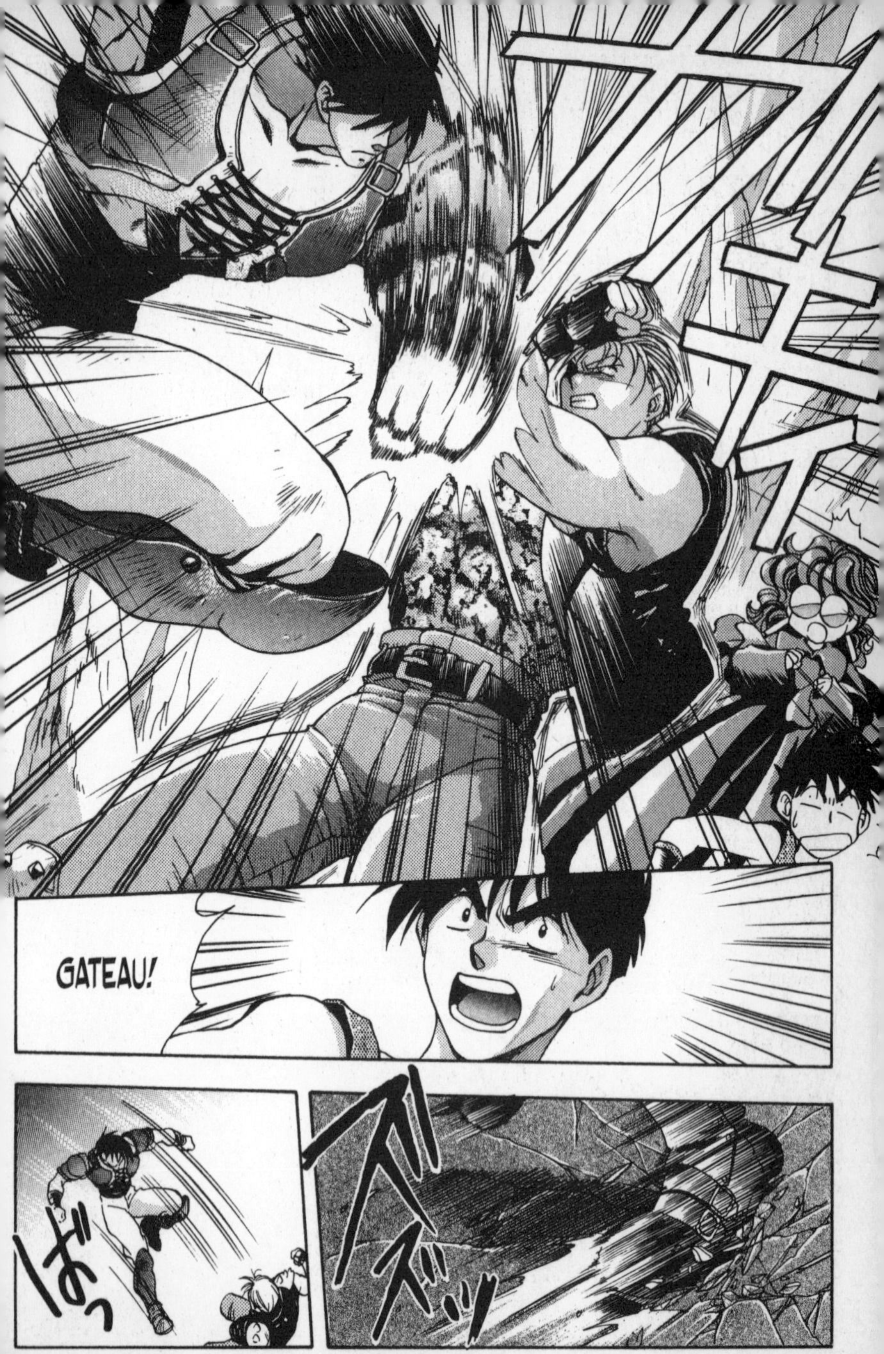
GATEAU!
ズズッ
ばっ

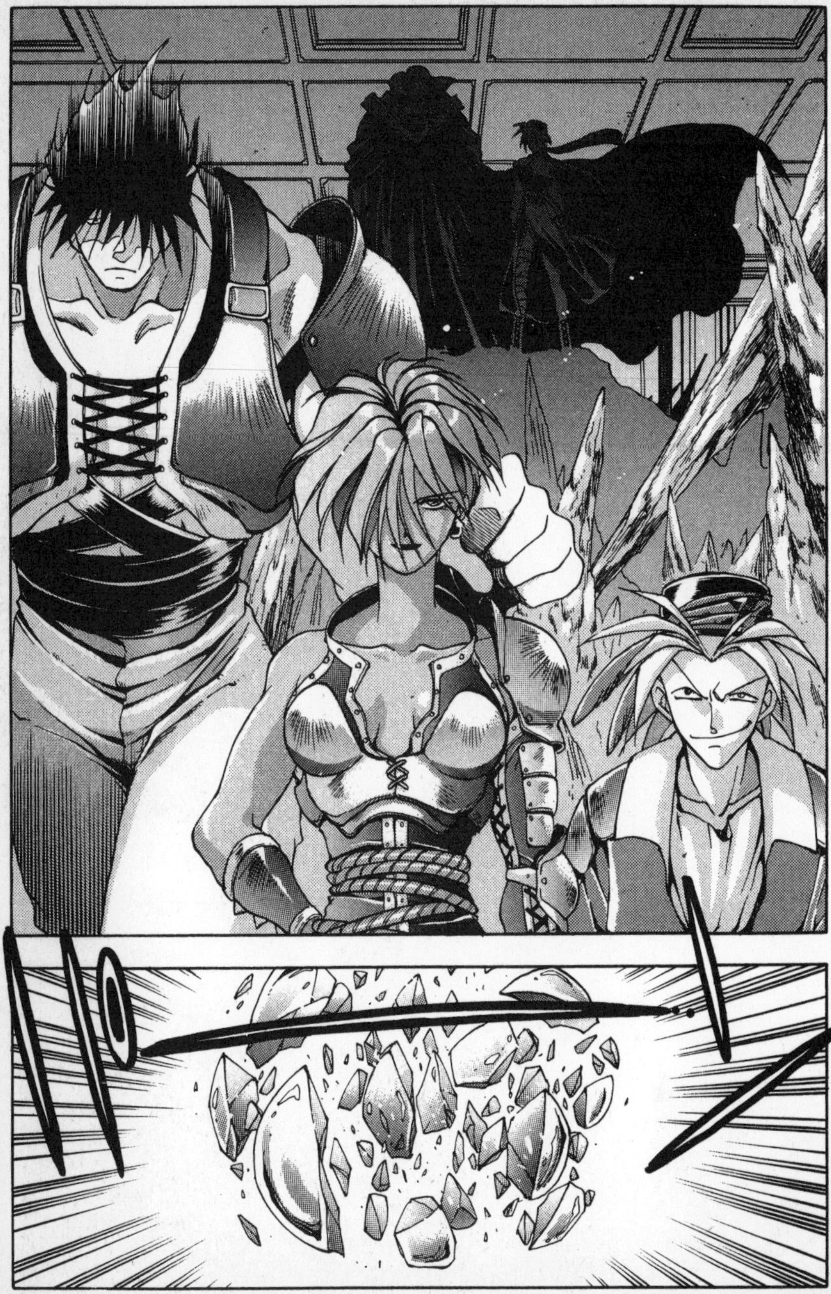

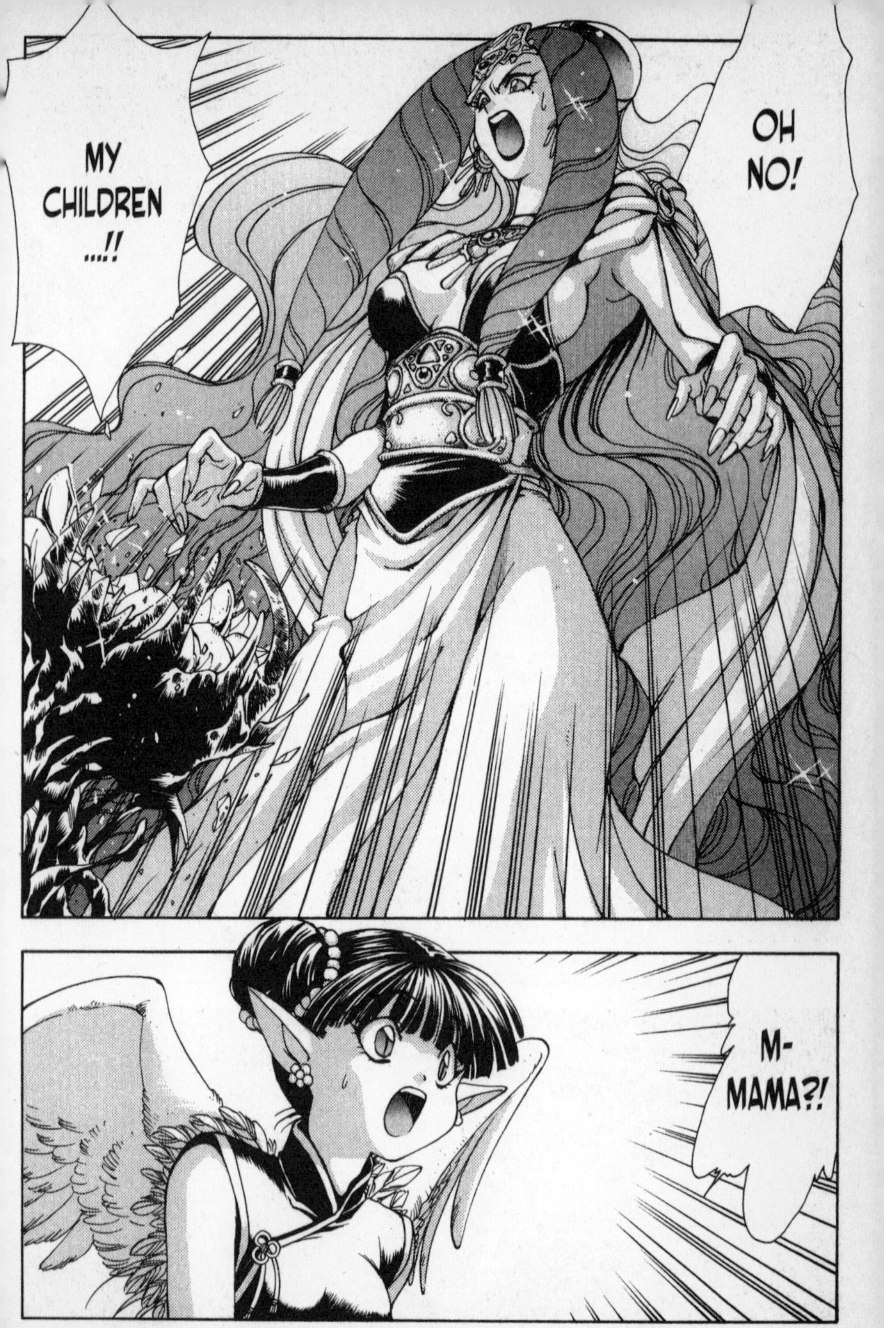
OH NO!
MY CHILDREN ...!!
M-MAMA?!

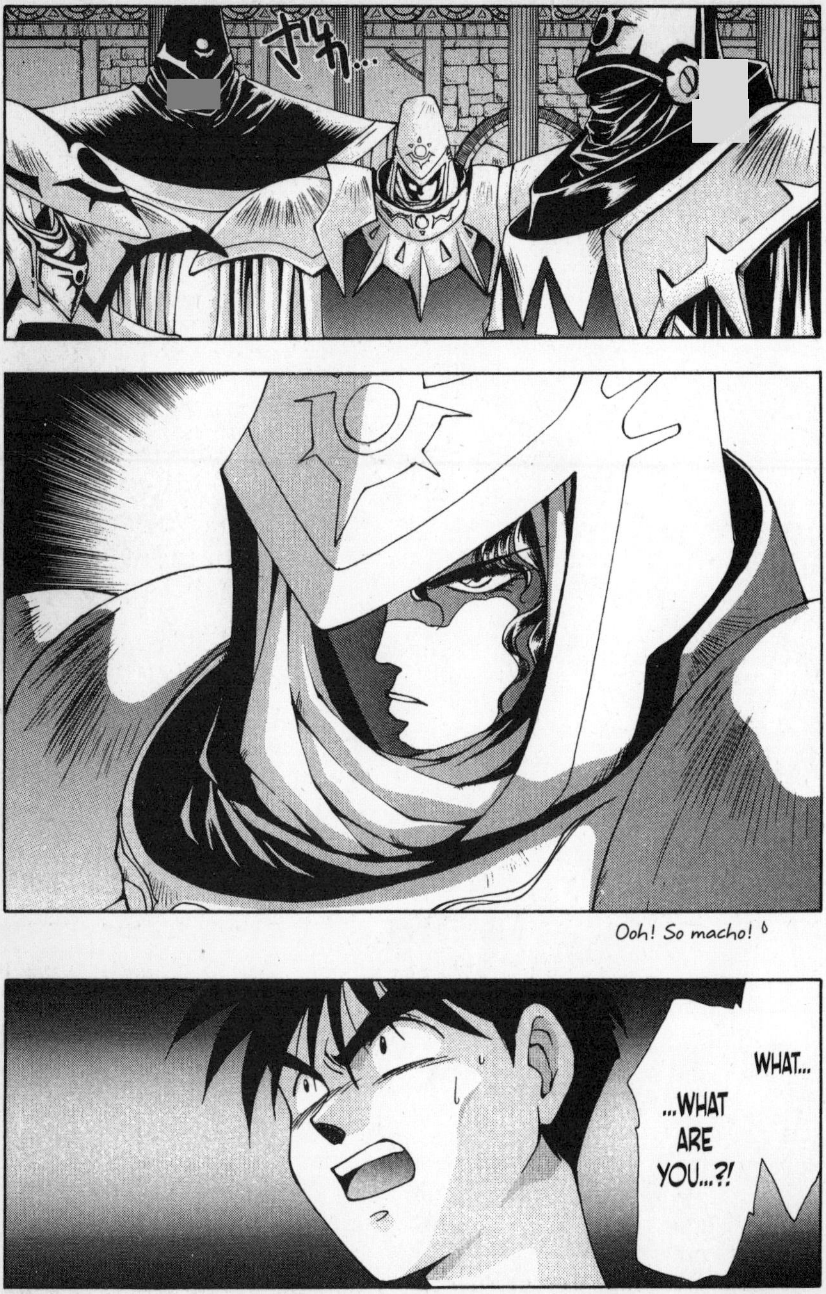
ざわ…
Ooh! So macho!
WHAT...
...WHAT ARE YOU...?!

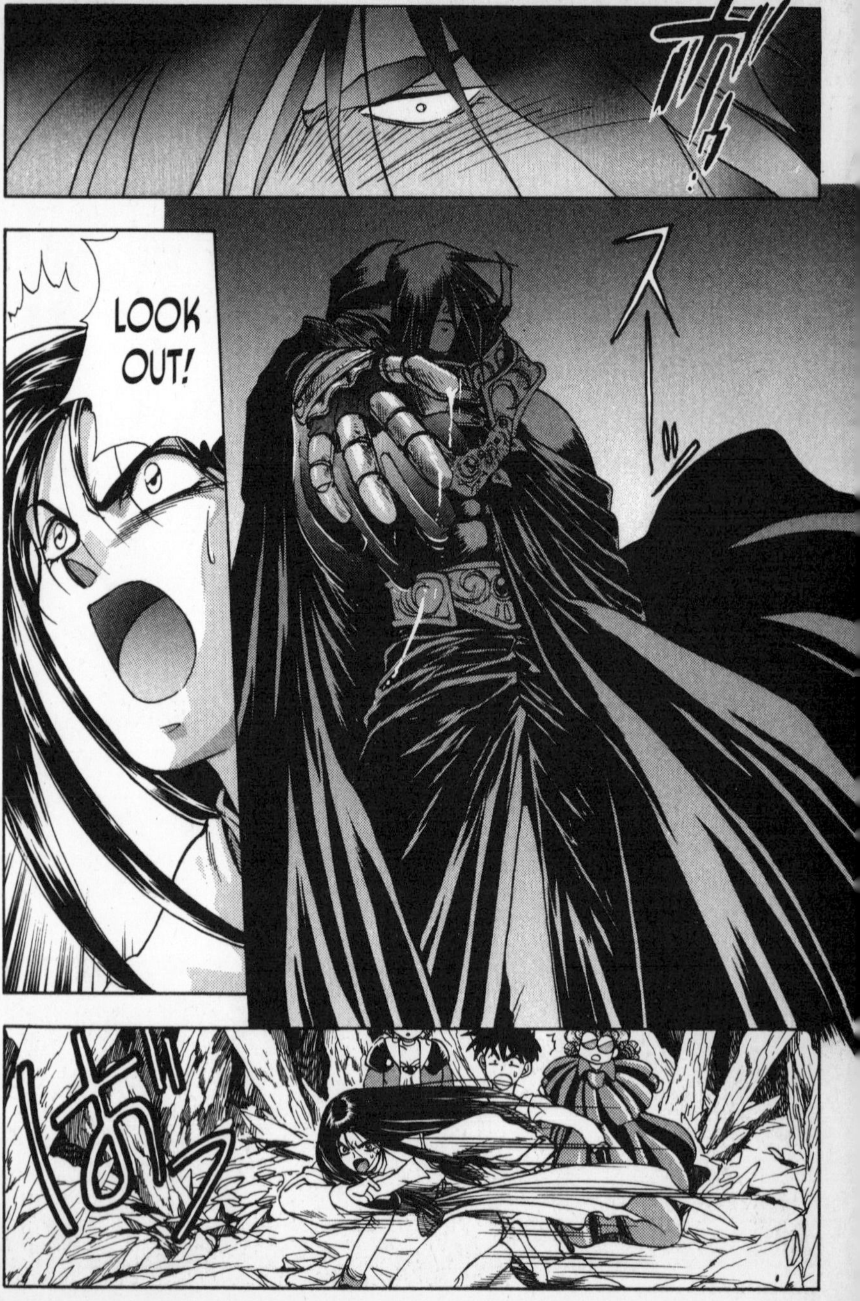
LOOK OUT!

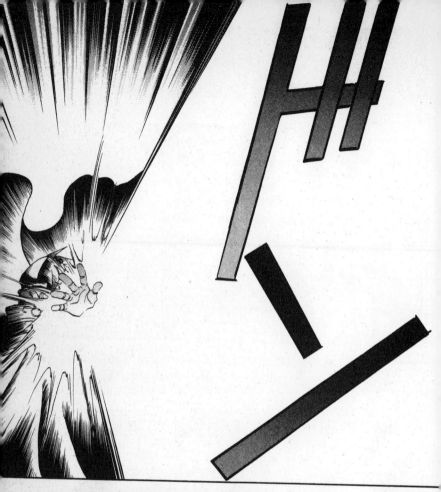

NNGH!!

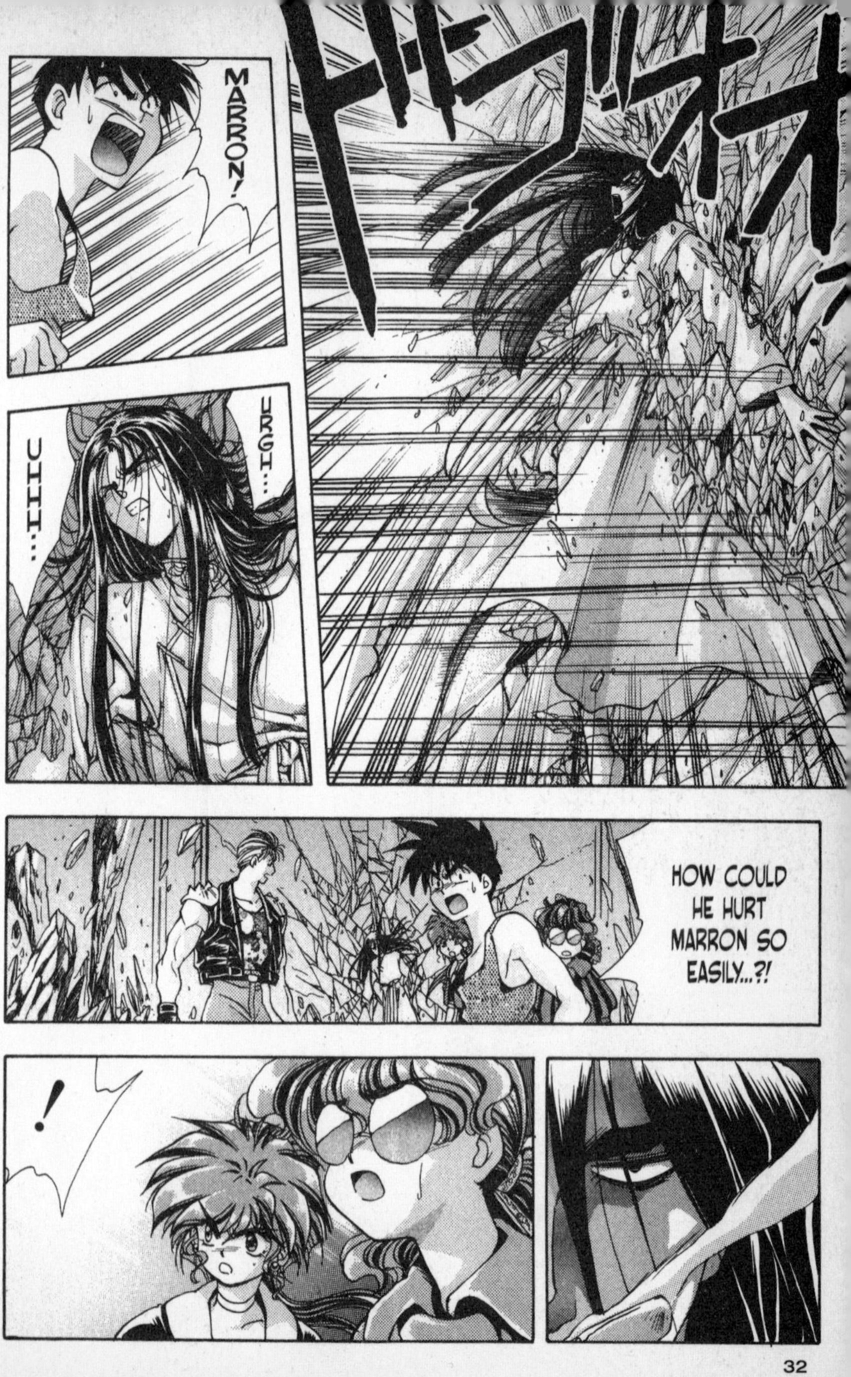
MARRON!
URGH...
UHHH...
HOW COULD HE HURT MARRON SO EASILY...?!
!

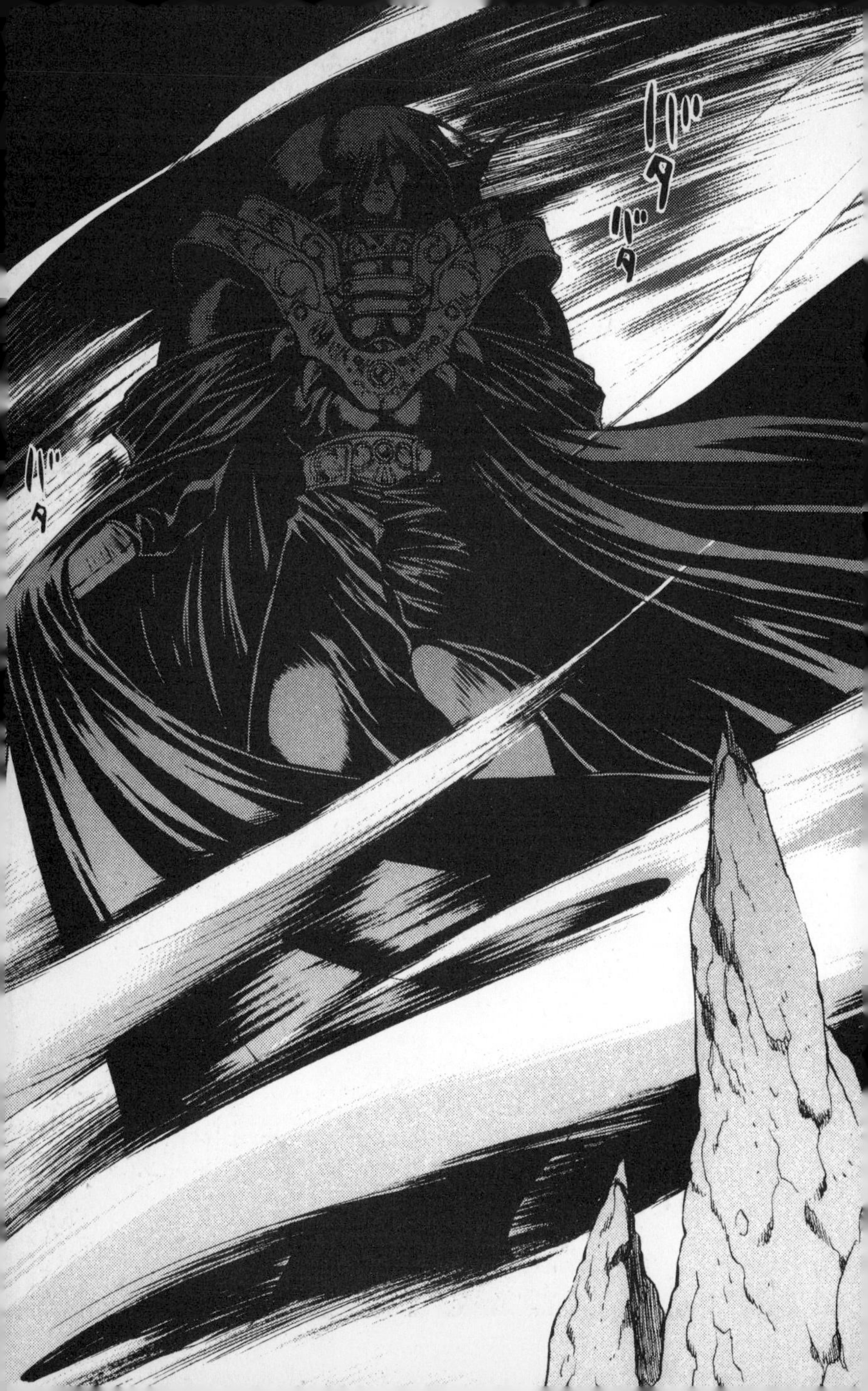
バタバタ
バタ

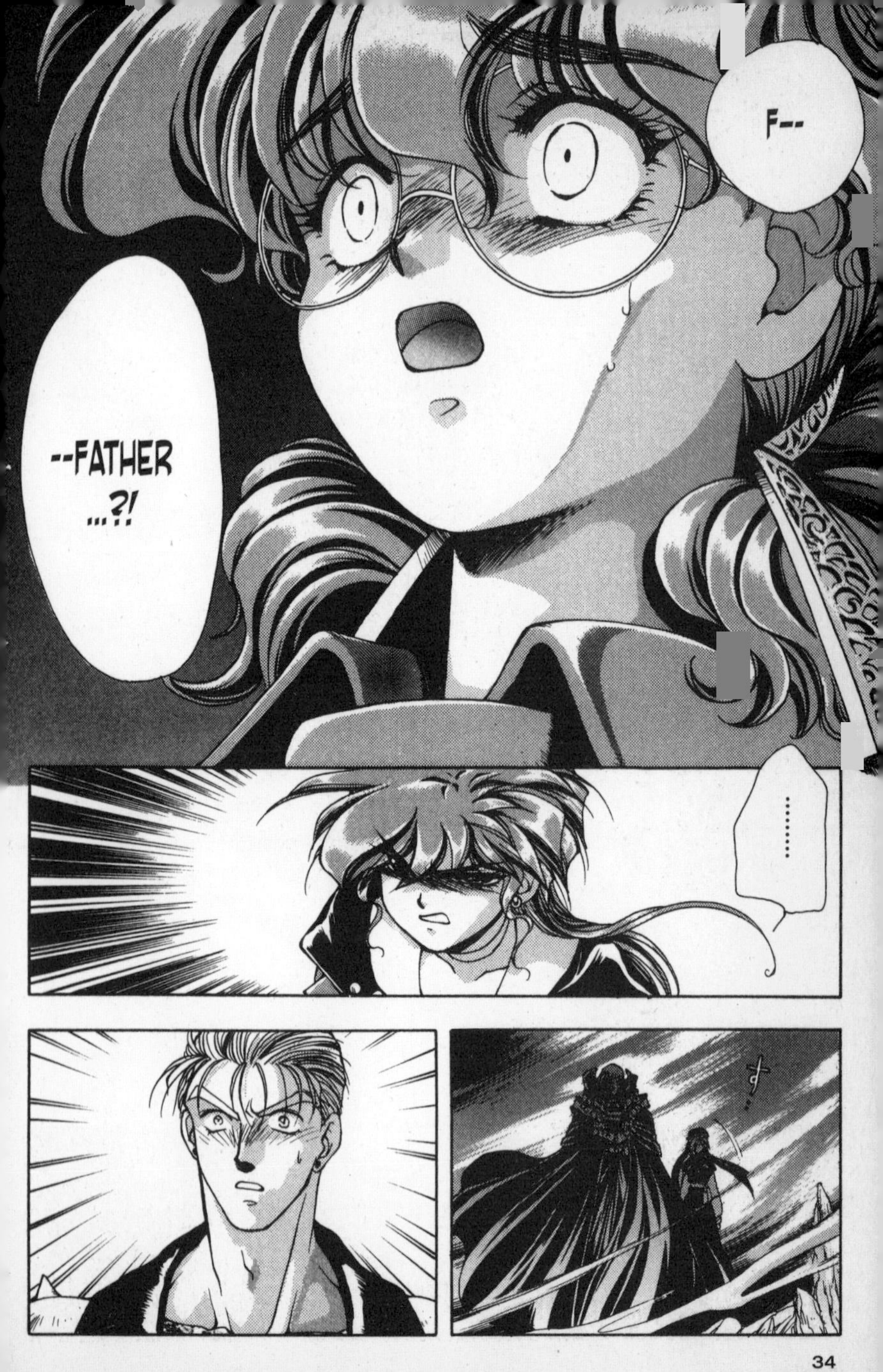
F--
--FATHER ...?!
....

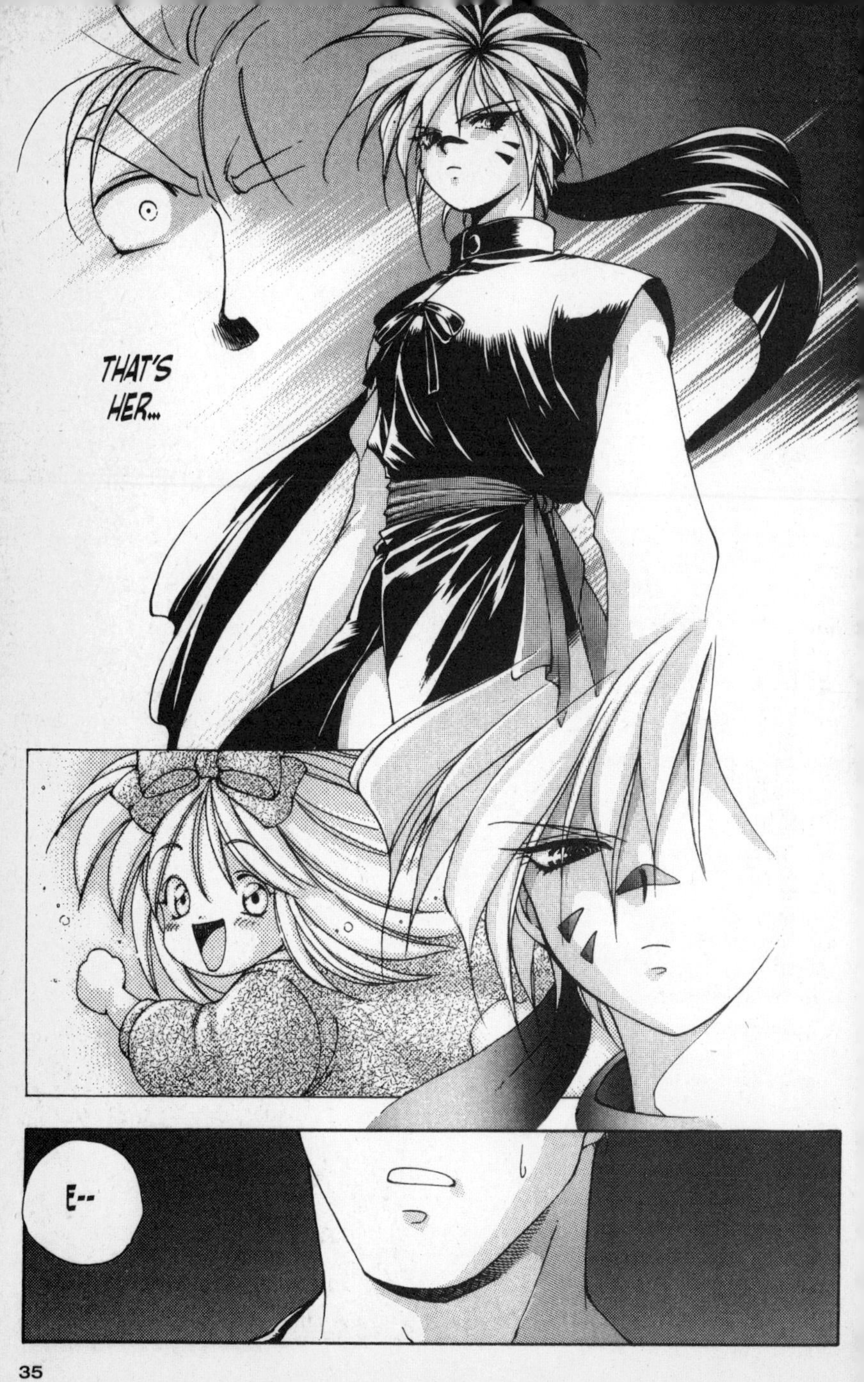
THAT'S HER...
E--

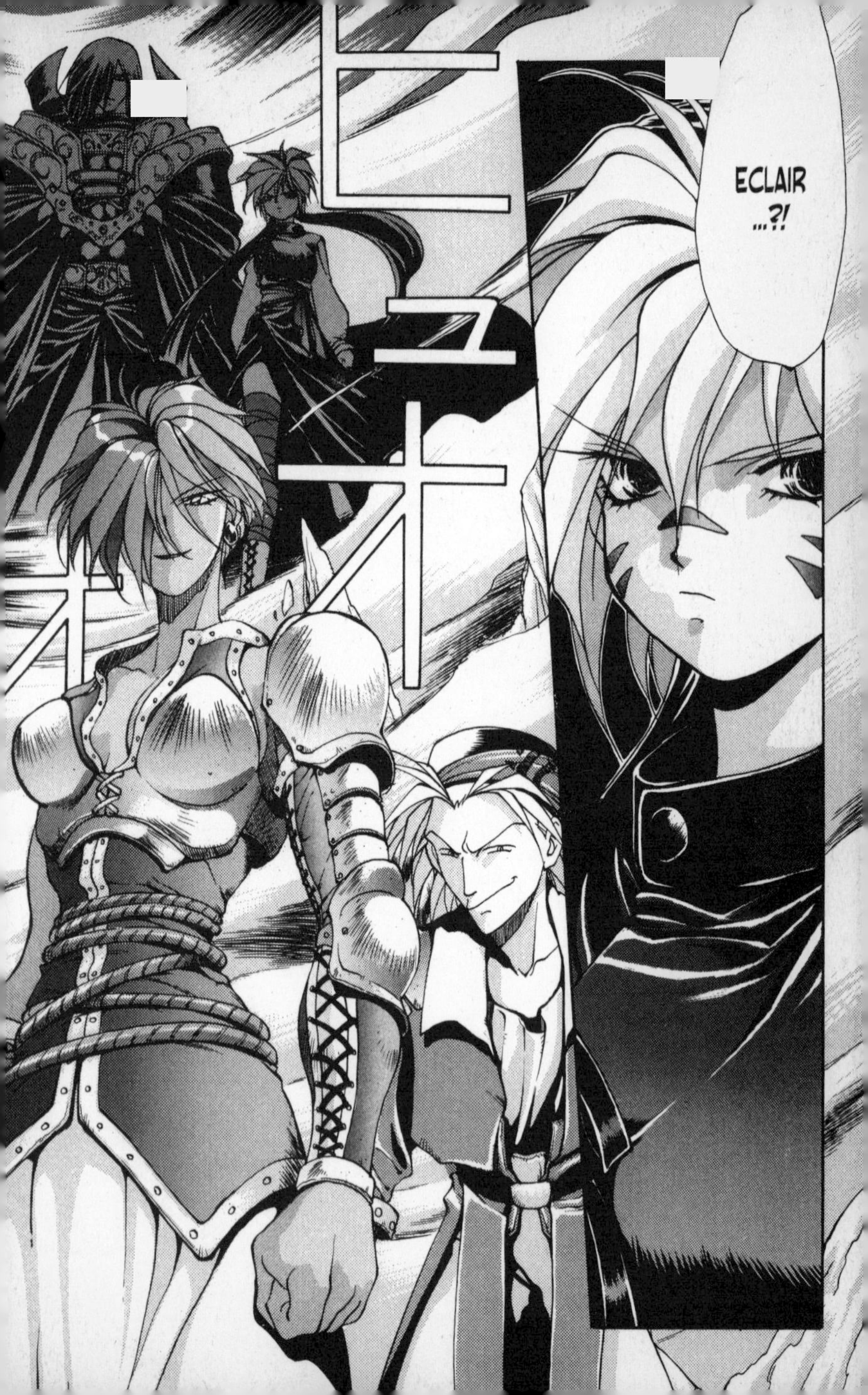
ECLAIR ...?!
ヒュオオ

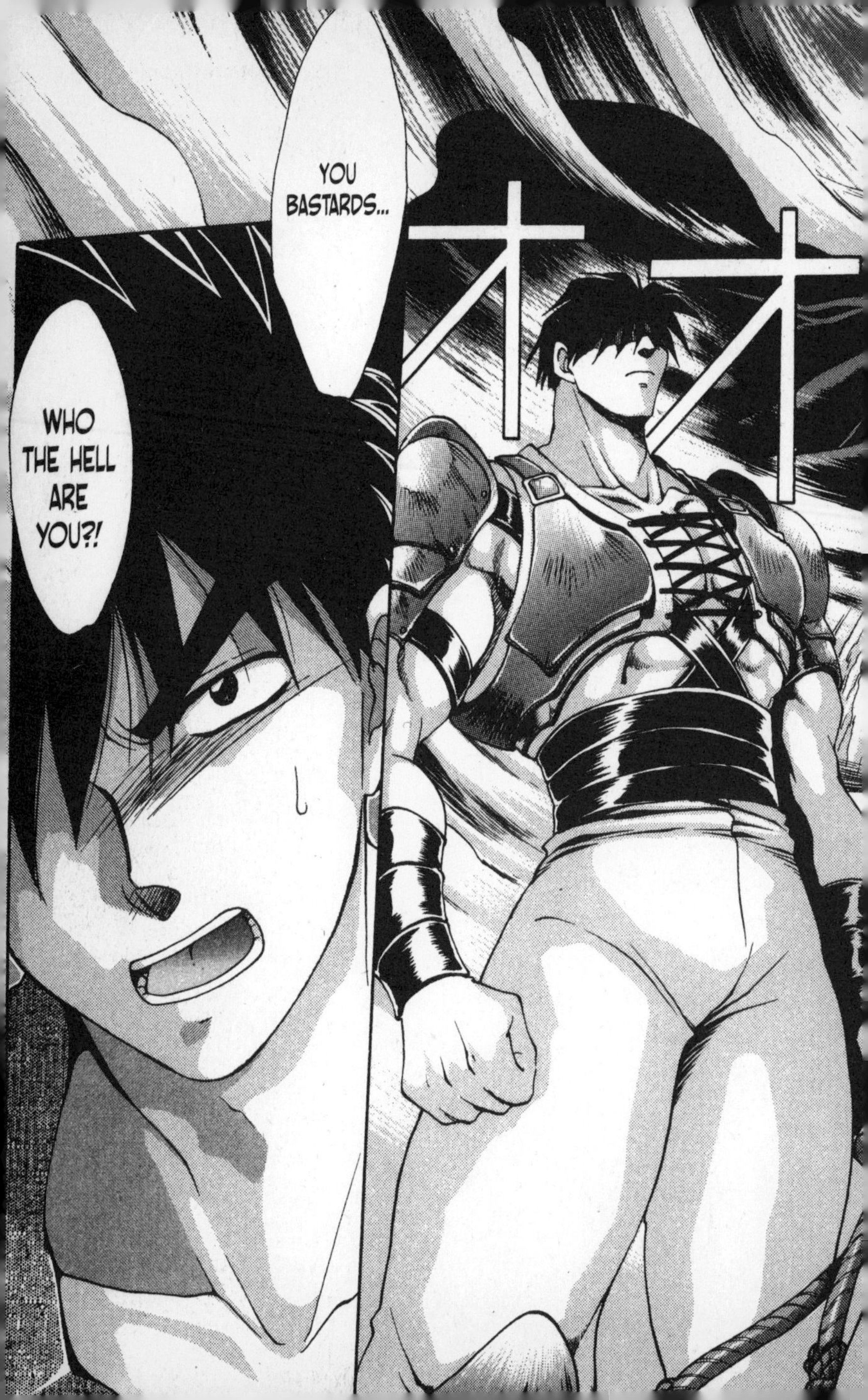
YOU BASTARDS...
WHO THE HELL ARE YOU?!

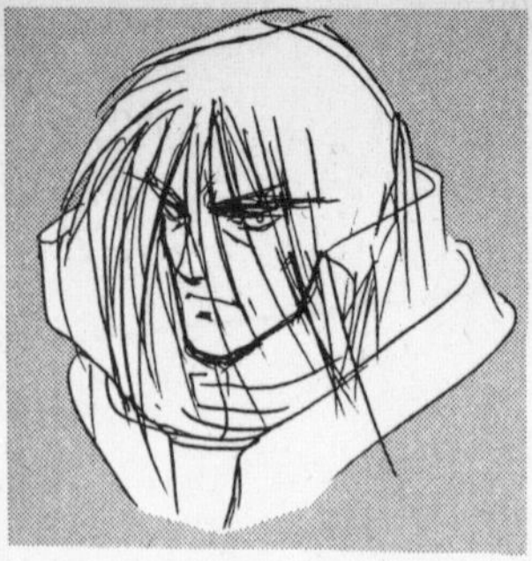

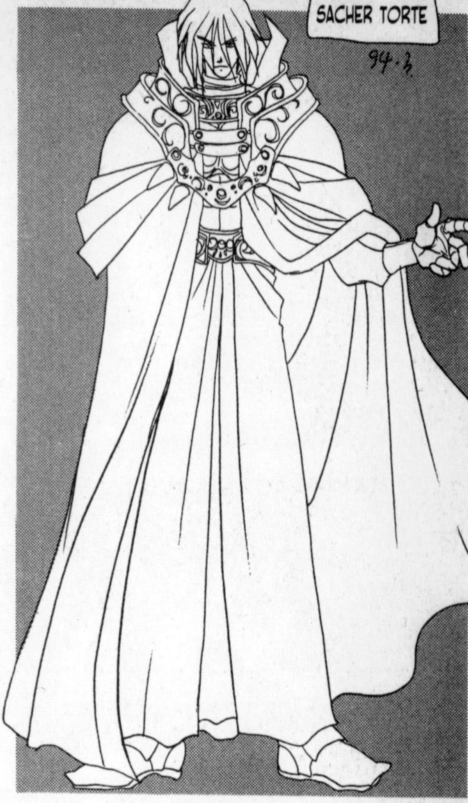
SACHER TORTE
94.3

• SACHER TORTE •

THE PAPA ABOVE IS THE FIRST ROUGH SKETCH I MADE OF HIM AS AN OLDER MAN. (BUT THIS COULD BE HIS TRUE FORM...) THE DRAWING ON THE RIGHT IS THE SECOND EDITION, WHICH IS ALSO THE FINAL ONE. I THOUGHT, "HEY, LET'S MAKE HIM COOL!" BUT, SADLY, I'M NOT TOO GOOD AT DRAWING COOL OR GENTLE GUYS. SNIFF, SOB... (I HAVEN'T HAD MUCH EXPERIENCE DRAWING THEM.) HE'S THE ONE WHO RAISED TIRA AND CHOCOLAT (AT LEAST DURING THEIR EARLY CHILDHOOD)...OR SO IT SEEMS. (HEY!) I LOVE HIM, BUT I CAN'T DRAW HIM!

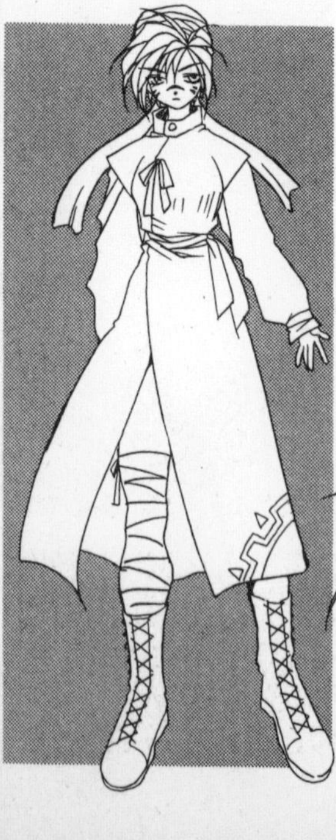

NATA DE COCO

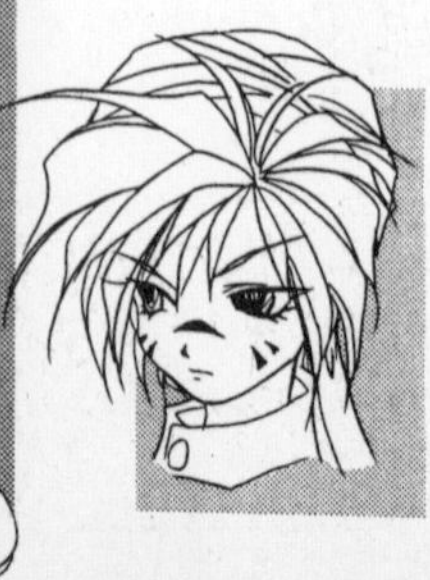

• NATA DE COCO •

SOME PEOPLE MIGHT REALIZE THIS, BUT HER INSPIRATION COMES FROM A CERTAIN FEMALE CHARACTER IN A CERTAIN FIGHTING GAME. (WHO COULD THAT BE?) IN TERMS OF DESIGN AND PERSONALITY, SHE'S MY FAVORITE FEMALE CHARACTER RIGHT NOW. SHE STARTED OUT WITH BRAIDS, BUT NOW SHE HAS SHORT HAIR. THERE WERE TOO MANY GIRLS WITH LONG HAIR, SO I WANTED TO DRAW ONE WITH SHORT HAIR. I GOT HER DESIGN DOWN IN ONE TRY. (BUT IS THIS REALLY HER PERSONALITY? I LIKE THE EXPRESSIONLESS LOOK, BUT...) I DREW SHOTS OF HER WITHOUT THE CLOTHES, BUT THIS IS ALL I HAVE READY NOW.

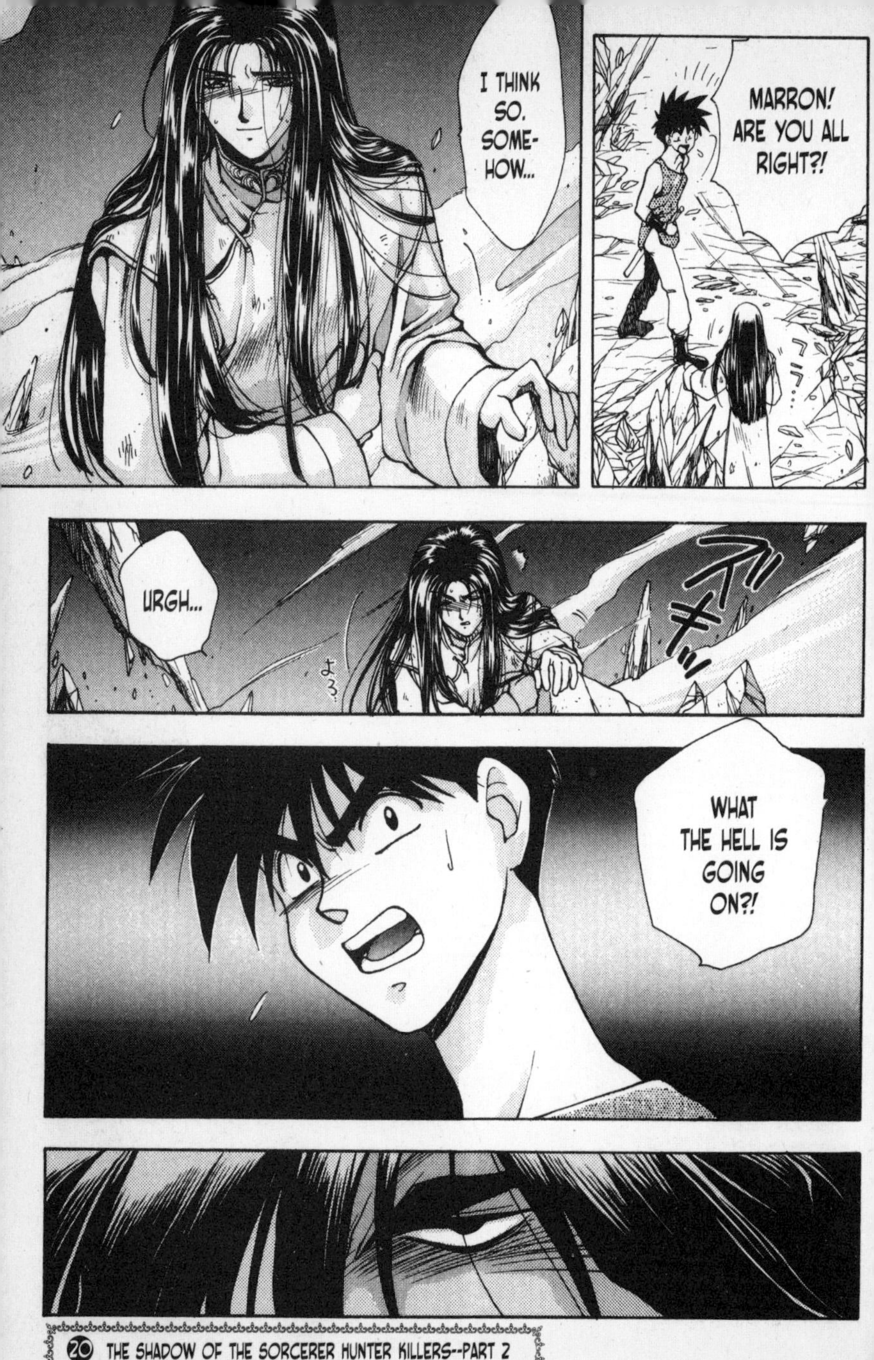
MARRON! ARE YOU ALL RIGHT?!
I THINK SO. SOME-HOW...
URGH...
WHAT THE HELL IS GOING ON?!

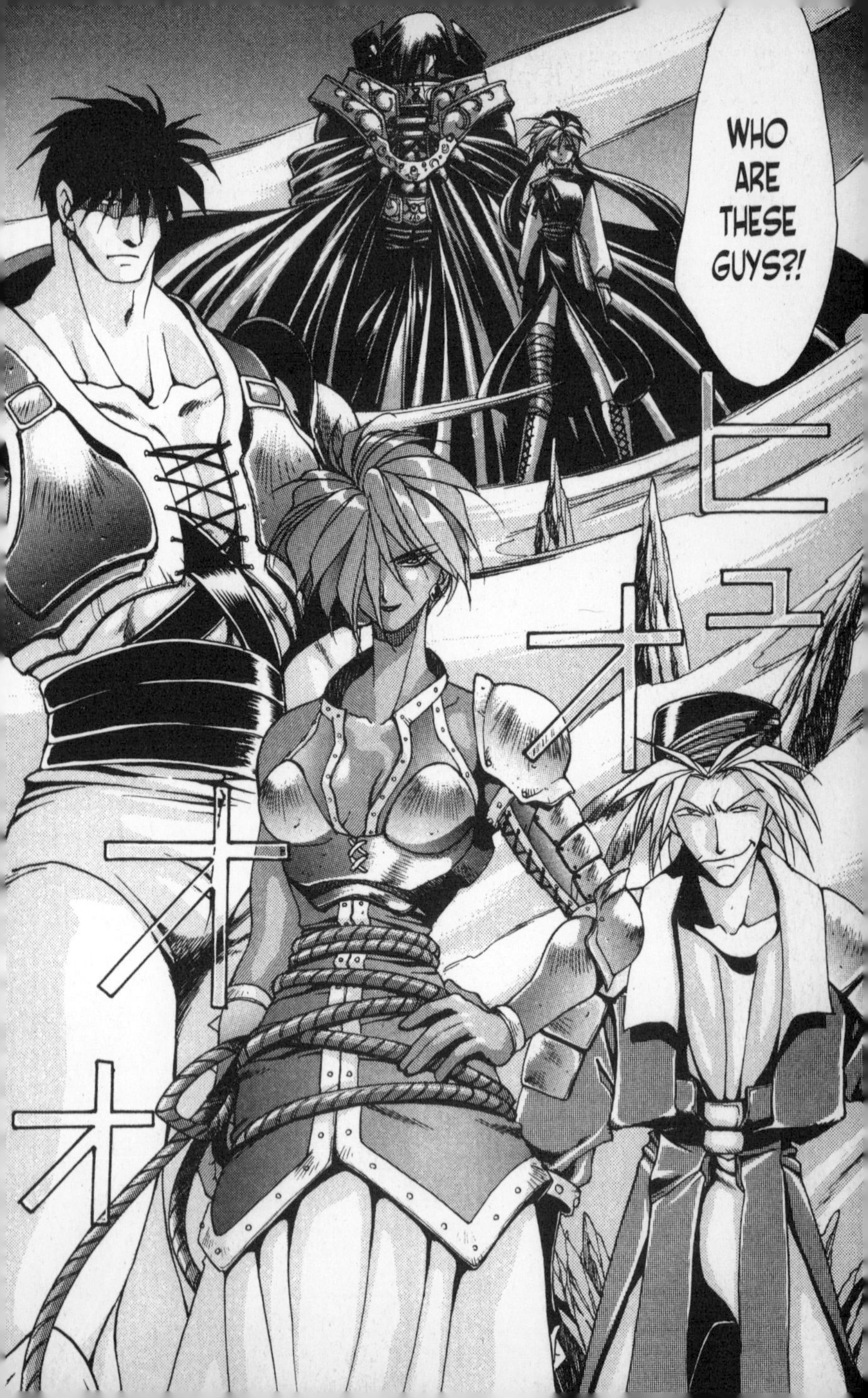
WHO ARE THESE GUYS?!
ヒュオオオ

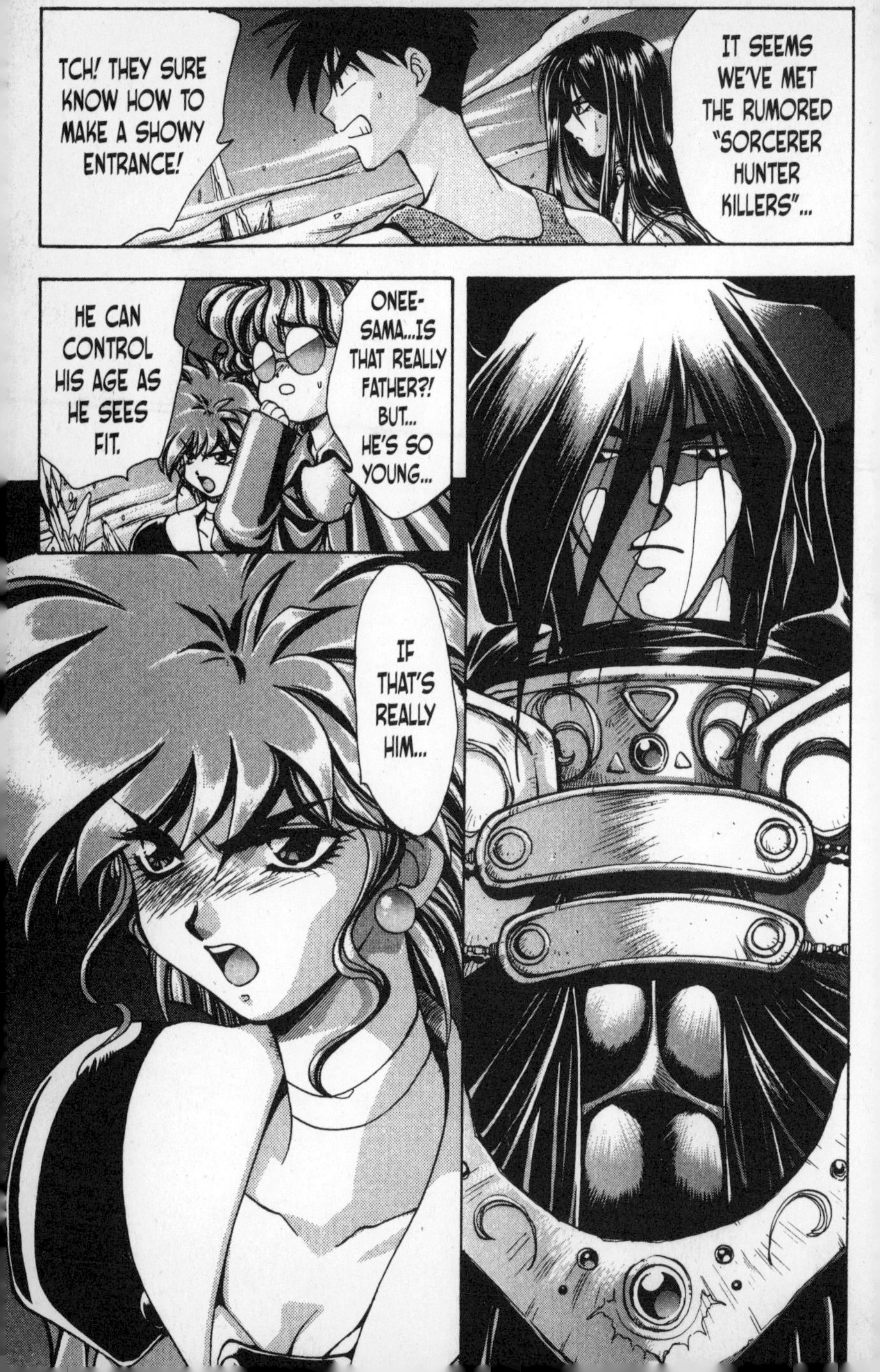
IT SEEMS WE'VE MET THE RUMORED "SORCERER HUNTER KILLERS"...
TCH! THEY SURE KNOW HOW TO MAKE A SHOWY ENTRANCE!
ONEE-SAMA...IS THAT REALLY FATHER?! BUT... HE'S SO YOUNG...
HE CAN CONTROL HIS AGE AS HE SEES FIT.
IF THAT'S REALLY HIM...

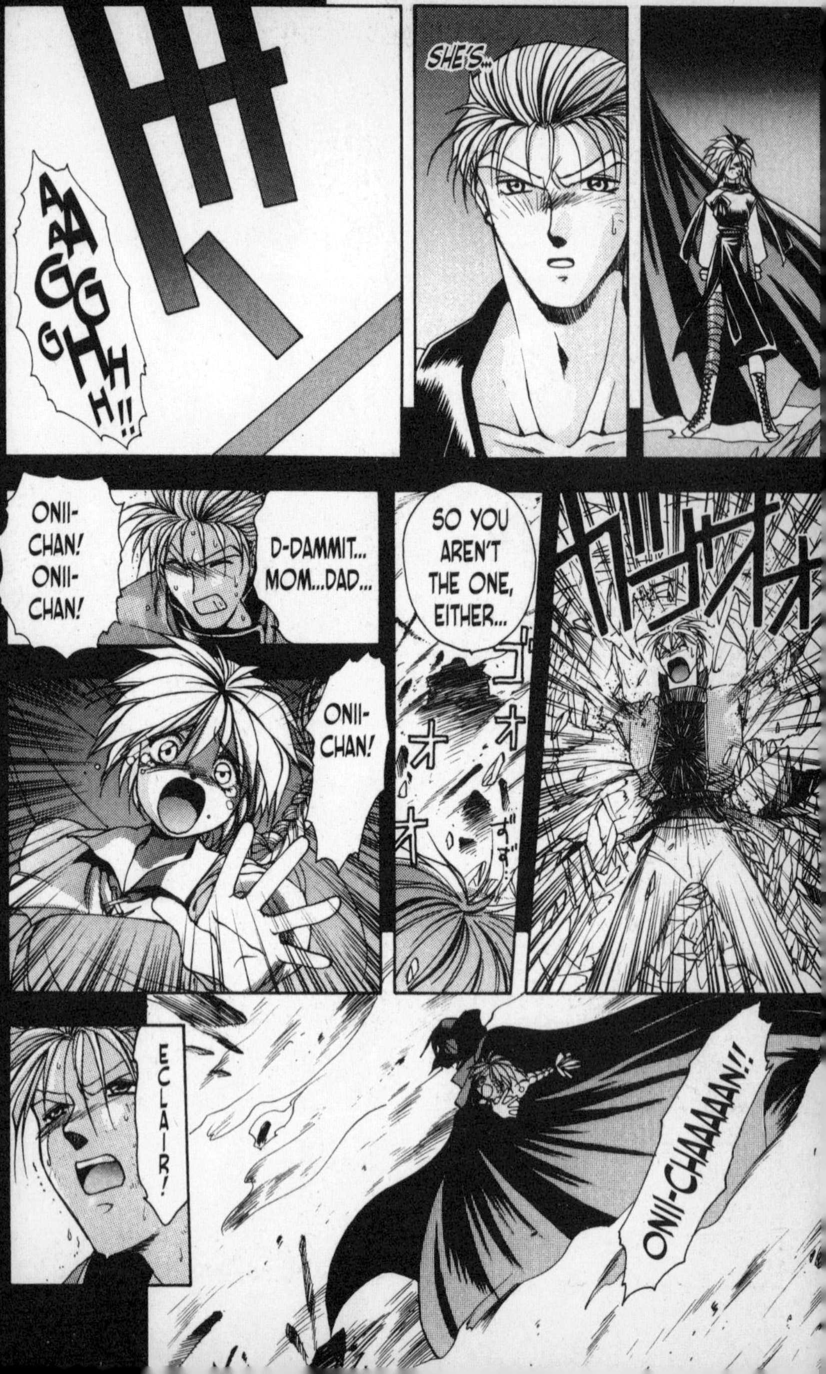
SHE'S...
AAAGGGHHHH!!
ゴオオオ
ずず
SO YOU AREN'T THE ONE, EITHER...
D-DAMMIT... MOM...DAD...
ONII-CHAN! ONII-CHAN!
ONII-CHAN!
ONII-CHAAAAN!!
ECLAIR!

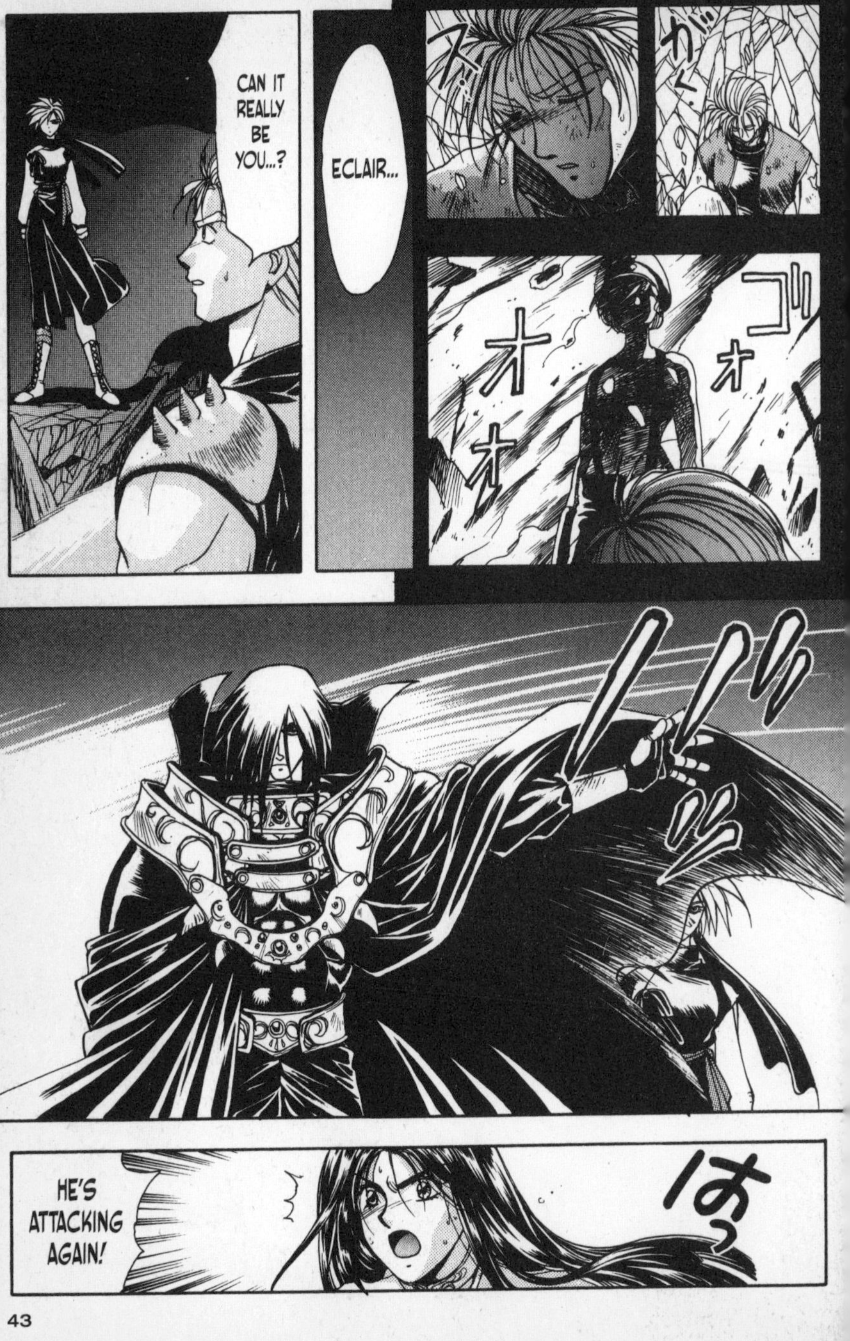
がく…
ズ…
ゴォ
オォ
ECLAIR...
CAN IT REALLY BE YOU...?
はっ
HE'S ATTACKING AGAIN!

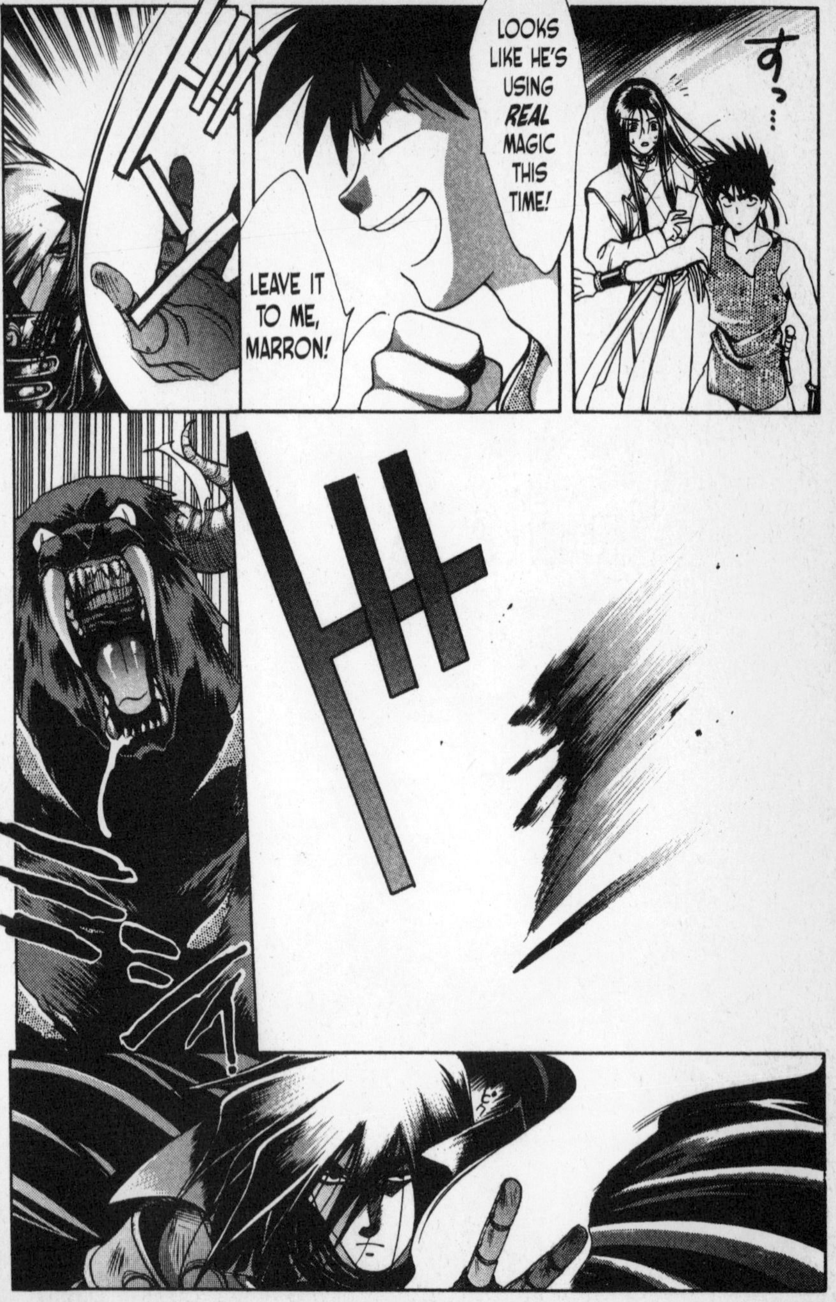
すっ…
LOOKS LIKE HE'S USING *REAL* MAGIC THIS TIME!
LEAVE IT TO ME, MARRON!

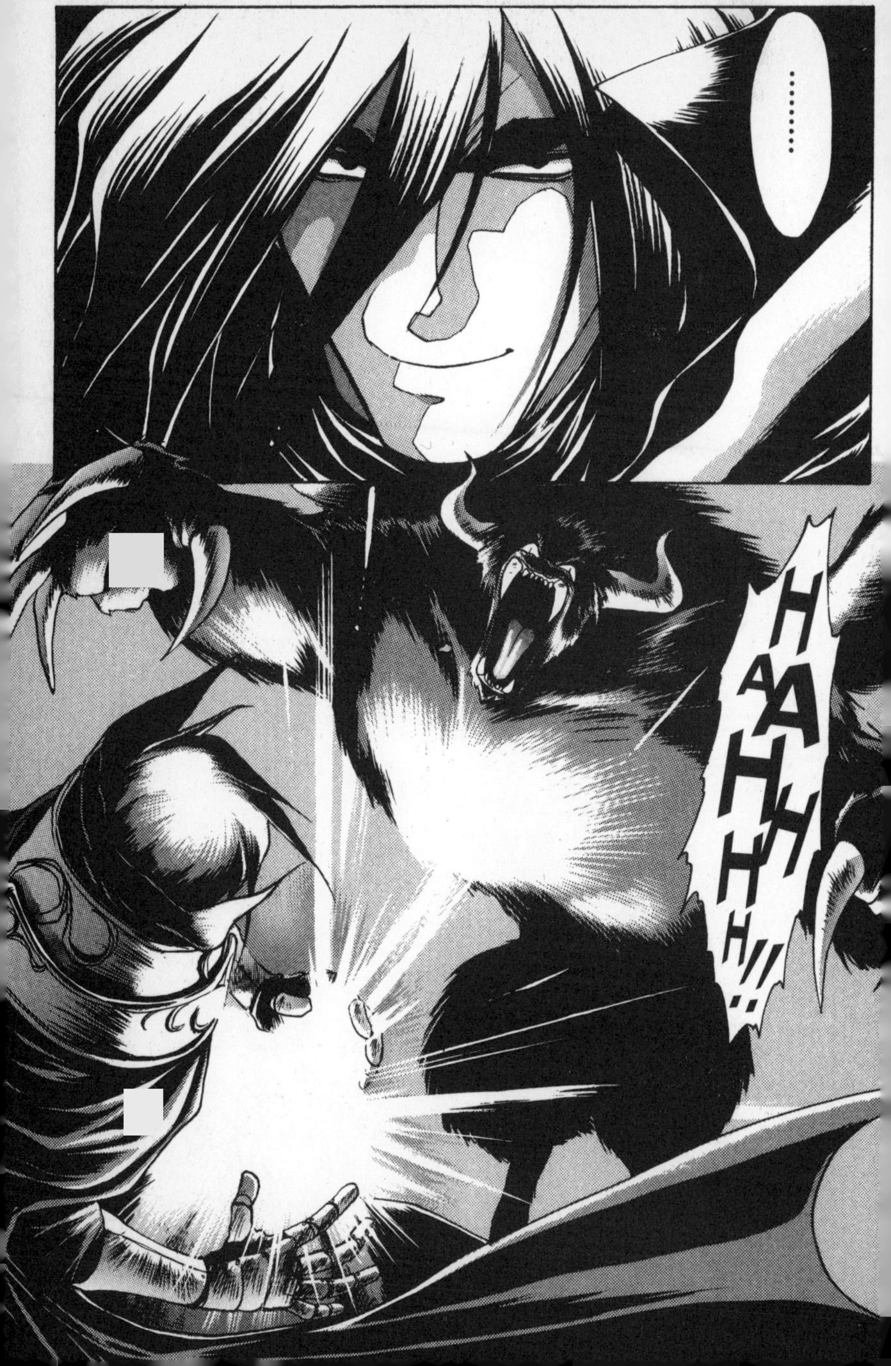
......
HAAHHHHH!!

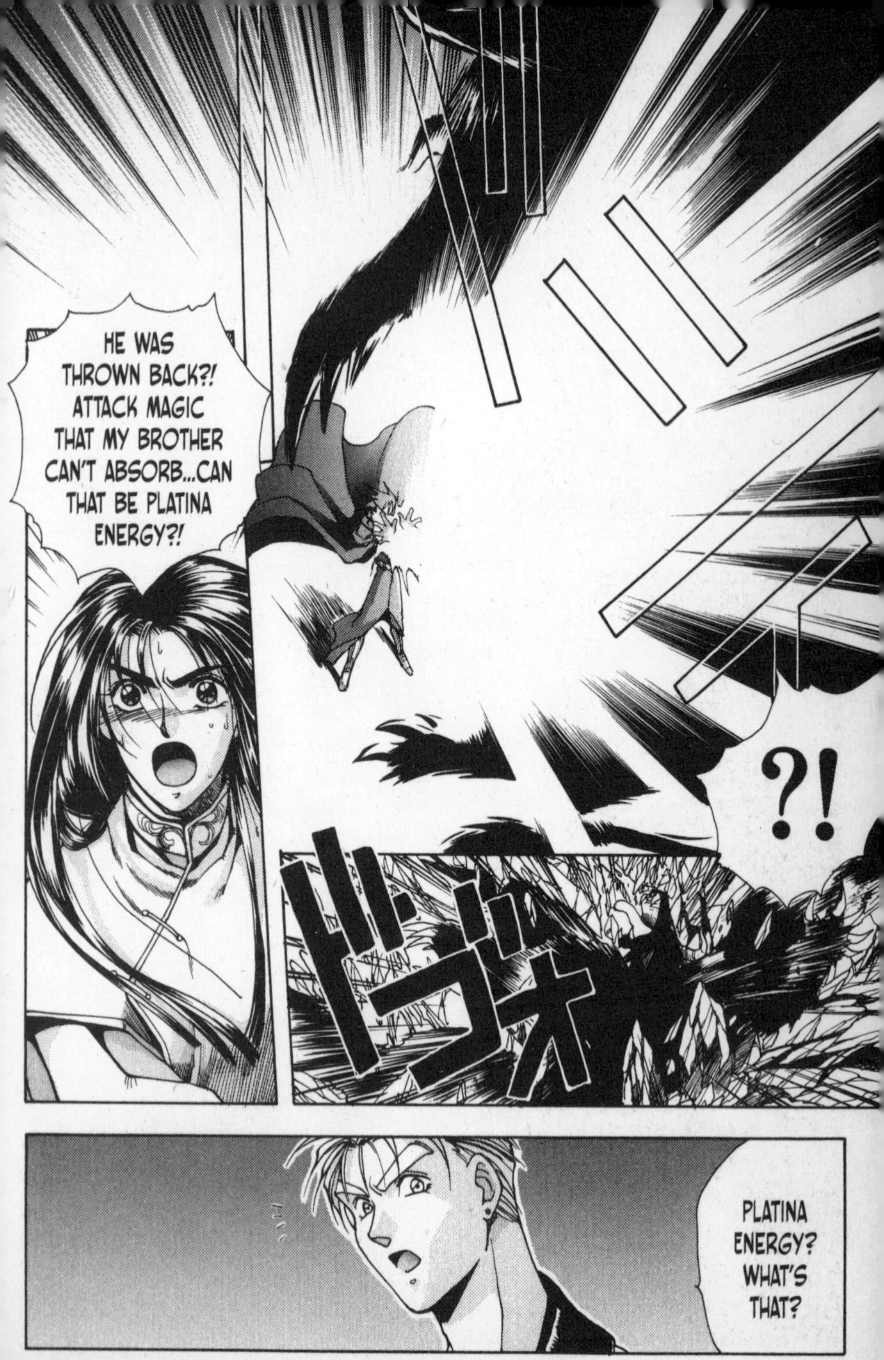
?!
ドゴオ
HE WAS THROWN BACK?! ATTACK MAGIC THAT MY BROTHER CAN'T ABSORB...CAN THAT BE PLATINA ENERGY?!
PLATINA ENERGY? WHAT'S THAT?

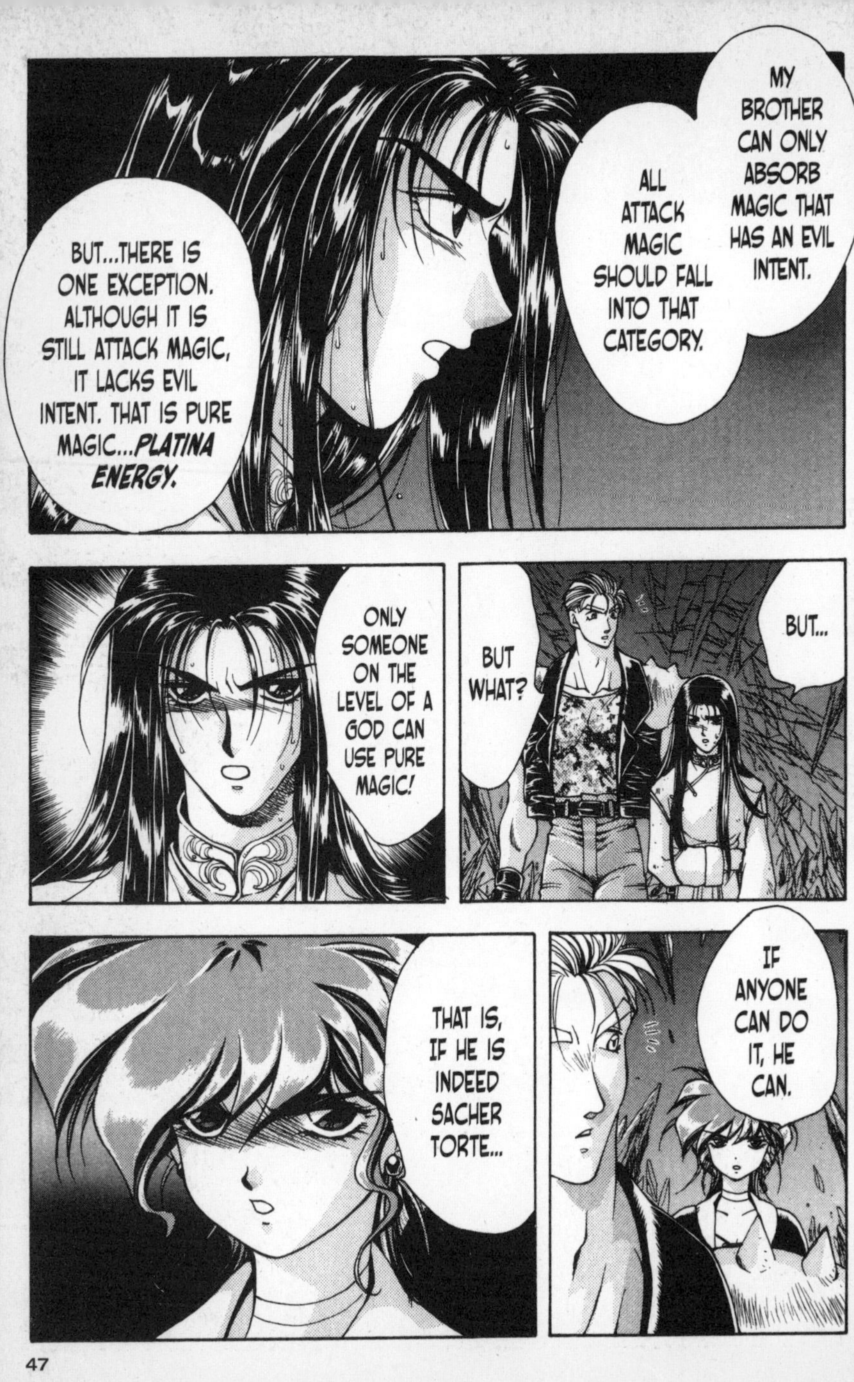
MY BROTHER CAN ONLY ABSORB MAGIC THAT HAS AN EVIL INTENT.
ALL ATTACK MAGIC SHOULD FALL INTO THAT CATEGORY.
BUT...THERE IS ONE EXCEPTION. ALTHOUGH IT IS STILL ATTACK MAGIC, IT LACKS EVIL INTENT. THAT IS PURE MAGIC...*PLATINA ENERGY.*
BUT...
BUT WHAT?
ONLY SOMEONE ON THE LEVEL OF A GOD CAN USE PURE MAGIC!
IF ANYONE CAN DO IT, HE CAN.
THAT IS, IF HE IS INDEED SACHER TORTE...

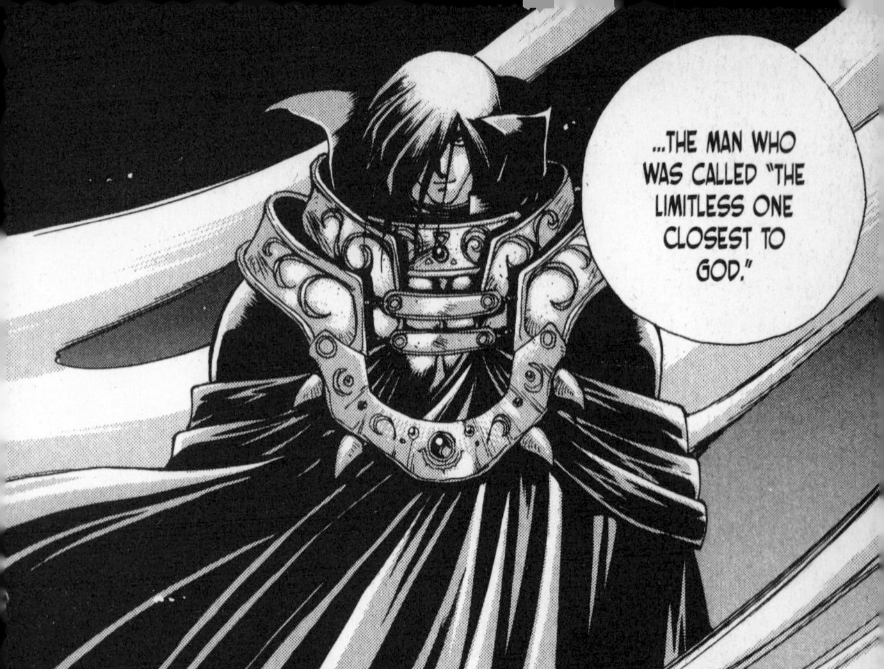
...THE MAN WHO WAS CALLED "THE LIMITLESS ONE CLOSEST TO GOD."

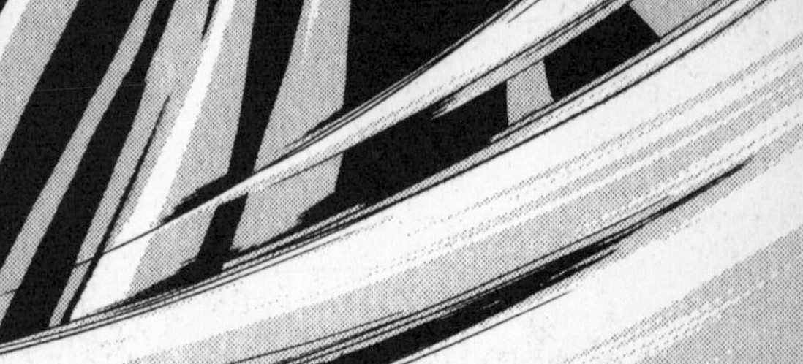
THE ONE CLOSEST TO GOD...

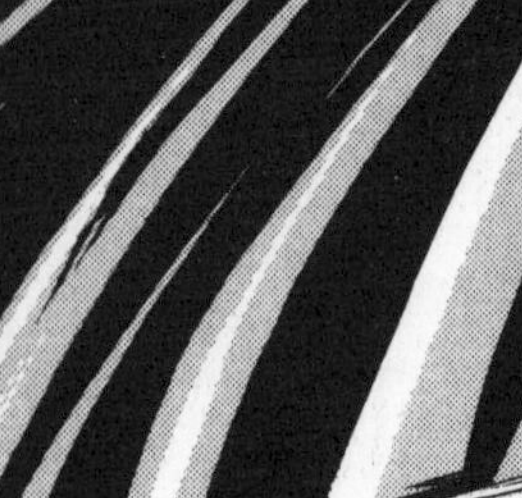
OW WOW WOW ...

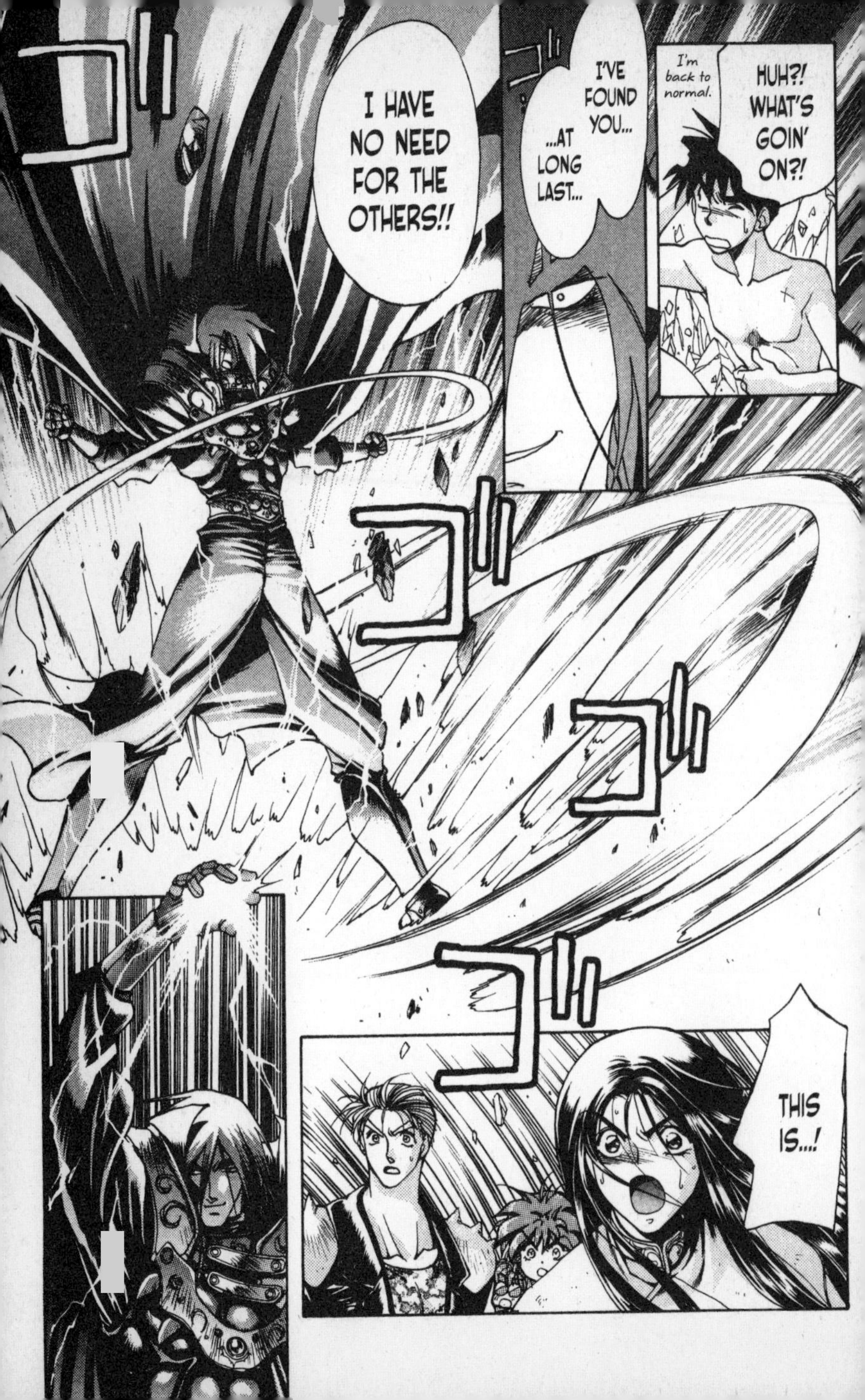
HUH?! WHAT'S GOIN' ON?!
I'm back to normal.
I'VE FOUND YOU...
...AT LONG LAST...
ゴ
I HAVE NO NEED FOR THE OTHERS!!
ゴ
ゴ
ゴ
ゴ
THIS IS...!

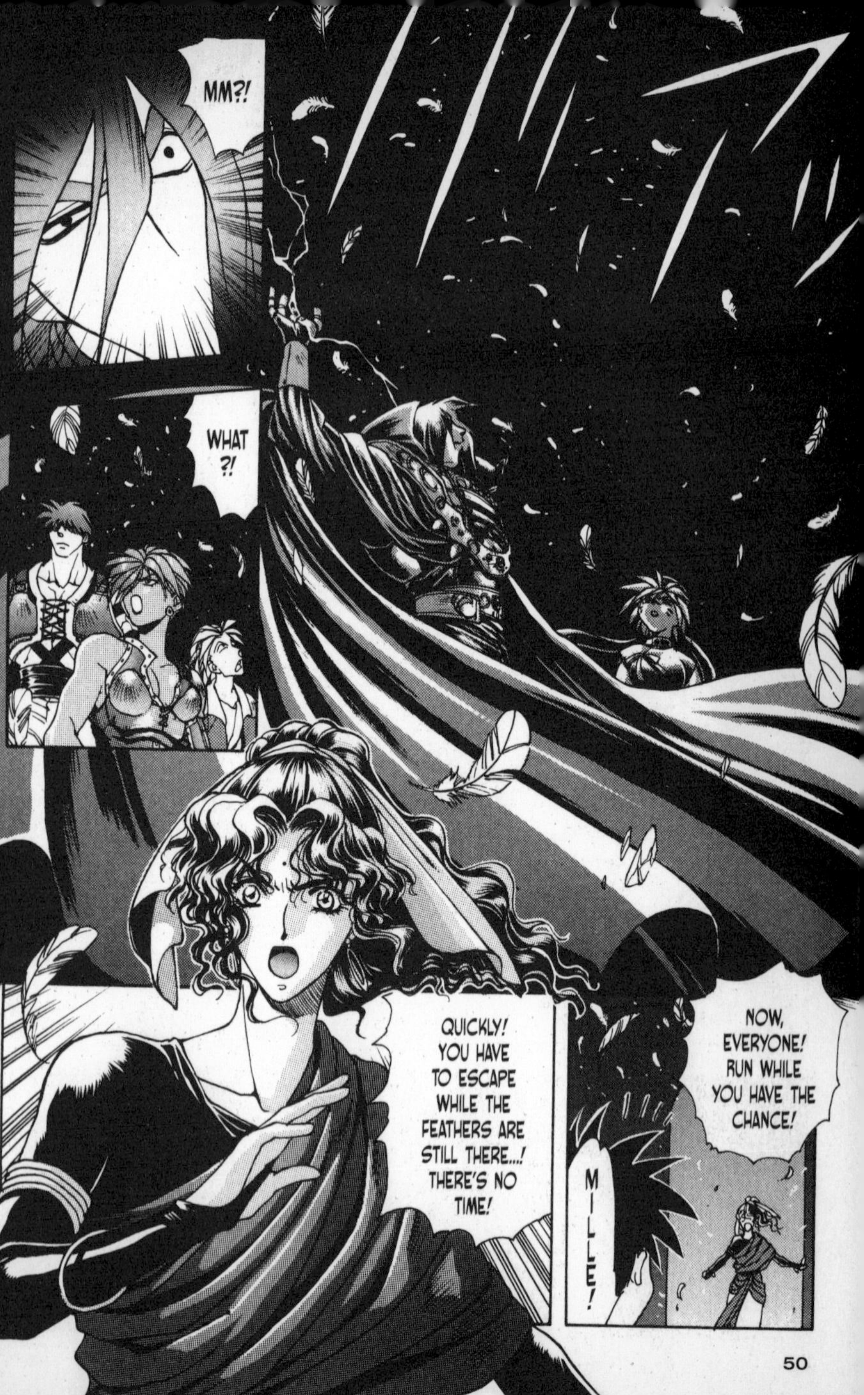
MM?!
WHAT ?!
NOW, EVERYONE! RUN WHILE YOU HAVE THE CHANCE!
MILLE!
QUICKLY! YOU HAVE TO ESCAPE WHILE THE FEATHERS ARE STILL THERE...! THERE'S NO TIME!

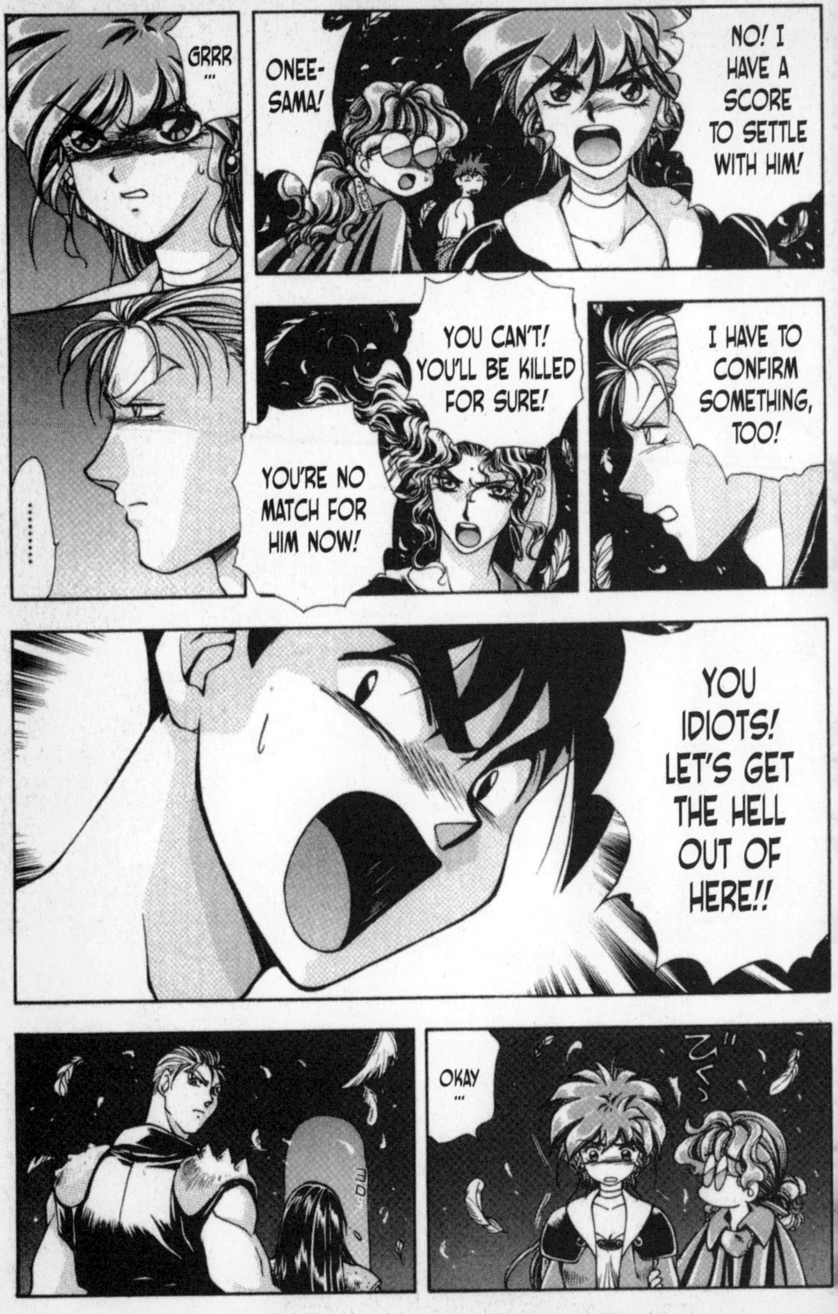
NO! I HAVE A SCORE TO SETTLE WITH HIM!
ONEE-SAMA!
I HAVE TO CONFIRM SOMETHING, TOO!
YOU CAN'T! YOU'LL BE KILLED FOR SURE!
YOU'RE NO MATCH FOR HIM NOW!
GRRR ...
....
YOU IDIOTS! LET'S GET THE HELL OUT OF HERE!!
OKAY ...

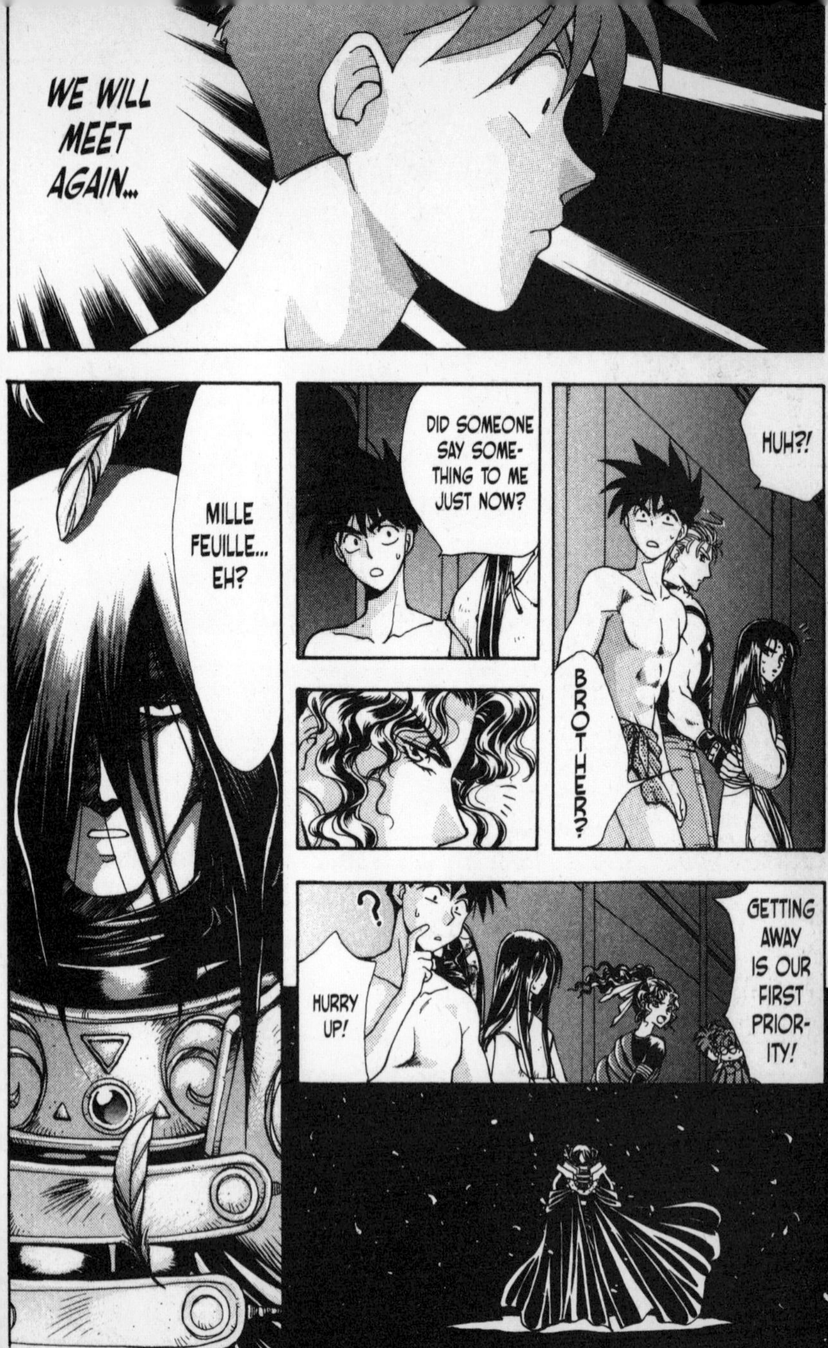
WE WILL MEET AGAIN...
HUH?!
BROTHER?
DID SOMEONE SAY SOME-THING TO ME JUST NOW?
GETTING AWAY IS OUR FIRST PRIOR-ITY!
HURRY UP!
MILLE FEUILLE... EH?

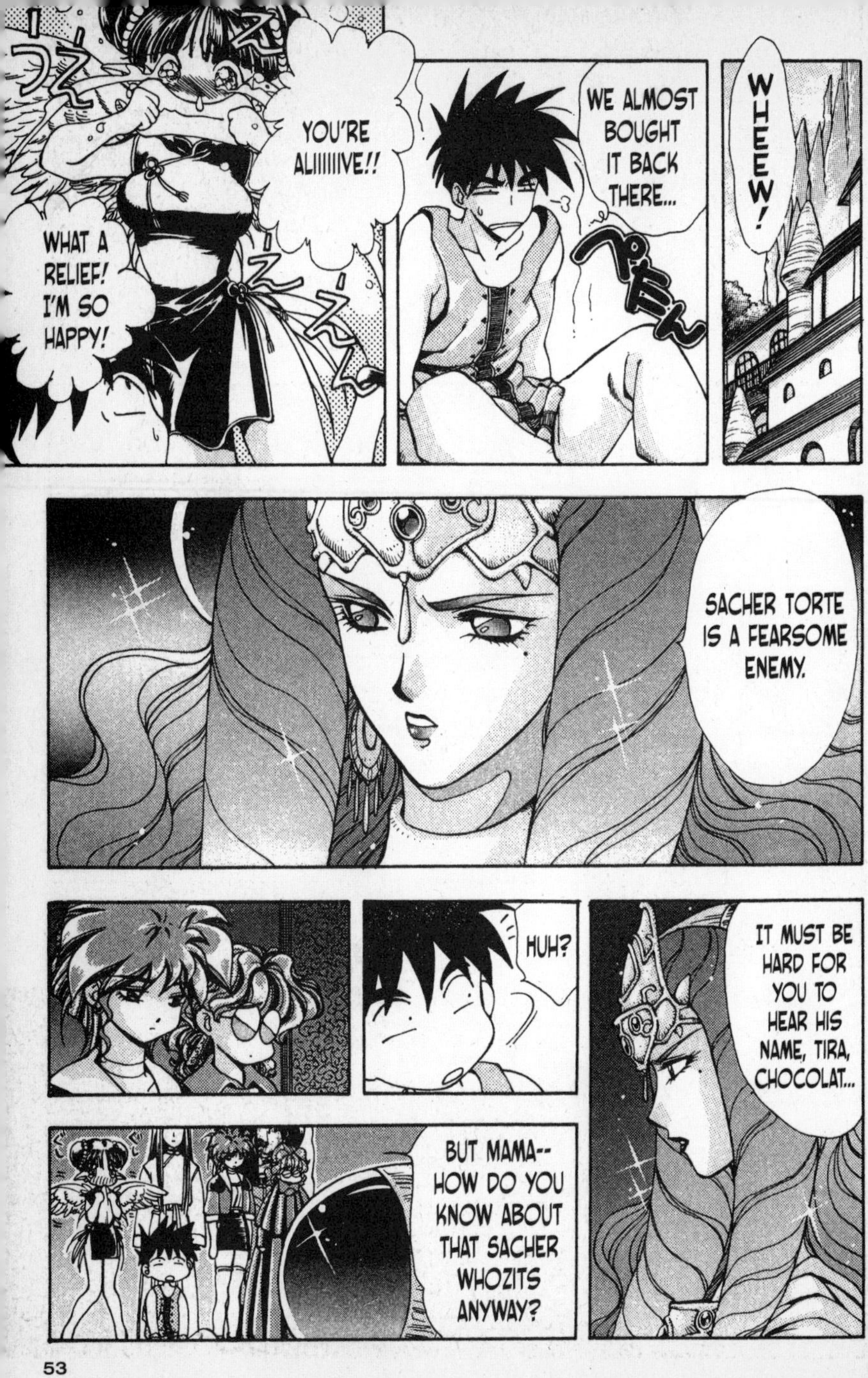
WHEEEW!
WE ALMOST BOUGHT IT BACK THERE...
YOU'RE ALIIIIIIVE!!
WHAT A RELIEF! I'M SO HAPPY!
SACHER TORTE IS A FEARSOME ENEMY.
IT MUST BE HARD FOR YOU TO HEAR HIS NAME, TIRA, CHOCOLAT...
HUH?
BUT MAMA-- HOW DO YOU KNOW ABOUT THAT SACHER WHOZITS ANYWAY?

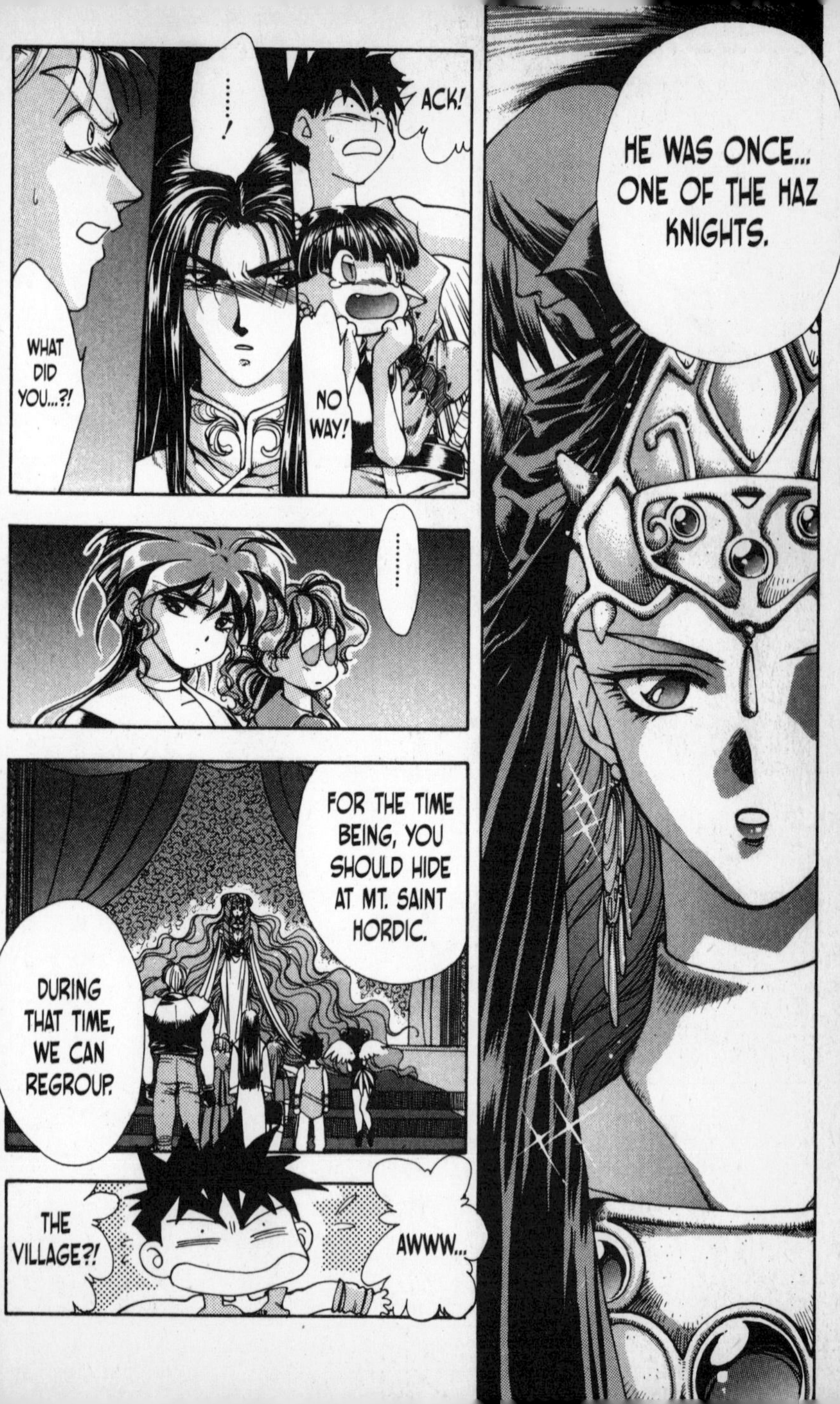
HE WAS ONCE... ONE OF THE HAZ KNIGHTS.
ACK!
......!
NO WAY!
WHAT DID YOU...?!
....
FOR THE TIME BEING, YOU SHOULD HIDE AT MT. SAINT HORDIC.
DURING THAT TIME, WE CAN REGROUP.
AWWW...
THE VILLAGE?!

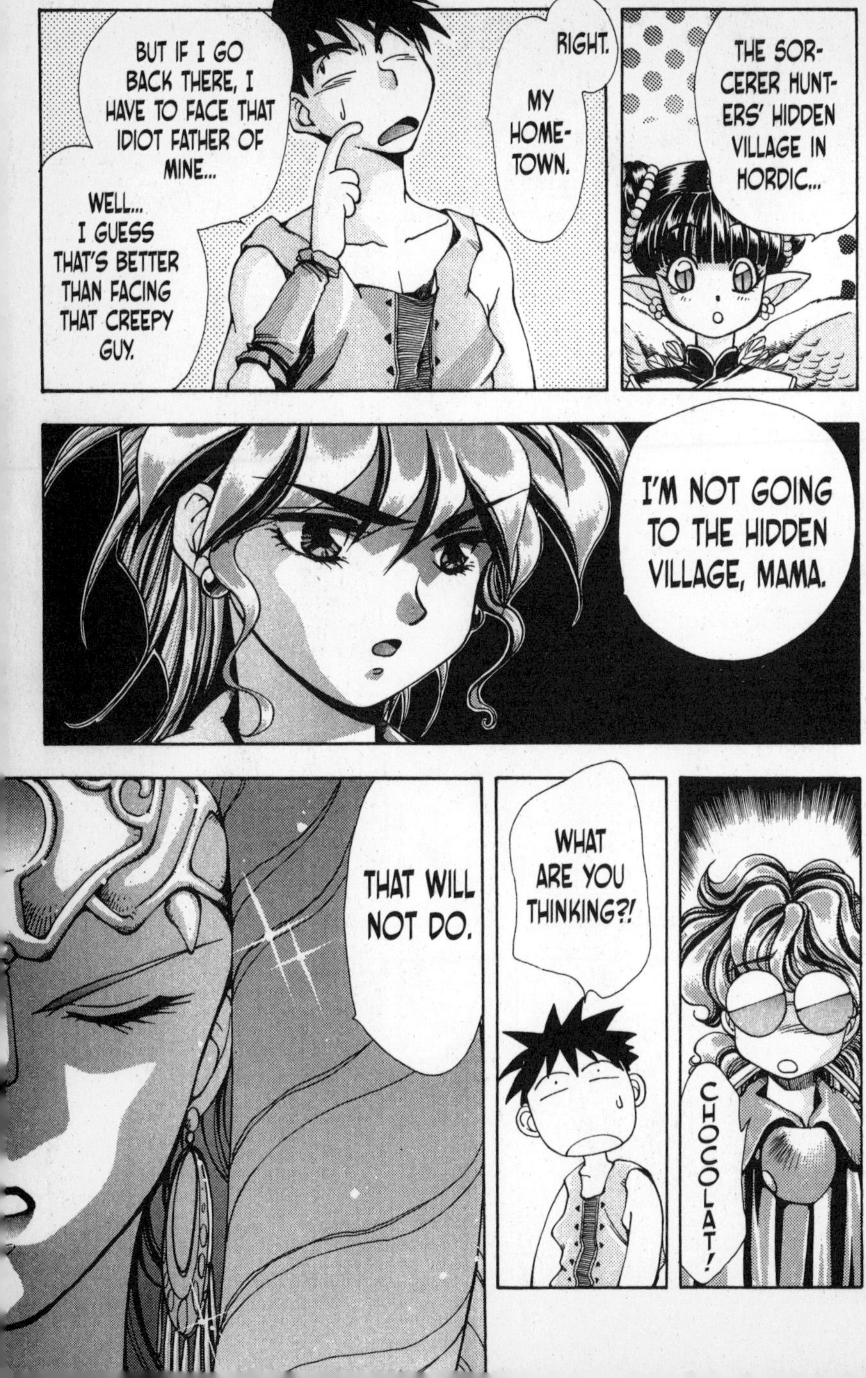
THE SORCERER HUNTERS' HIDDEN VILLAGE IN HORDIC...
RIGHT.
MY HOMETOWN.
BUT IF I GO BACK THERE, I HAVE TO FACE THAT IDIOT FATHER OF MINE...
WELL... I GUESS THAT'S BETTER THAN FACING THAT CREEPY GUY.
I'M NOT GOING TO THE HIDDEN VILLAGE, MAMA.
CHOCOLAT!
WHAT ARE YOU THINKING?!
THAT WILL NOT DO.

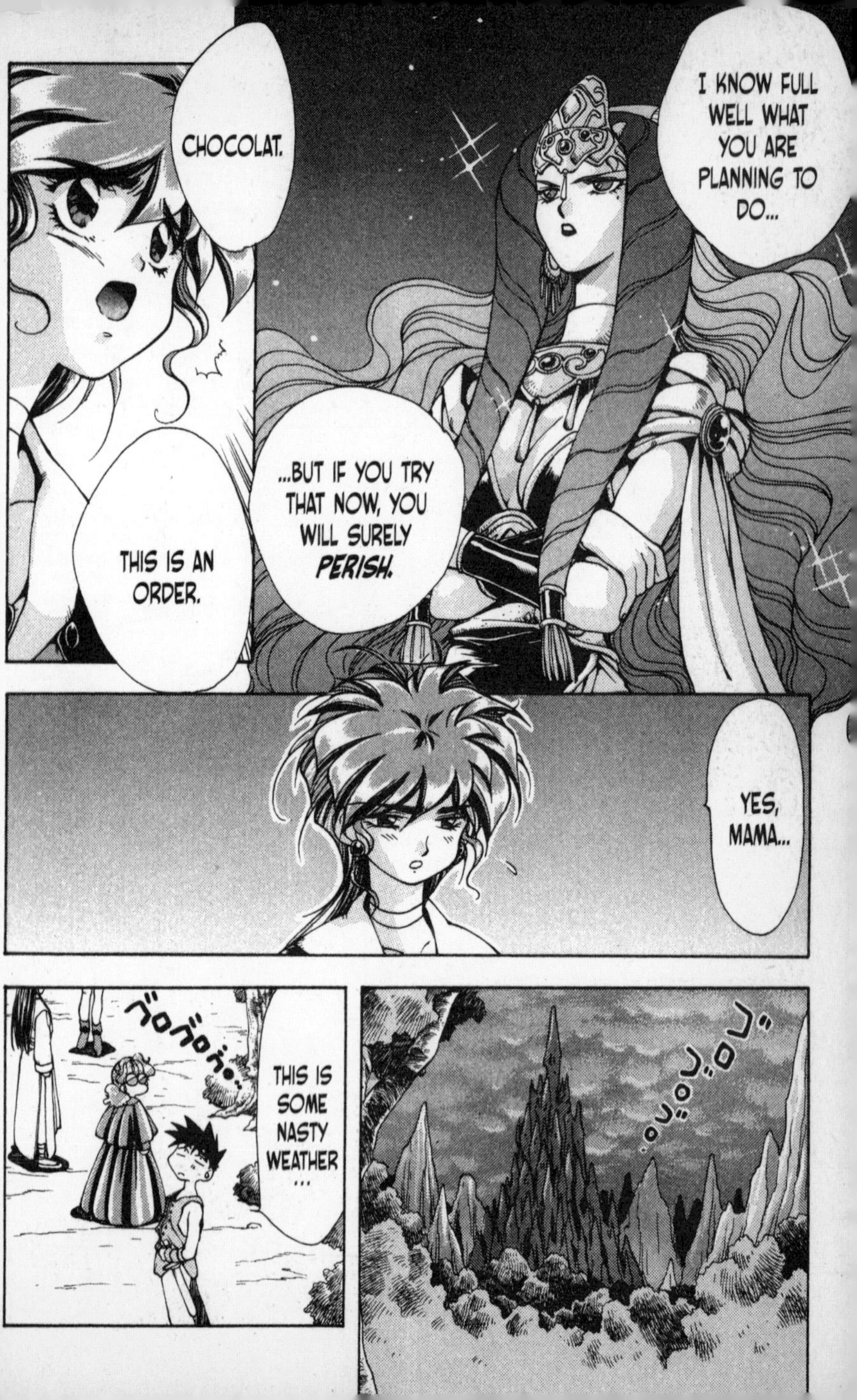

I KNOW FULL WELL WHAT YOU ARE PLANNING TO DO...
...BUT IF YOU TRY THAT NOW, YOU WILL SURELY *PERISH.*
CHOCOLAT.
THIS IS AN ORDER.
YES, MAMA...
ゴロゴロ…
THIS IS SOME NASTY WEATHER ...

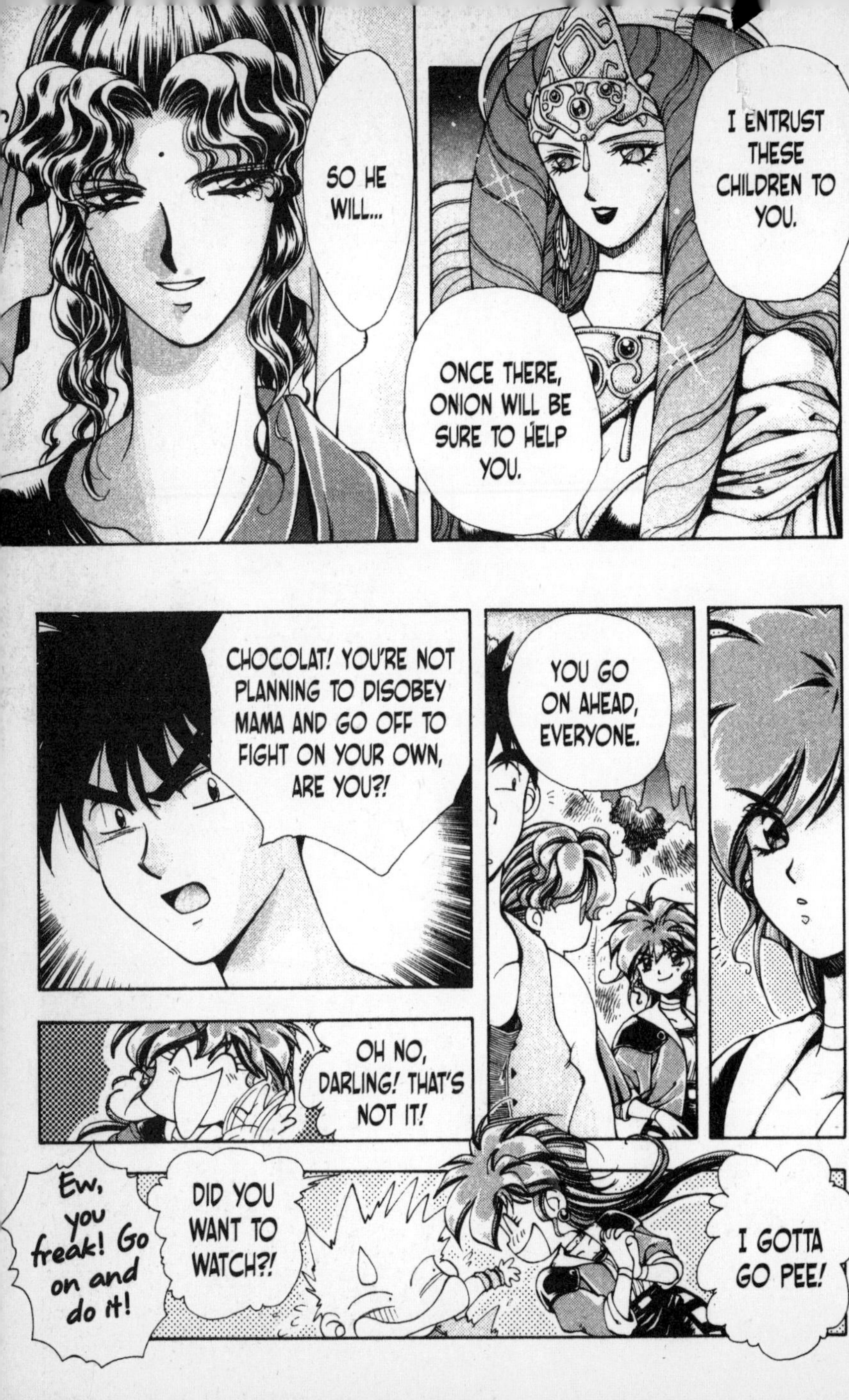
I ENTRUST THESE CHILDREN TO YOU.
ONCE THERE, ONION WILL BE SURE TO HELP YOU.
SO HE WILL...
YOU GO ON AHEAD, EVERYONE.
CHOCOLAT! YOU'RE NOT PLANNING TO DISOBEY MAMA AND GO OFF TO FIGHT ON YOUR OWN, ARE YOU?!
OH NO, DARLING! THAT'S NOT IT!
I GOTTA GO PEE!
DID YOU WANT TO WATCH?!
Ew, you freak! Go on and do it!

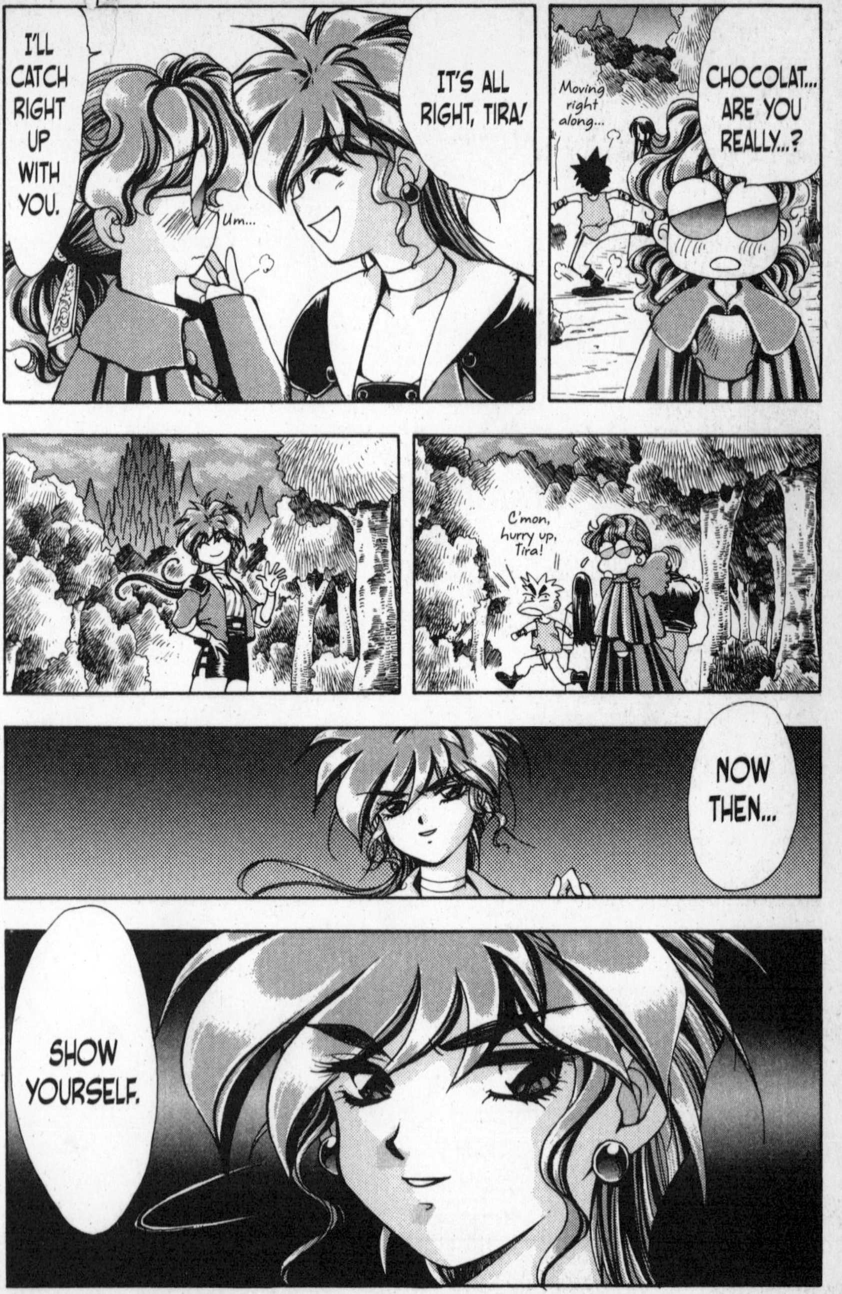
CHOCOLAT... ARE YOU REALLY...?
Moving right along...
IT'S ALL RIGHT, TIRA!
I'LL CATCH RIGHT UP WITH YOU.
Um...
C'mon, hurry up, Tira!
NOW THEN...
SHOW YOURSELF.

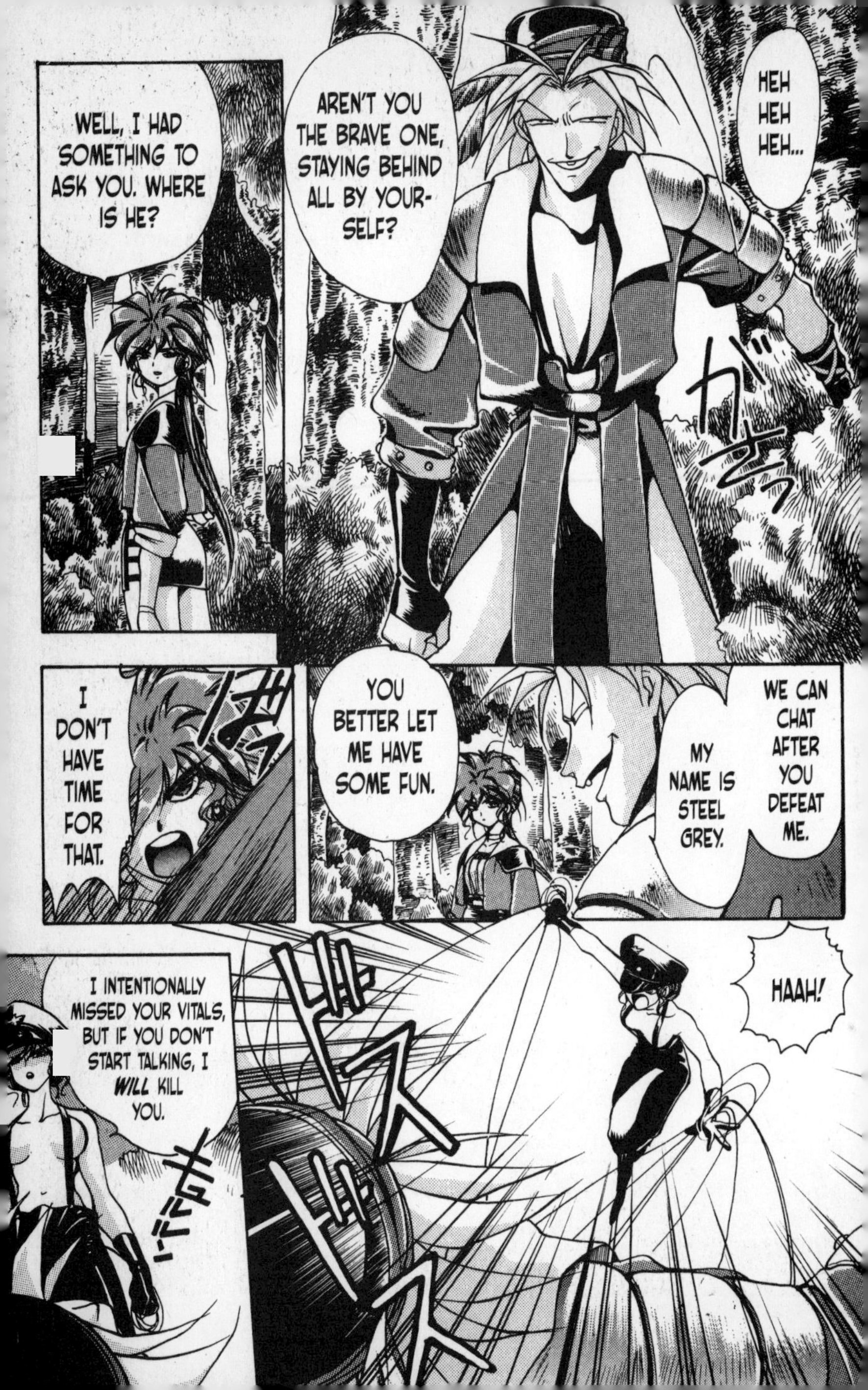
HEH HEH HEH...
AREN'T YOU THE BRAVE ONE, STAYING BEHIND ALL BY YOURSELF?
WELL, I HAD SOMETHING TO ASK YOU. WHERE IS HE?
WE CAN CHAT AFTER YOU DEFEAT ME.
MY NAME IS STEEL GREY.
YOU BETTER LET ME HAVE SOME FUN.
I DON'T HAVE TIME FOR THAT.
HAAH!
I INTENTIONALLY MISSED YOUR VITALS, BUT IF YOU DON'T START TALKING, I *WILL* KILL YOU.

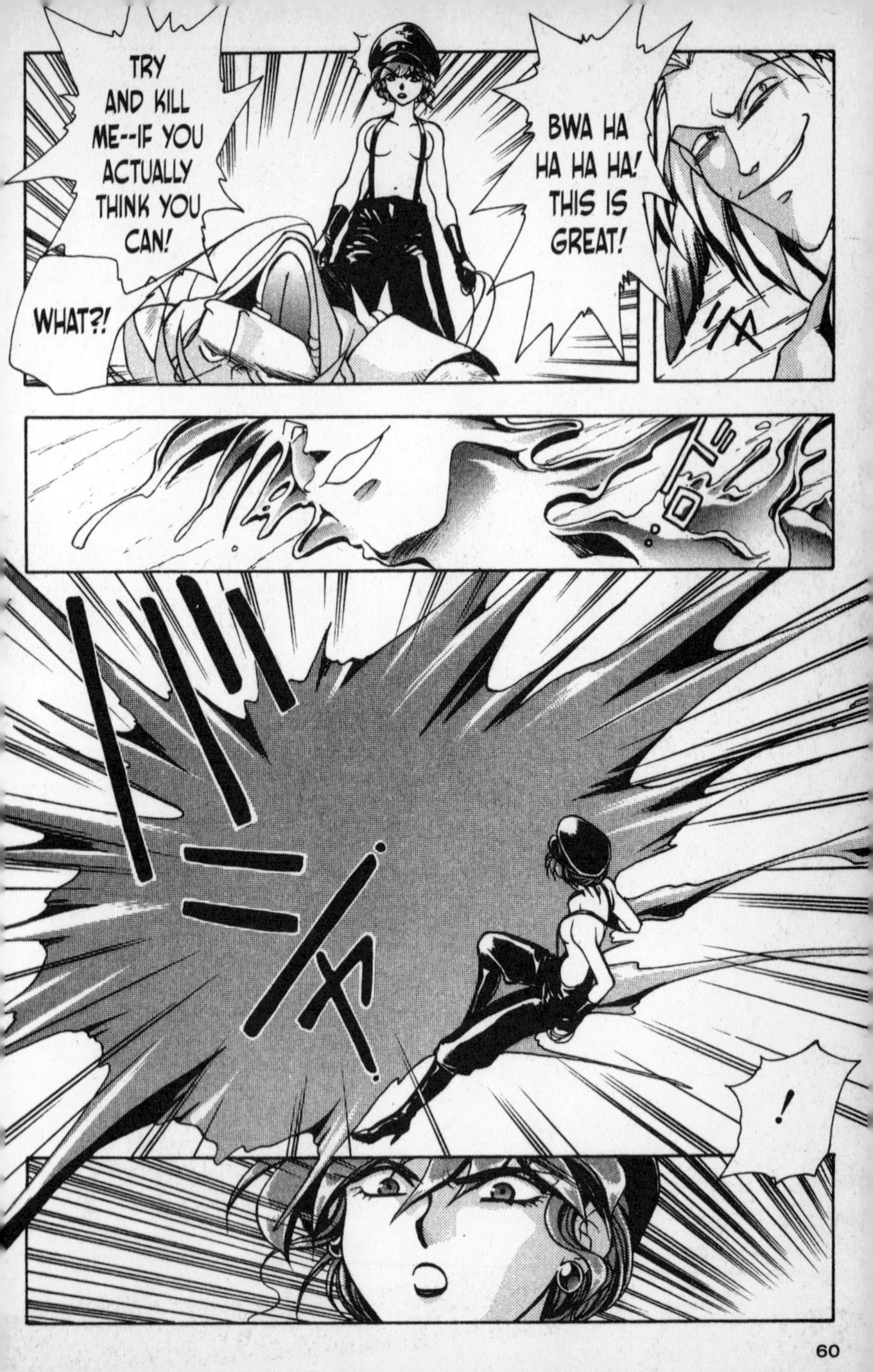
BWA HA HA HA HA! THIS IS GREAT!
TRY AND KILL ME--IF YOU ACTUALLY THINK YOU CAN!
WHAT?!
!

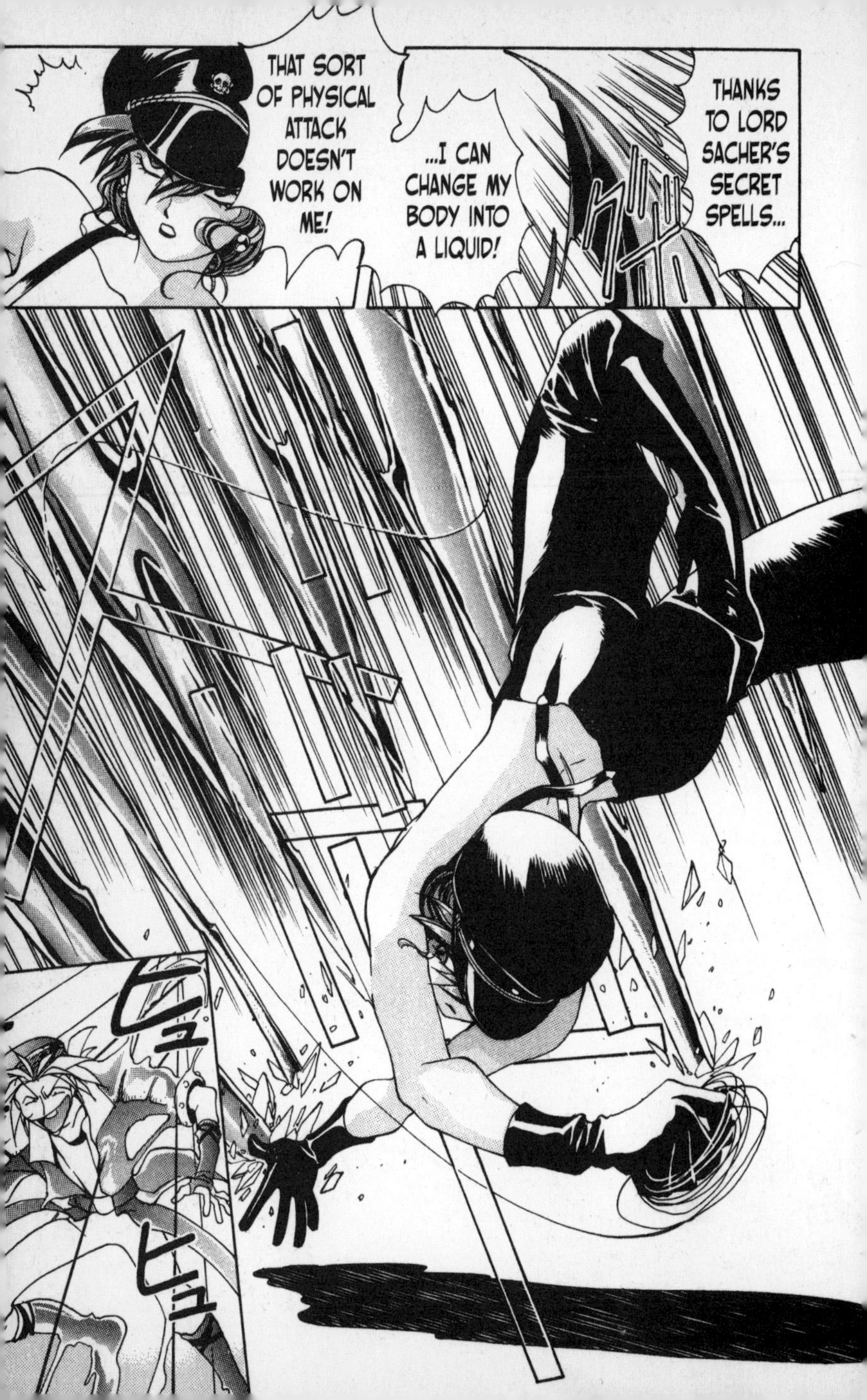
THANKS TO LORD SACHER'S SECRET SPELLS...
...I CAN CHANGE MY BODY INTO A LIQUID!
THAT SORT OF PHYSICAL ATTACK DOESN'T WORK ON ME!
ヒュ
ヒュ

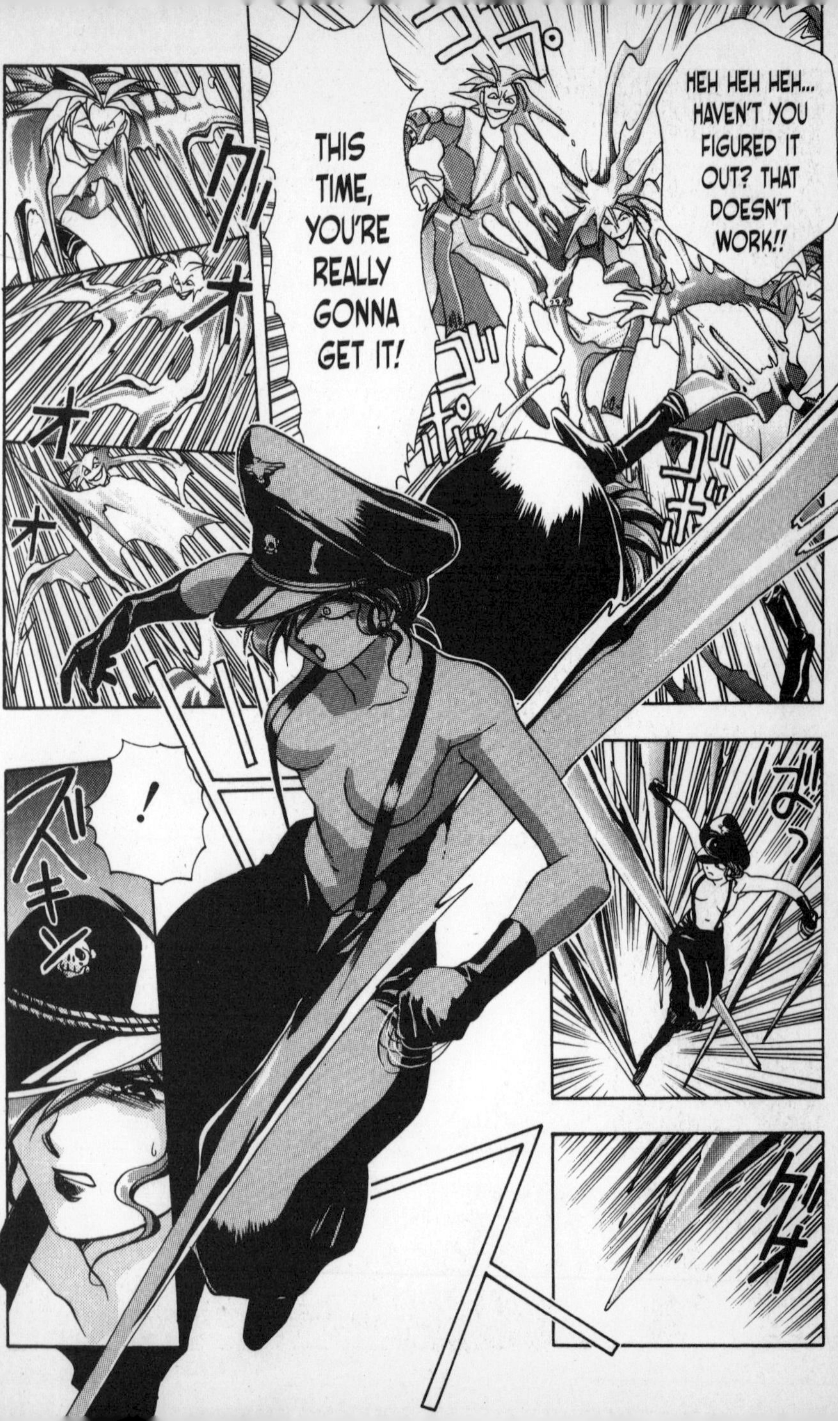
HEH HEH HEH... HAVEN'T YOU FIGURED IT OUT? THAT DOESN'T WORK!!
THIS TIME, YOU'RE REALLY GONNA GET IT!
!

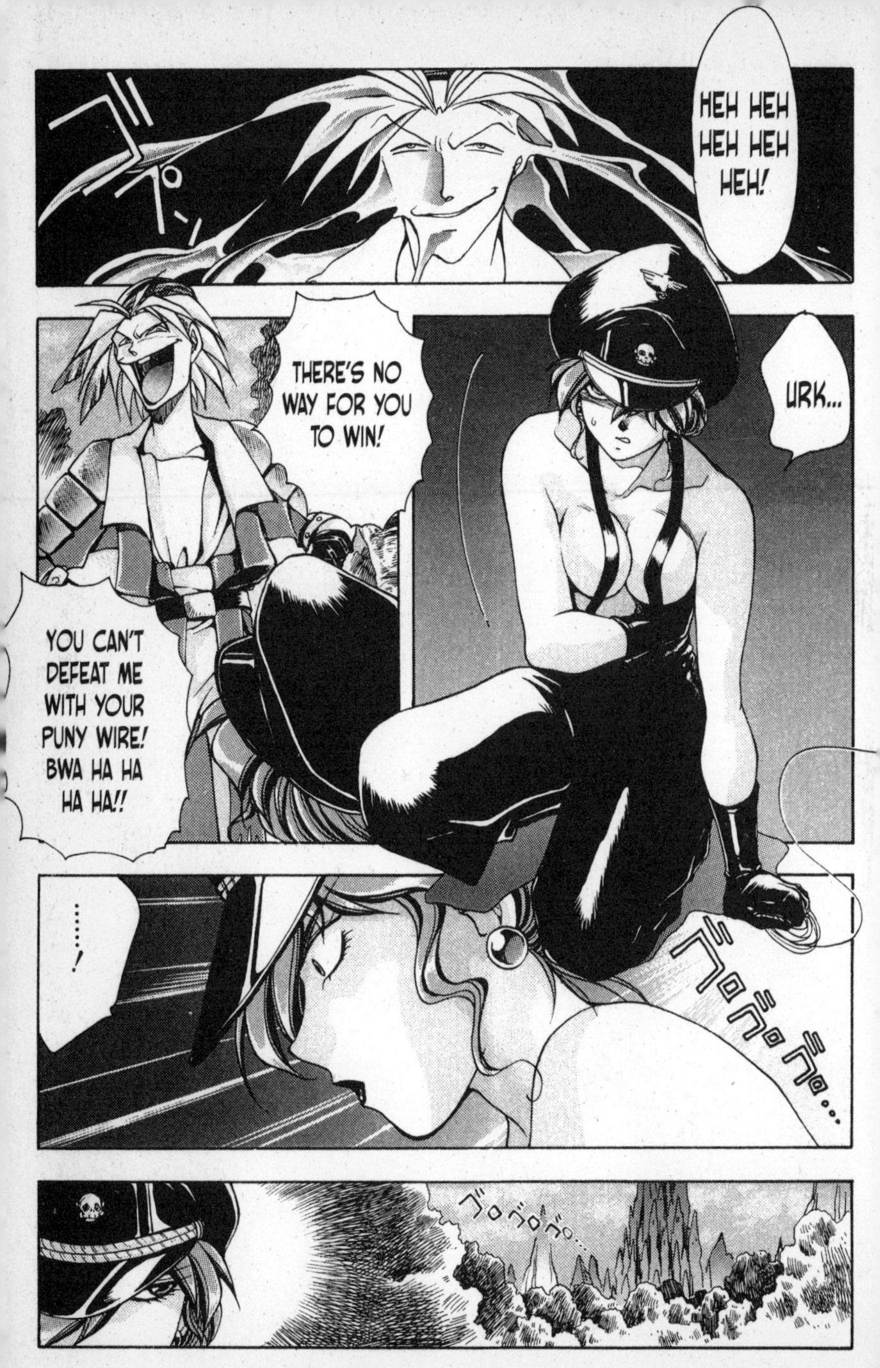

HEH HEH HEH HEH HEH!
URK...
THERE'S NO WAY FOR YOU TO WIN!
YOU CAN'T DEFEAT ME WITH YOUR PUNY WIRE! BWA HA HA HA HA!!
......!

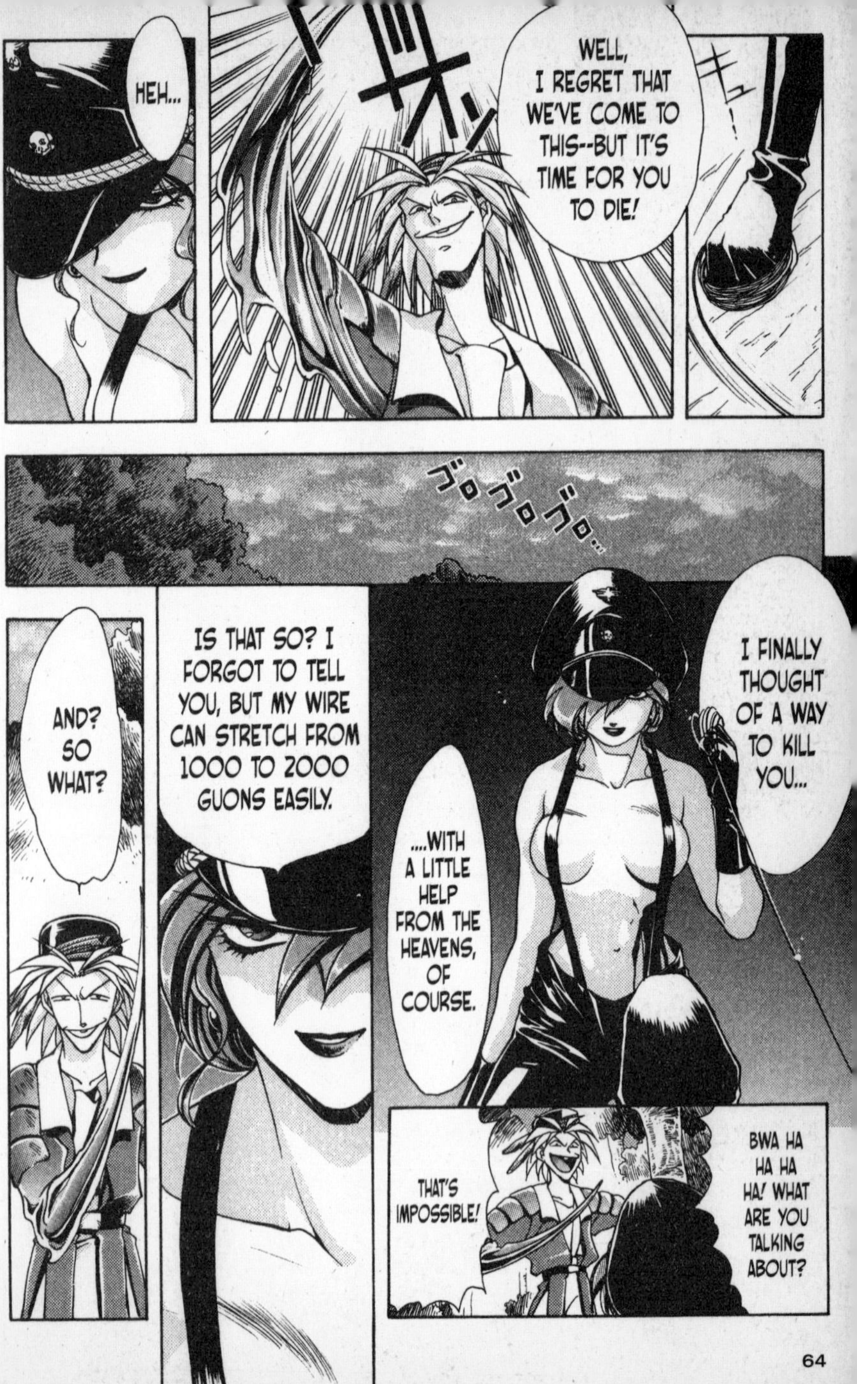
WELL, I REGRET THAT WE'VE COME TO THIS--BUT IT'S TIME FOR YOU TO DIE!
HEH...
ゴロゴロゴロ...
I FINALLY THOUGHT OF A WAY TO KILL YOU...
....WITH A LITTLE HELP FROM THE HEAVENS, OF COURSE.
BWA HA HA HA HA! WHAT ARE YOU TALKING ABOUT?
THAT'S IMPOSSIBLE!
IS THAT SO? I FORGOT TO TELL YOU, BUT MY WIRE CAN STRETCH FROM 1000 TO 2000 GUONS EASILY.
AND? SO WHAT?
...

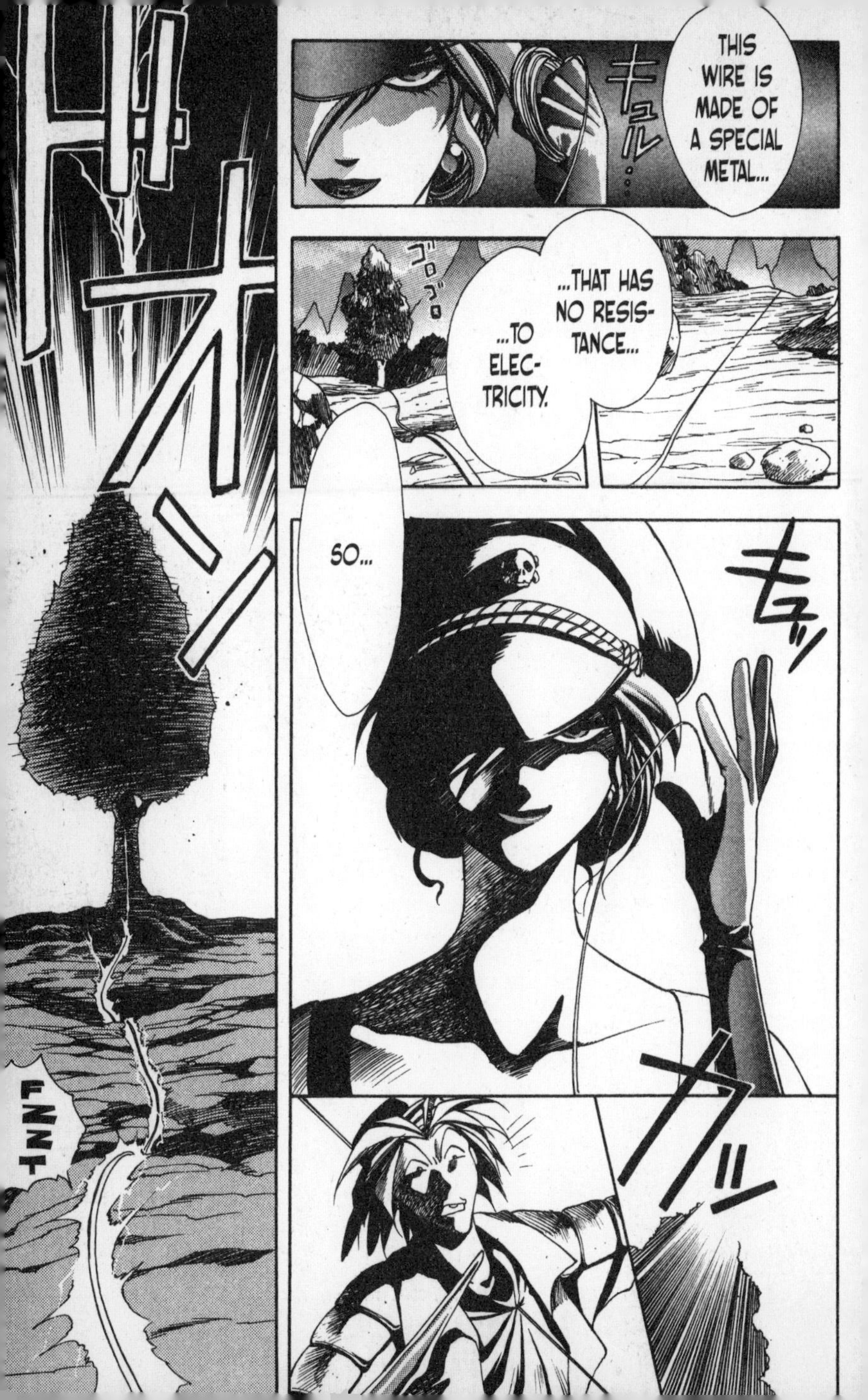
THIS WIRE IS MADE OF A SPECIAL METAL...
キュル...
...THAT HAS NO RESISTANCE...
...TO ELECTRICITY.
ゴロゴロ
SO...
FZZT

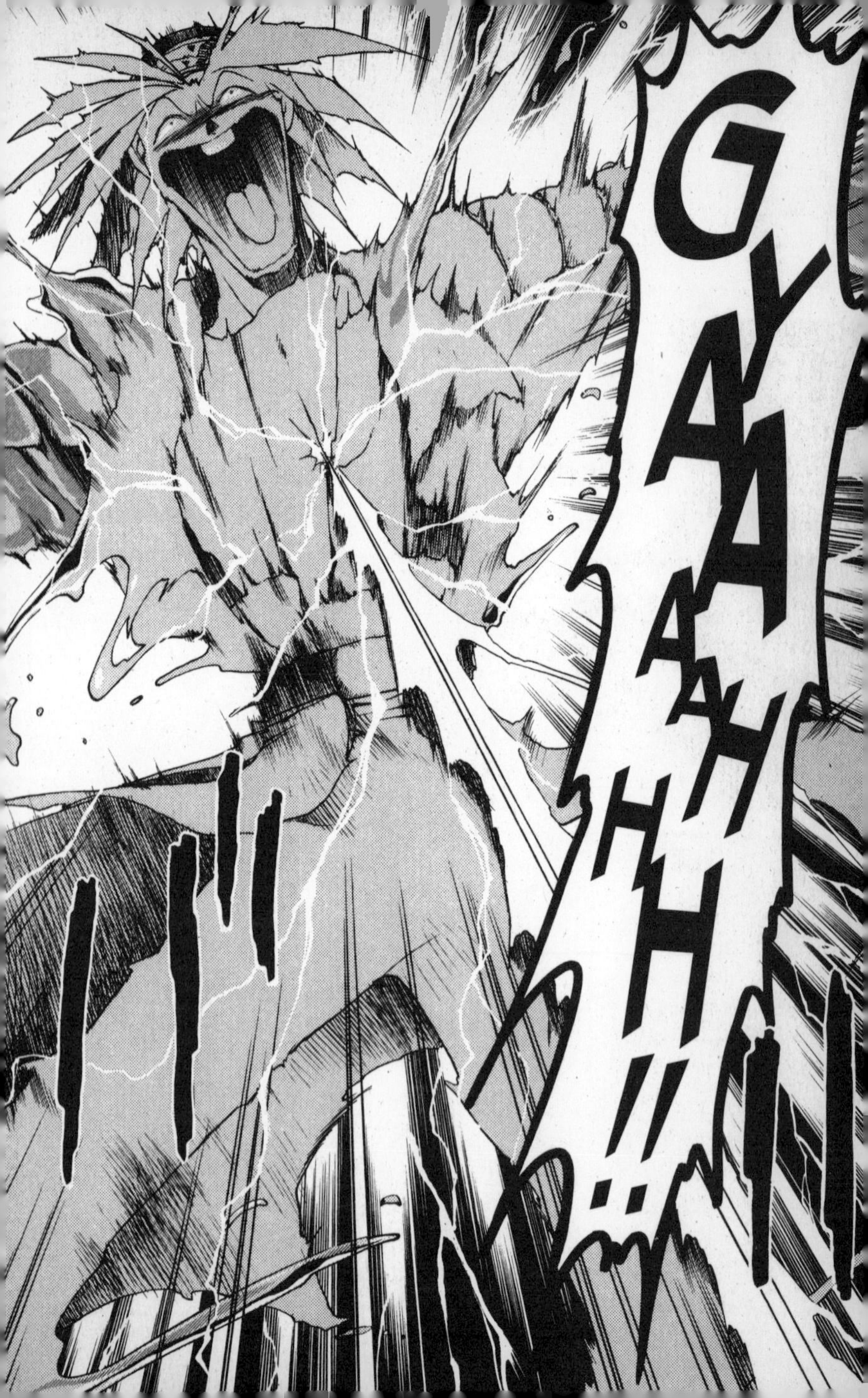
GYAAAAHHH!!

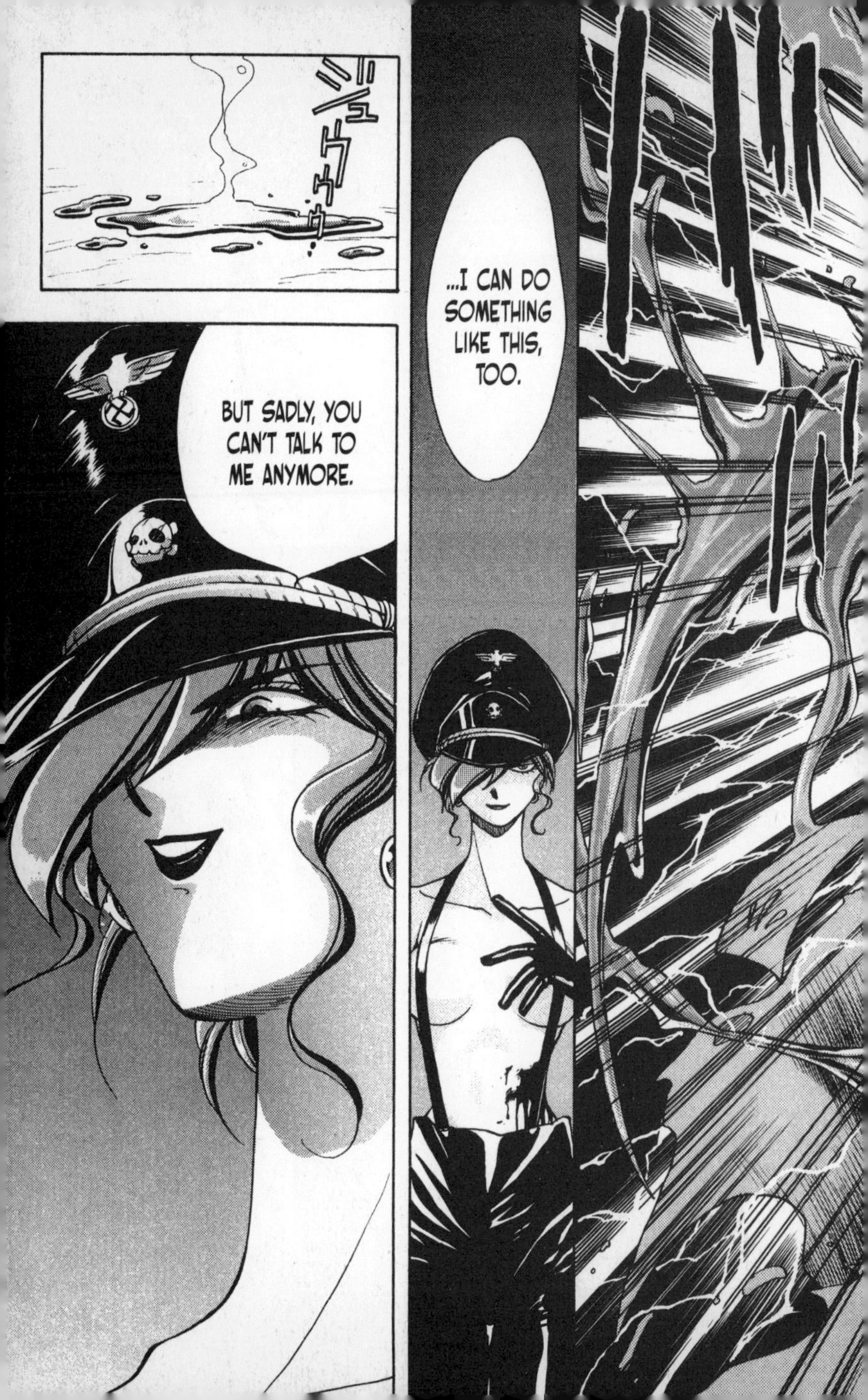
...I CAN DO SOMETHING LIKE THIS, TOO.
ジュウゥゥ
BUT SADLY, YOU CAN'T TALK TO ME ANYMORE.

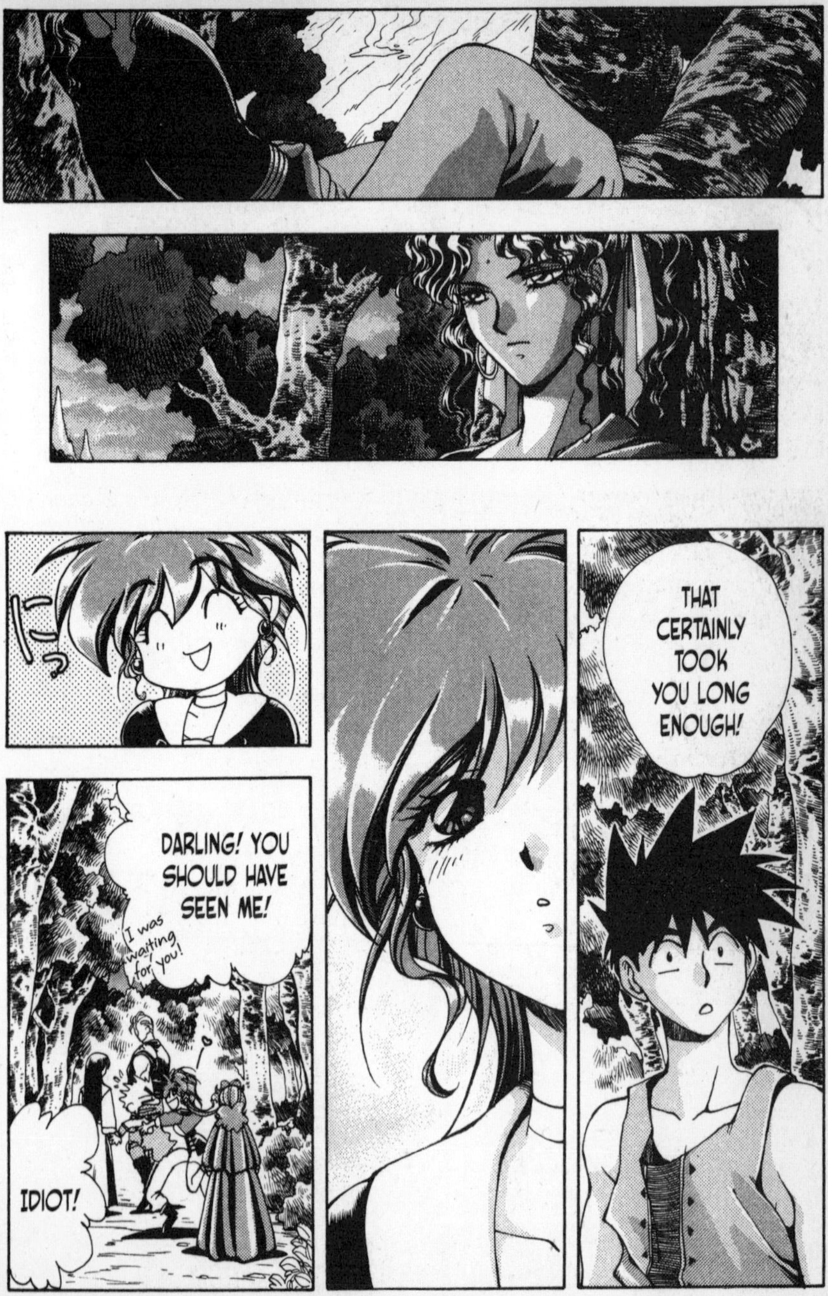
THAT CERTAINLY TOOK YOU LONG ENOUGH!
DARLING! YOU SHOULD HAVE SEEN ME!
I was waiting for you!
IDIOT!

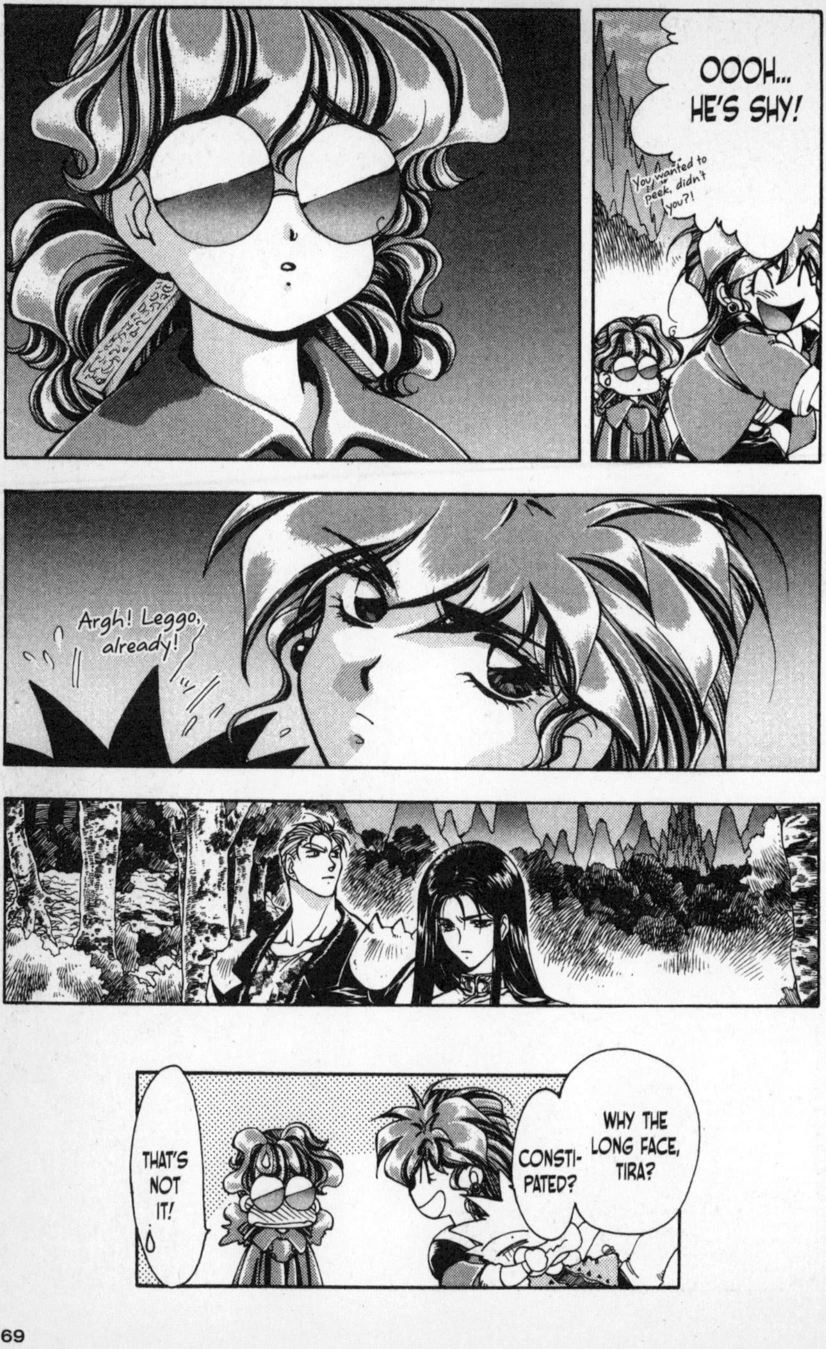
OOOH... HE'S SHY!
You wanted to peek, didn't you?!
Argh! Leggo, already!
WHY THE LONG FACE, TIRA?
CONSTI-PATED?
THAT'S NOT IT!

SORCERER HUNTER KILLER

• GIA PURPLE •

THE MYSTERIOUS MUSCLEMAN! AH...◊ I HAVE NOTHING TO WRITE ABOUT HIM.◊ I GOT THE DESIGNS DONE QUICKLY FOR ALL OF THESE THREE. INSTEAD OF LOADING STUFF ON GIA, I THOUGHT LEAVING HIS UPPER BODY ALMOST BARE MADE HIM LOOK STRONGER. THOUGH, STRIPPING THE ARMOR OFF HIM...WAS A PAIN. ◊

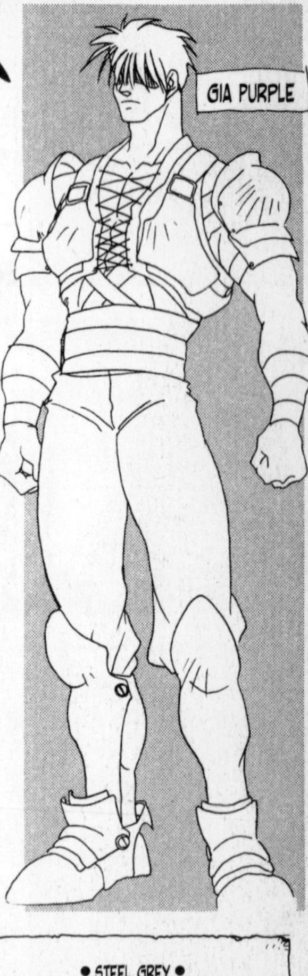
GIA PURPLE

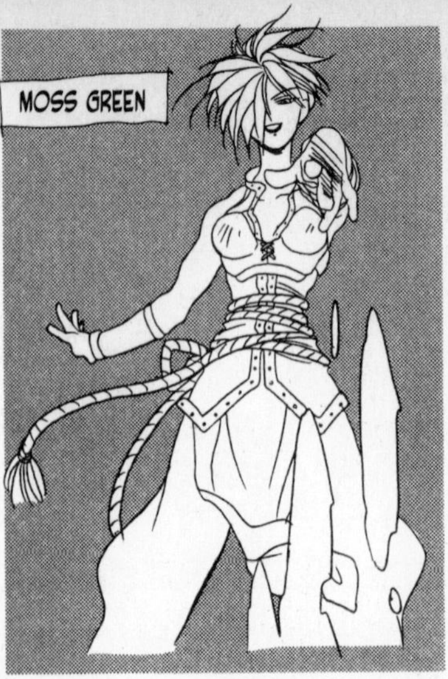
MOSS GREEN

• MOSS GREEN •

I LIKE SHORT HAIR AND TAN SKIN!◊ I'M SORRY!◊ (WHAT AM I APOLOGIZING FOR?◊) IT'S A PAIN TO APPLY THE TONE FOR DARKER SKIN...SO I AVOIDED IT UNTIL NOW. BUT I'M GLAD I FINALLY DID IT. AND WHAT'S MORE...IF SHE WERE NUDE...I...I'D BE SO HAPPY!◊ BUT SHE'S SURROUNDED BY EARTH SPEARS ALL THE TIME. MY POOR ASSISTANT WAS HALLUCINATING ABOUT EARTH SPEARS. I LIKED HER CLOTHES AND ARMOR, TOO.

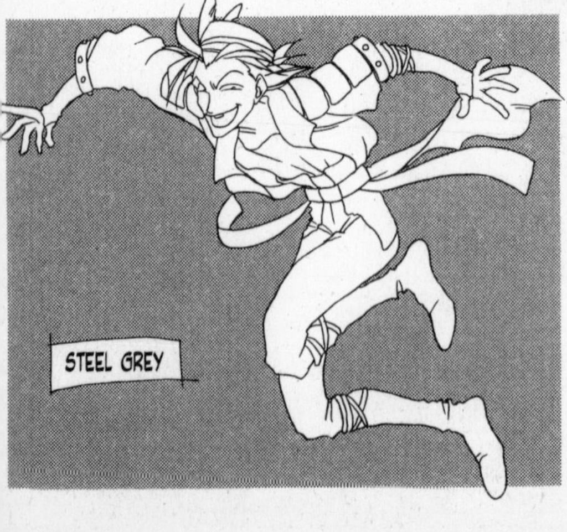
STEEL GREY

• STEEL GREY •

THE CHARACTER MODEL FOR STEEL GREY IS, OF COURSE, SUNEO!◊ HE'S SKINNY AND SHORT AND LIGHT... AT FIRST, STEEL GREY HAD GIA PURPLE'S NAME. HE WAS THE UNLUCKY FIRST AMONG THE THREE TO DIE.◊ BECAUSE OF HIS FACE, PERHAPS...?◊

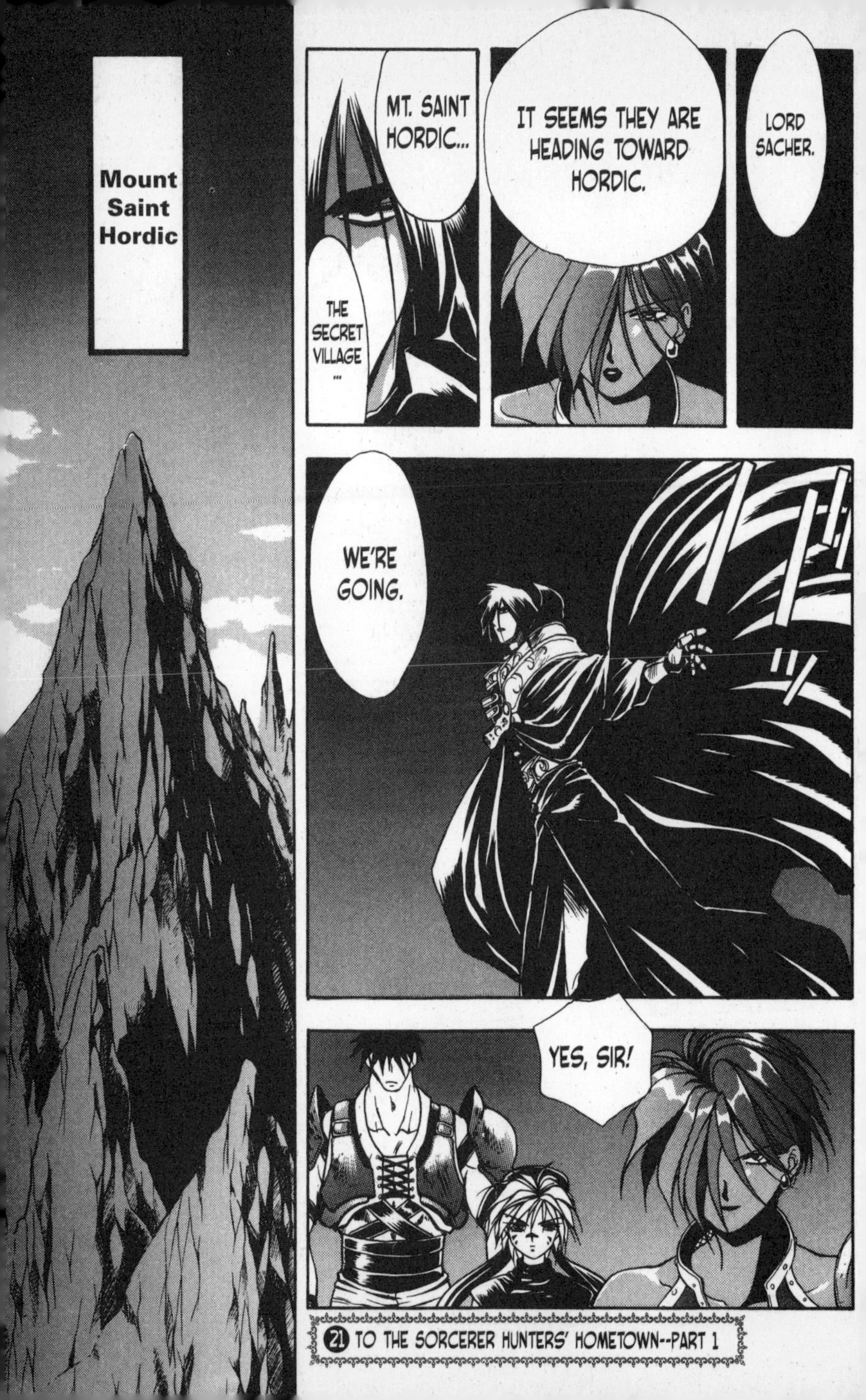
LORD SACHER.
IT SEEMS THEY ARE HEADING TOWARD HORDIC.
MT. SAINT HORDIC...
THE SECRET VILLAGE ...
WE'RE GOING.
YES, SIR!
21 TO THE SORCERER HUNTERS' HOMETOWN--PART 1
Mount Saint Hordic

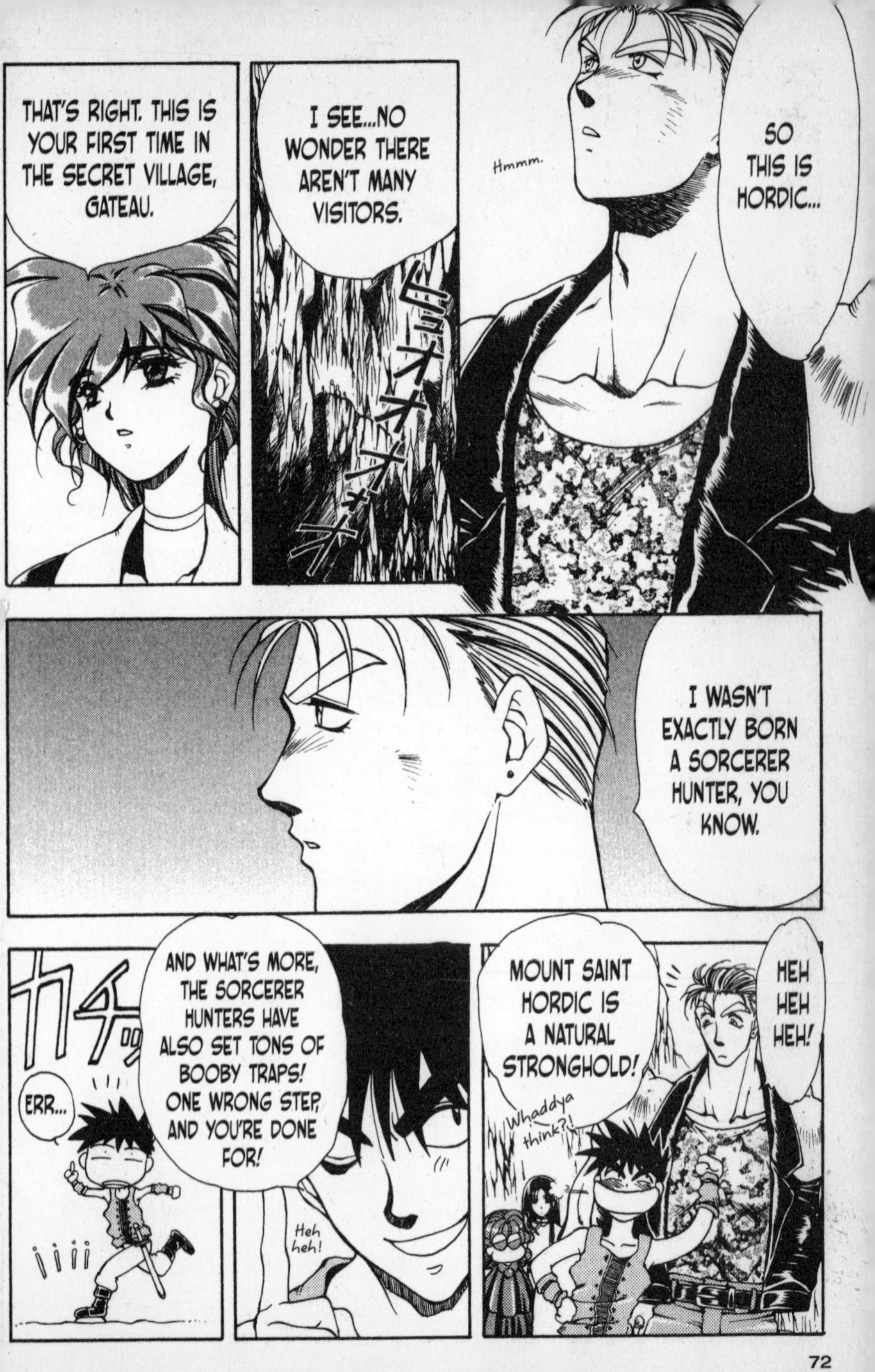

Hmmm.
SO THIS IS HORDIC...
I SEE...NO WONDER THERE AREN'T MANY VISITORS.
THAT'S RIGHT. THIS IS YOUR FIRST TIME IN THE SECRET VILLAGE, GATEAU.
I WASN'T EXACTLY BORN A SORCERER HUNTER, YOU KNOW.
HEH HEH HEH!
MOUNT SAINT HORDIC IS A NATURAL STRONGHOLD!
Whaddya think?!
AND WHAT'S MORE, THE SORCERER HUNTERS HAVE ALSO SET TONS OF BOOBY TRAPS! ONE WRONG STEP, AND YOU'RE DONE FOR!
Heh heh!
ERR...

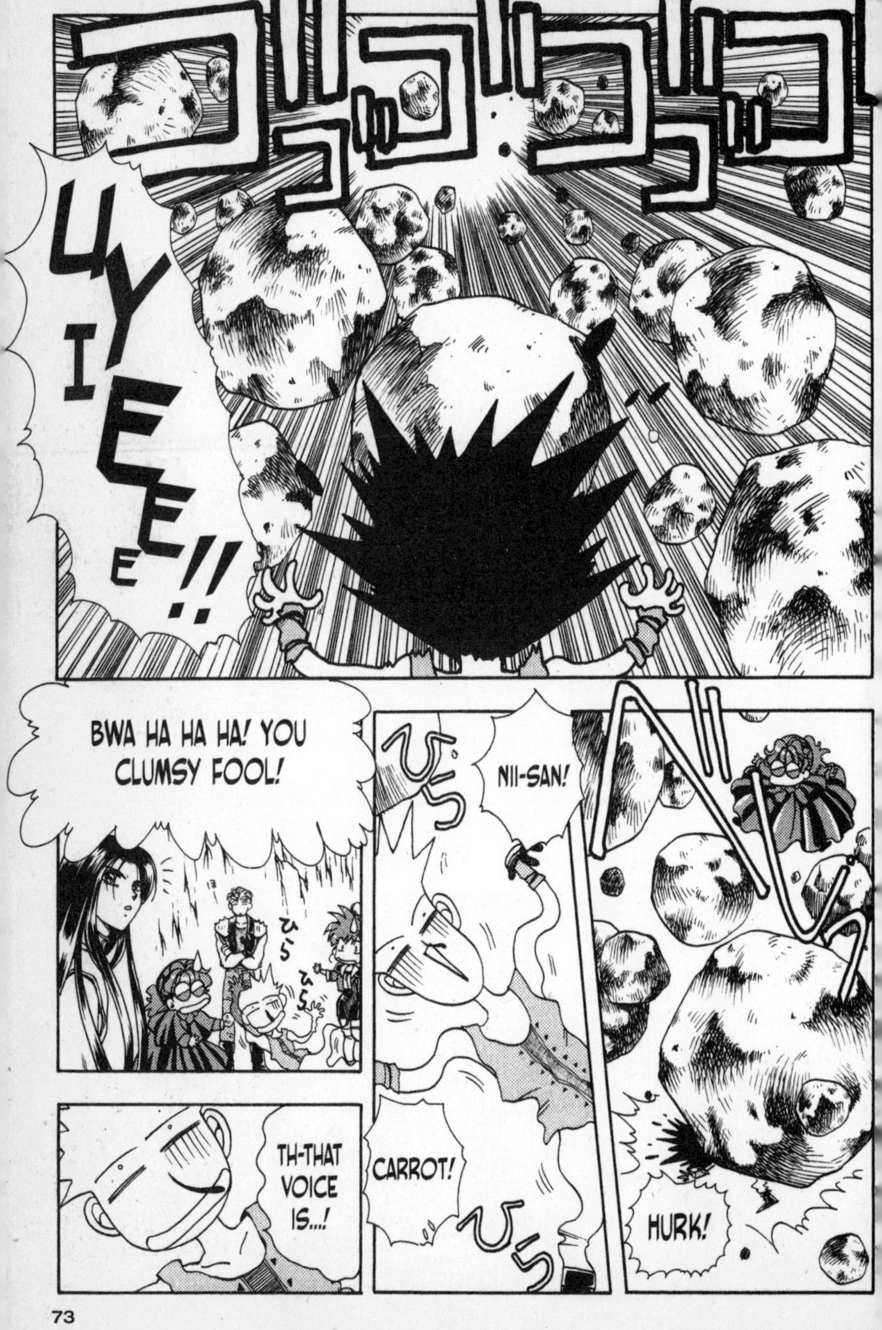

ゴッゴッゴッ
UYIEEEE!!
HURK!
NII-SAN!
ひら
CARROT!
ひら
BWA HA HA HA! YOU CLUMSY FOOL!
ひら ひら
TH-THAT VOICE IS...!

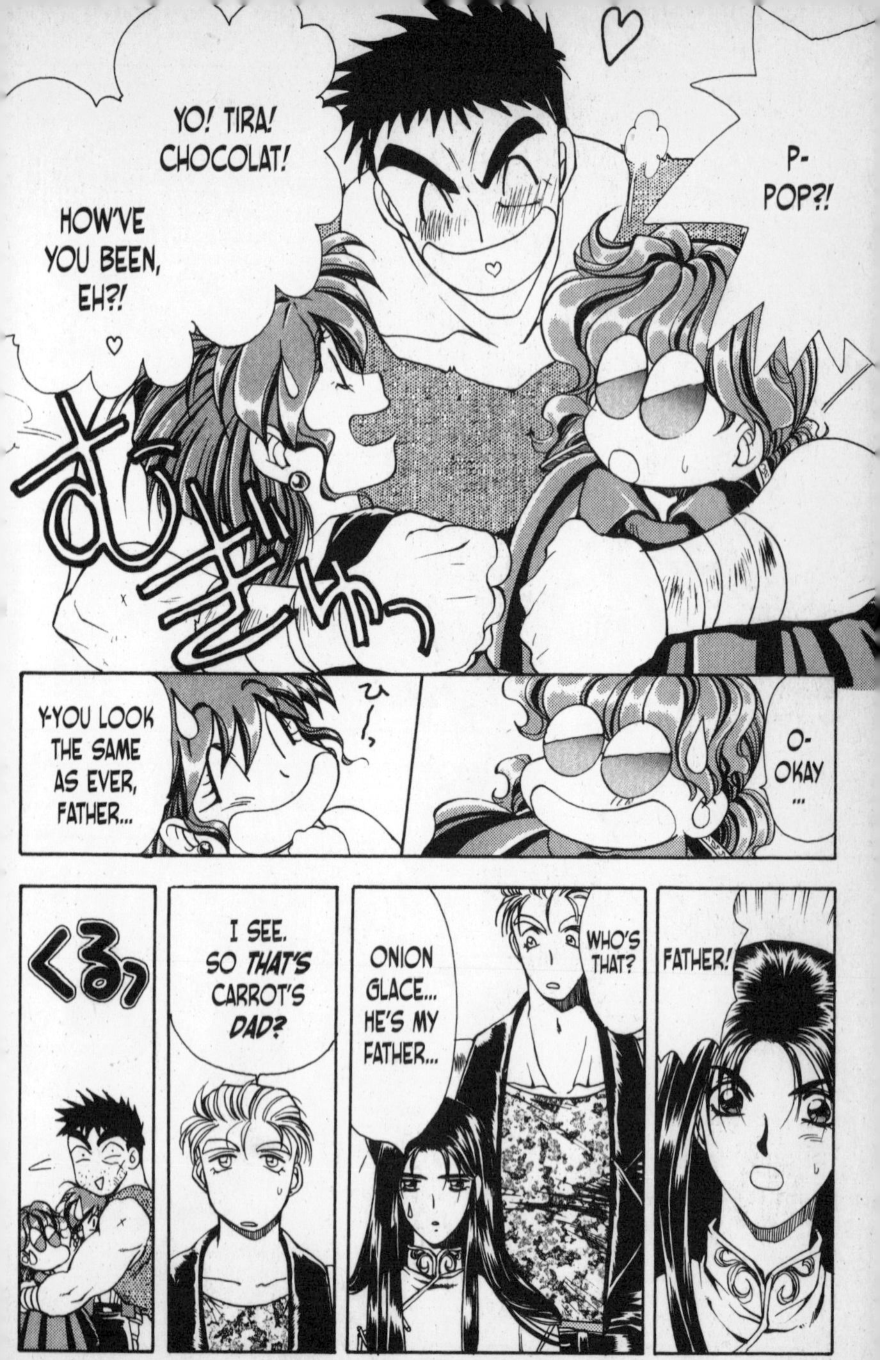
YO! TIRA! CHOCOLAT!
HOW'VE YOU BEEN, EH?! ♡
P- POP?!
むぎゅっ
O- OKAY ...
ひー
Y-YOU LOOK THE SAME AS EVER, FATHER...
FATHER!
WHO'S THAT?
ONION GLACE... HE'S MY FATHER...
I SEE. SO *THAT'S* CARROT'S *DAD*?
くるっ

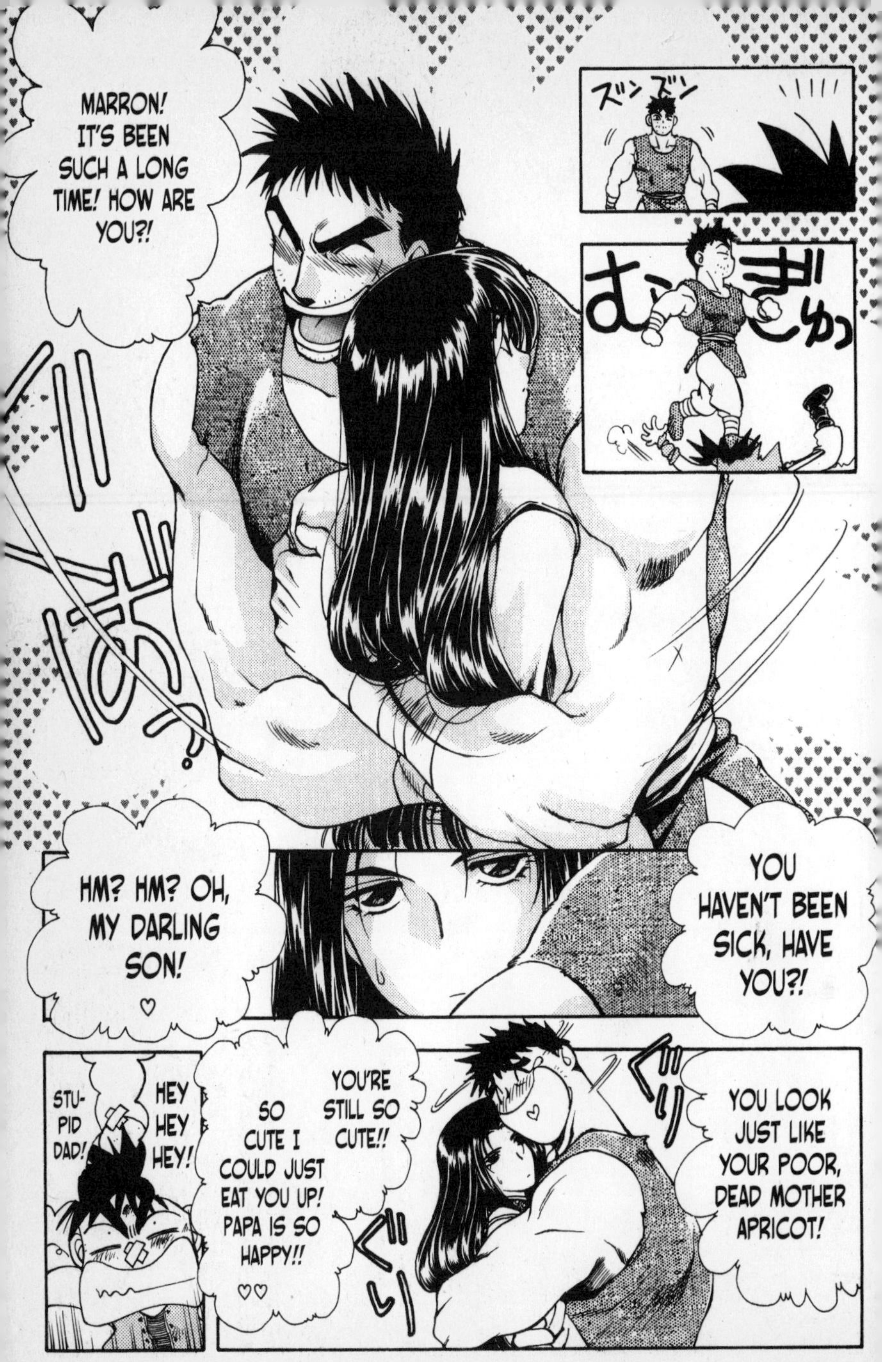
ズンズン
むぎゅっ
MARRON! IT'S BEEN SUCH A LONG TIME! HOW ARE YOU?!
はっ?!
YOU HAVEN'T BEEN SICK, HAVE YOU?!
HM? HM? OH, MY DARLING SON! ♡
YOU LOOK JUST LIKE YOUR POOR, DEAD MOTHER APRICOT!
ぐりぐり
YOU'RE STILL SO CUTE!!
SO CUTE I COULD JUST EAT YOU UP! PAPA IS SO HAPPY!! ♡♡
HEY HEY HEY!
STU-PID DAD!

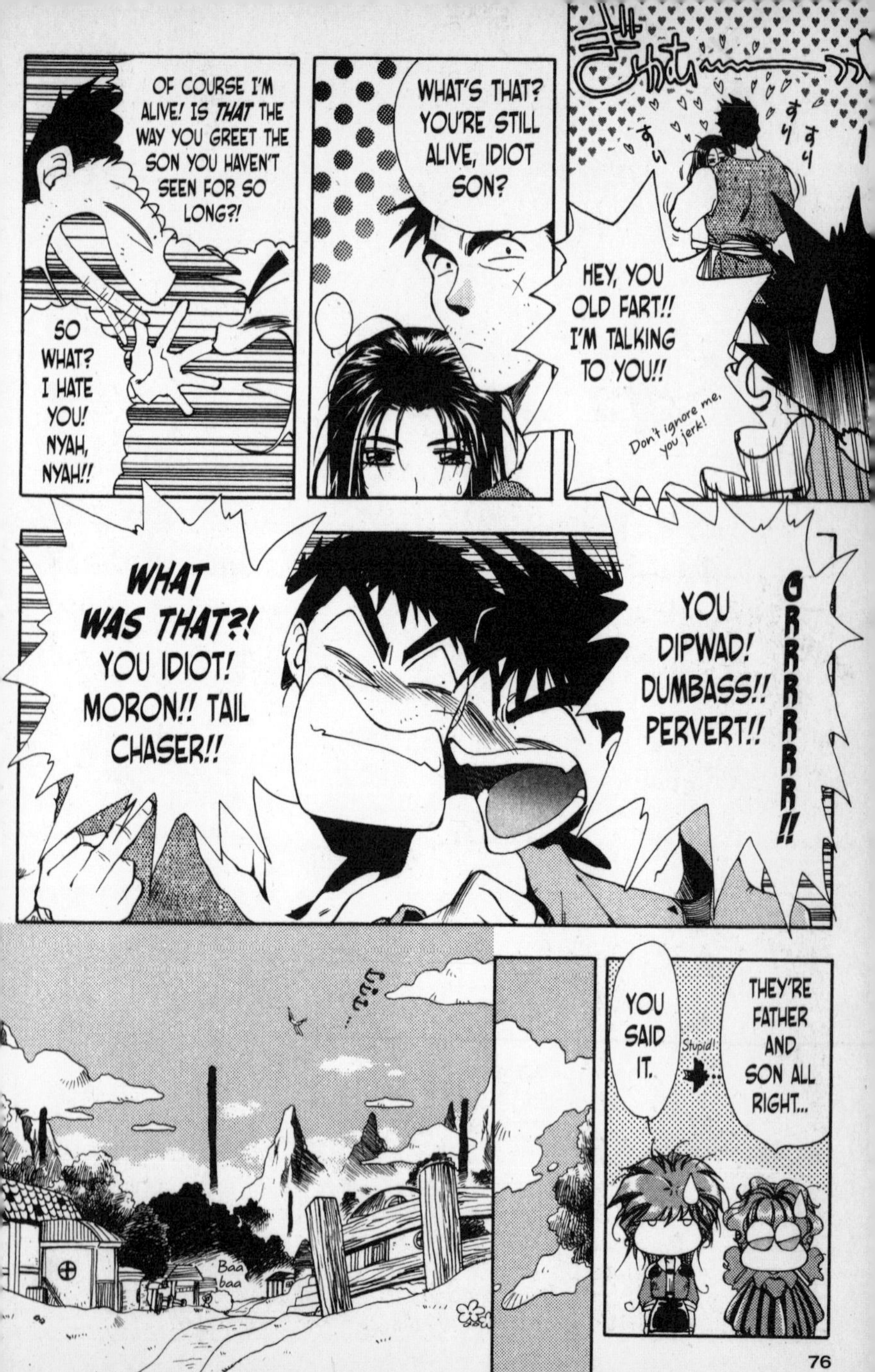
すり すり
すい
HEY, YOU OLD FART!! I'M TALKING TO YOU!!
Don't ignore me, you jerk!
WHAT'S THAT? YOU'RE STILL ALIVE, IDIOT SON?
OF COURSE I'M ALIVE! IS *THAT* THE WAY YOU GREET THE SON YOU HAVEN'T SEEN FOR SO LONG?!
SO WHAT? I HATE YOU! NYAH, NYAH!!
GRRRRRR!!
YOU DIPWAD! DUMBASS!! PERVERT!!
WHAT WAS THAT?! YOU IDIOT! MORON!! TAIL CHASER!!
THEY'RE FATHER AND SON ALL RIGHT...
Stupid!
YOU SAID IT.
Baa baa

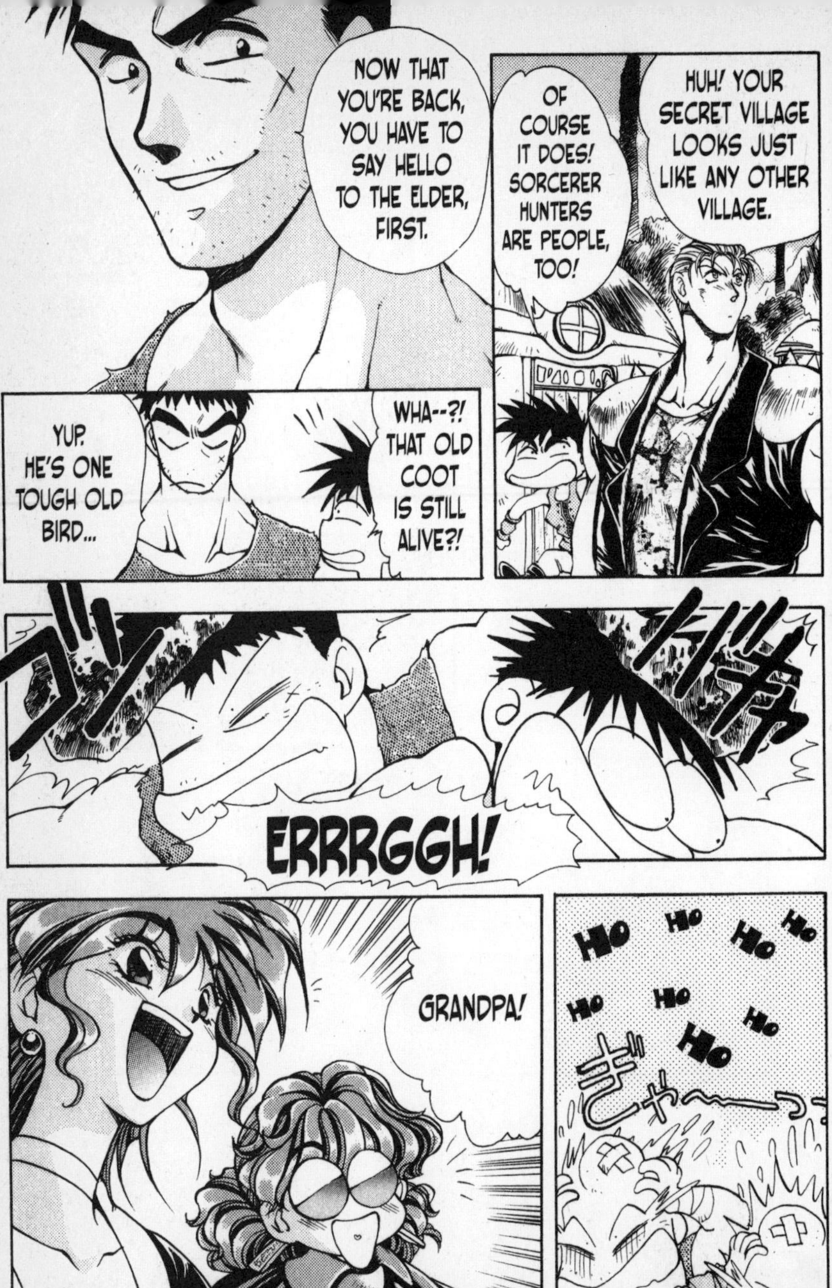
HUH! YOUR SECRET VILLAGE LOOKS JUST LIKE ANY OTHER VILLAGE.
OF COURSE IT DOES! SORCERER HUNTERS ARE PEOPLE, TOO!
NOW THAT YOU'RE BACK, YOU HAVE TO SAY HELLO TO THE ELDER, FIRST.
WHA--?! THAT OLD COOT IS STILL ALIVE?!
YUP. HE'S ONE TOUGH OLD BIRD...
ERRRGGH!
HO HO HO HO HO HO HO HO HO
ぎゃ～っ
GRANDPA!

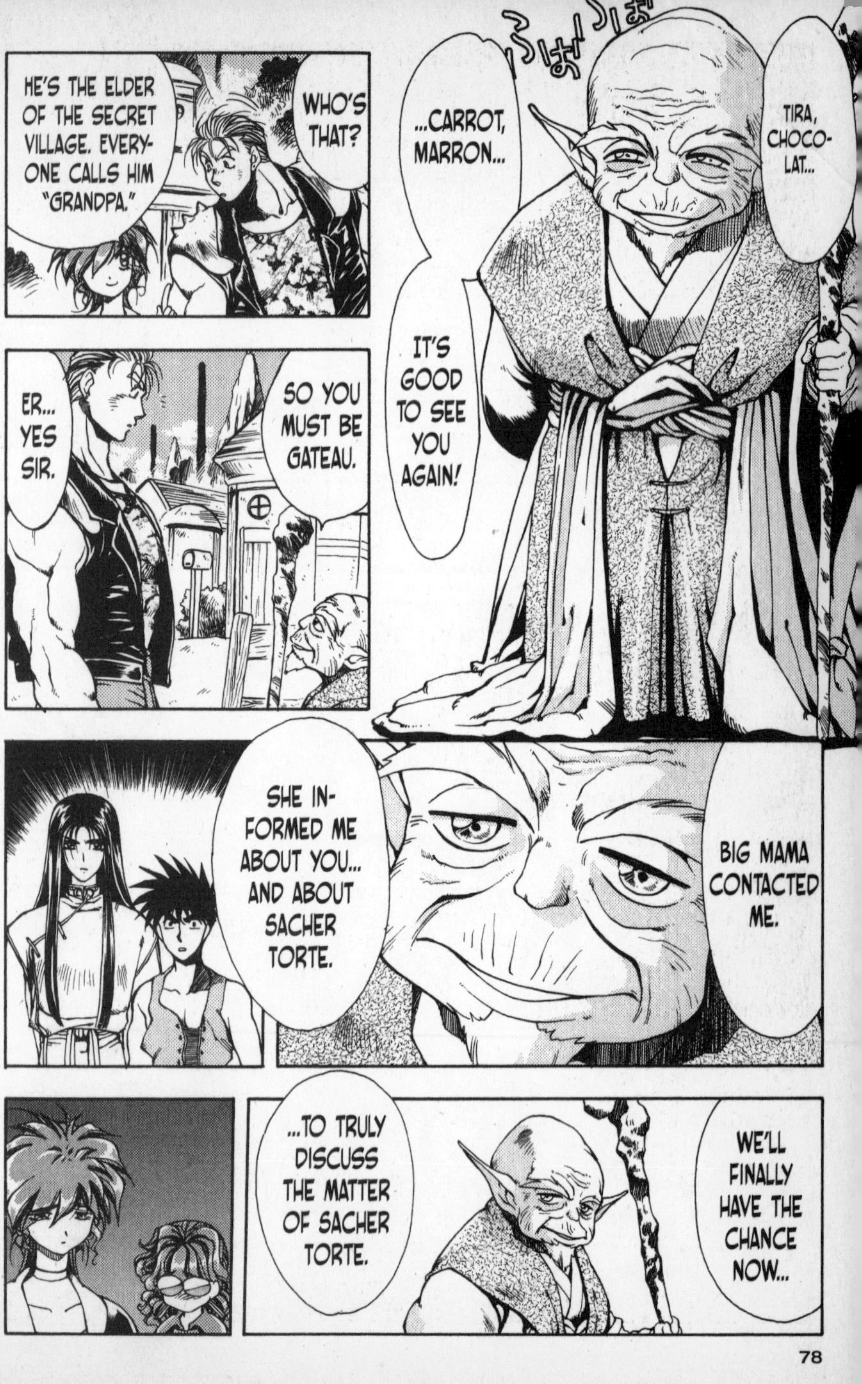
TIRA, CHOCO-LAT...
...CARROT, MARRON...
IT'S GOOD TO SEE YOU AGAIN!
WHO'S THAT?
HE'S THE ELDER OF THE SECRET VILLAGE. EVERY-ONE CALLS HIM "GRANDPA."
SO YOU MUST BE GATEAU.
ER... YES SIR.
BIG MAMA CONTACTED ME.
SHE IN-FORMED ME ABOUT YOU... AND ABOUT SACHER TORTE.
WE'LL FINALLY HAVE THE CHANCE NOW...
...TO TRULY DISCUSS THE MATTER OF SACHER TORTE.

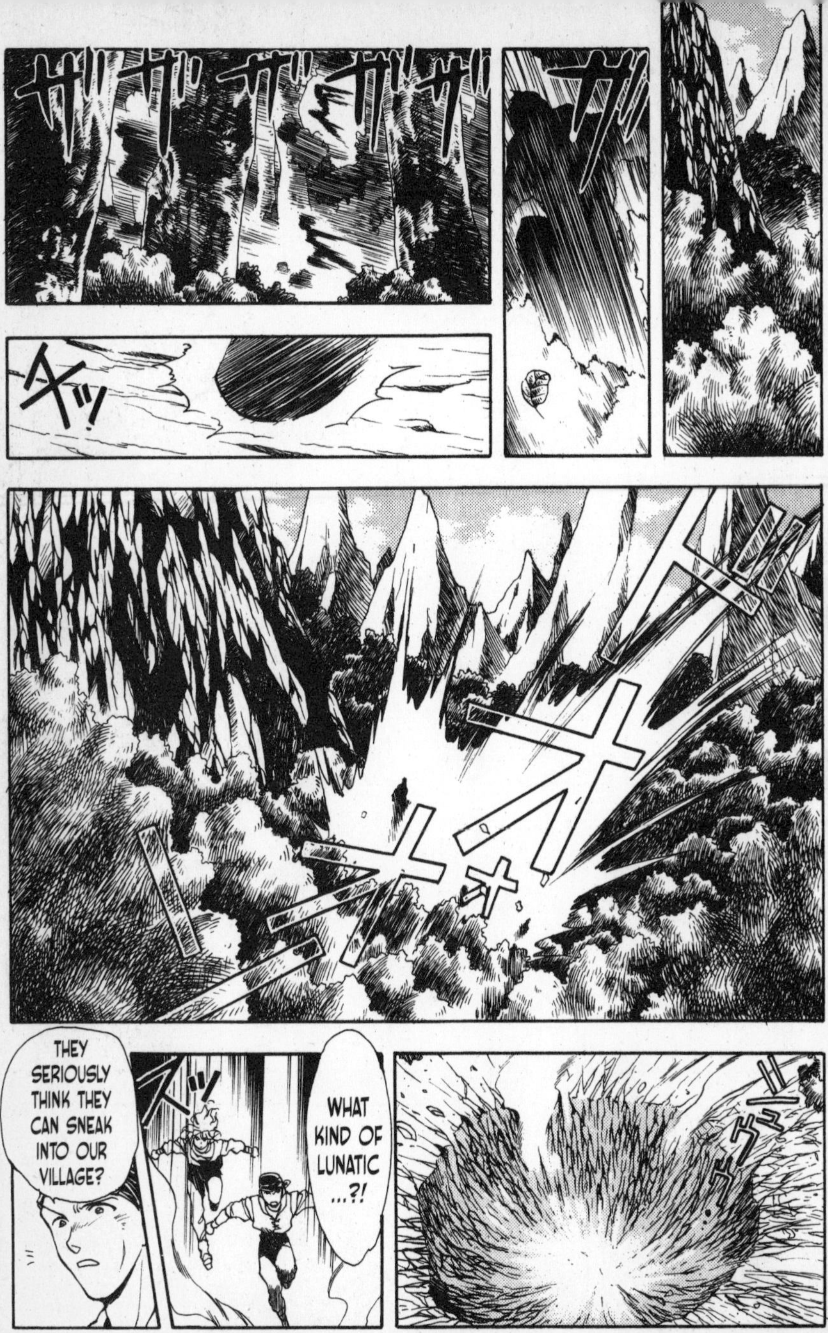
WHAT KIND OF LUNATIC ...?!
THEY SERIOUSLY THINK THEY CAN SNEAK INTO OUR VILLAGE?

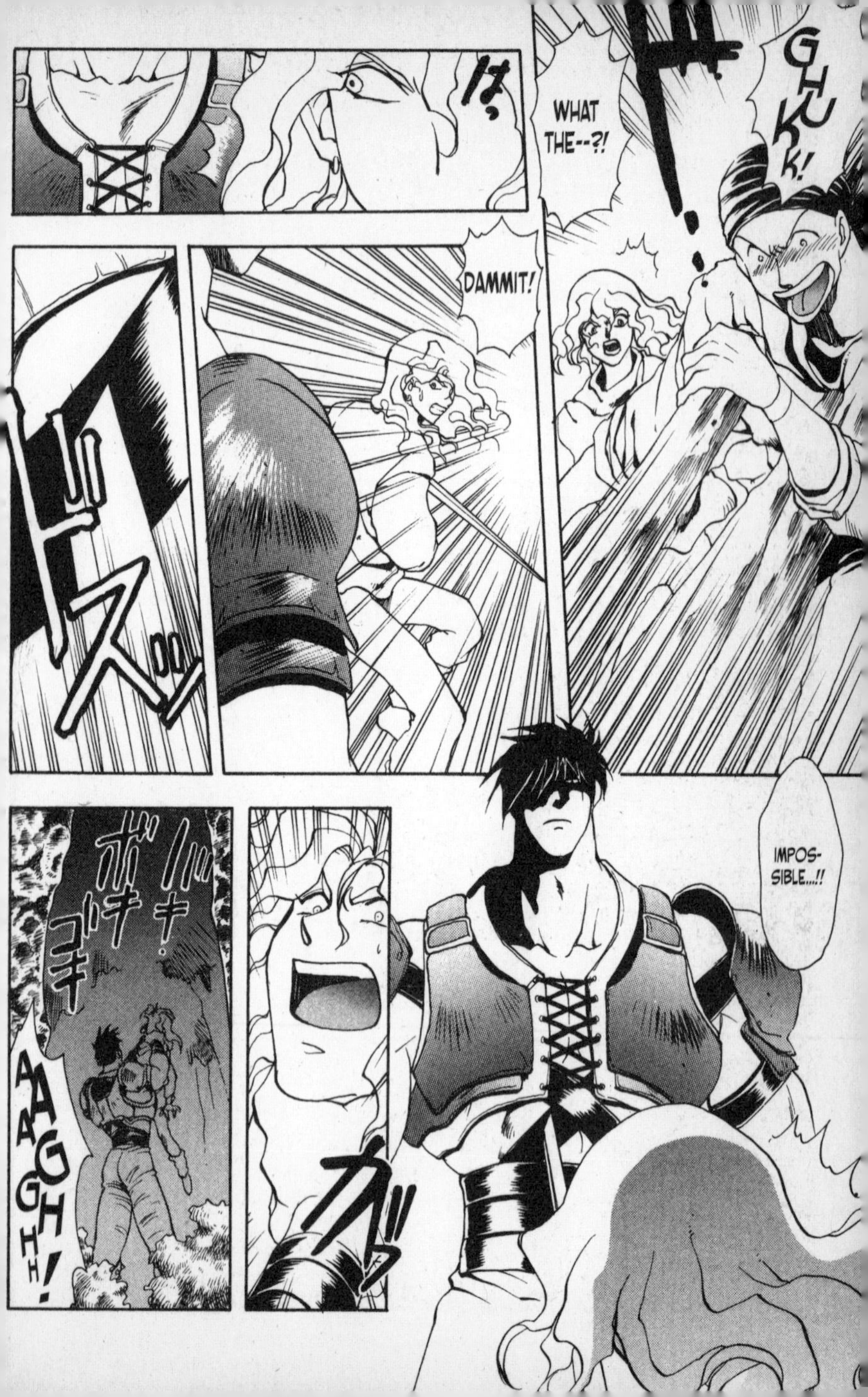
GHUKK!
WHAT THE--?!
は、
DAMMIT!
ドスッ
IMPOS-SIBLE...!!
ガッ
バキ！
ボキ
ゴキ
AAAGHHH!

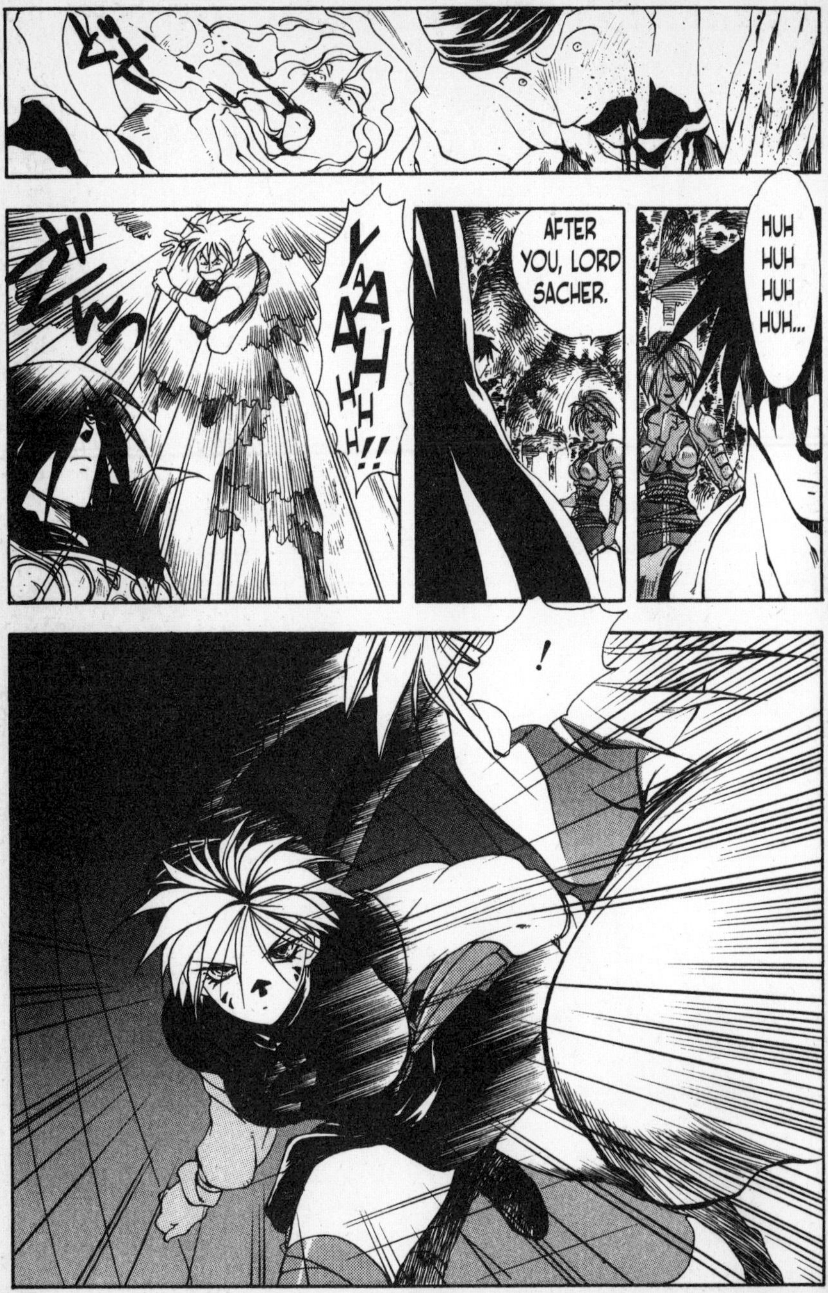
HUH HUH HUH HUH...
AFTER YOU, LORD SACHER.
YAAAHHHHH!!
!

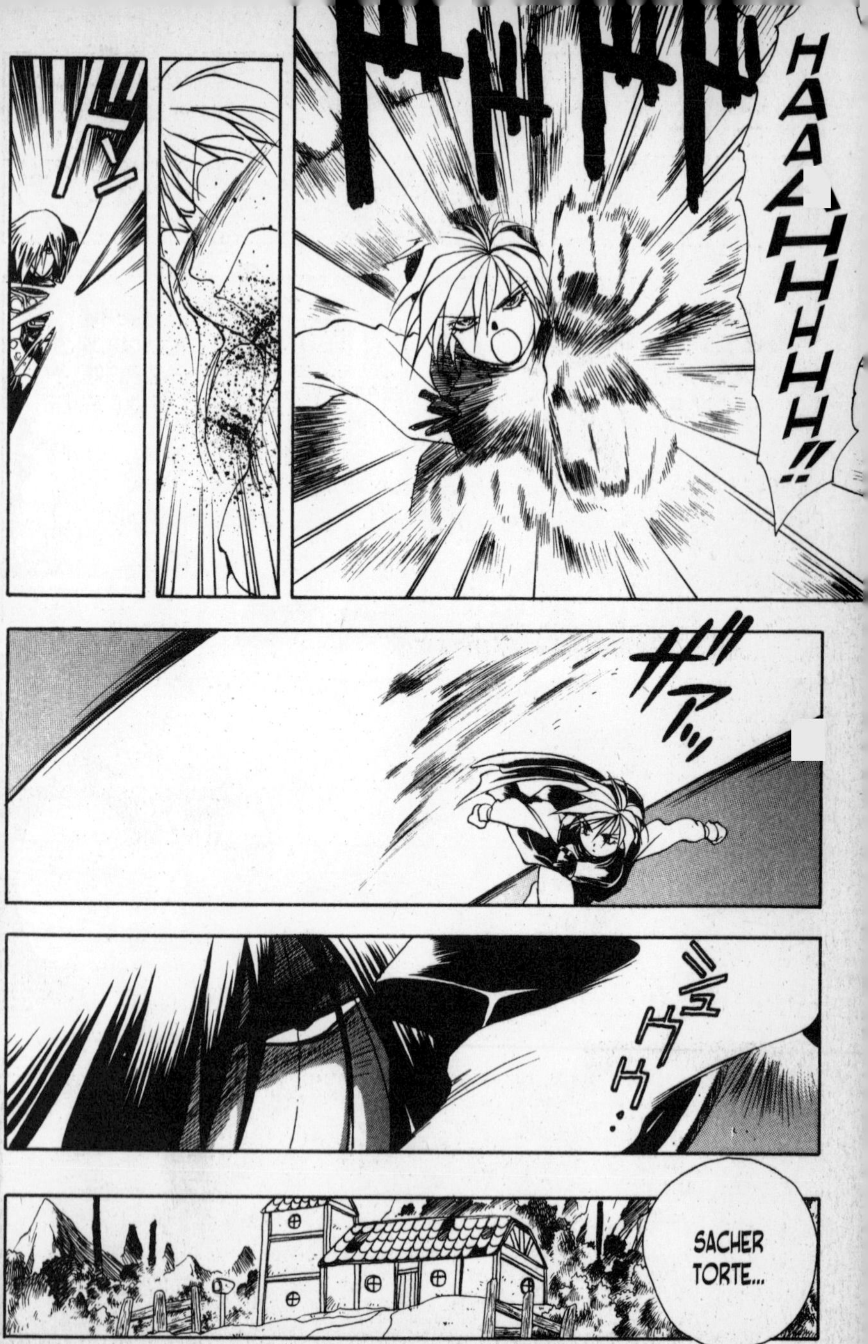
HAAAHHHHH!!
ザァッ
シュウウ…
SACHER TORTE...

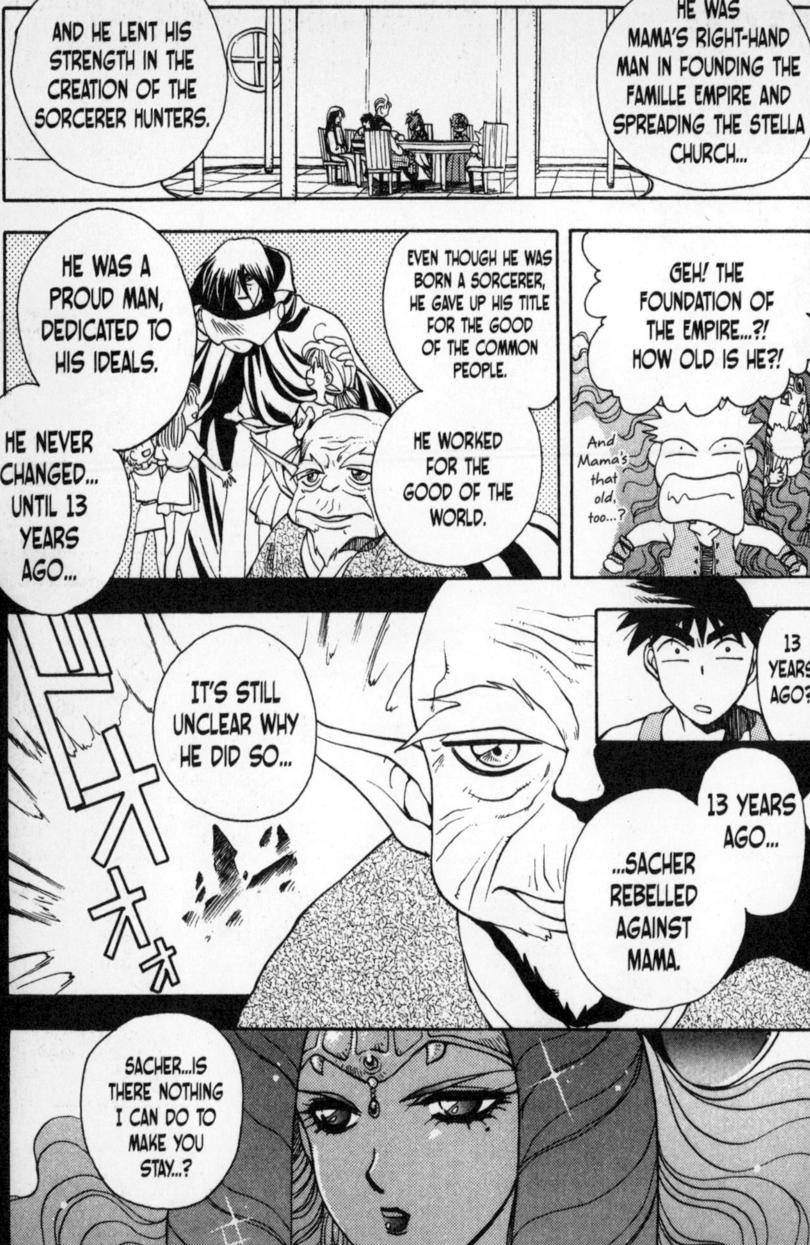
HE WAS MAMA'S RIGHT-HAND MAN IN FOUNDING THE FAMILLE EMPIRE AND SPREADING THE STELLA CHURCH...
AND HE LENT HIS STRENGTH IN THE CREATION OF THE SORCERER HUNTERS.
GEH! THE FOUNDATION OF THE EMPIRE...?! HOW OLD IS HE?!
And Mama's that old, too...?
EVEN THOUGH HE WAS BORN A SORCERER, HE GAVE UP HIS TITLE FOR THE GOOD OF THE COMMON PEOPLE.
HE WAS A PROUD MAN, DEDICATED TO HIS IDEALS.
HE WORKED FOR THE GOOD OF THE WORLD.
HE NEVER CHANGED... UNTIL 13 YEARS AGO...
13 YEARS AGO?
13 YEARS AGO...
...SACHER REBELLED AGAINST MAMA.
IT'S STILL UNCLEAR WHY HE DID SO...
SACHER...IS THERE NOTHING I CAN DO TO MAKE YOU STAY...?

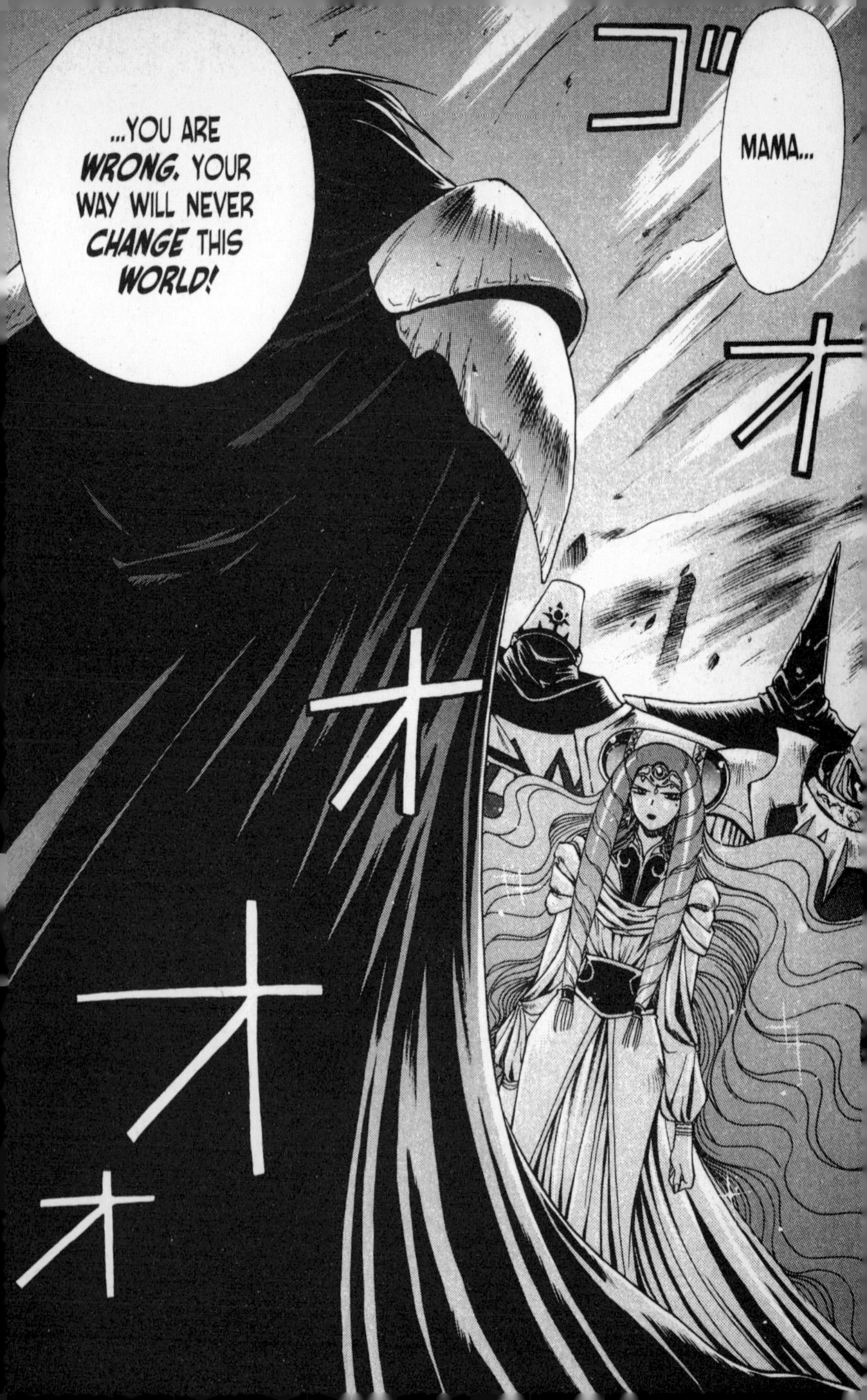
ゴオ
MAMA...
...YOU ARE WRONG. YOUR WAY WILL NEVER CHANGE THIS WORLD!
オオオ

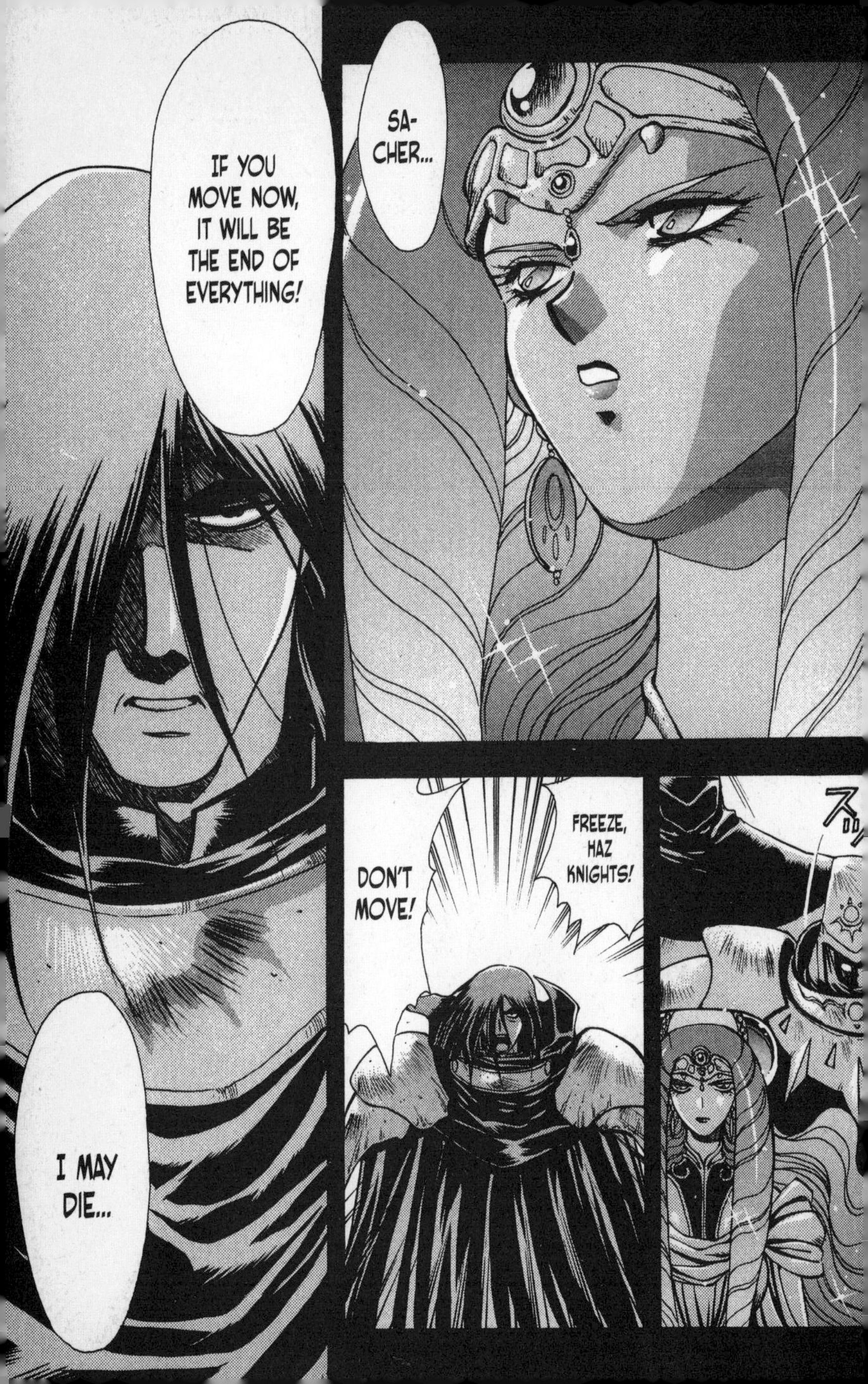

SA-CHER...
FREEZE, HAZ KNIGHTS!
DON'T MOVE!
IF YOU MOVE NOW, IT WILL BE THE END OF EVERYTHING!
I MAY DIE...

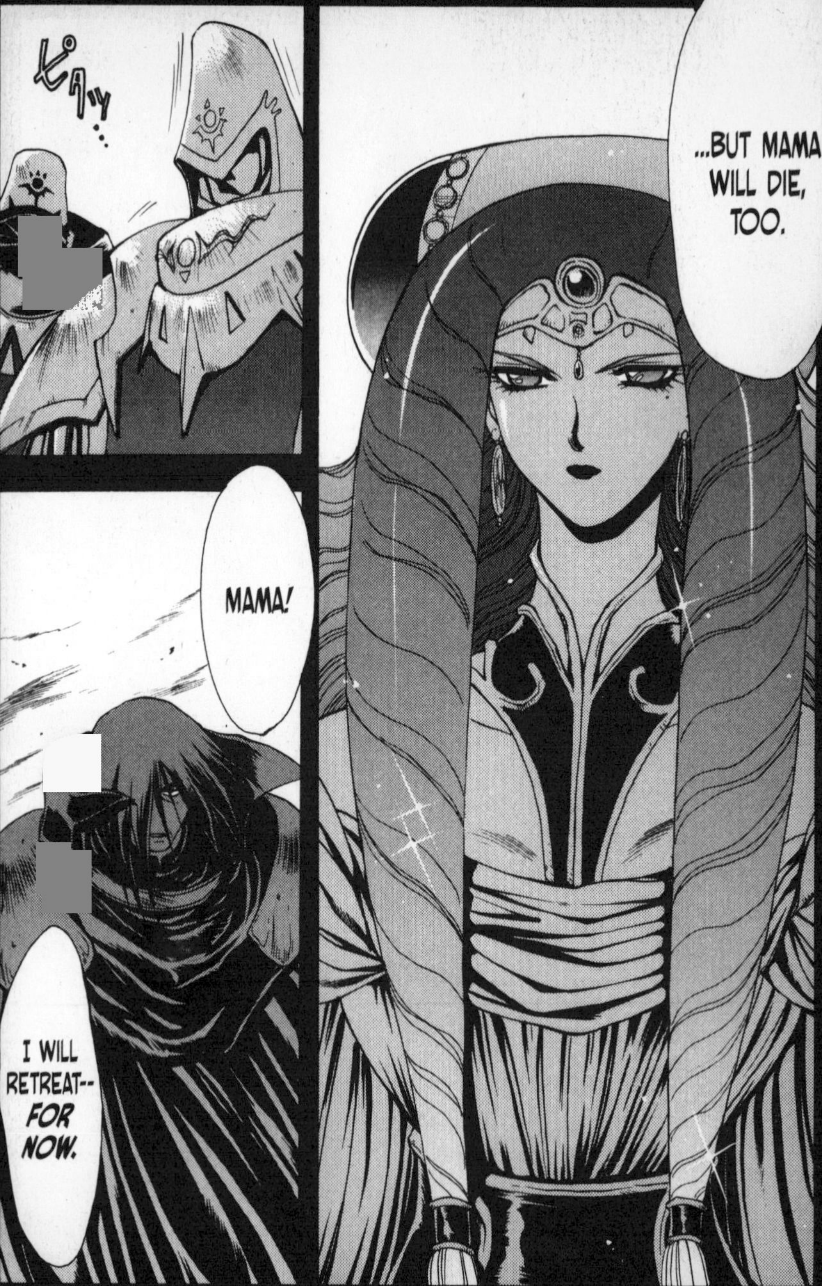
...BUT MAMA WILL DIE, TOO.
ピクッ...
MAMA!
I WILL RETREAT-- *FOR NOW.*

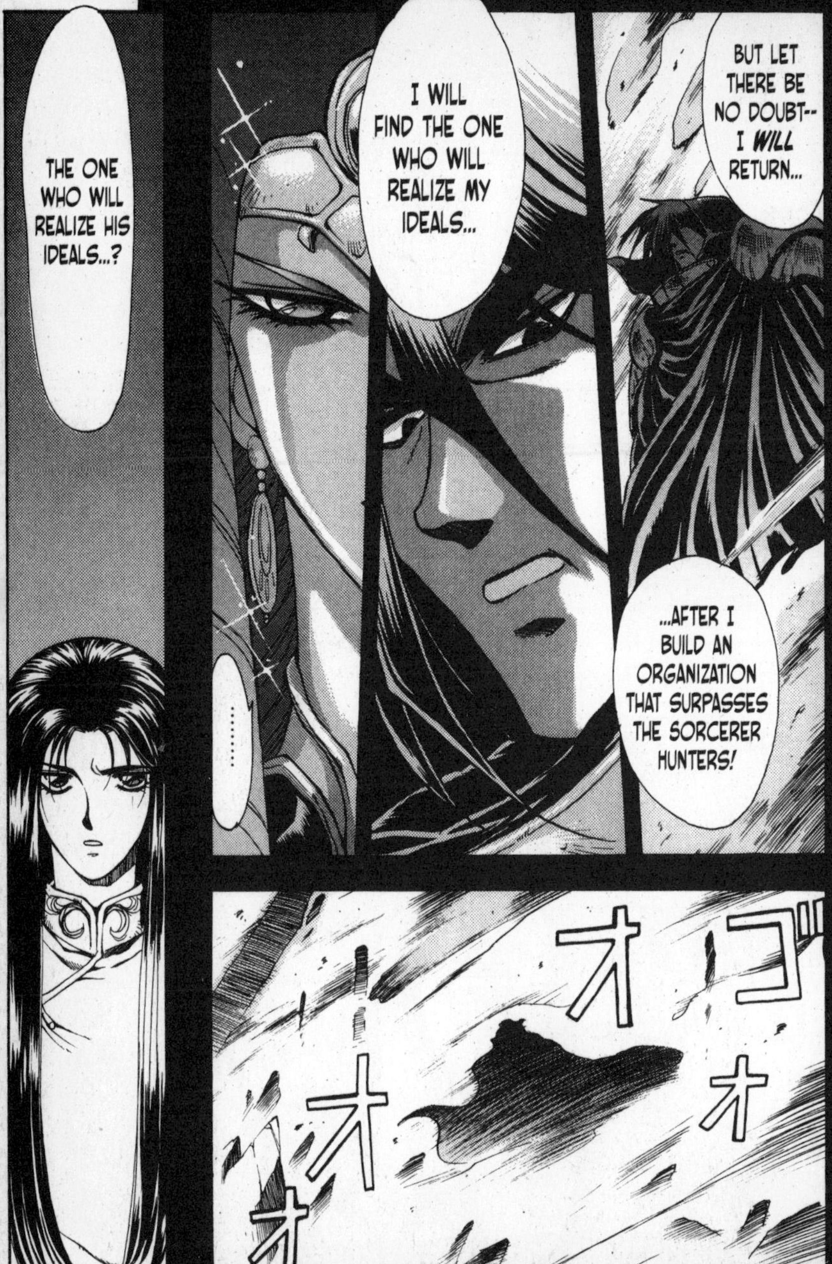
BUT LET THERE BE NO DOUBT-- I *WILL* RETURN...
...AFTER I BUILD AN ORGANIZATION THAT SURPASSES THE SORCERER HUNTERS!
I WILL FIND THE ONE WHO WILL REALIZE MY IDEALS...
......
ゴオオオオオ
THE ONE WHO WILL REALIZE HIS IDEALS...?

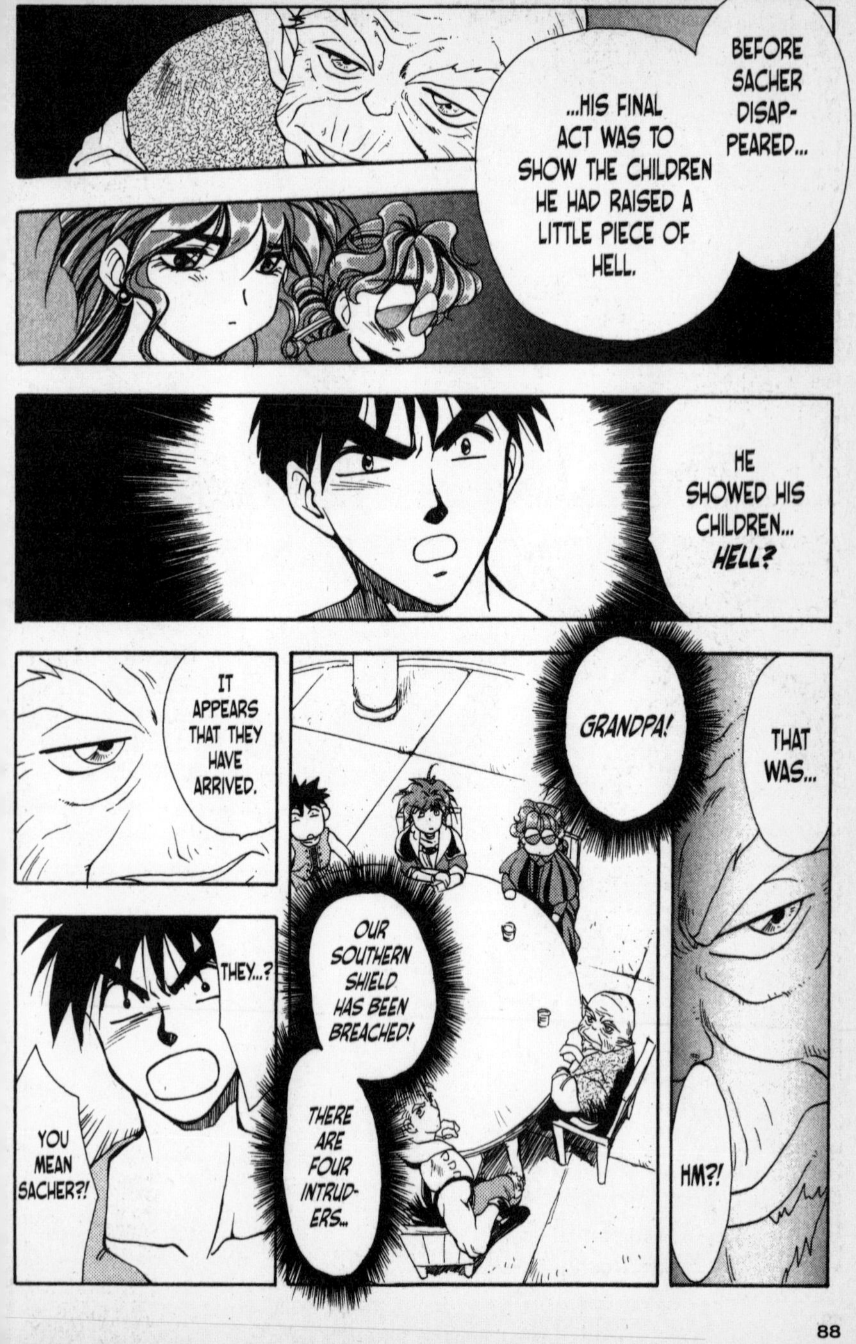
BEFORE SACHER DISAPPEARED...
...HIS FINAL ACT WAS TO SHOW THE CHILDREN HE HAD RAISED A LITTLE PIECE OF HELL.
HE SHOWED HIS CHILDREN... *HELL?*
THAT WAS...
HM?!
GRANDPA!
OUR SOUTHERN SHIELD HAS BEEN BREACHED!
THERE ARE FOUR INTRUDERS...
IT APPEARS THAT THEY HAVE ARRIVED.
THEY...?
YOU MEAN SACHER?!

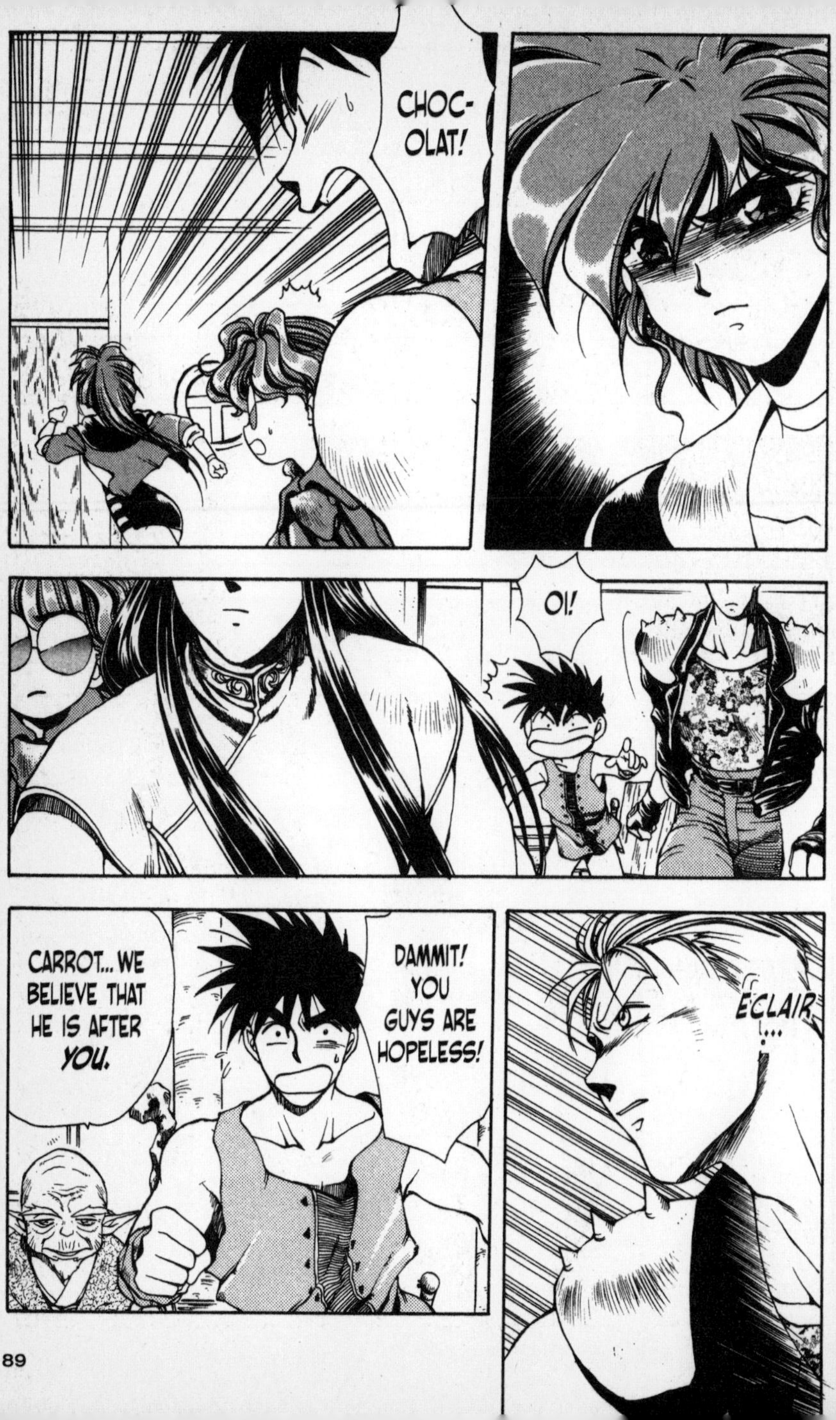
CHOC-OLAT!
OI!
ÉCLAIR...
DAMMIT! YOU GUYS ARE HOPELESS!
CARROT... WE BELIEVE THAT HE IS AFTER *YOU.*

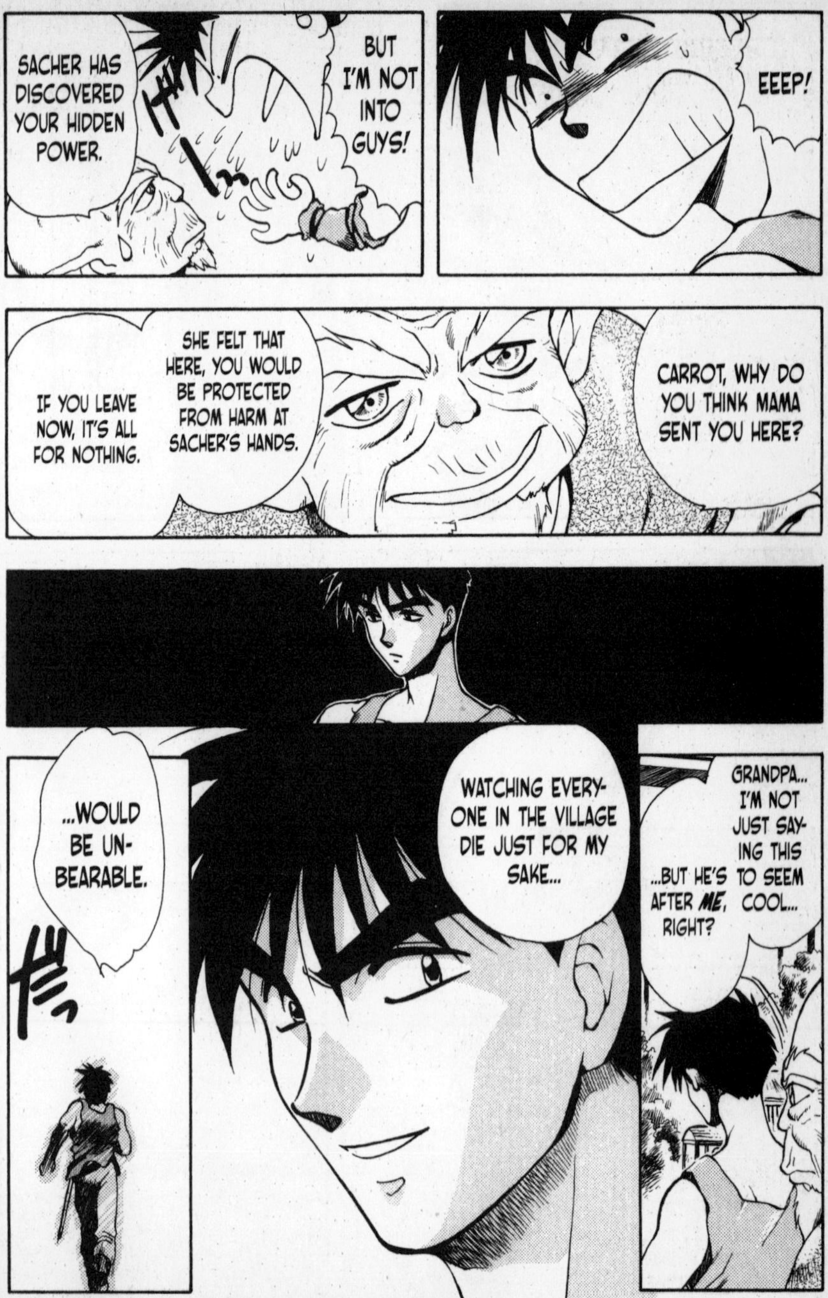
EEEP!
BUT I'M NOT INTO GUYS!
SACHER HAS DISCOVERED YOUR HIDDEN POWER.
CARROT, WHY DO YOU THINK MAMA SENT YOU HERE?
SHE FELT THAT HERE, YOU WOULD BE PROTECTED FROM HARM AT SACHER'S HANDS.
IF YOU LEAVE NOW, IT'S ALL FOR NOTHING.
GRANDPA... I'M NOT JUST SAYING THIS TO SEEM COOL...
...BUT HE'S AFTER *ME*, RIGHT?
WATCHING EVERYONE IN THE VILLAGE DIE JUST FOR MY SAKE...
...WOULD BE UNBEARABLE.

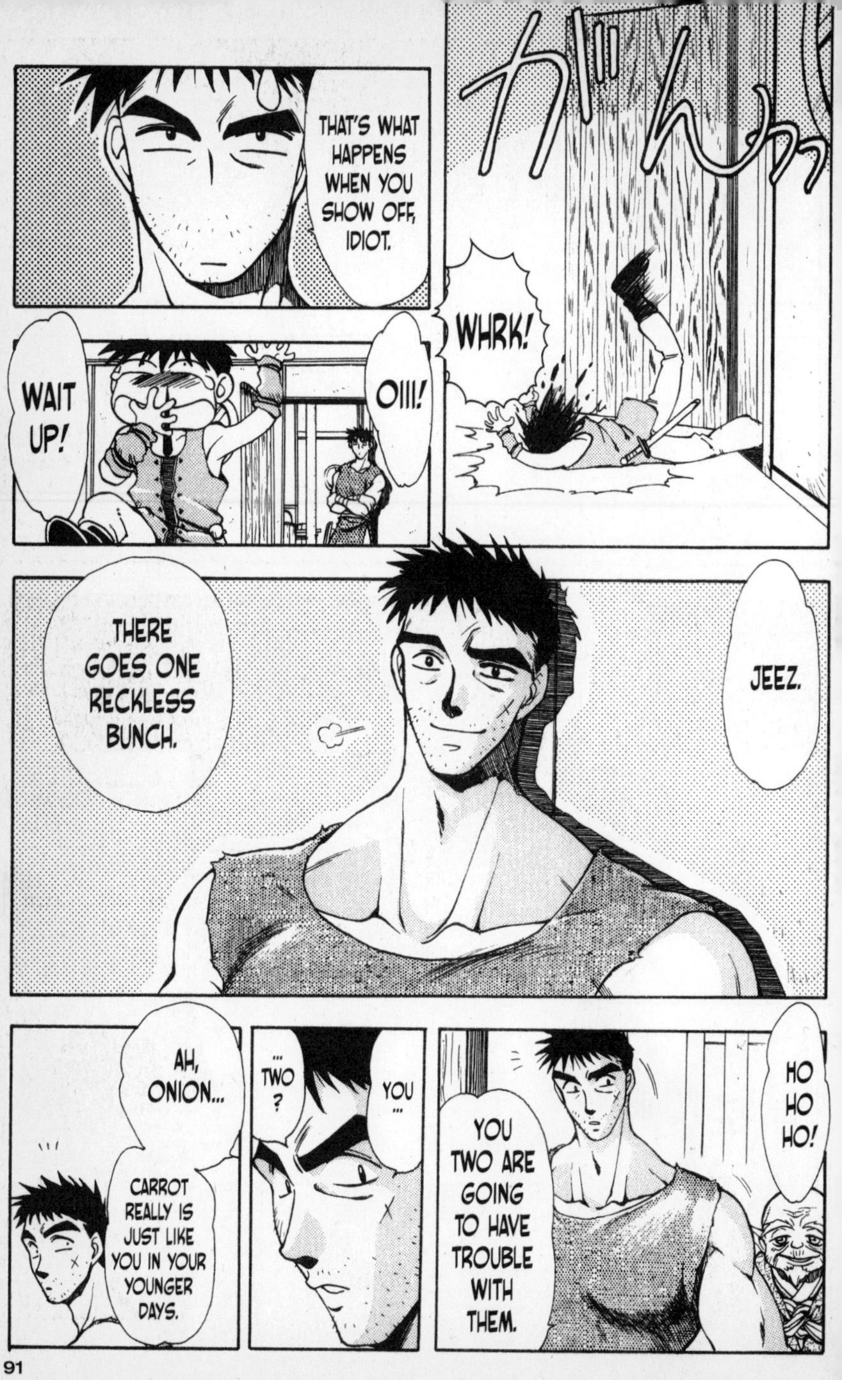
WHRK!
THAT'S WHAT HAPPENS WHEN YOU SHOW OFF, IDIOT.
OIII!
WAIT UP!
JEEZ.
THERE GOES ONE RECKLESS BUNCH.
HO HO HO!
YOU TWO ARE GOING TO HAVE TROUBLE WITH THEM.
YOU...
...TWO?
AH, ONION...
CARROT REALLY IS JUST LIKE YOU IN YOUR YOUNGER DAYS.

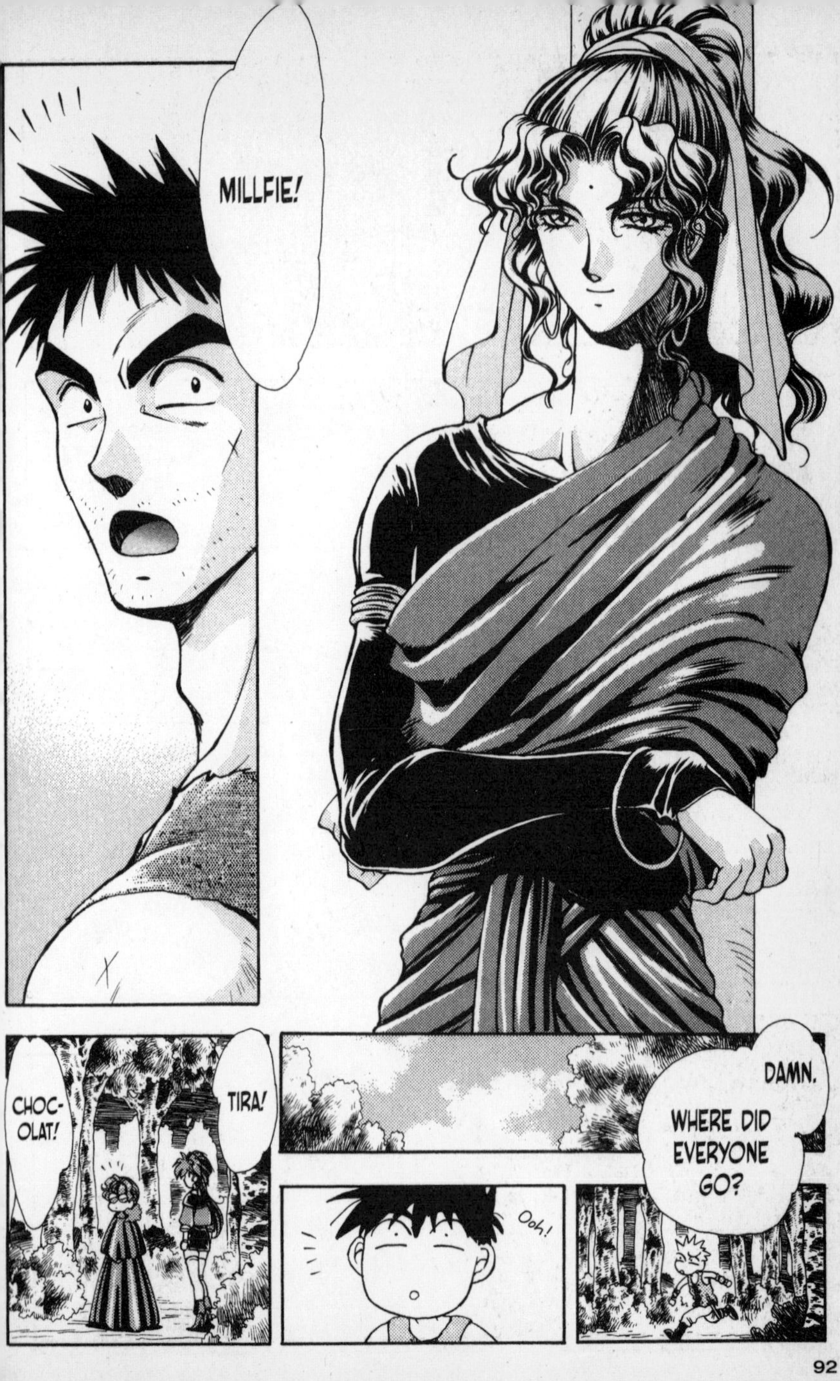
MILLFIE!
DAMN.
WHERE DID EVERYONE GO?
Ooh!
TIRA!
CHOC-OLAT!

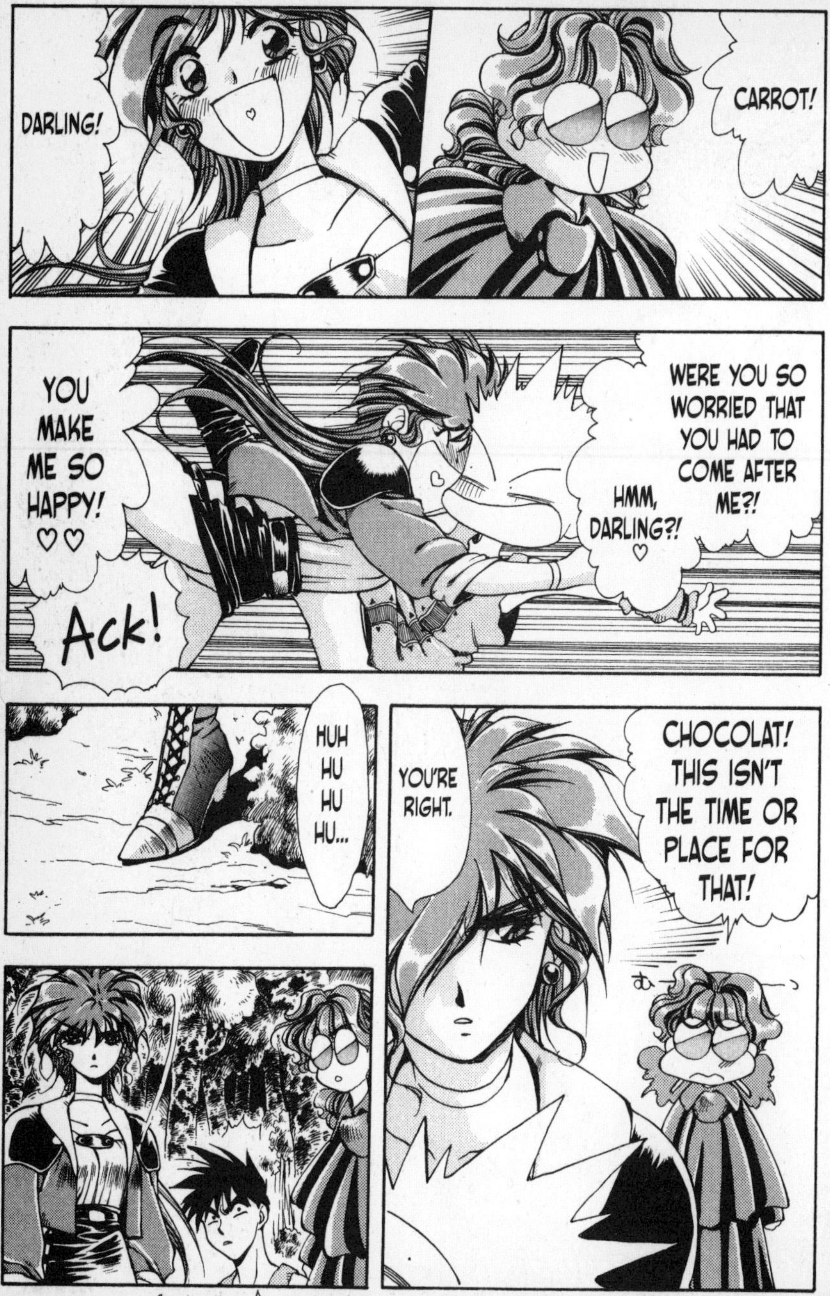
CARROT!
DARLING!
WERE YOU SO WORRIED THAT YOU HAD TO COME AFTER ME?!
HMM, DARLING?! ♡
YOU MAKE ME SO HAPPY! ♡ ♡
Ack!
CHOCOLAT! THIS ISN'T THE TIME OR PLACE FOR THAT!
YOU'RE RIGHT.
む――っ
HUH HU HU HU...

Carrot is sitting.

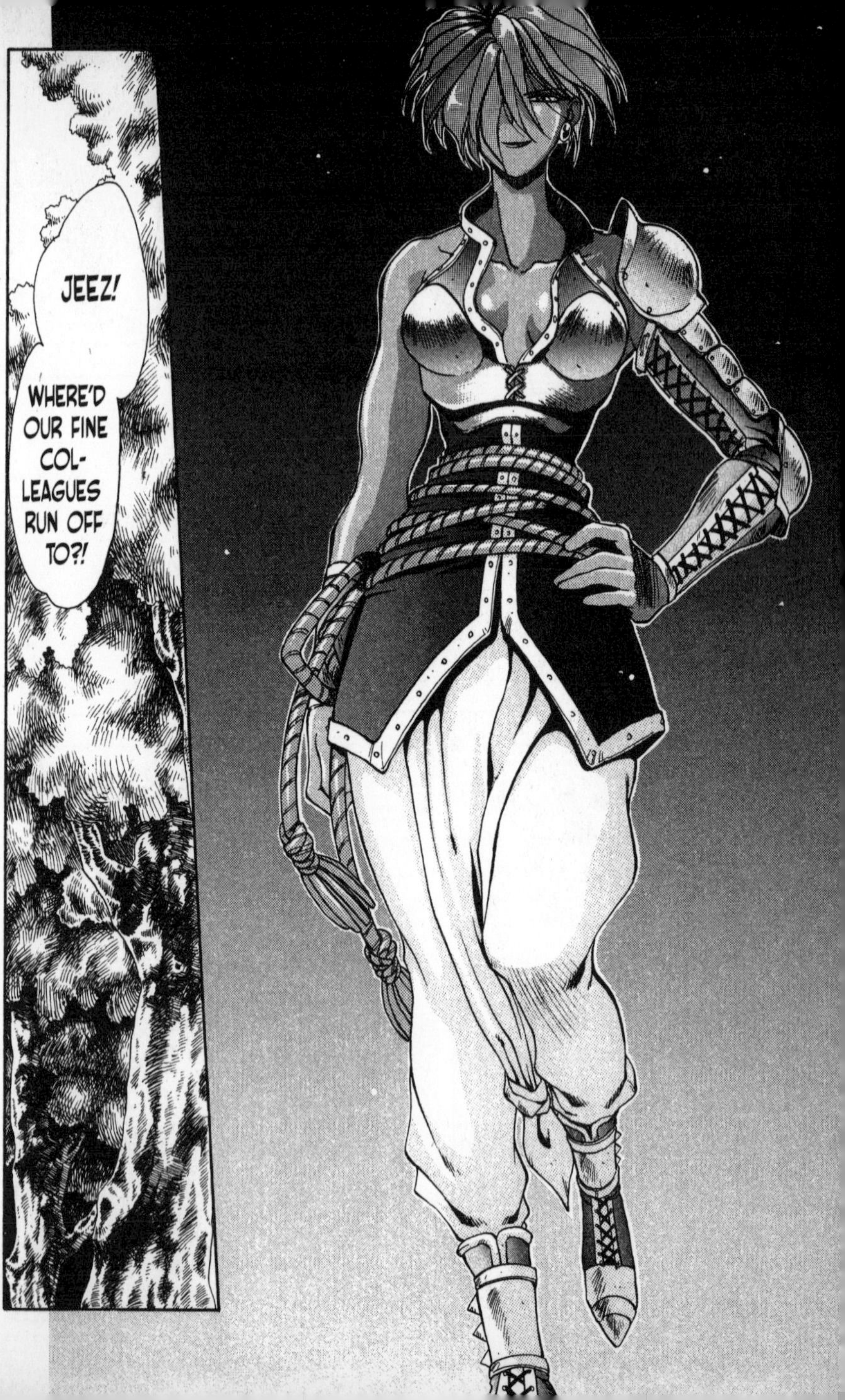
JEEZ!
WHERE'D OUR FINE COL-LEAGUES RUN OFF TO?!

SHH!

Om vajra dham ham

!

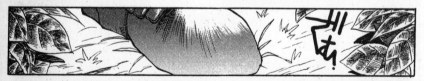

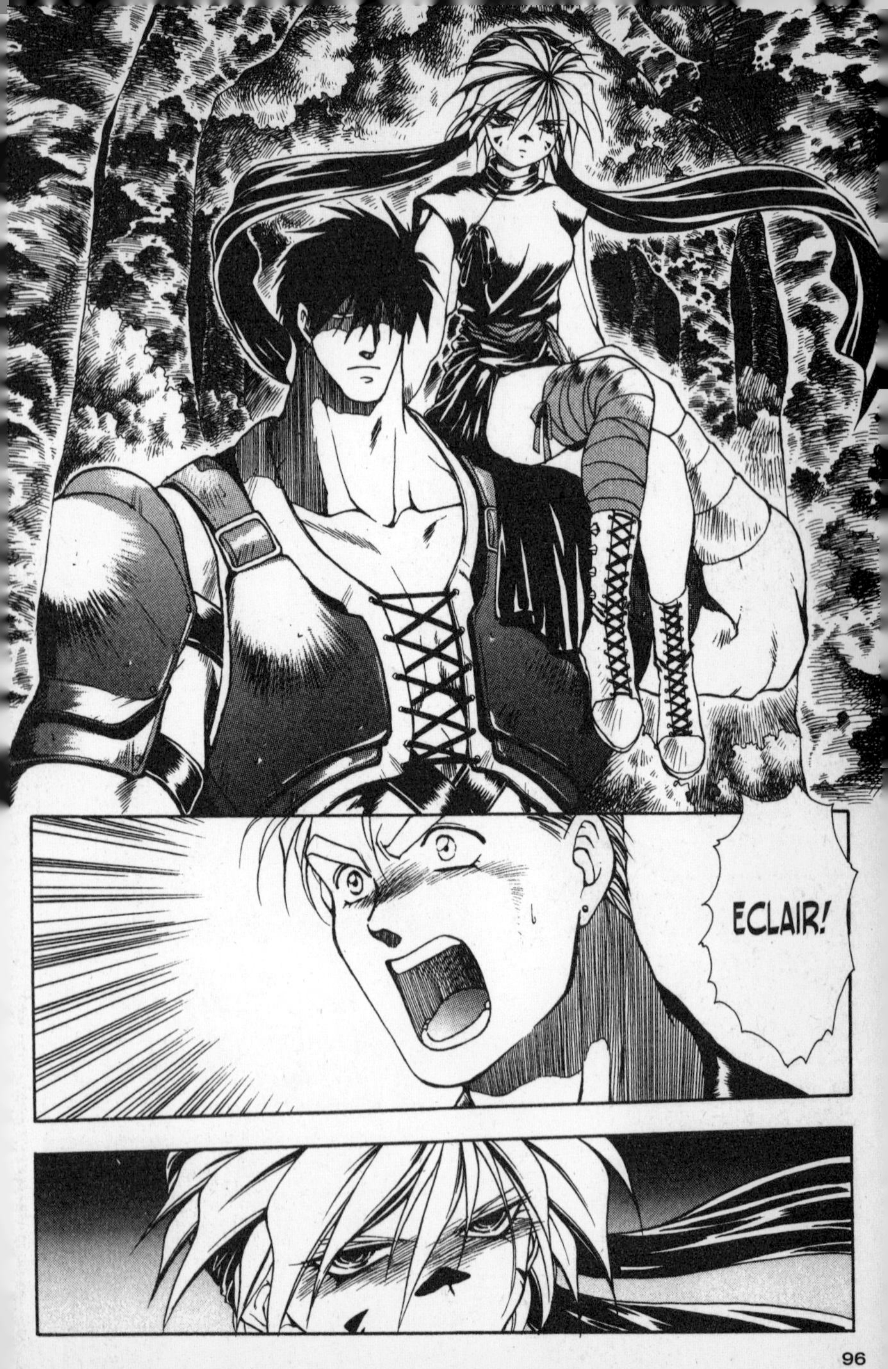
ECLAIR!

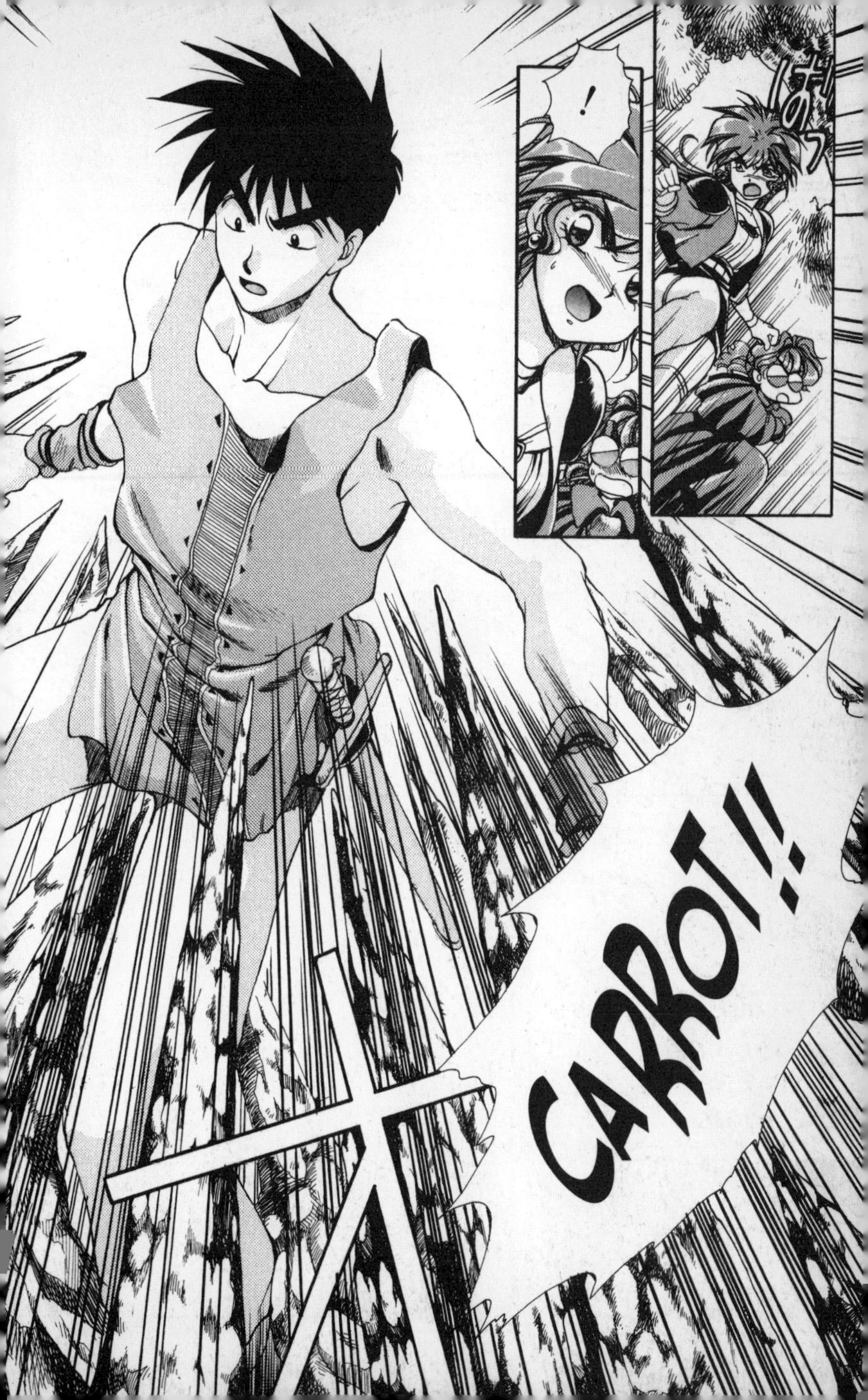
!
CAROT!!

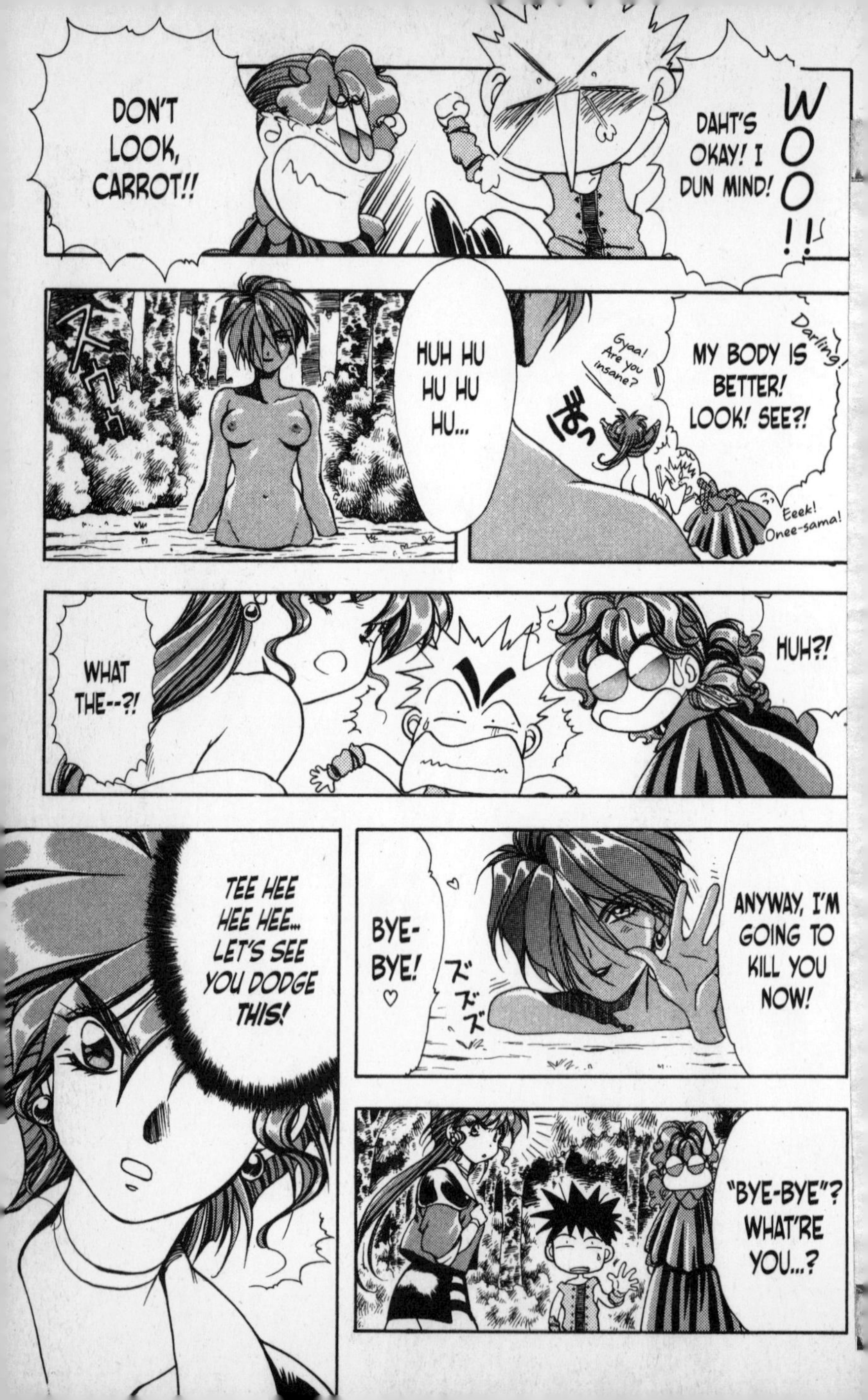
WOOO!!
DAHT'S OKAY! I DUN MIND!
DON'T LOOK, CARROT!!
Darling!
MY BODY IS BETTER! LOOK! SEE?!
Gyaa! Are you insane?
Eeek! Onee-sama!
HUH HU HU HU HU...
HUH?!
WHAT THE--?!
ANYWAY, I'M GOING TO KILL YOU NOW!
BYE-BYE! ♡
ズズズ
"BYE-BYE"? WHAT'RE YOU...?
TEE HEE HEE HEE... LET'S SEE YOU DODGE THIS!

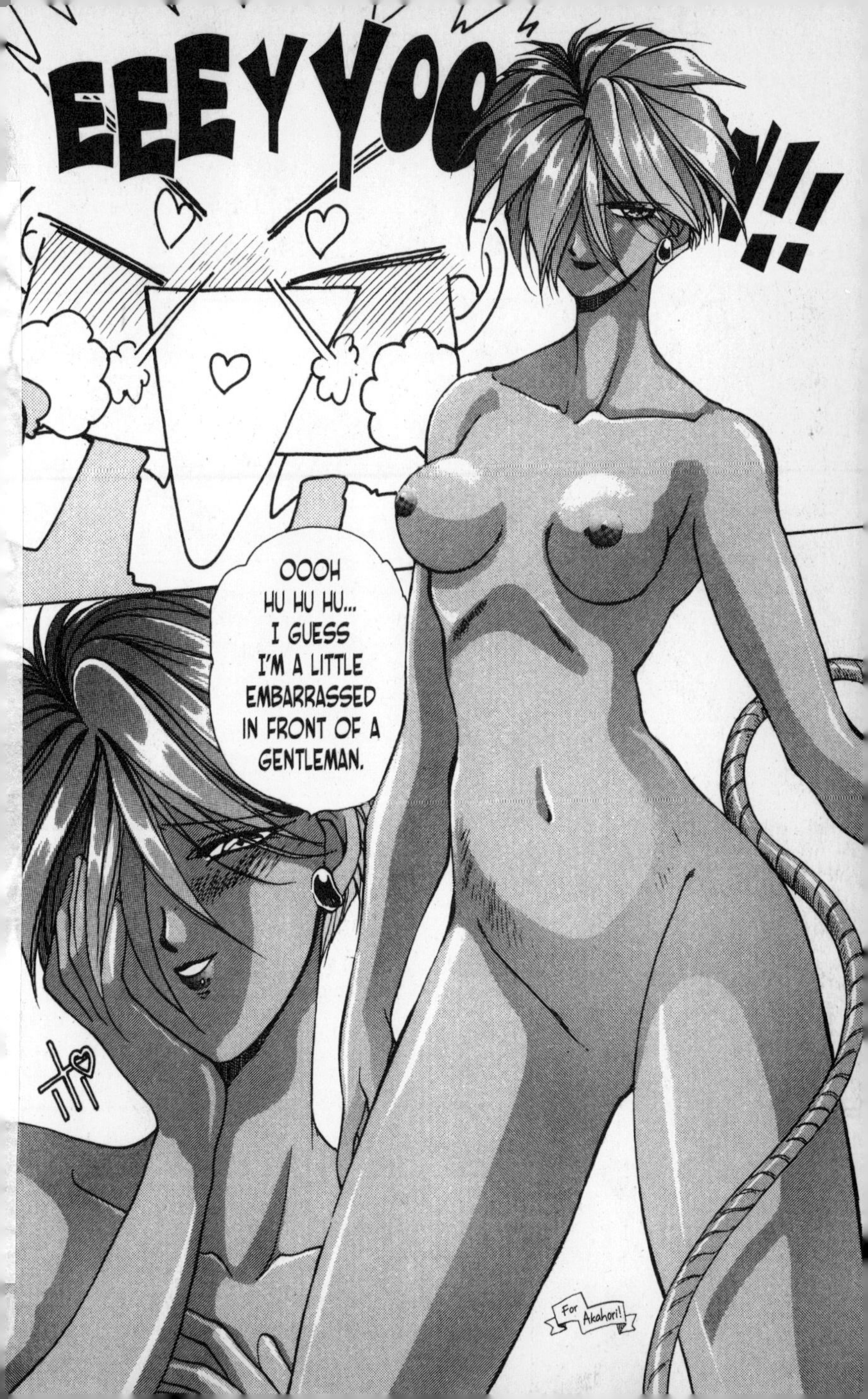
EEEYYOO
OOOH HU HU HU... I GUESS I'M A LITTLE EMBARRASSED IN FRONT OF A GENTLEMAN.
For Akahori!

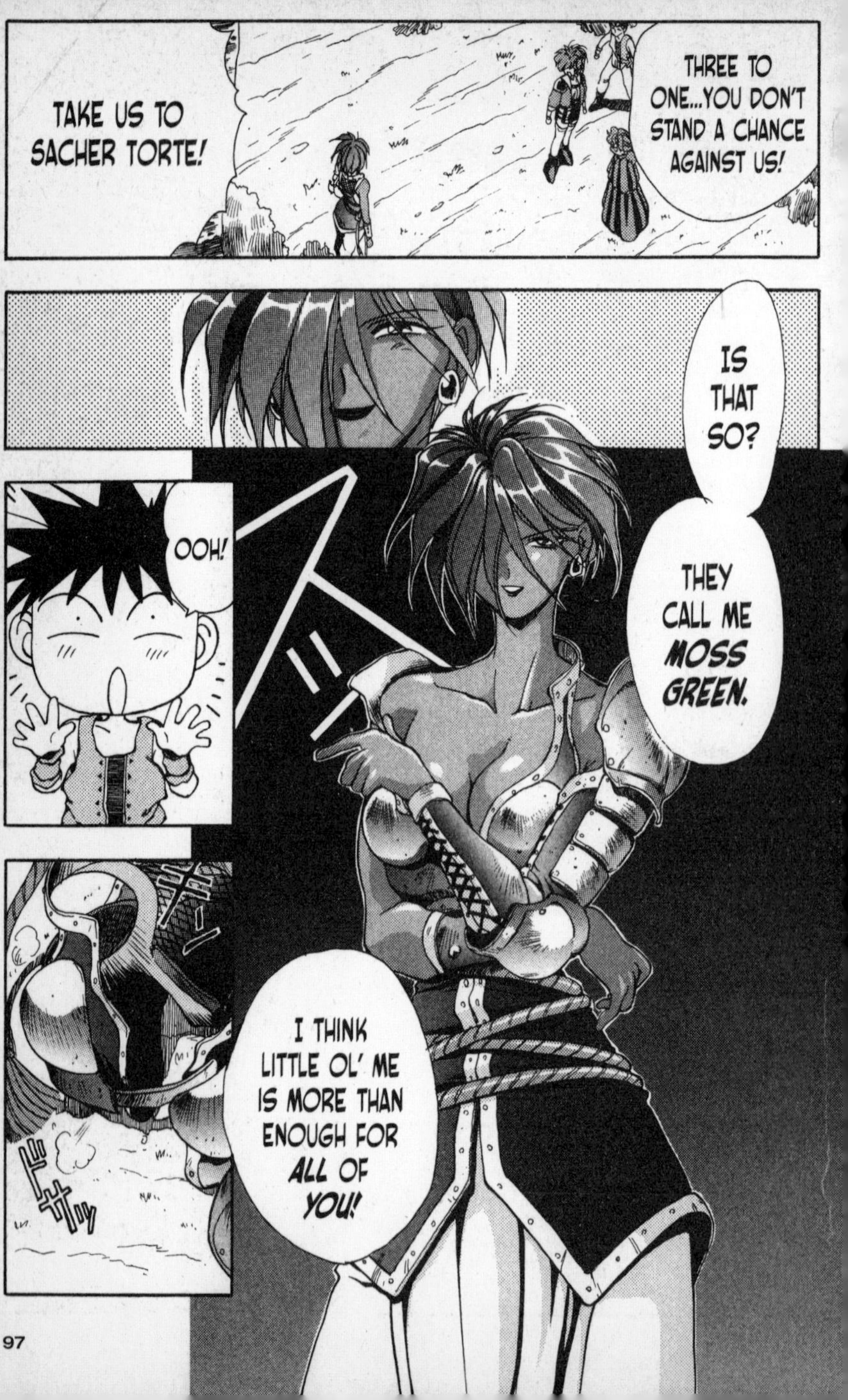
THREE TO ONE...YOU DON'T STAND A CHANCE AGAINST US!
TAKE US TO SACHER TORTE!
IS THAT SO?
THEY CALL ME MOSS GREEN.
I THINK LITTLE OL' ME IS MORE THAN ENOUGH FOR ALL OF YOU!
OOH!

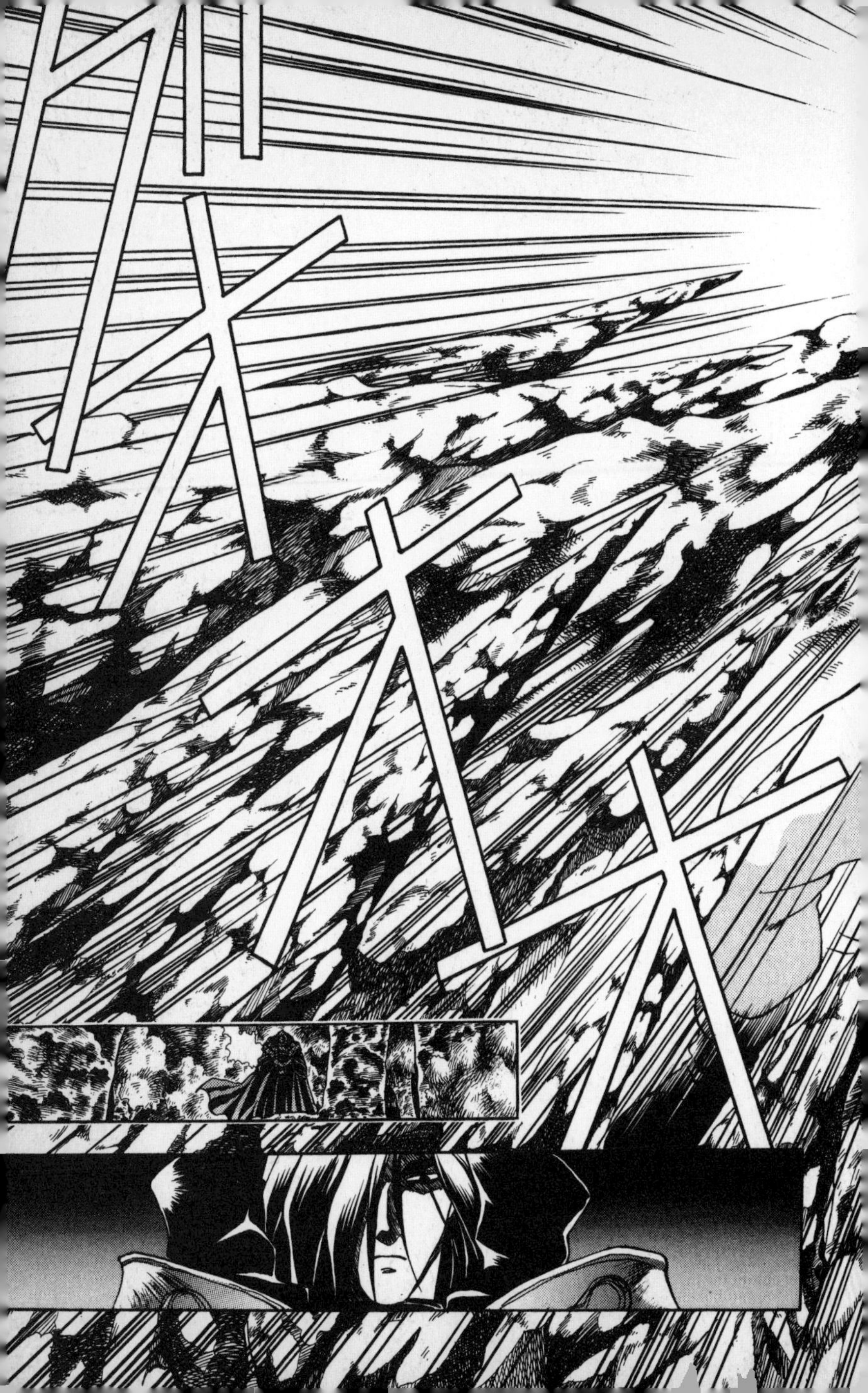

TOCHÔGAKI

RAY. OMISHI

HELLO! THIS IS OMISHI. I DECIDED TO PUT IN AN INTERMISSION. I BET THERE ARE SOME PEOPLE WONDERING, "WHAT'S GOING ON IN THE FOURTH BOOK?!" WELL...I FELT BLANK PAGES BETWEEN THE STORIES WERE A WASTE...DON'T YOU AGREE? OMISHI LIKES TO READ THE CHITCHAT DONE IN EXTRA PAGES. HOW ABOUT YOU GUYS? I REALLY SHOULD HAVE STARTED IN THE FIRST BOOK, BUT...UH...I'M REALLY PRETTY LAME FOR STARTING IN THE MIDDLE. AND I'M SURE I'M GOING TO DO STUFF THAT IS TOTALLY UNRELATED TO THE STORY. (I WANT TO DO SOMETHING COMPLETELY DIFFERENT IN THE NEXT BOOK.) IS THAT REALLY OKAY? NOW THAT I'VE DECIDED TO DO IT, THOUGH, I DON'T KNOW WHAT TO USE. IT'S NOT THAT I DON'T HAVE IDEAS...MUMBLE MUMBLE...IN THE END, I WENT WITH THE ORIGINAL CHARACTER DESIGNS, WHICH IS NEITHER HERE NOR THERE. AND THIS BOOK IS WHERE THE SORCERER HUNTER KILLERS FIRST APPEAR, TOO...OHHH. I'M SORRY. WHAT'S GOING ON HERE? OMISHI'S LITTLE BRAIN IS JUST DYING... SO I'LL CONTINUE THIS LATER. (IT'S JUST AN INTERMISSION, AFTER ALL.) STILL, THE INTERMISSION HAS TO BE LONGER THAN THE AFTERWORD... WELL, SEE YOU LATER IN THE AFTERWORD...♥

12/1994 RAY OMISHI

So...is this a "Middleword," then?

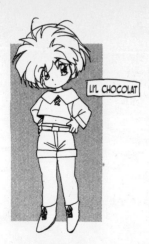

LI'L CHOCOLAT

I WONDER IF YOU HAVE TO HAVE BROTHERS OR SISTERS TO BE A SORCERER HUNTER?

NAAH... THAT CAN'T BE.

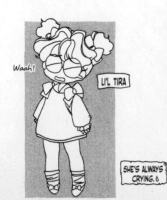

Waah!
LI'L TIRA
SHE'S ALWAYS CRYING.

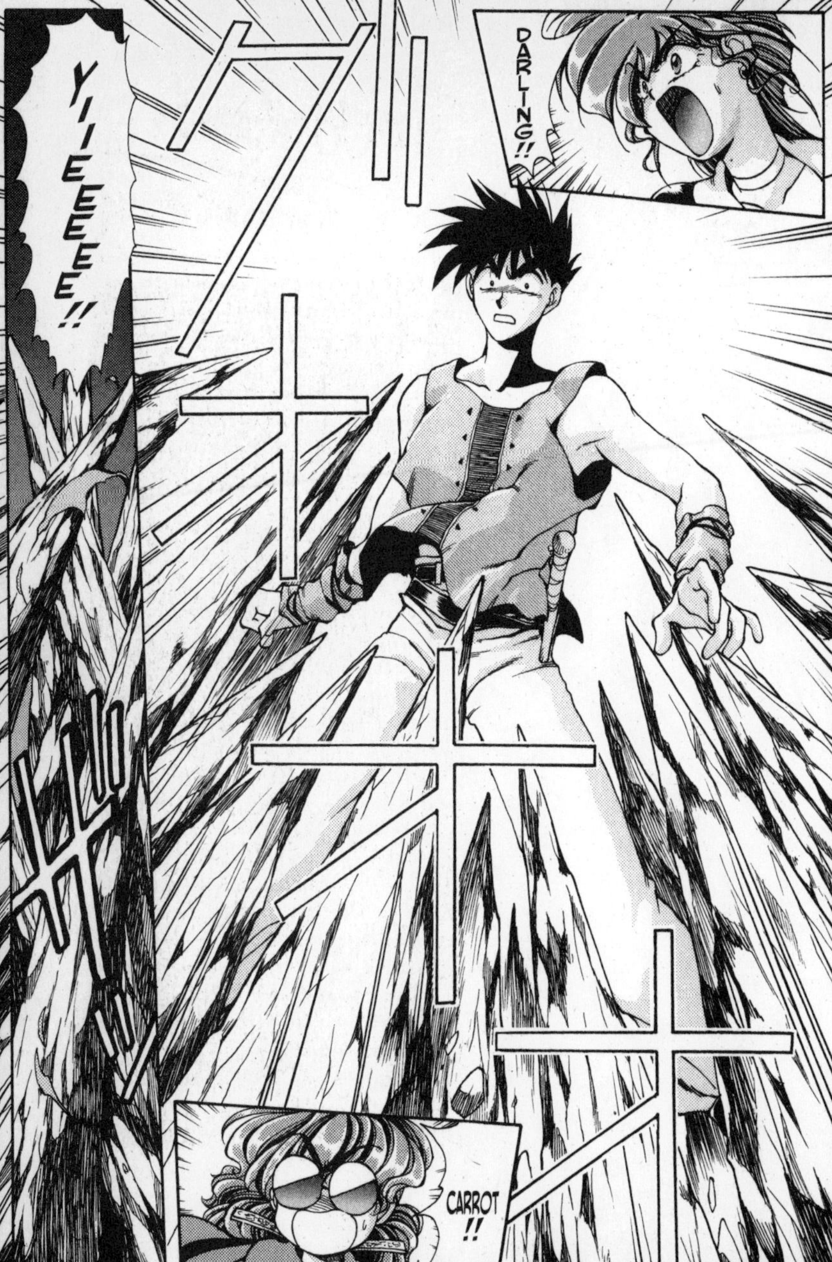
DARLING!!
YIIIEEEEEE!!
CARROT!!

22 TO THE SORCERER HUNTERS' HOMETOWN--PART 2

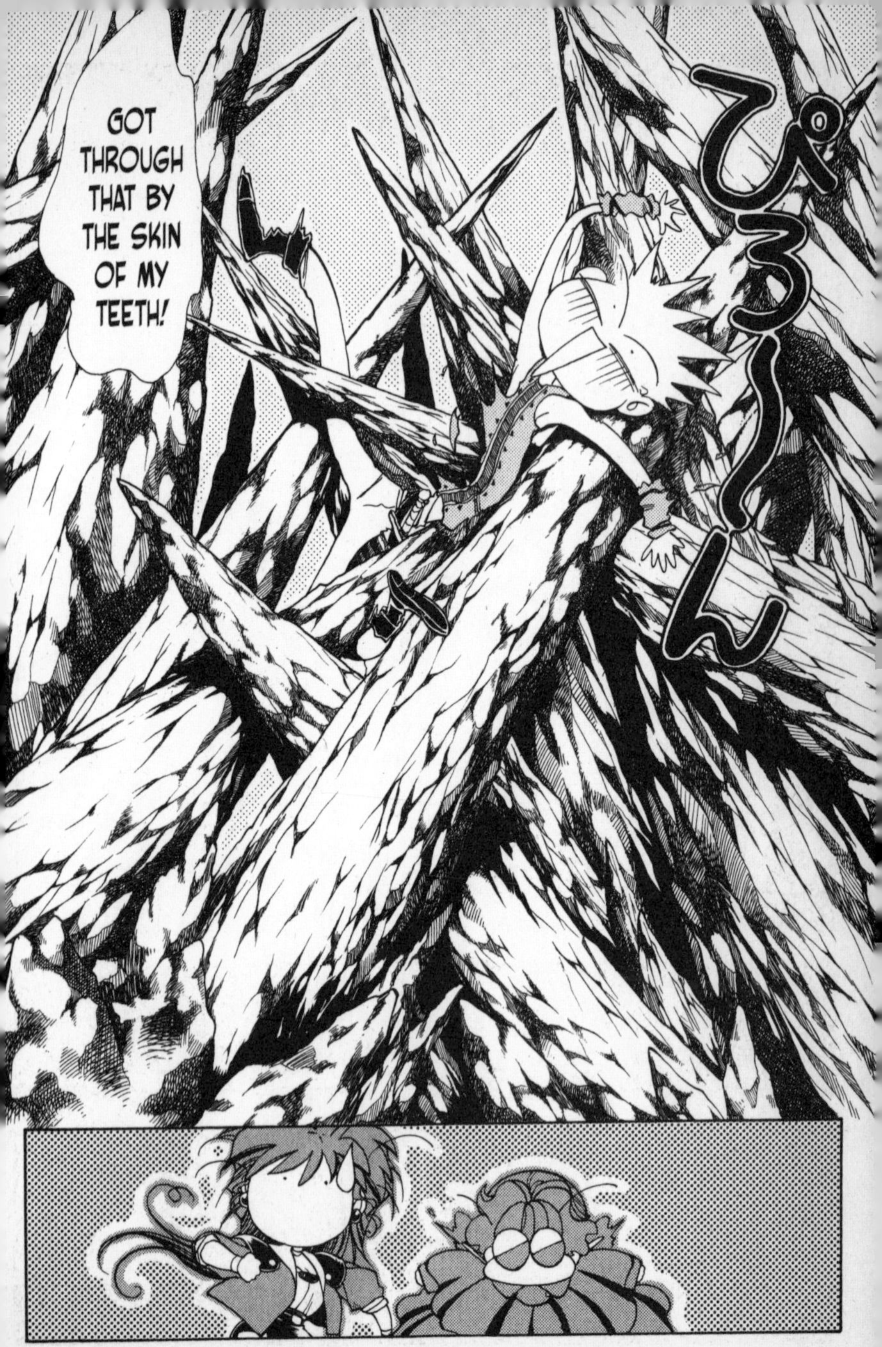
ぴろーん
GOT THROUGH THAT BY THE SKIN OF MY TEETH!

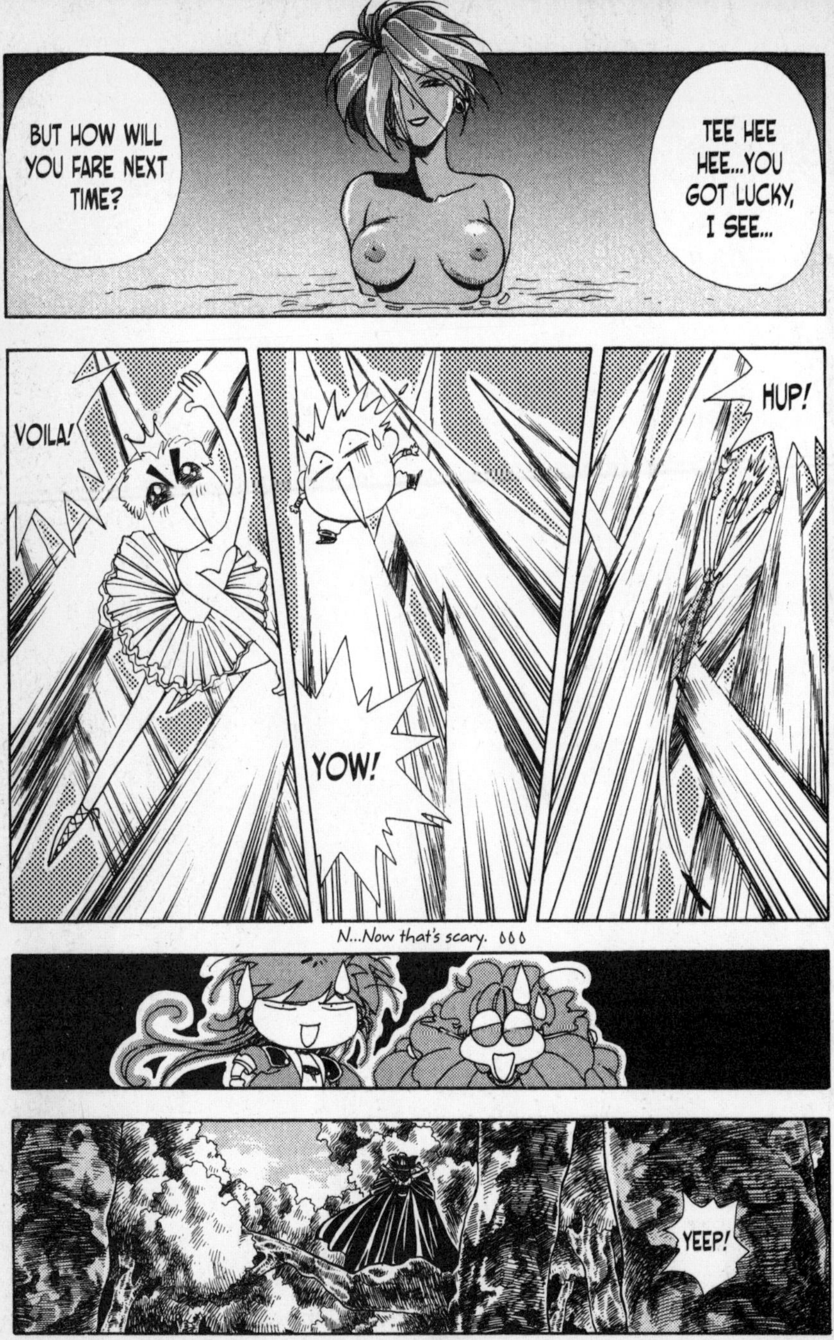
TEE HEE HEE...YOU GOT LUCKY, I SEE...
BUT HOW WILL YOU FARE NEXT TIME?
HUP!
YOW!
VOILA!
N...Now that's scary.
YEEP!

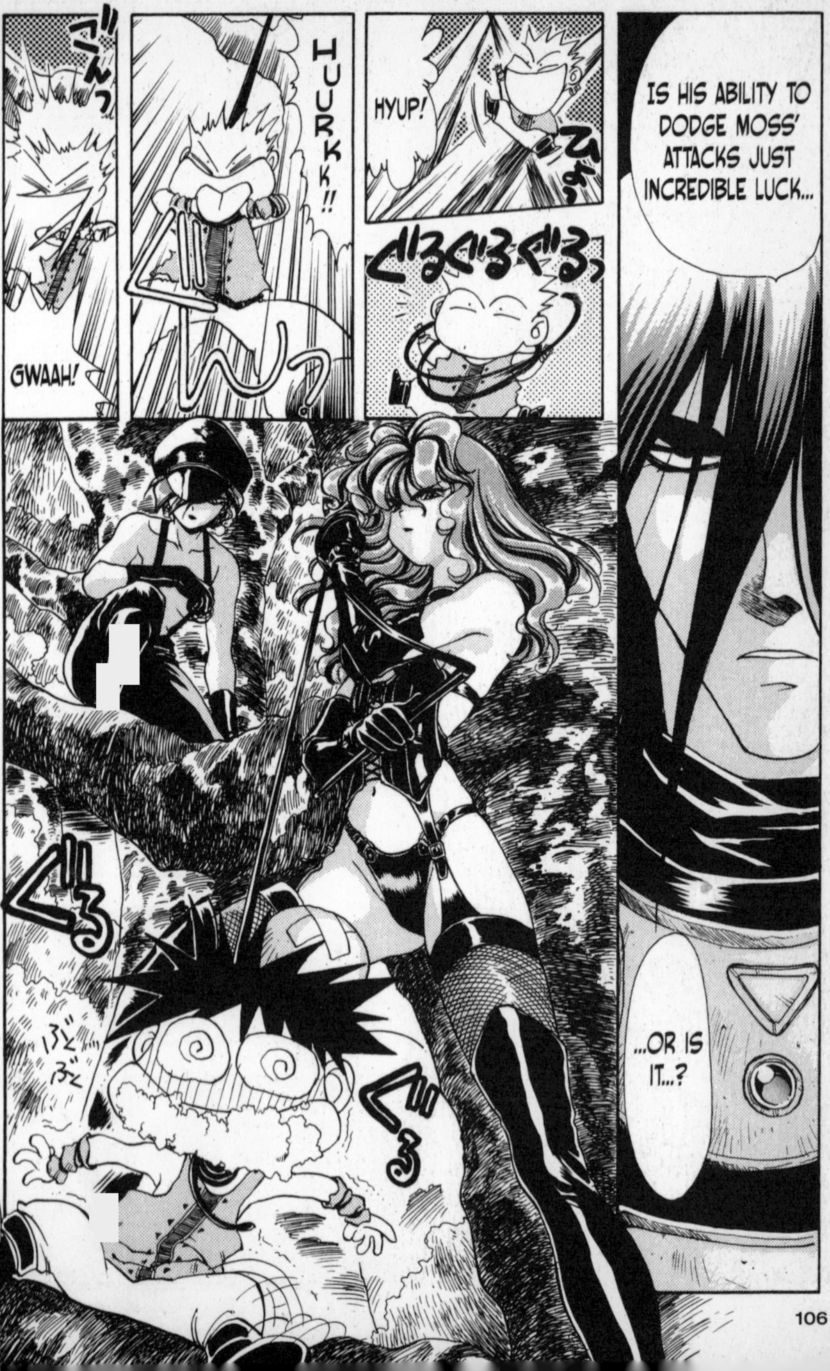
IS HIS ABILITY TO DODGE MOSS' ATTACKS JUST INCREDIBLE LUCK...
...OR IS IT...?
HYUP!
HUURKK!!
GWAAH!

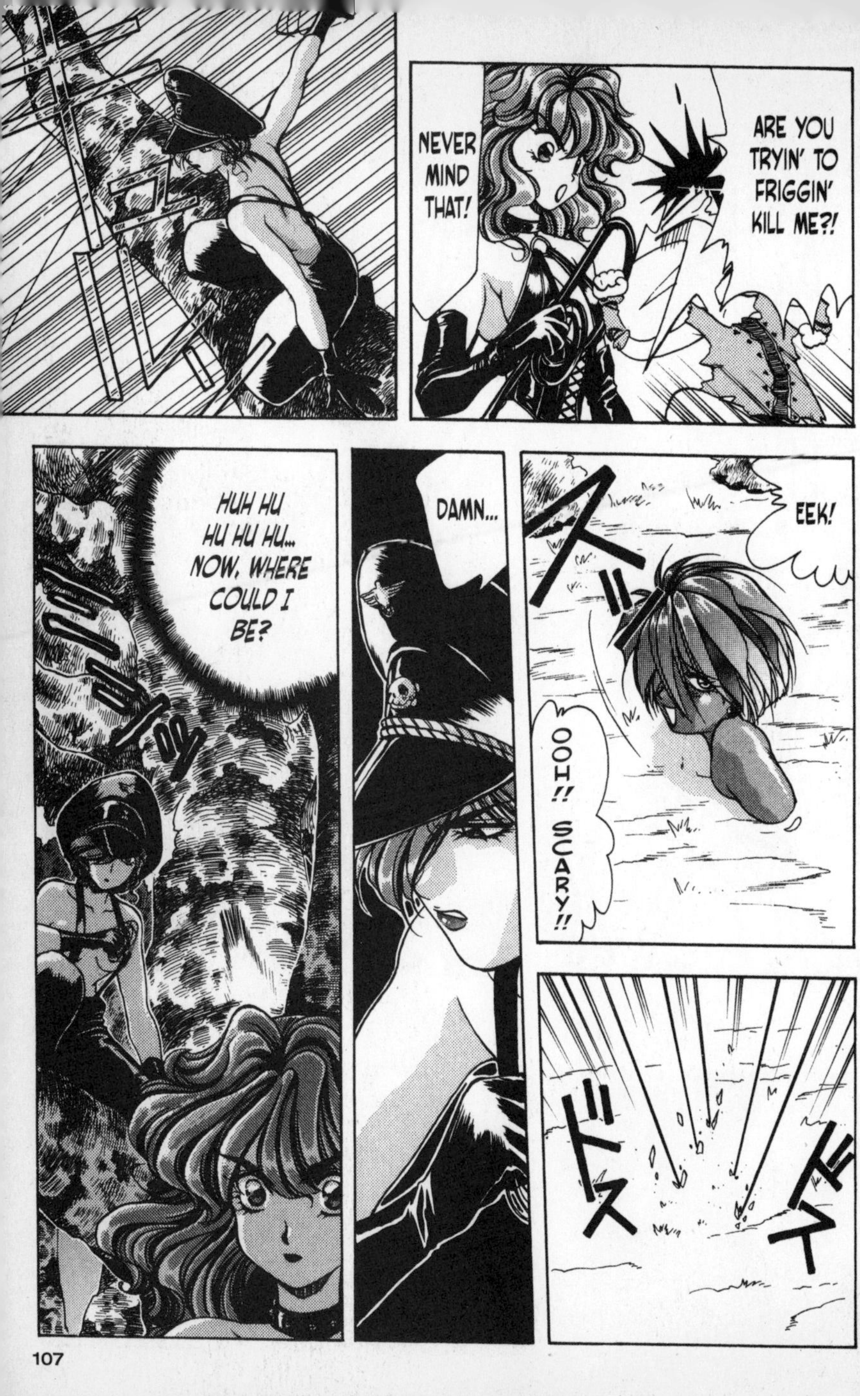
ARE YOU TRYIN' TO FRIGGIN' KILL ME?!
NEVER MIND THAT!
EEK!
OOH!! SCARY!!
DAMN...
HUH HU HU HU HU... NOW, WHERE COULD I BE?

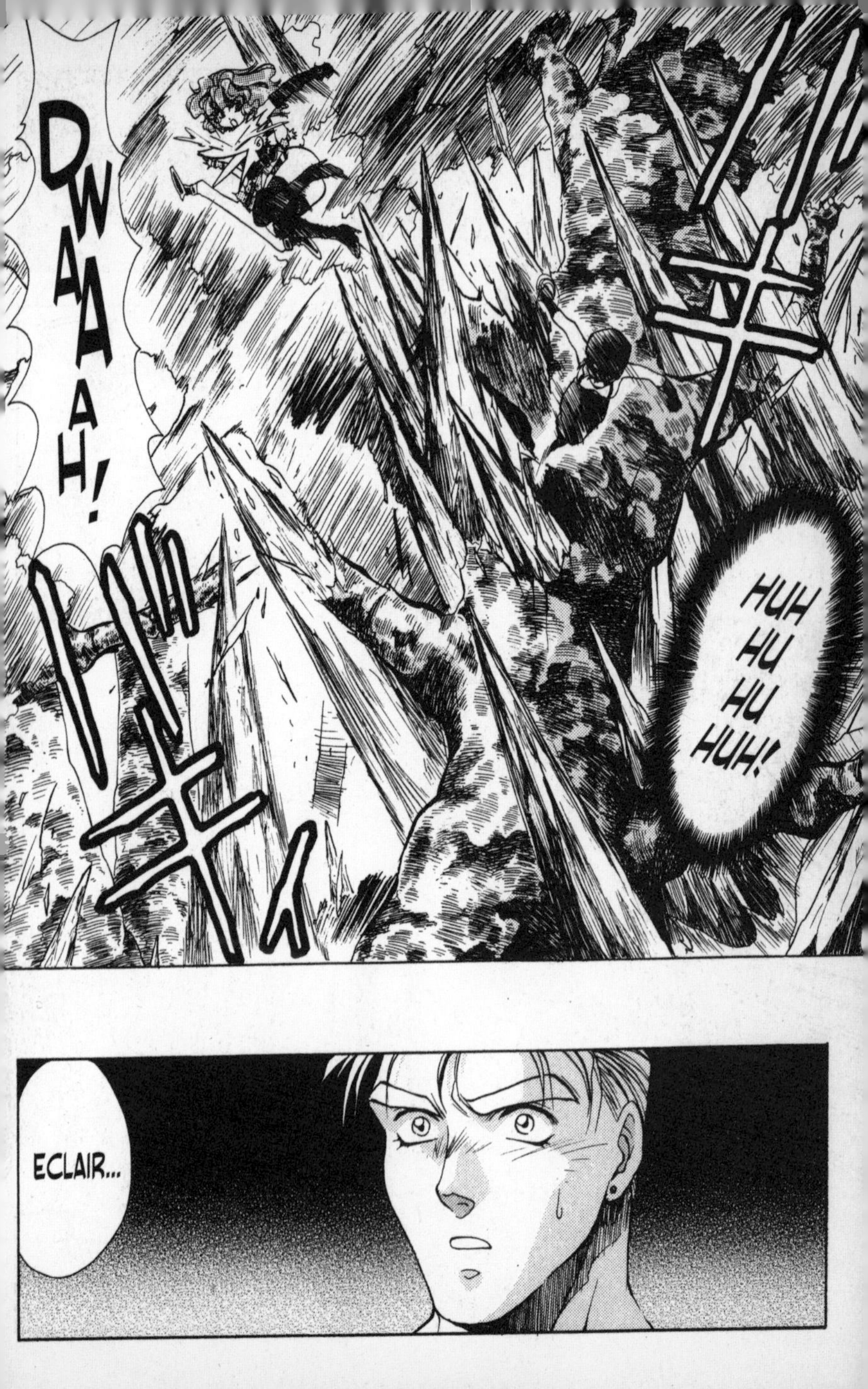
DWAAAH!
HUH HU HU HUH!
ECLAIR...

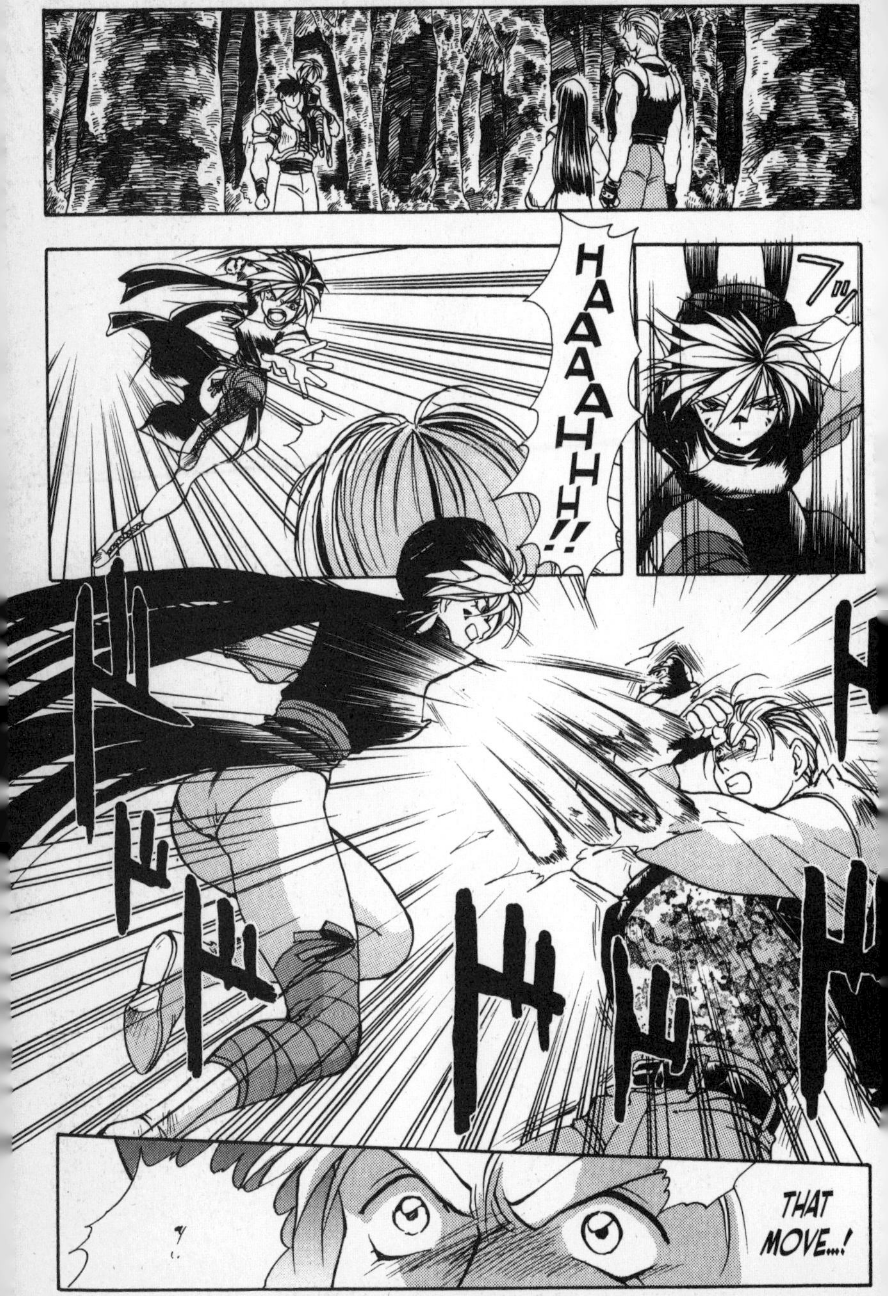
HAAAAAHHH!!
THAT MOVE...!

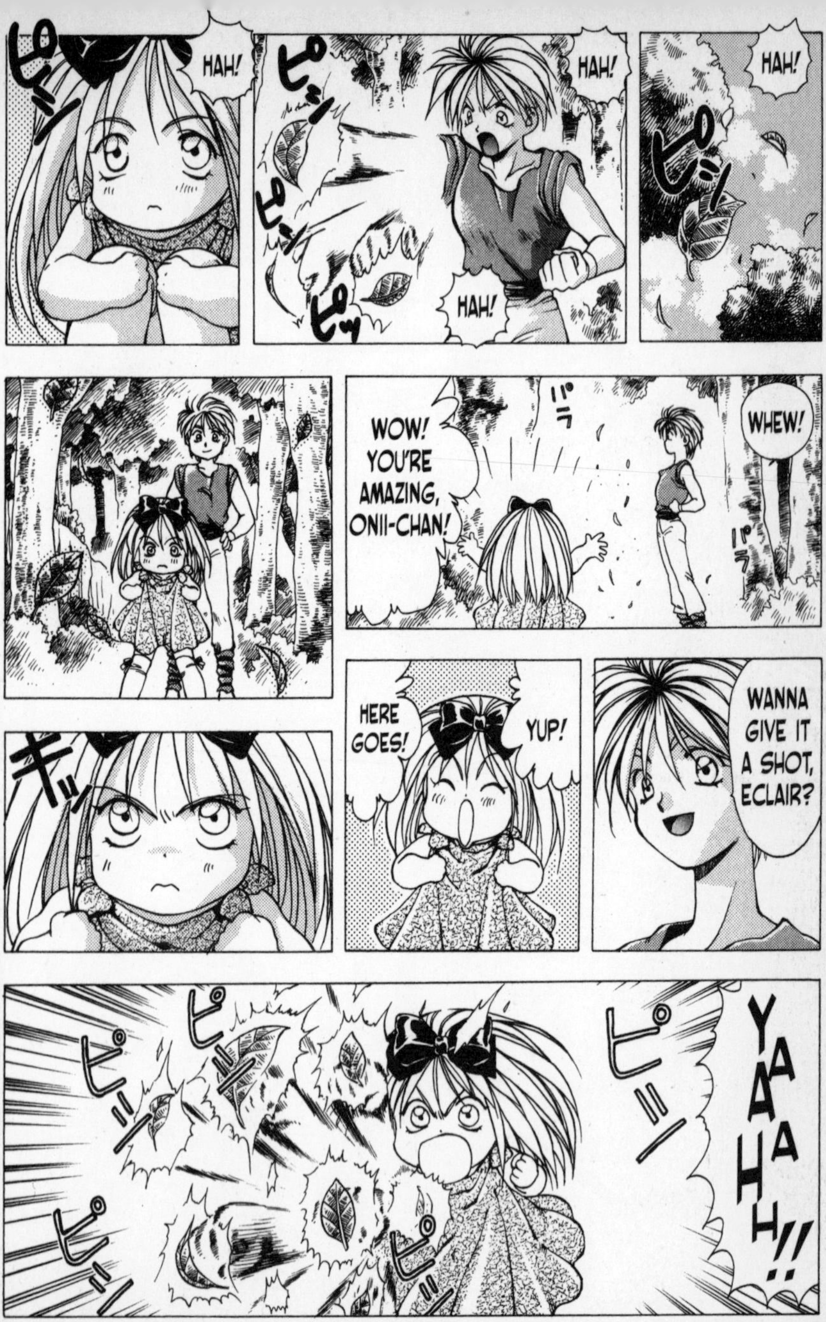
HAH!
HAH!
HAH!
HAH!
WHEW!
WOW! YOU'RE AMAZING, ONII-CHAN!
WANNA GIVE IT A SHOT, ECLAIR?
YUP!
HERE GOES!
YAAAHH!!

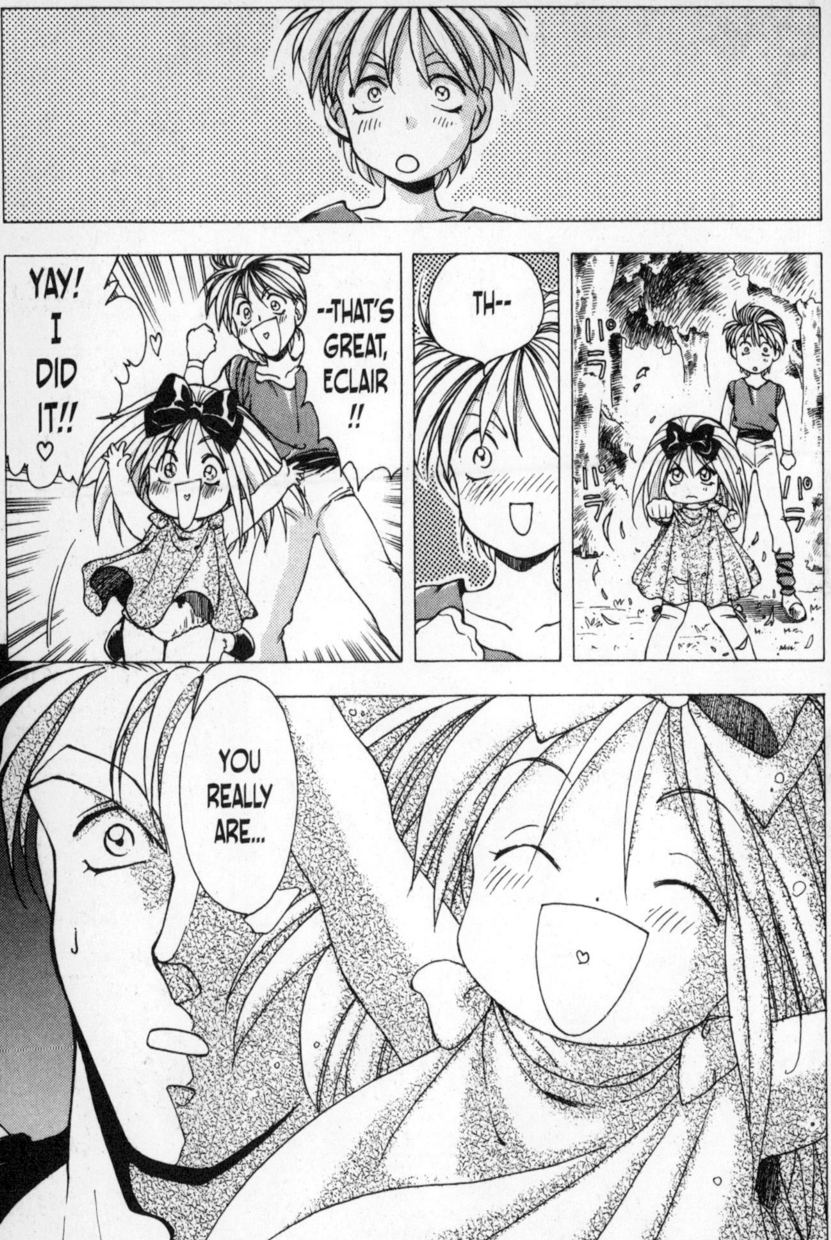
パラ
パラ
TH--
--THAT'S GREAT, ECLAIR !!
YAY! I DID IT!! ♡
YOU REALLY ARE...

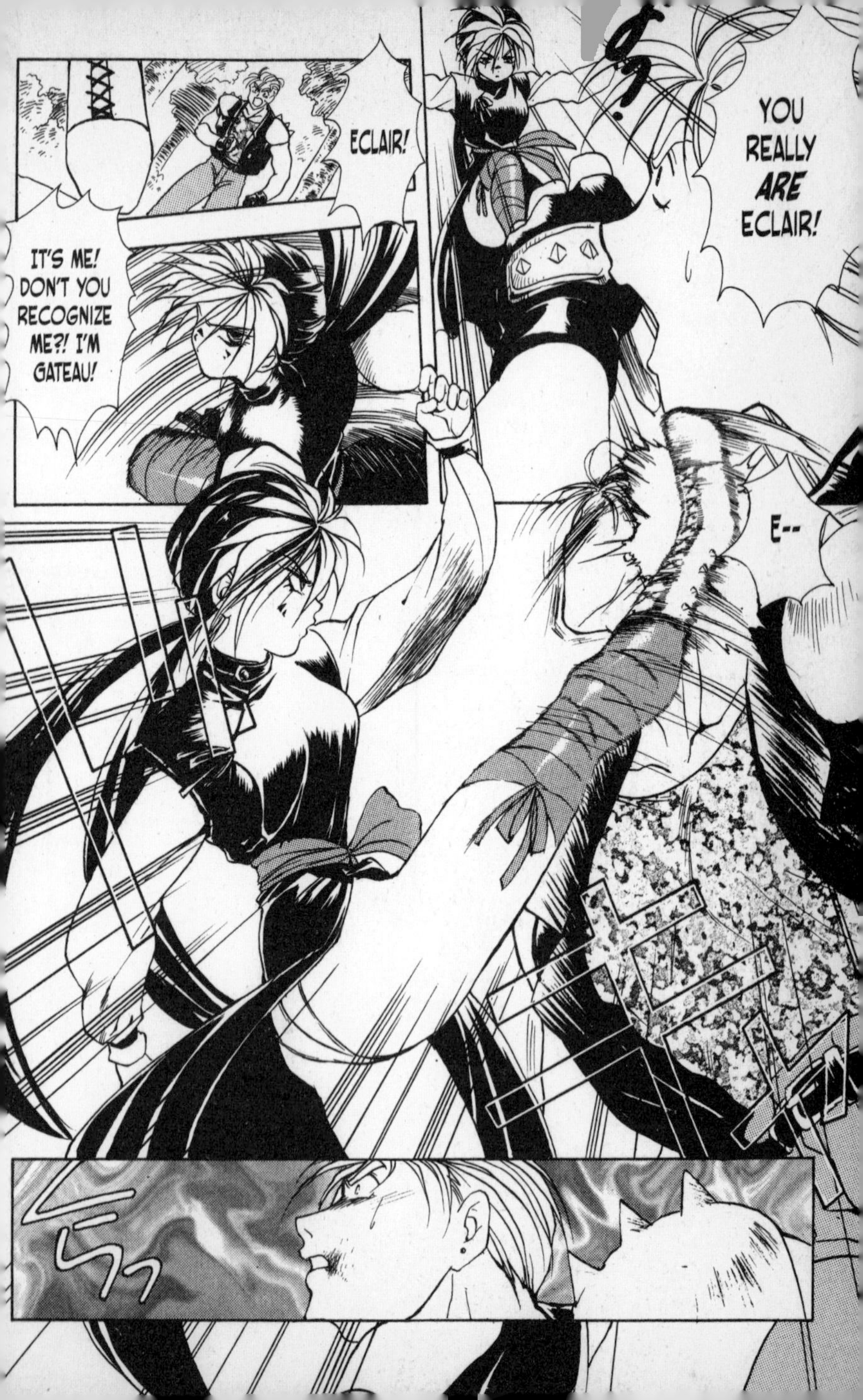
YOU REALLY **ARE** ECLAIR!
ECLAIR!
IT'S ME! DON'T YOU RECOGNIZE ME?! I'M GATEAU!
E--

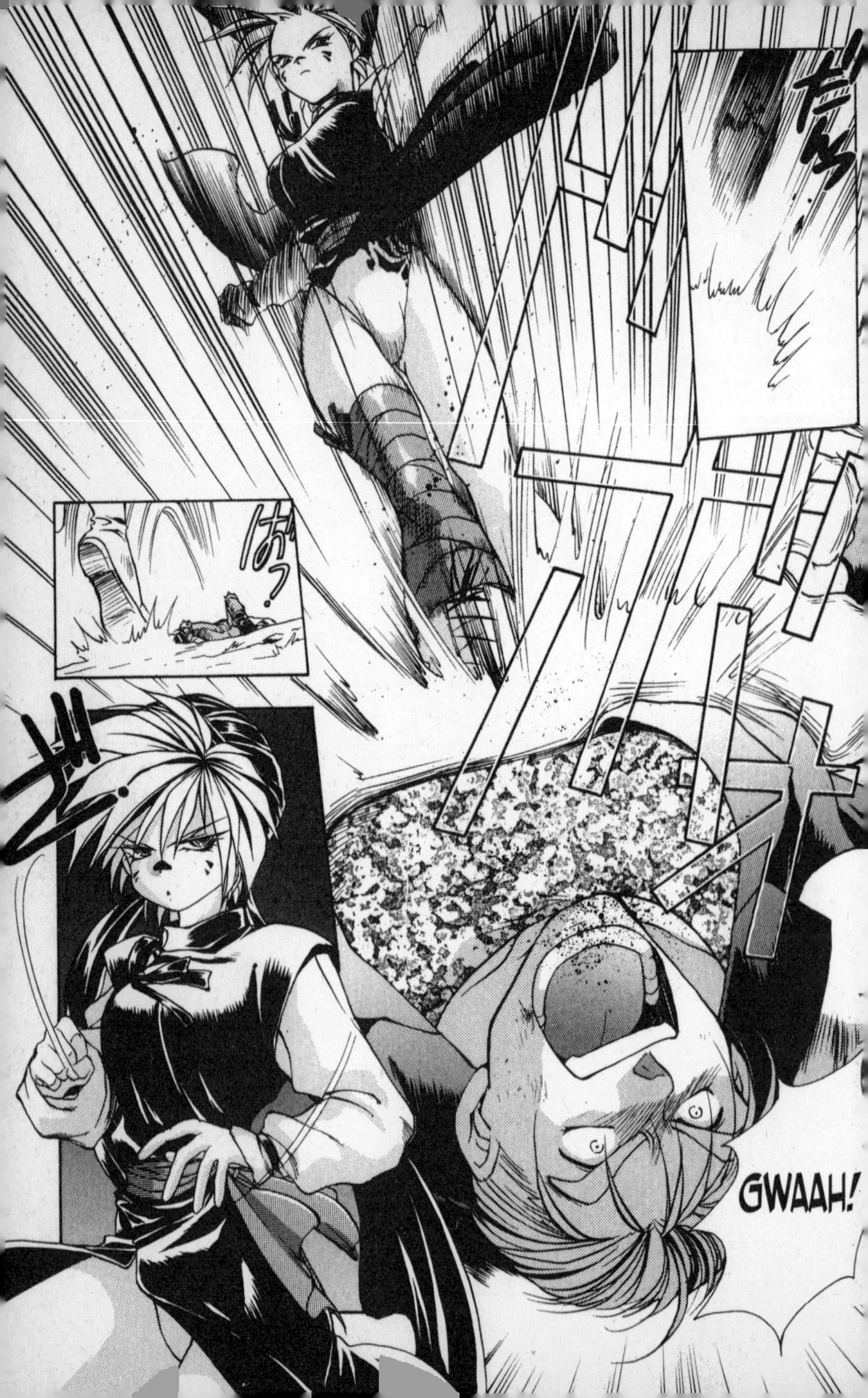
はっ?
GWAAH!

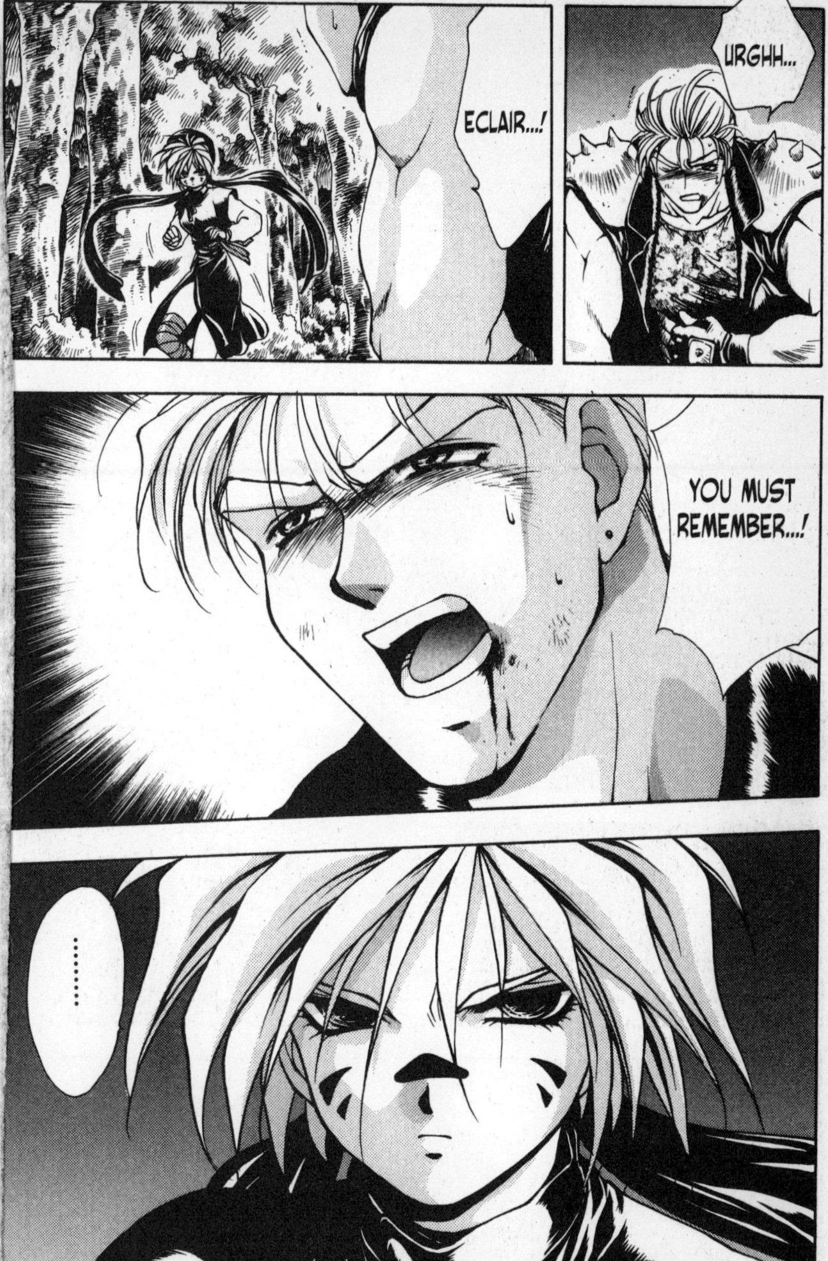
URGHH...
ECLAIR...!
YOU MUST REMEMBER...!
....

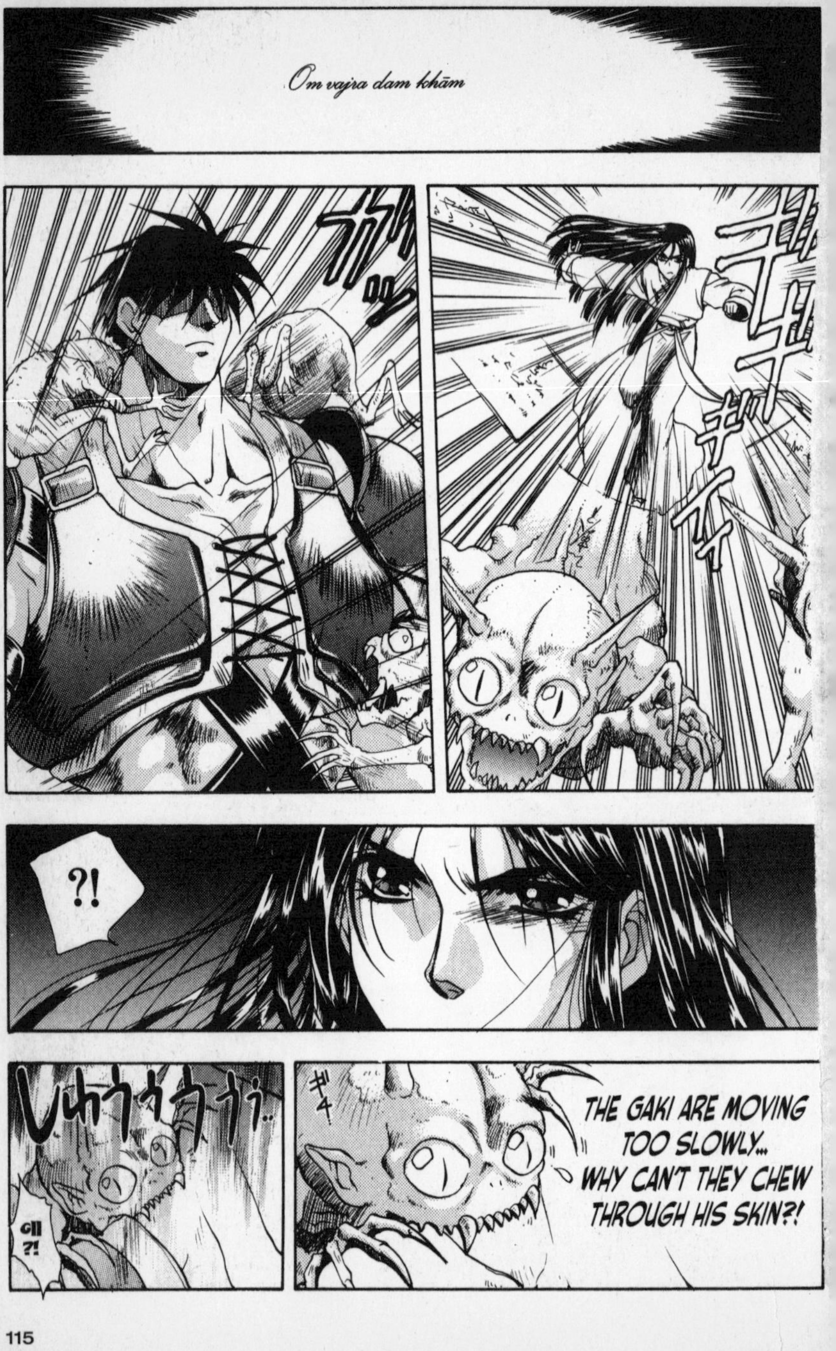
Ōm vajra dam khām
?!
THE GAKI ARE MOVING TOO SLOWLY... WHY CAN'T THEY CHEW THROUGH HIS SKIN?!
GII ?!

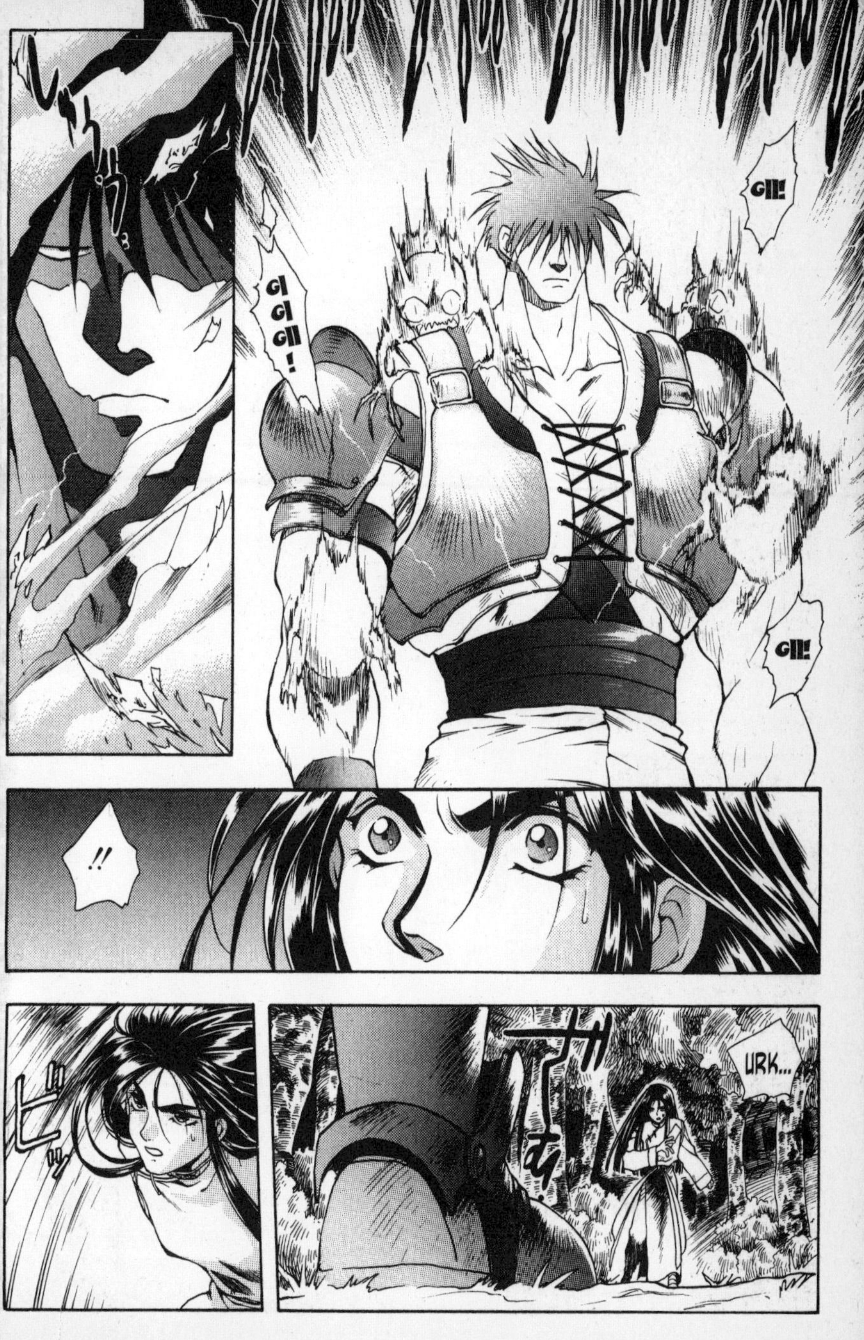
GII!
GI GI GII!
GII!
!!
URK...

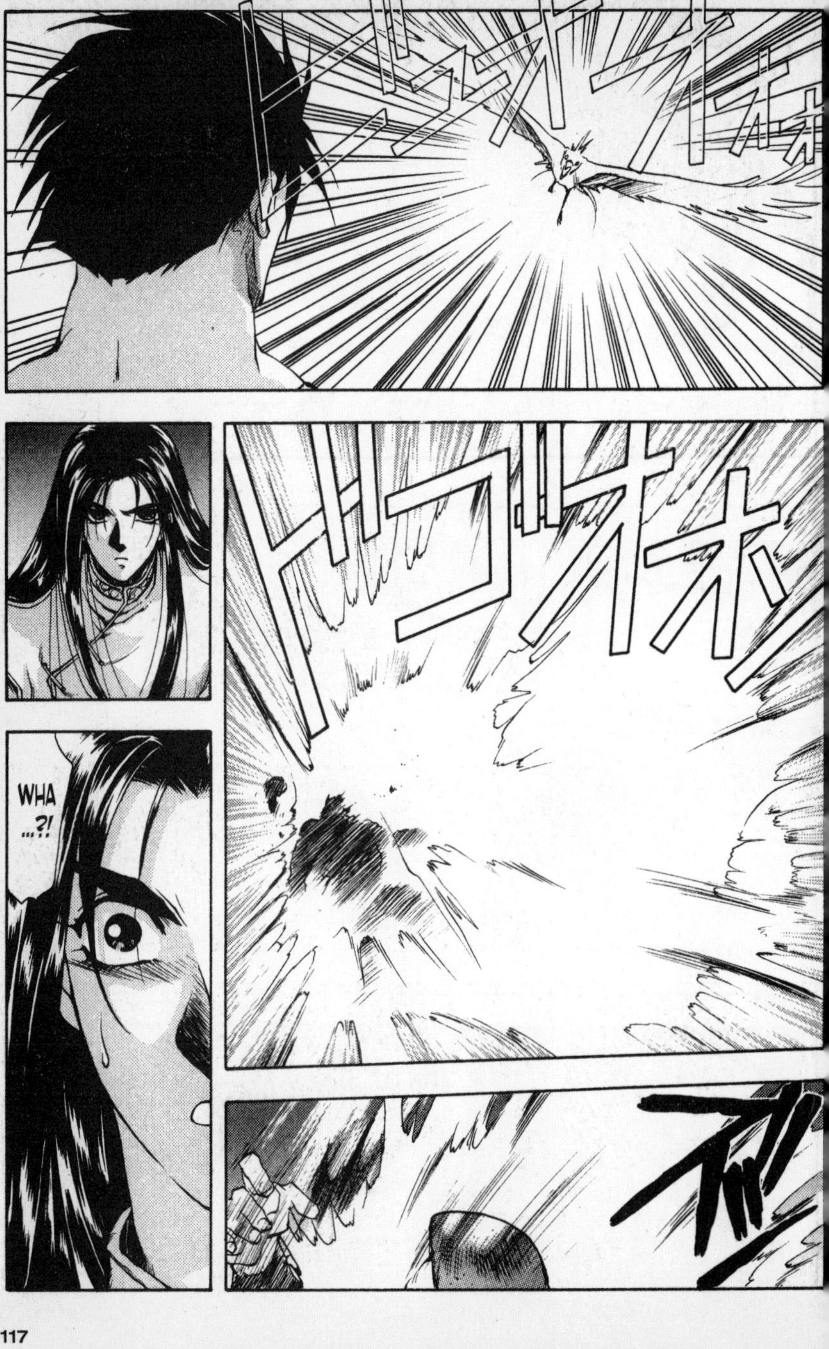
WHA ...?!

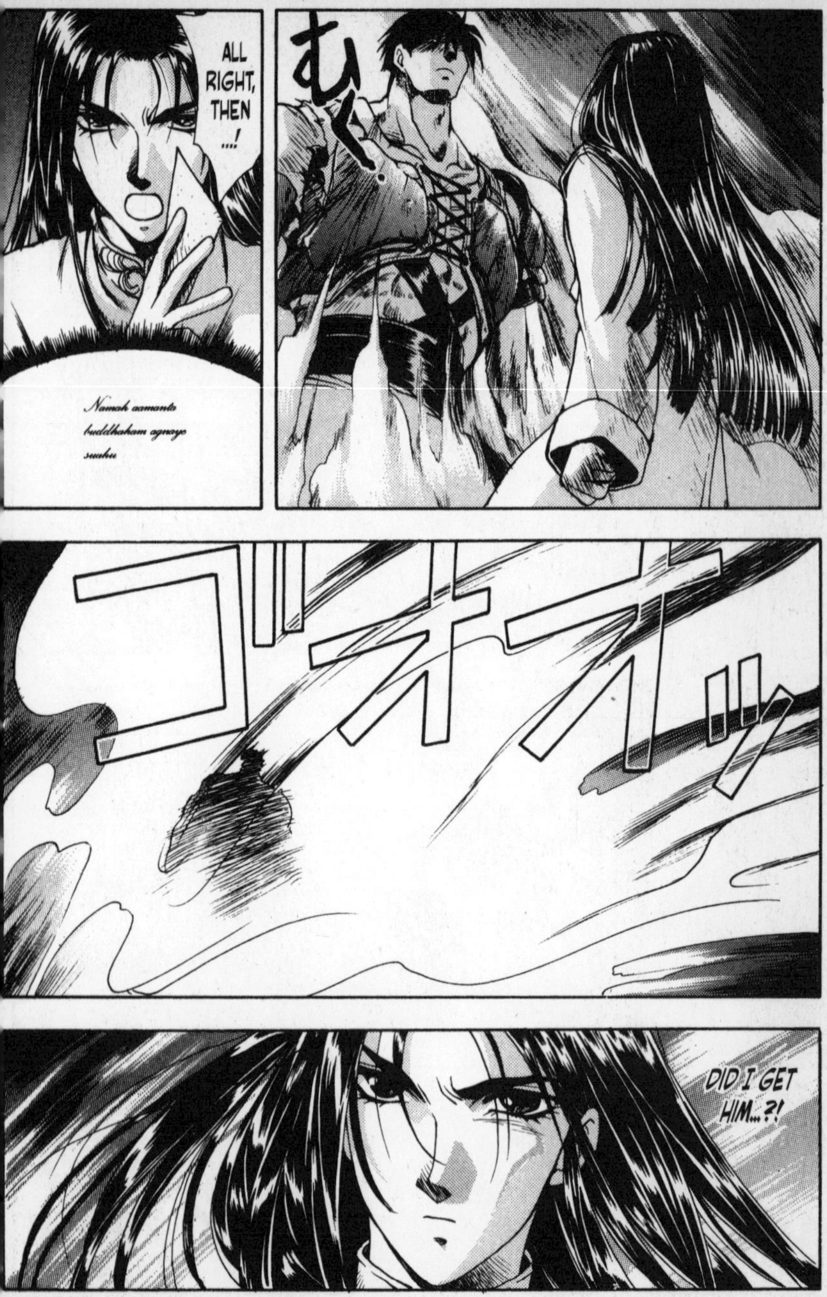
む
ALL RIGHT, THEN ...!
Namah samanta buddhanam agnaye svaha
ゴオオッ
DID I GET HIM...?!

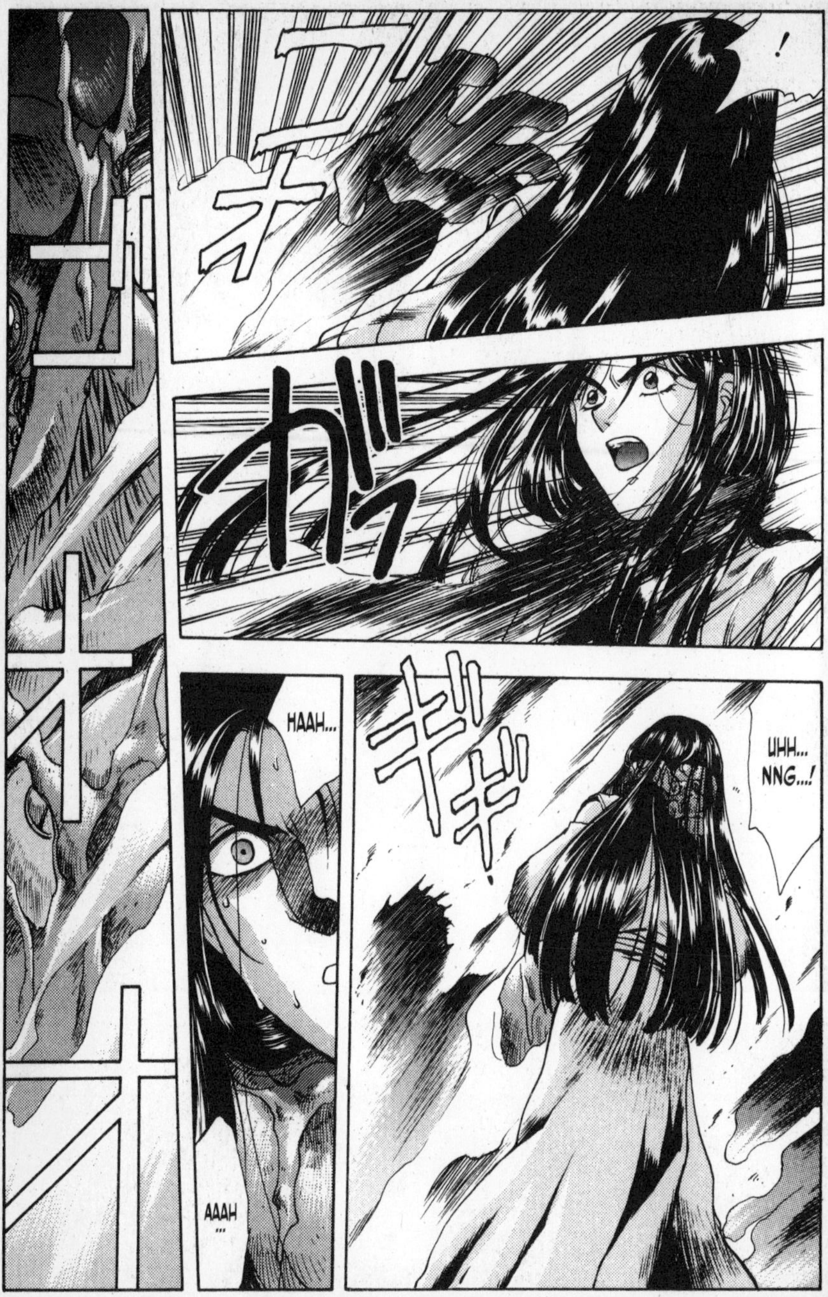
!
UHH... NNG...!
HAAH...
AAAH ...

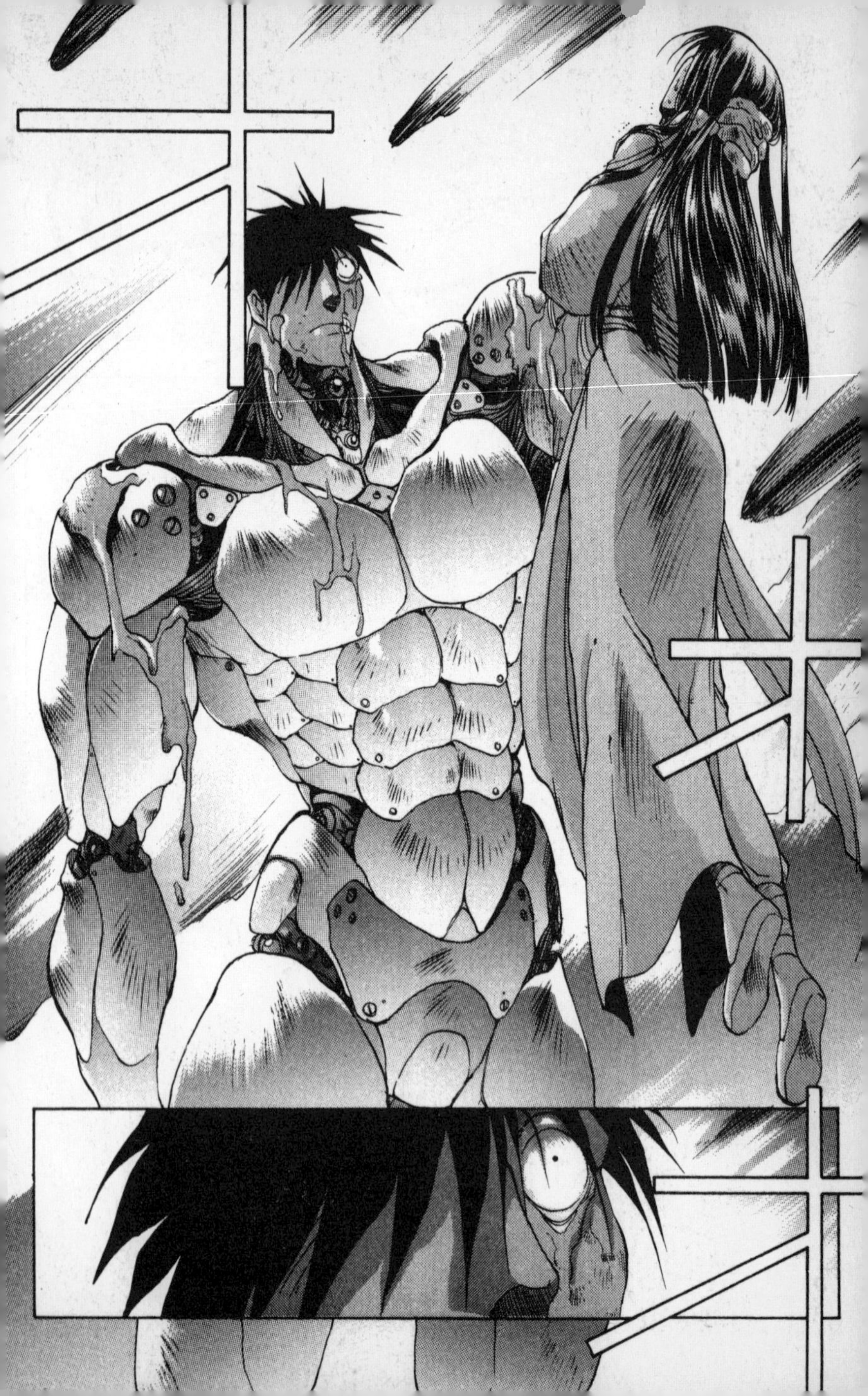

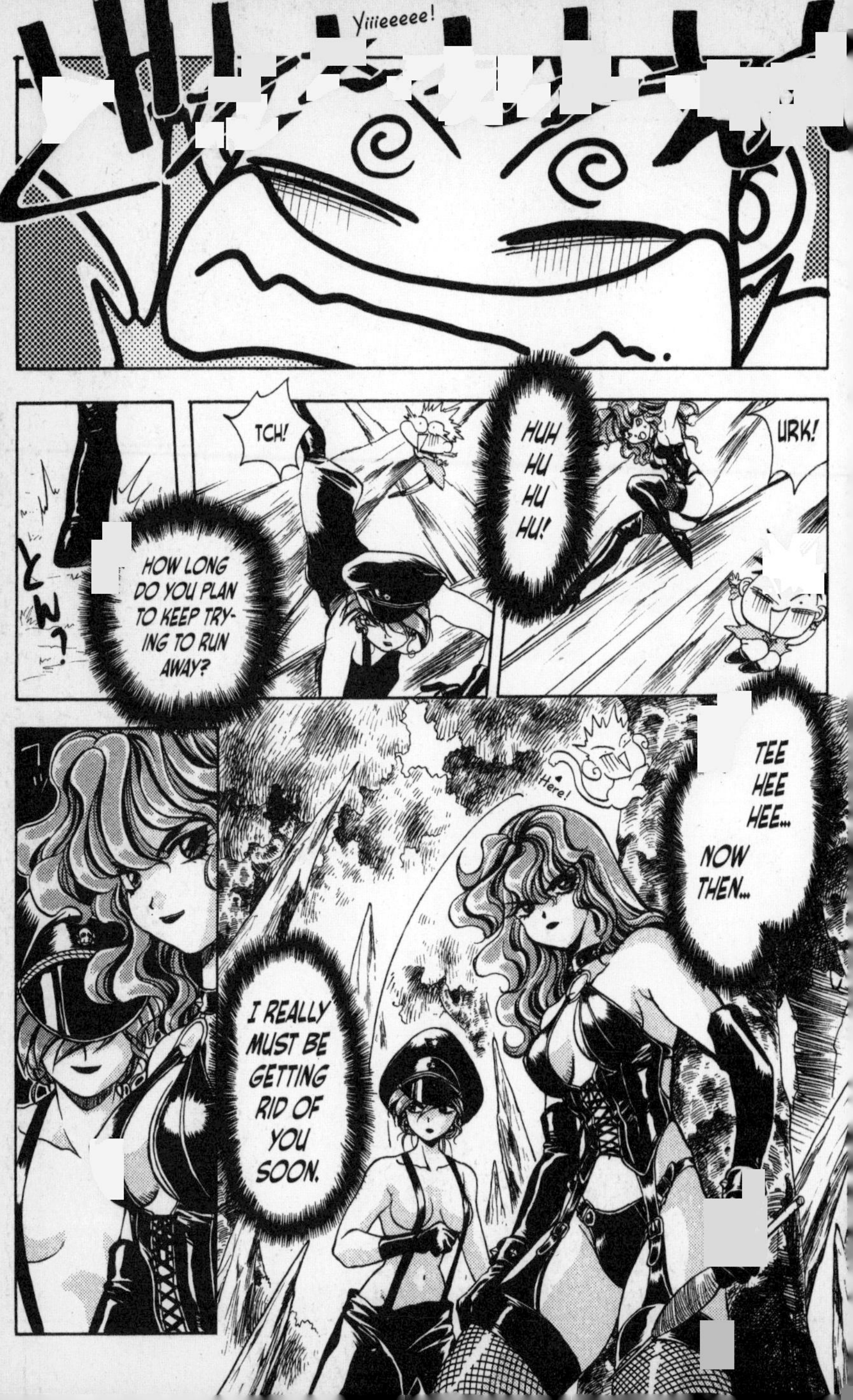
Yiiieeeee!
URK!
HUH HU HU HU!
TCH!
HOW LONG DO YOU PLAN TO KEEP TRY-ING TO RUN AWAY?
TEE HEE HEE... NOW THEN...
Here!
I REALLY MUST BE GETTING RID OF YOU SOON.

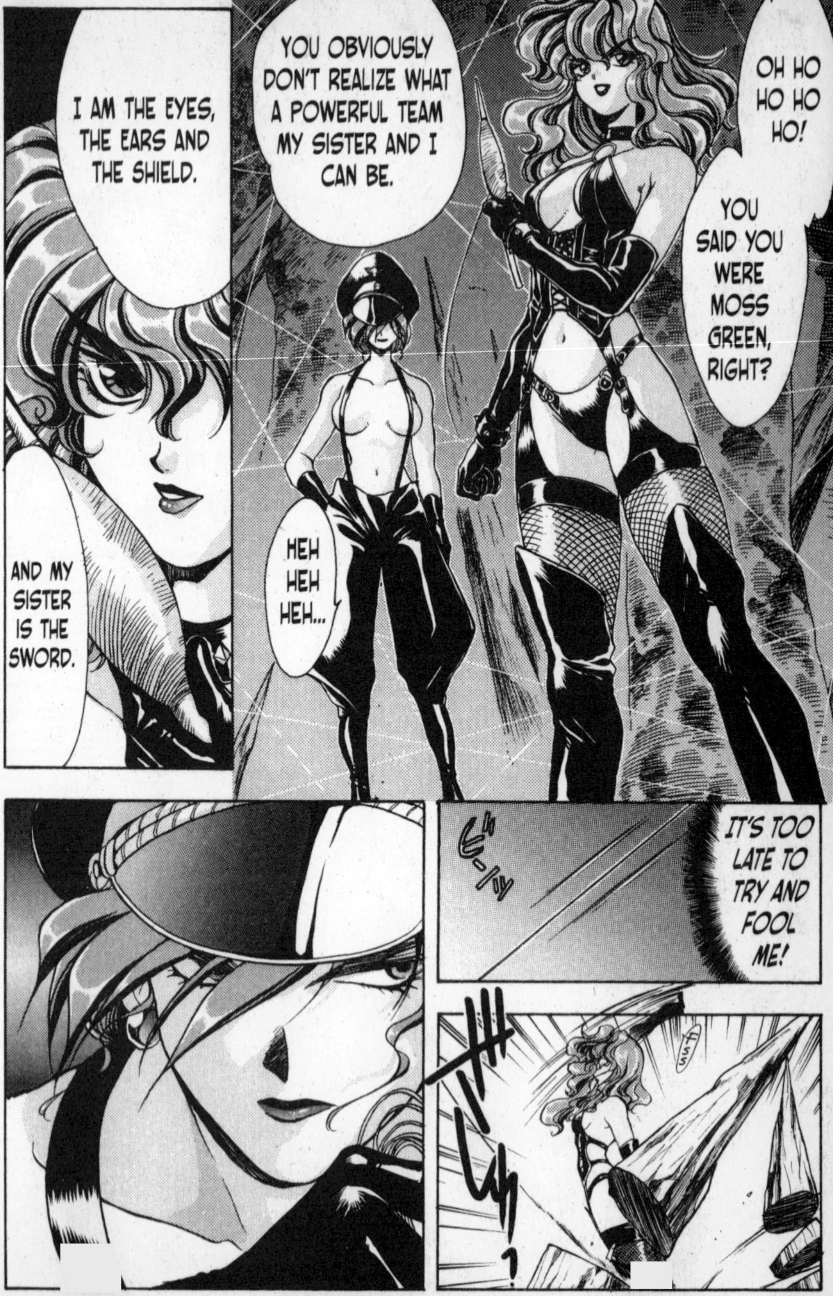
OH HO HO HO HO!
YOU SAID YOU WERE MOSS GREEN, RIGHT?
YOU OBVIOUSLY DON'T REALIZE WHAT A POWERFUL TEAM MY SISTER AND I CAN BE.
HEH HEH HEH...
I AM THE EYES, THE EARS AND THE SHIELD.
AND MY SISTER IS THE SWORD.
IT'S TOO LATE TO TRY AND FOOL ME!

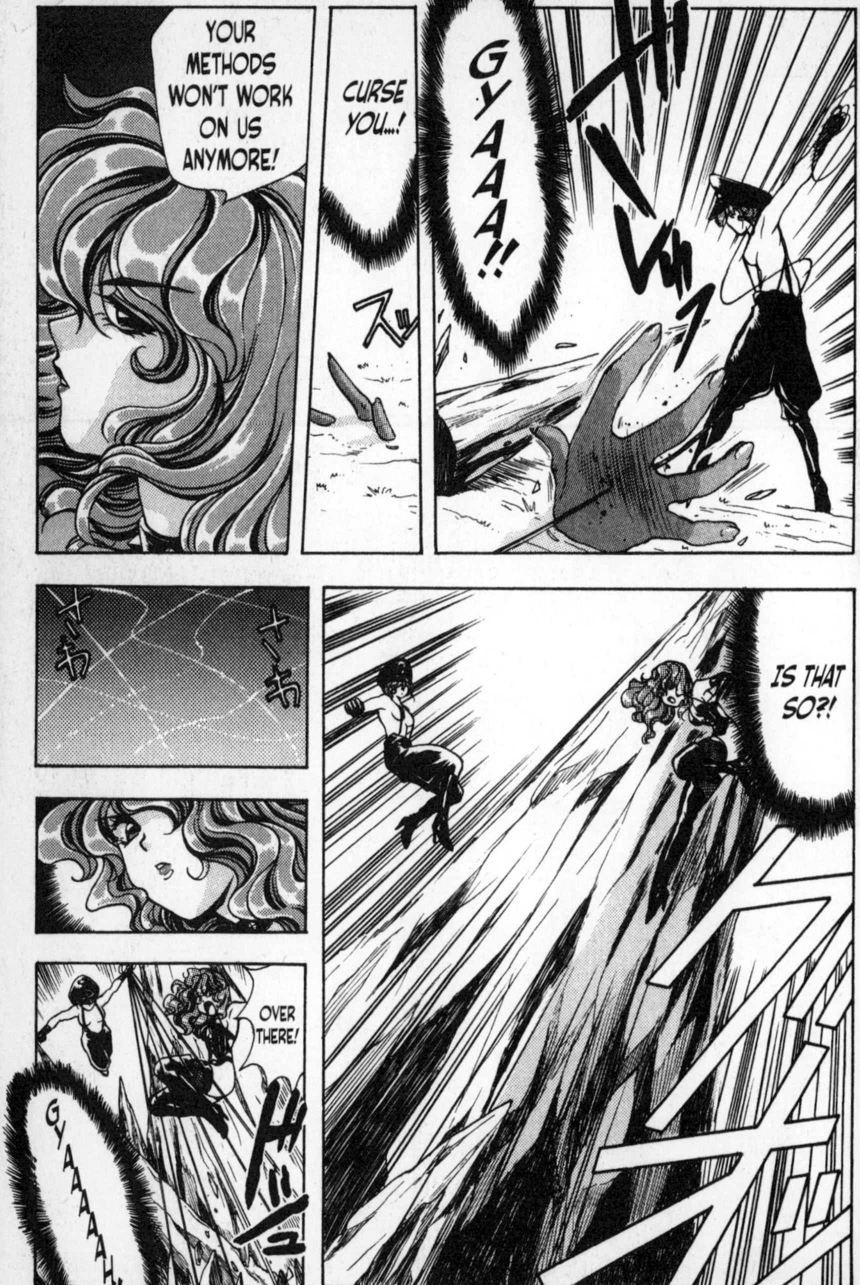
GYAAAA!!
CURSE YOU...!
YOUR METHODS WON'T WORK ON US ANYMORE!
IS THAT SO?!
OVER THERE!
GYAAAAAH!!

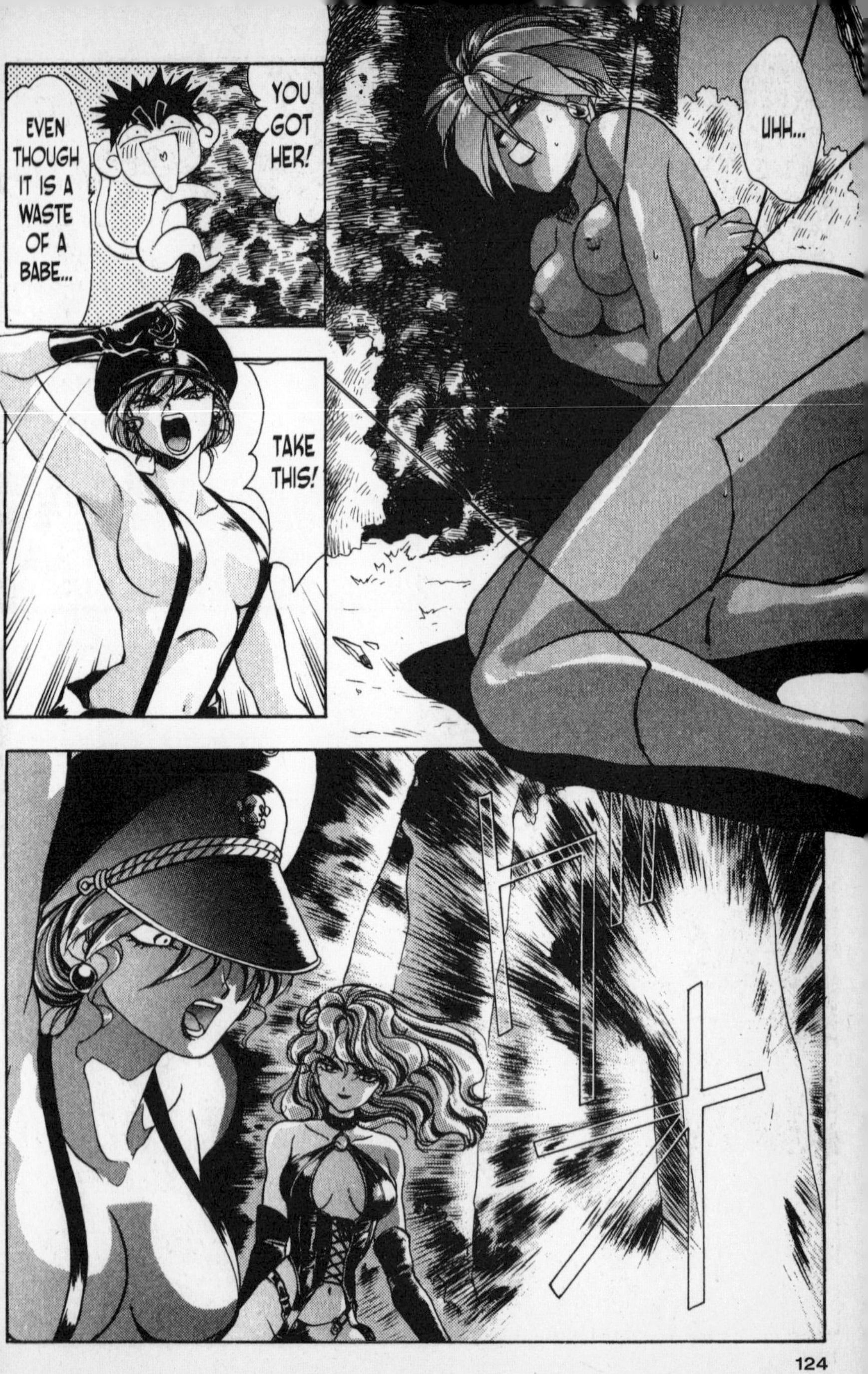
UHH...
YOU GOT HER!
EVEN THOUGH IT IS A WASTE OF A BABE...
TAKE THIS!

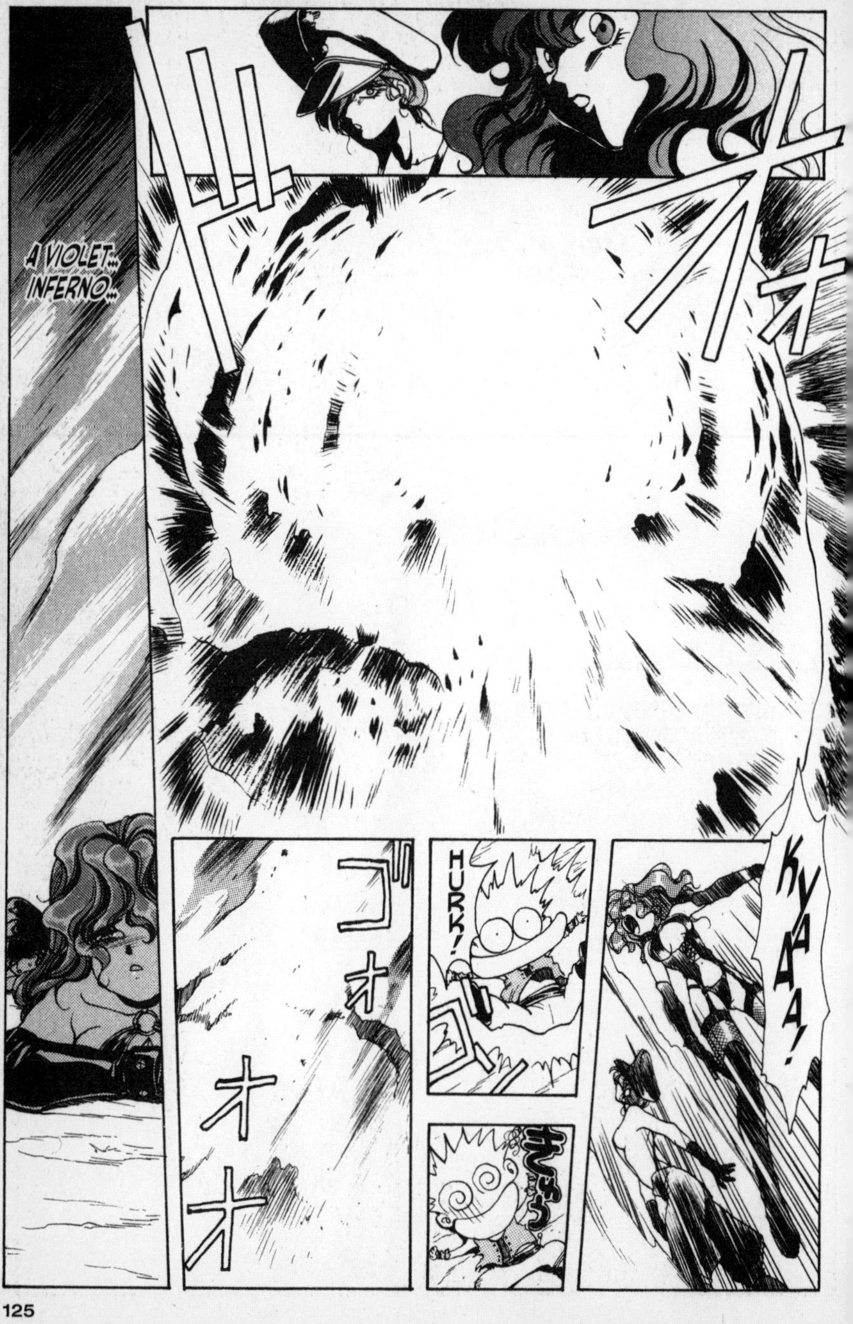

ドォ
オ
A VIOLET... INFERNO...
KYAAAA!
HURK!
きゅう
ゴォオオ

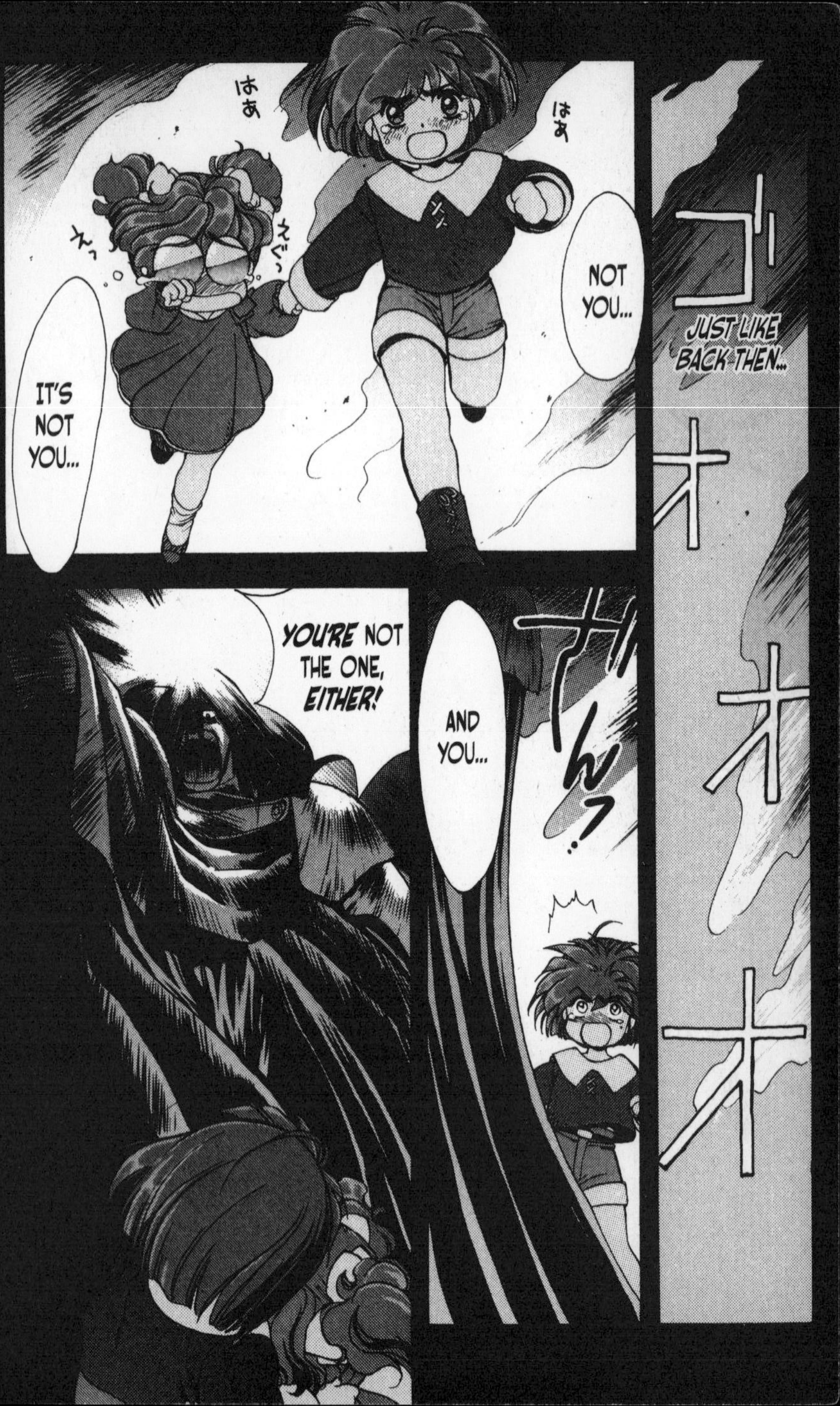
ゴーオオオ
JUST LIKE BACK THEN...
はあ
はあ
NOT YOU...
えぐっ
えっ
IT'S NOT YOU...
AND YOU...
がんっ!?
YOU'RE NOT THE ONE, EITHER!

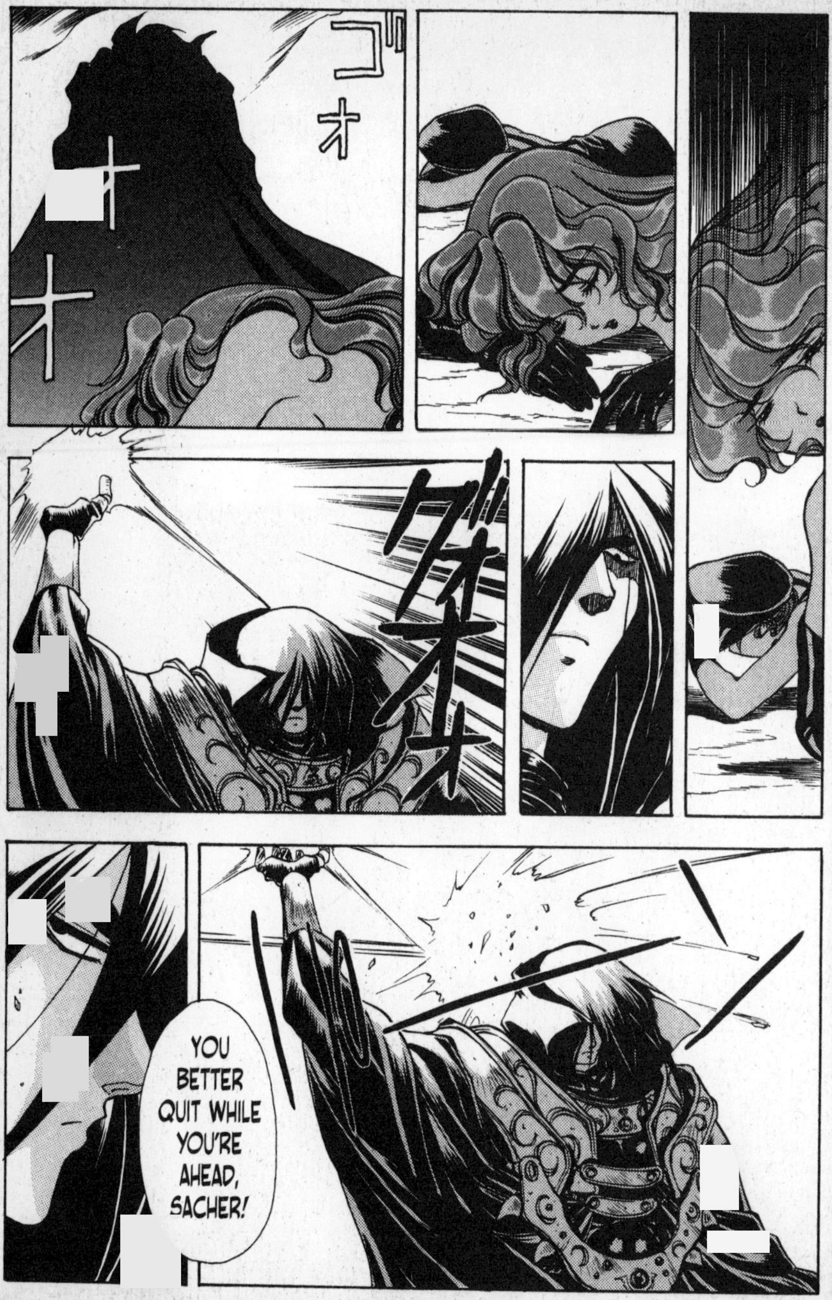
YOU BETTER QUIT WHILE YOU'RE AHEAD, SACHER!

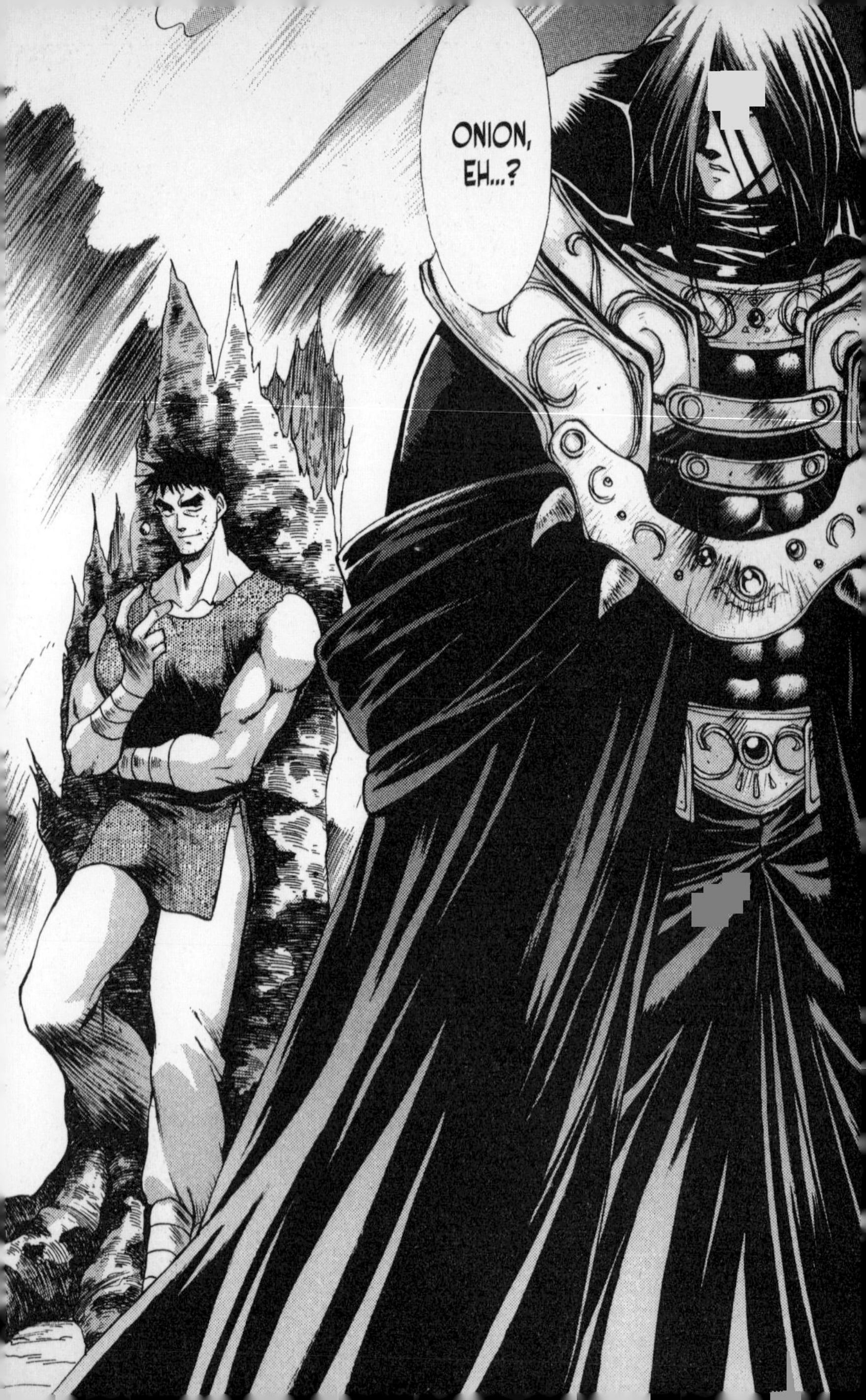
ONION, EH...?

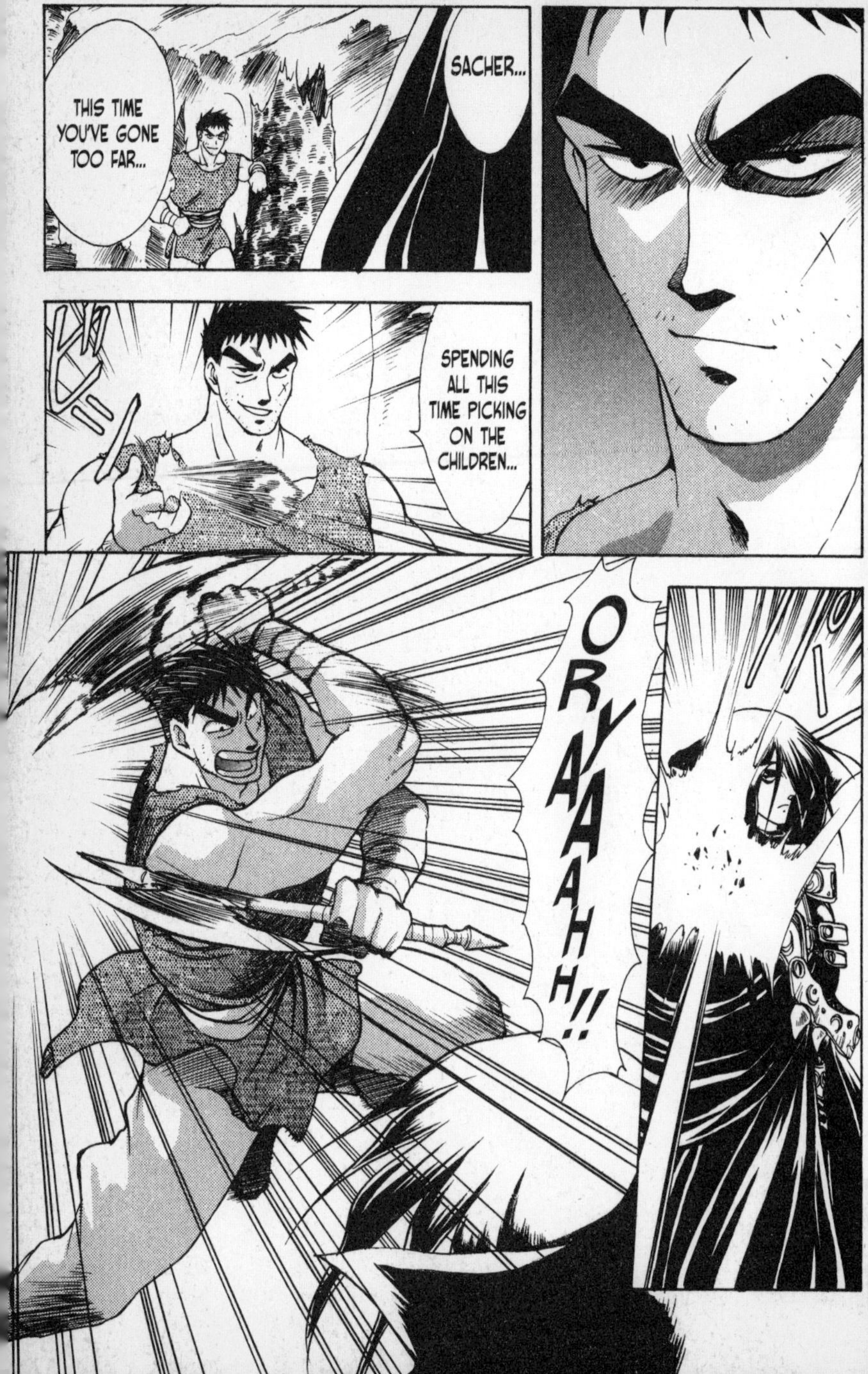
SACHER...
THIS TIME YOU'VE GONE TOO FAR...
SPENDING ALL THIS TIME PICKING ON THE CHILDREN...
ORYAAAAHH!!

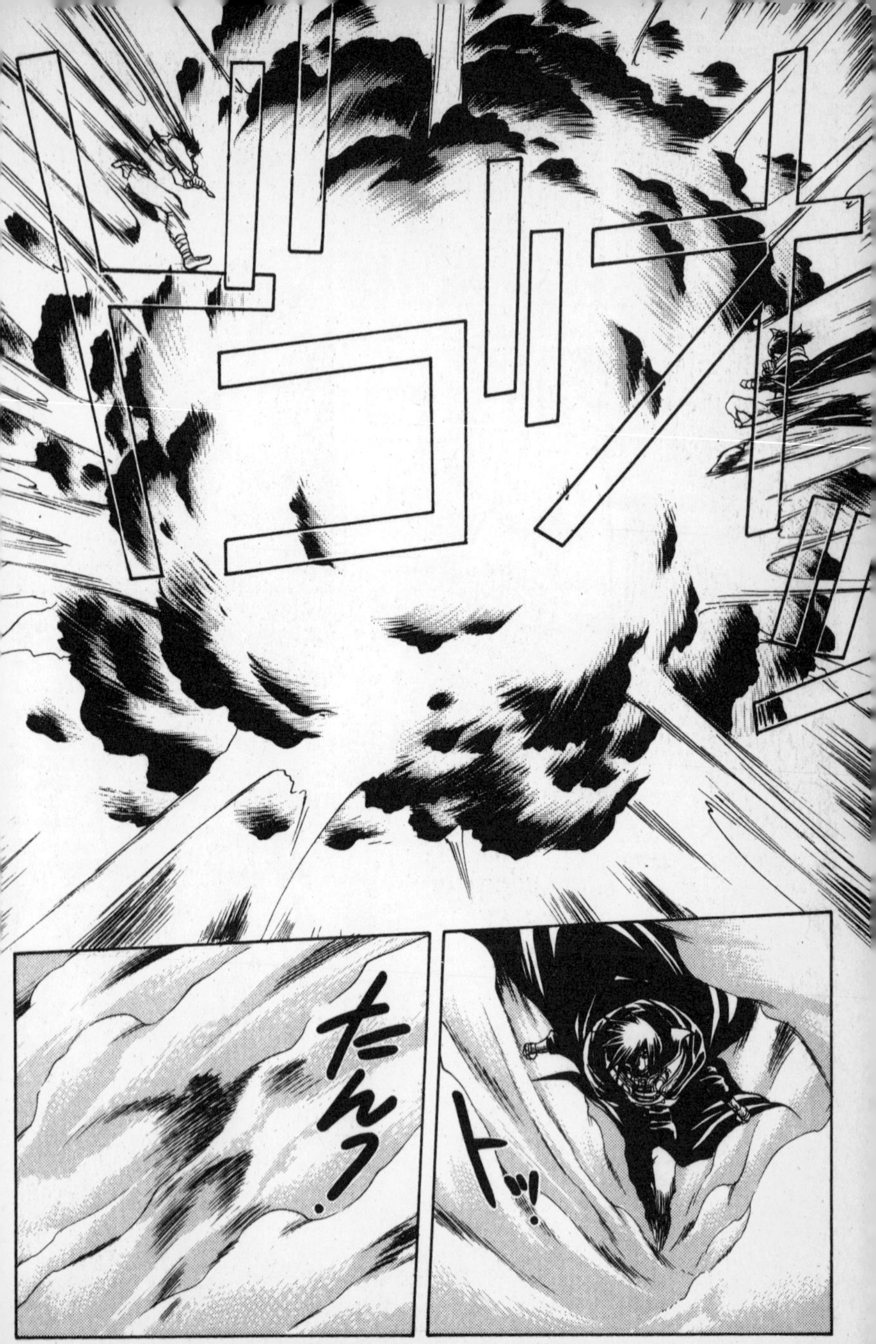
ドゴオッ
トッ!
たんっ!

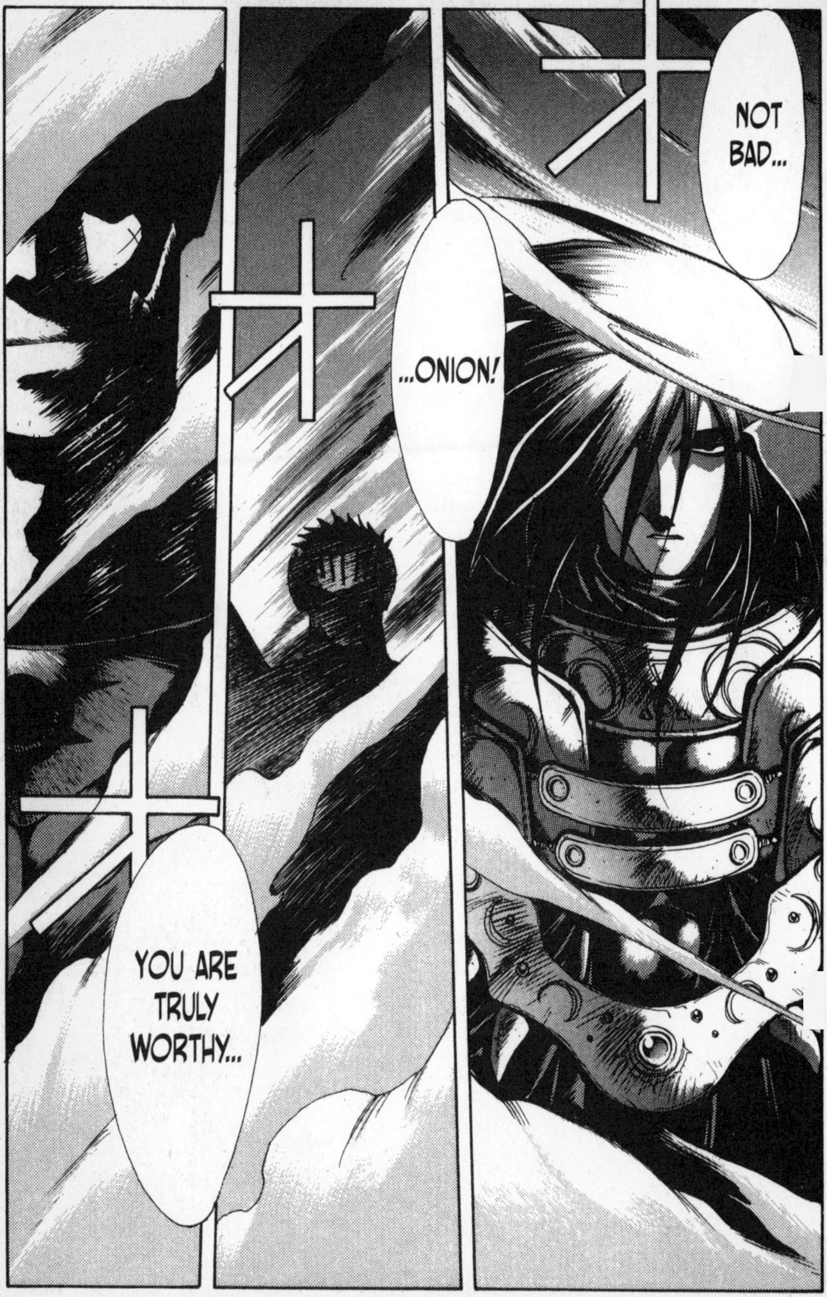
NOT BAD...
...ONION!
YOU ARE TRULY WORTHY...

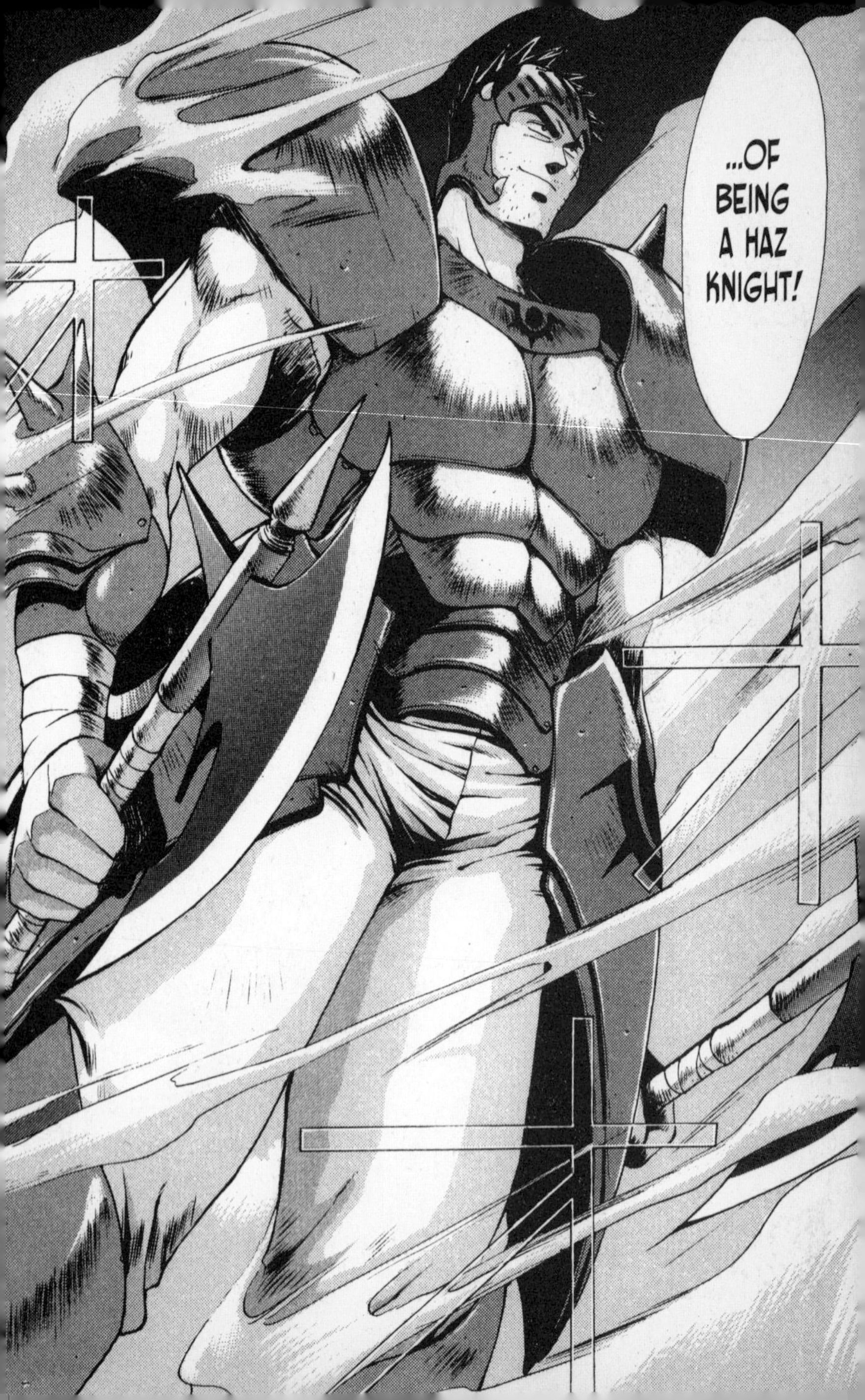
...OF BEING A HAZ KNIGHT!

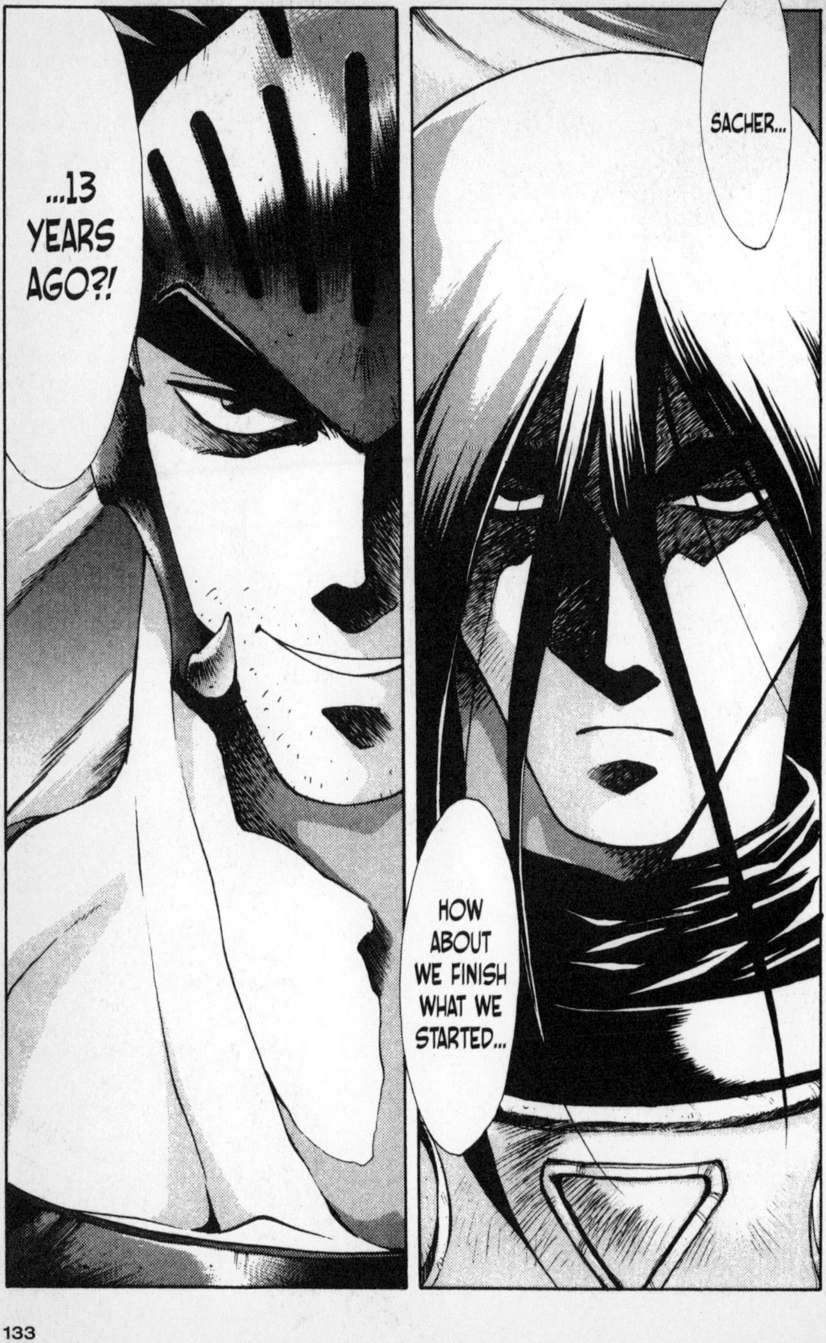
SACHER...
HOW ABOUT WE FINISH WHAT WE STARTED...
...13 YEARS AGO?!

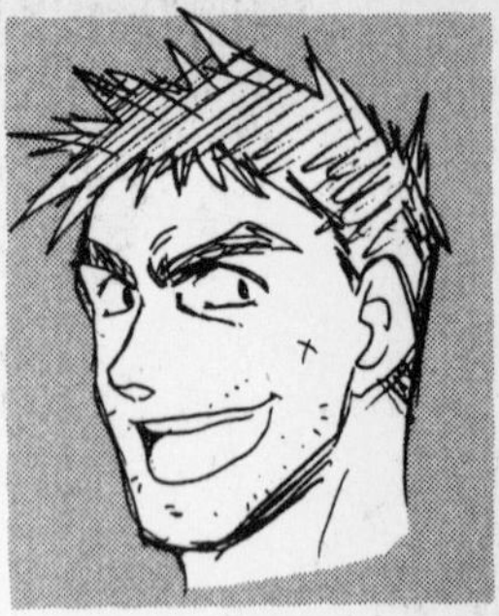

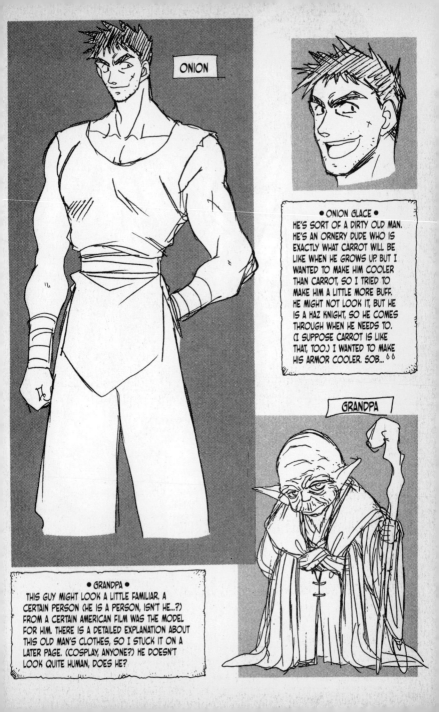

• ONION GLACE •
HE'S SORT OF A DIRTY OLD MAN. HE'S AN ORNERY DUDE WHO IS EXACTLY WHAT CARROT WILL BE LIKE WHEN HE GROWS UP. BUT I WANTED TO MAKE HIM COOLER THAN CARROT, SO I TRIED TO MAKE HIM A LITTLE MORE BUFF. HE MIGHT NOT LOOK IT, BUT HE IS A HAZ KNIGHT, SO HE COMES THROUGH WHEN HE NEEDS TO. (I SUPPOSE CARROT IS LIKE THAT, TOO.) I WANTED TO MAKE HIS ARMOR COOLER. SOB...

GRANDPA

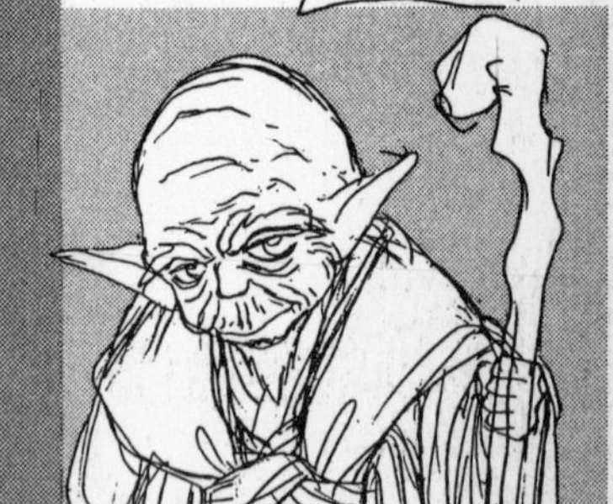

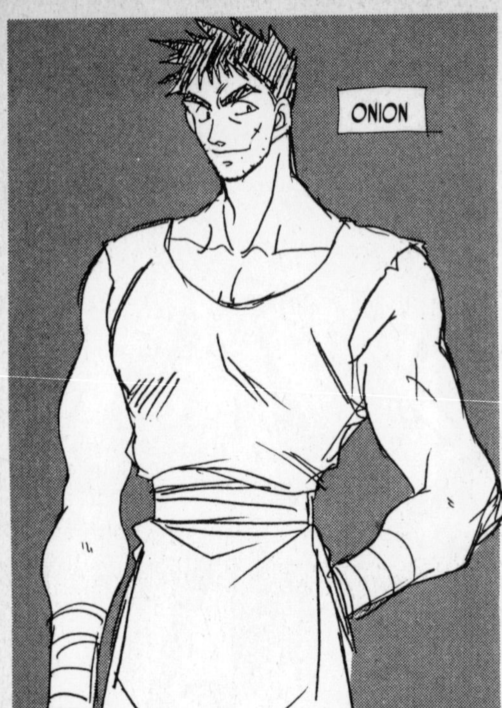
ONION

• GRANDPA •
THIS GUY MIGHT LOOK A LITTLE FAMILIAR. A CERTAIN PERSON (HE IS A PERSON, ISN'T HE...?) FROM A CERTAIN AMERICAN FILM WAS THE MODEL FOR HIM. THERE IS A DETAILED EXPLANATION ABOUT THIS OLD MAN'S CLOTHES, SO I STUCK IT ON A LATER PAGE. (COSPLAY, ANYONE?) HE DOESN'T LOOK QUITE HUMAN, DOES HE?

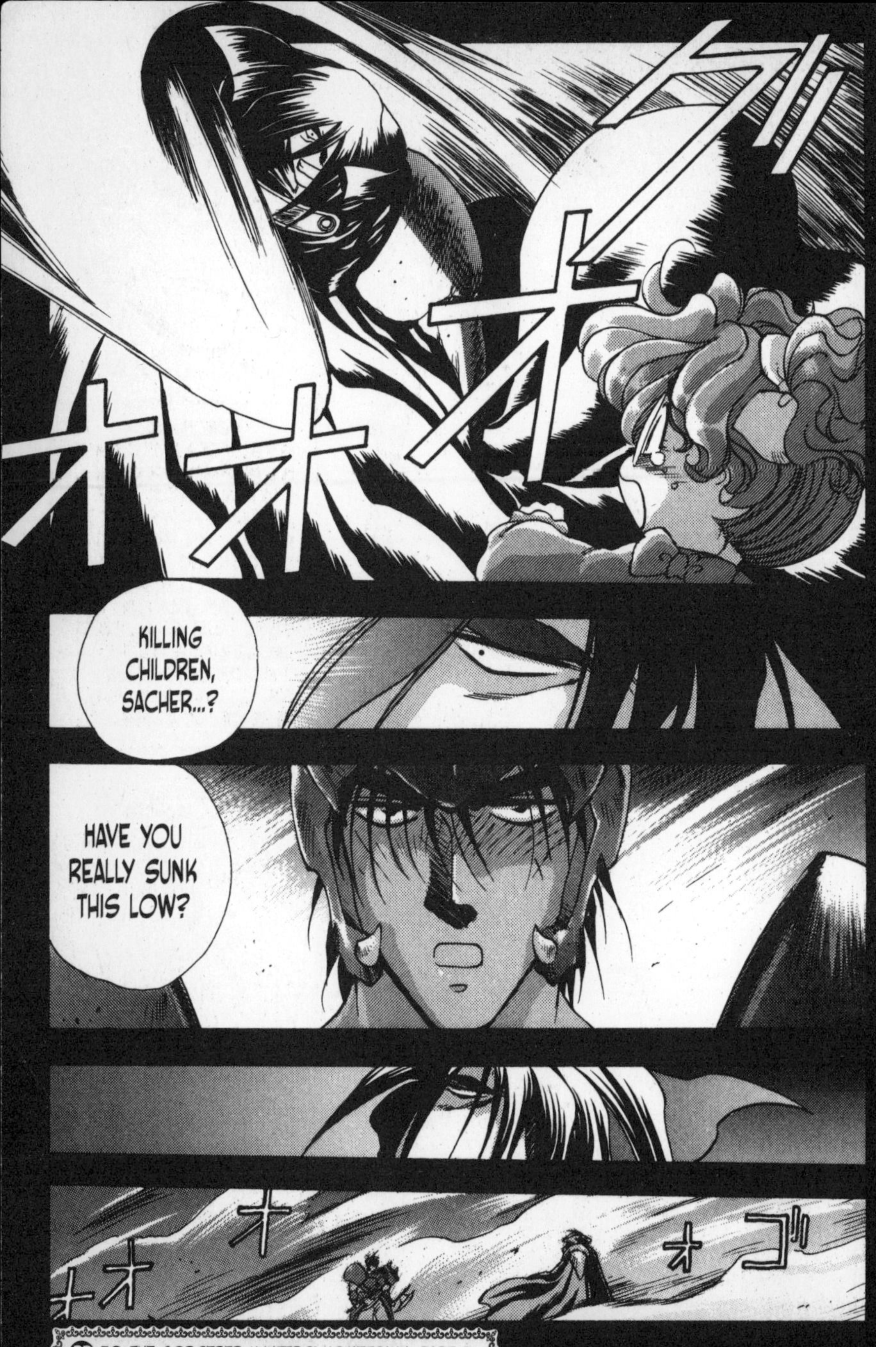
KILLING CHILDREN, SACHER...?
HAVE YOU REALLY SUNK THIS LOW?

㉓ TO THE SORCERER HUNTERS' HOMETOWN--PART 3

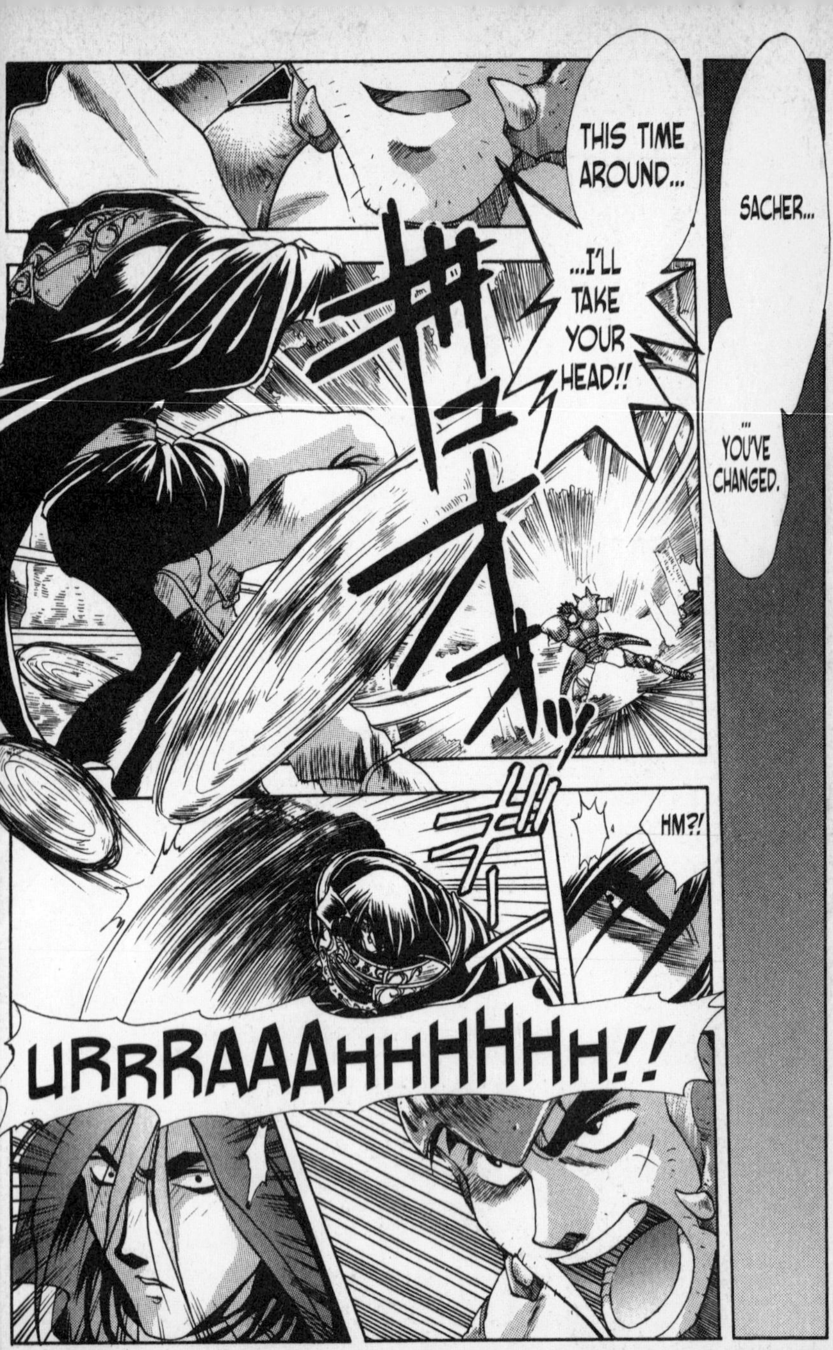
SACHER...
...YOU'VE CHANGED.
THIS TIME AROUND...
...I'LL TAKE YOUR HEAD!!
HM?!
URRRAAAHHHHHH!!

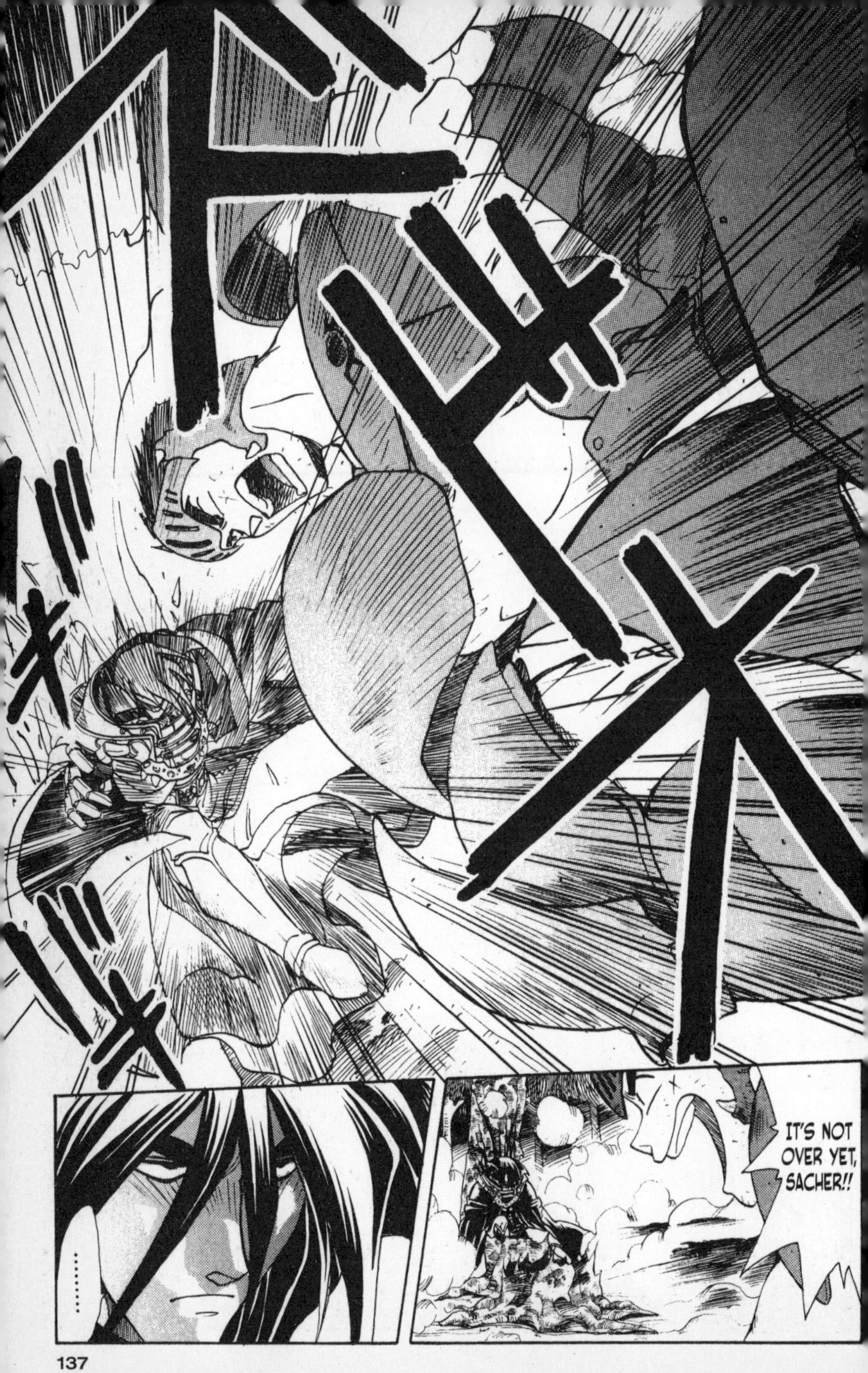
IT'S NOT OVER YET, SACHER!!
......

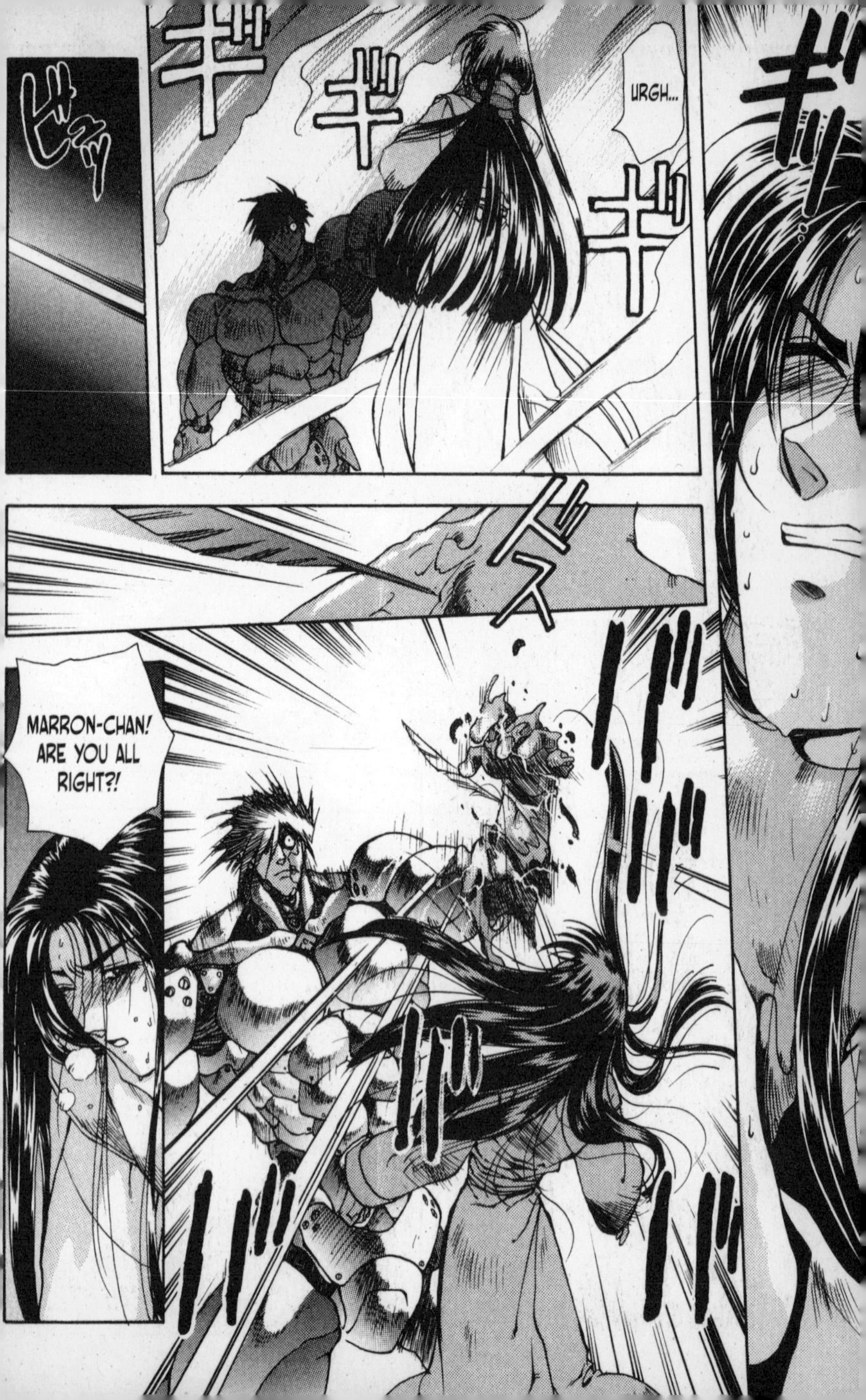
ギギギ
URGH...
ドス
MARRON-CHAN! ARE YOU ALL RIGHT?!

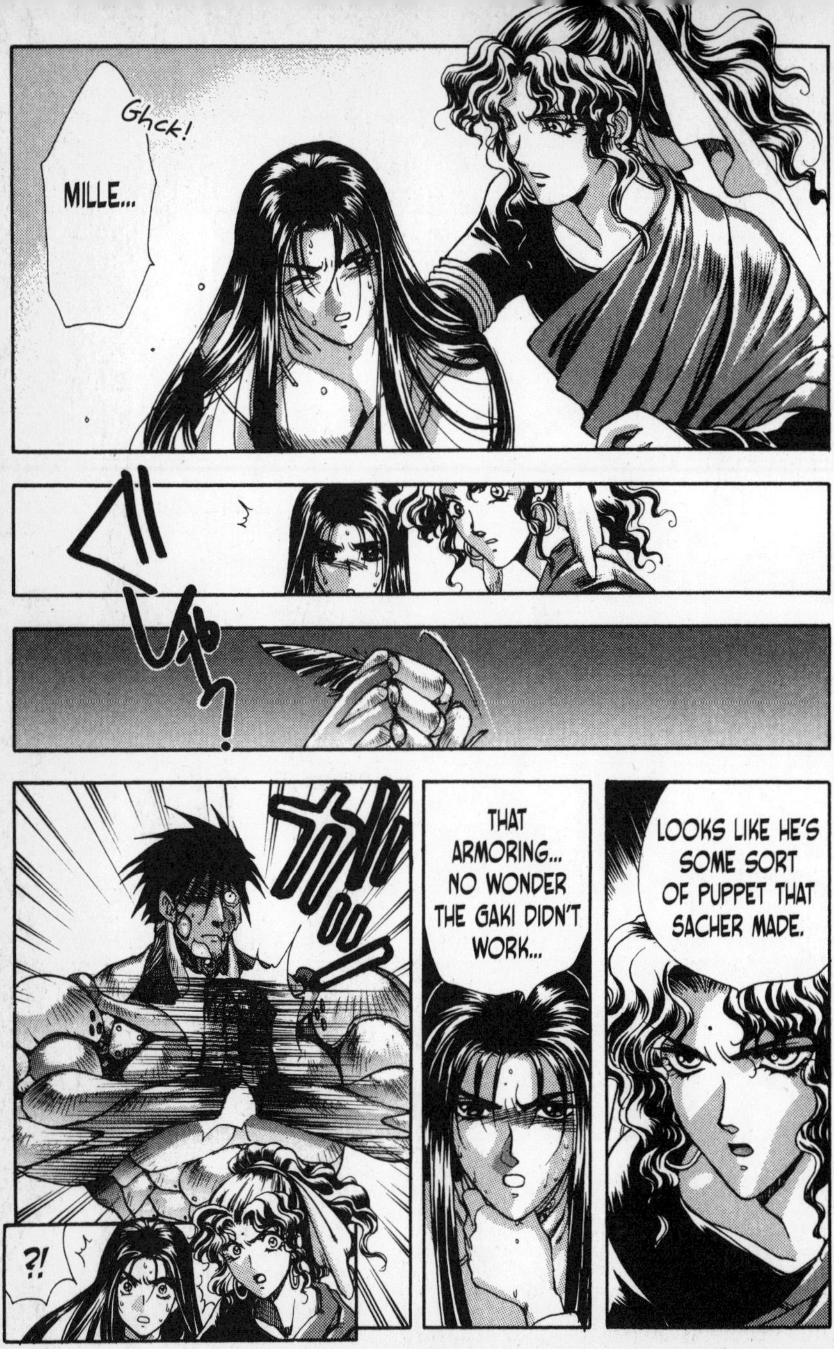
Ghck!
MILLE...
LOOKS LIKE HE'S SOME SORT OF PUPPET THAT SACHER MADE.
THAT ARMORING... NO WONDER THE GAKI DIDN'T WORK...
?!

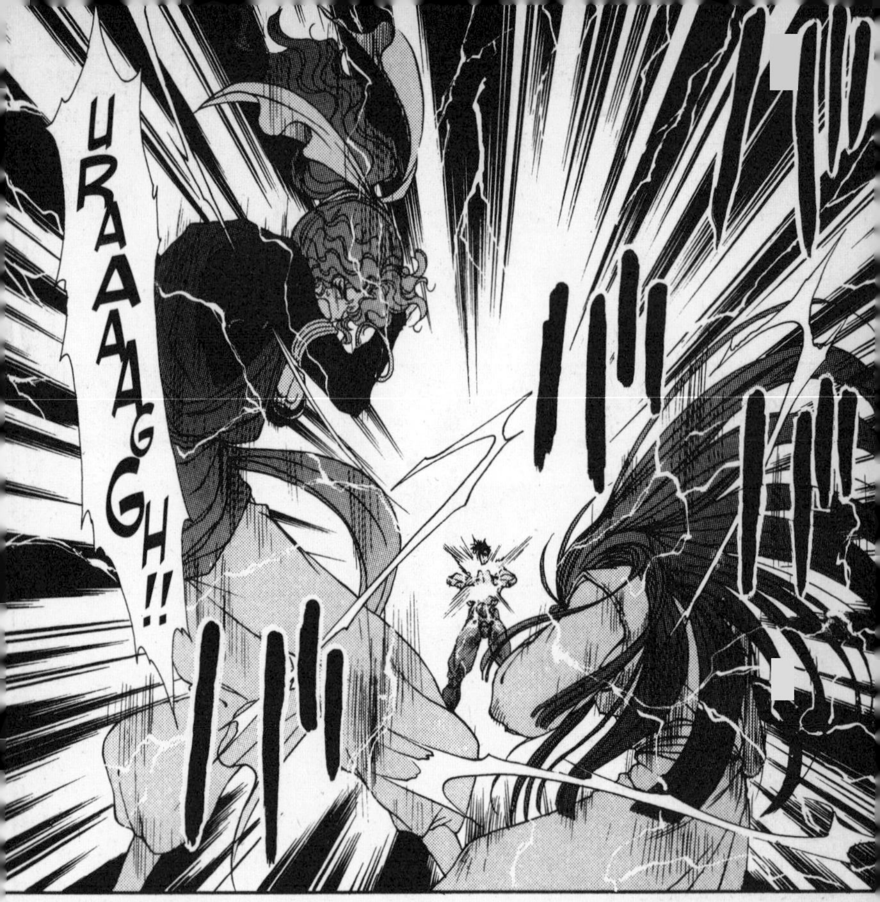
URAAAAGGH!!

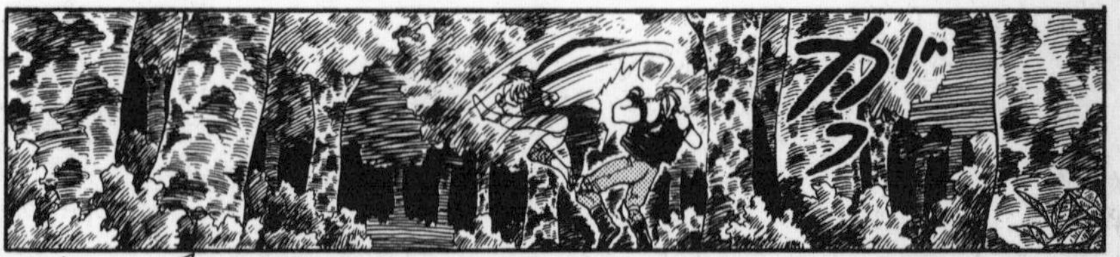
ガッ

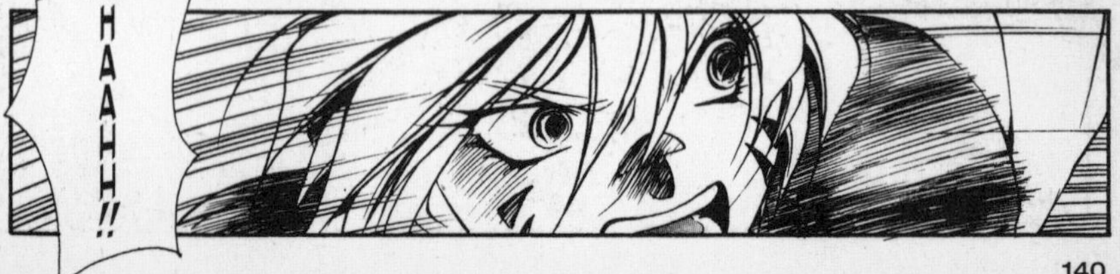
HAAHH!!

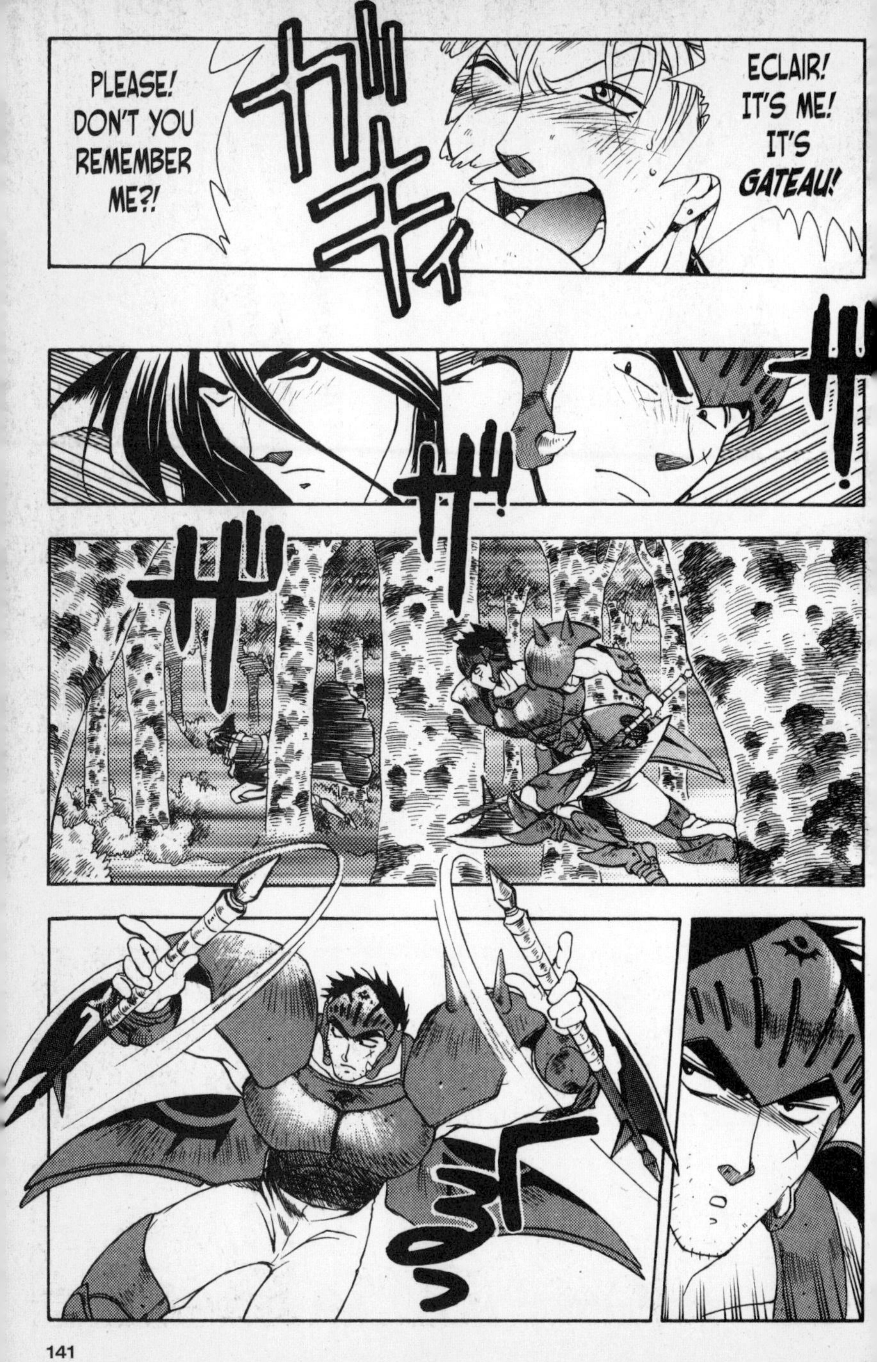
ECLAIR! IT'S ME! IT'S GATEAU!
PLEASE! DON'T YOU REMEMBER ME?!
ガキィ
ザ!
ザ!
ザ
ゴ

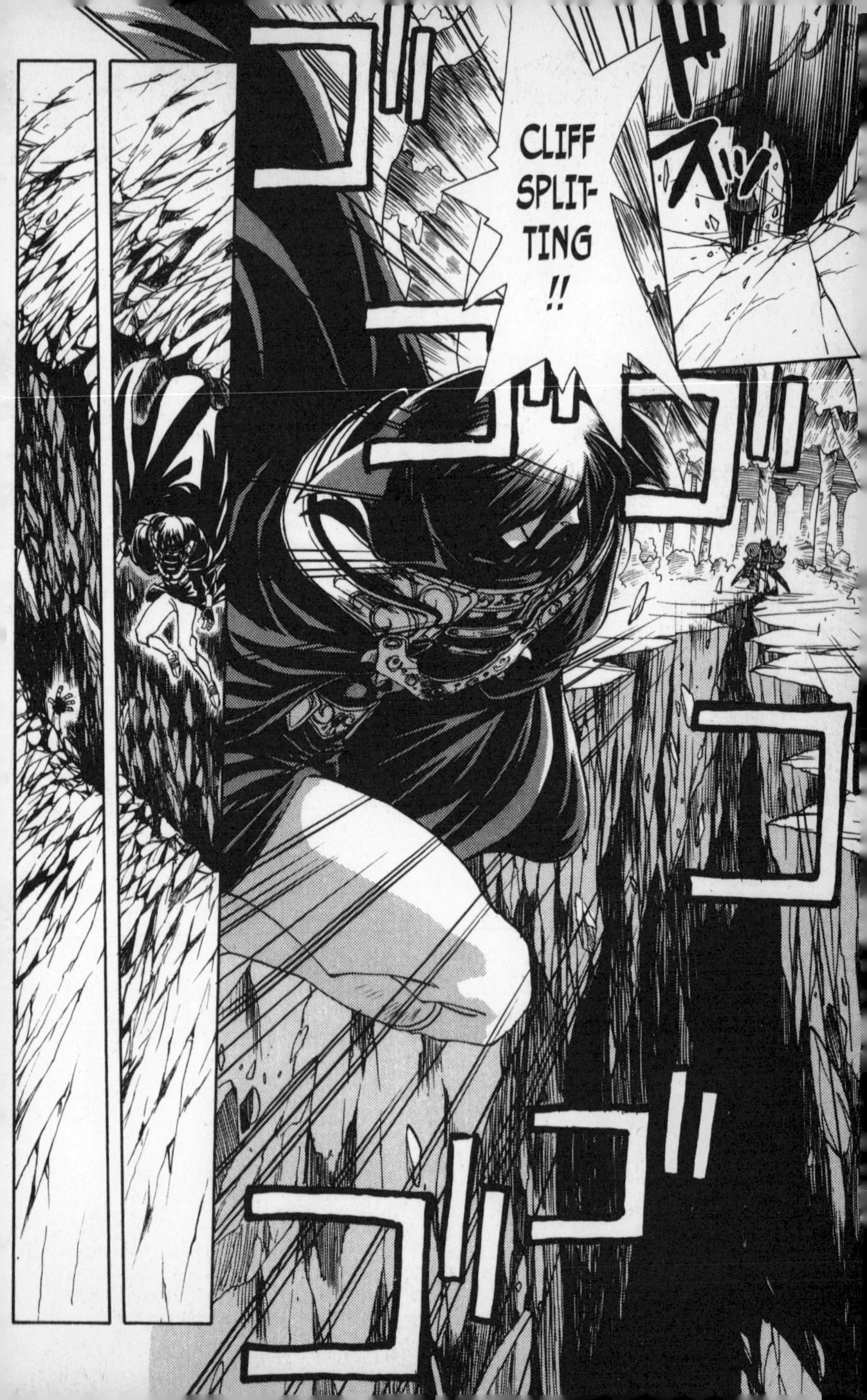
CLIFF SPLIT-TING !!

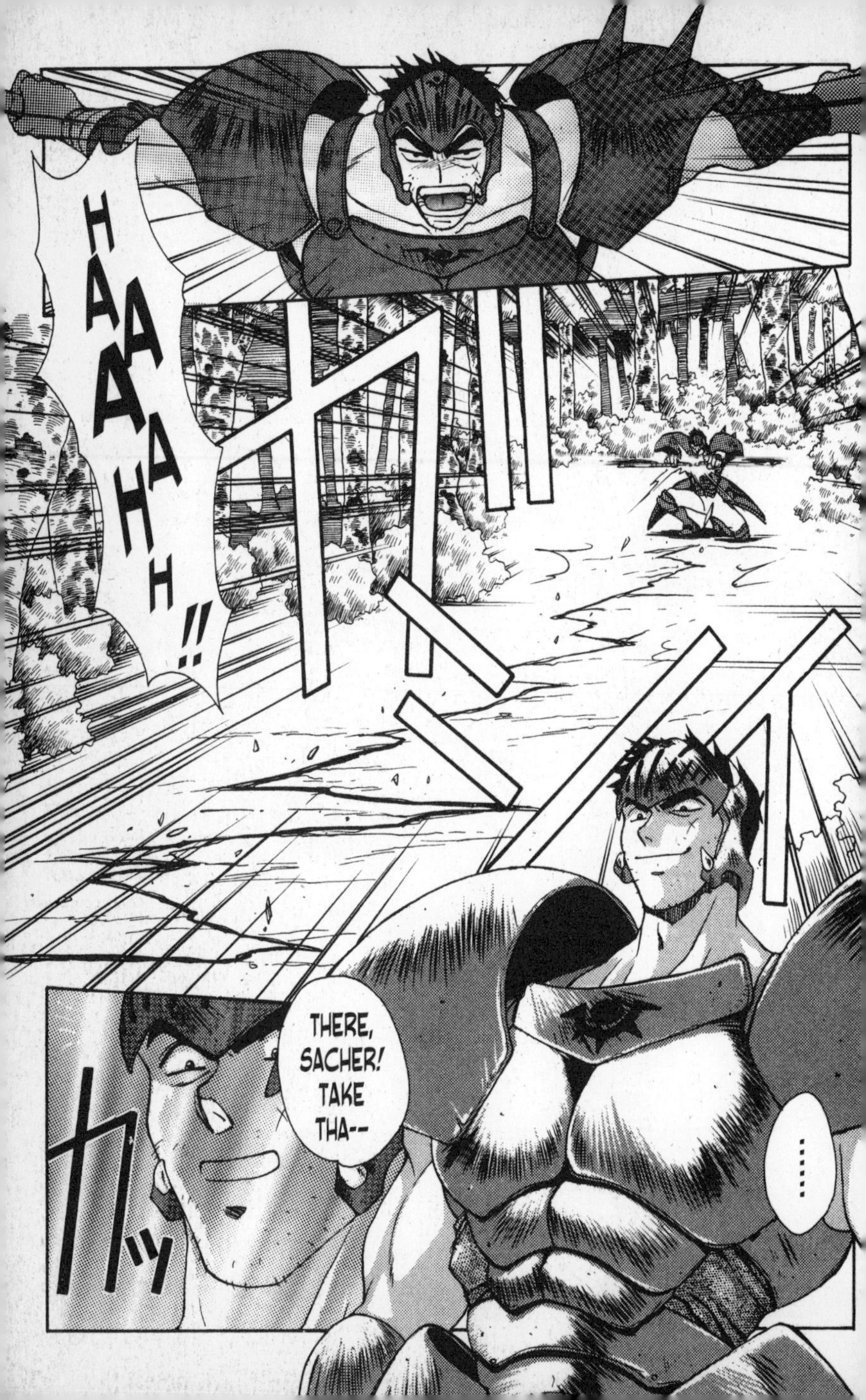
HAAAAHHH!!
THERE, SACHER! TAKE THA--
......

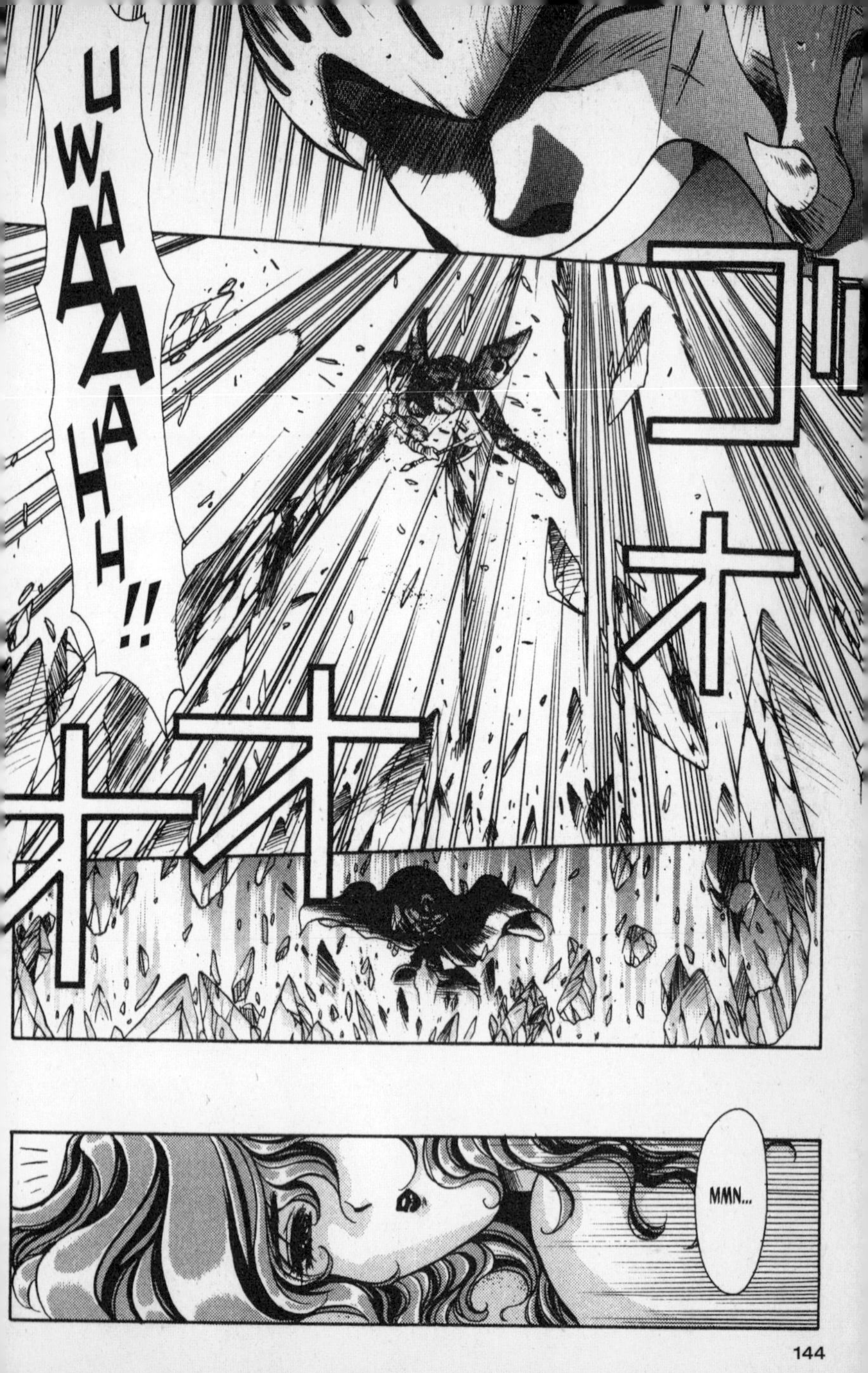
ゴオオオ
UWAAAAHH!!
MMN...

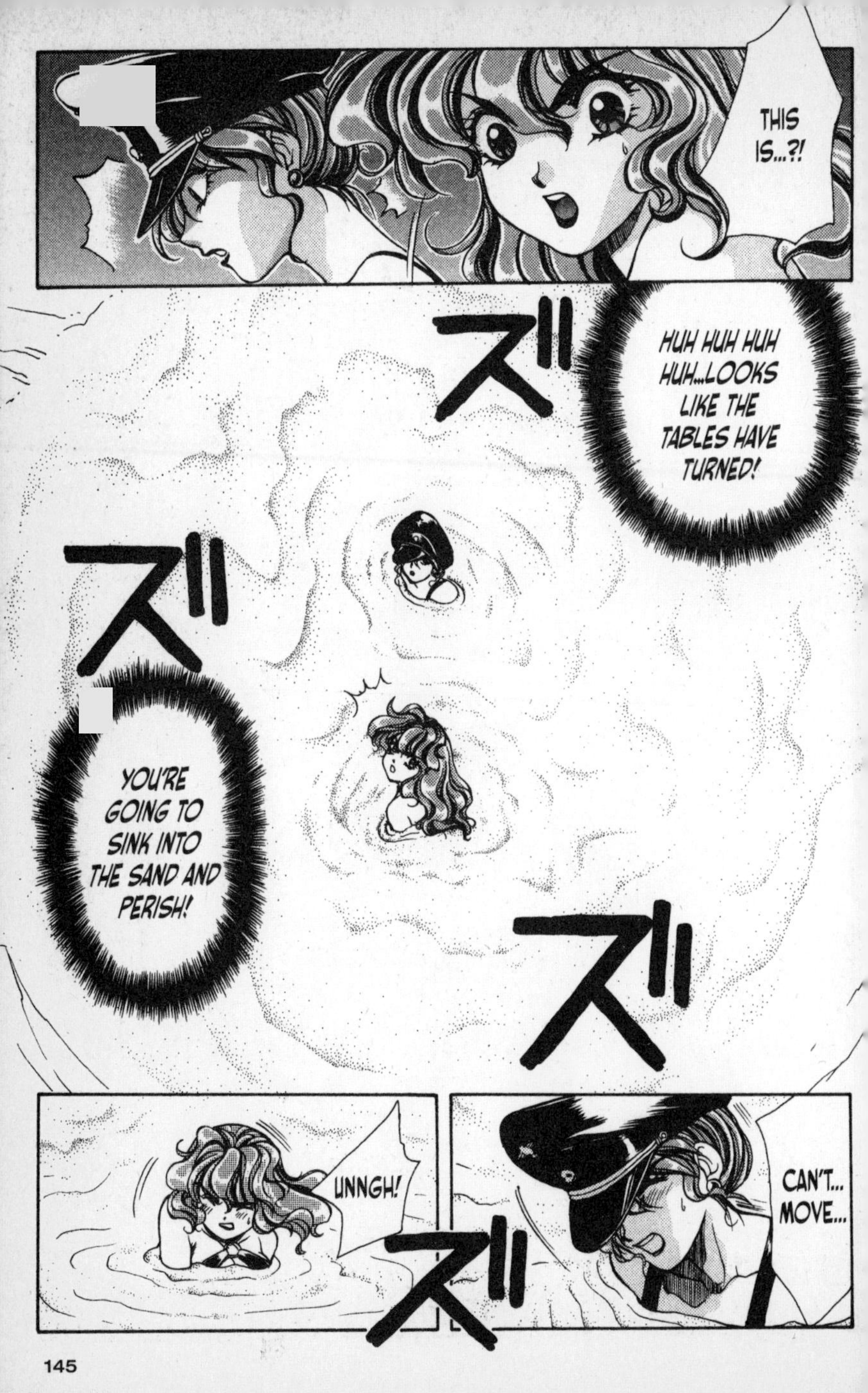
THIS IS...?!
ズ
HUH HUH HUH HUH...LOOKS LIKE THE TABLES HAVE TURNED!
ズ
YOU'RE GOING TO SINK INTO THE SAND AND PERISH!
ズ
CAN'T... MOVE...
UNNGH!
ズ

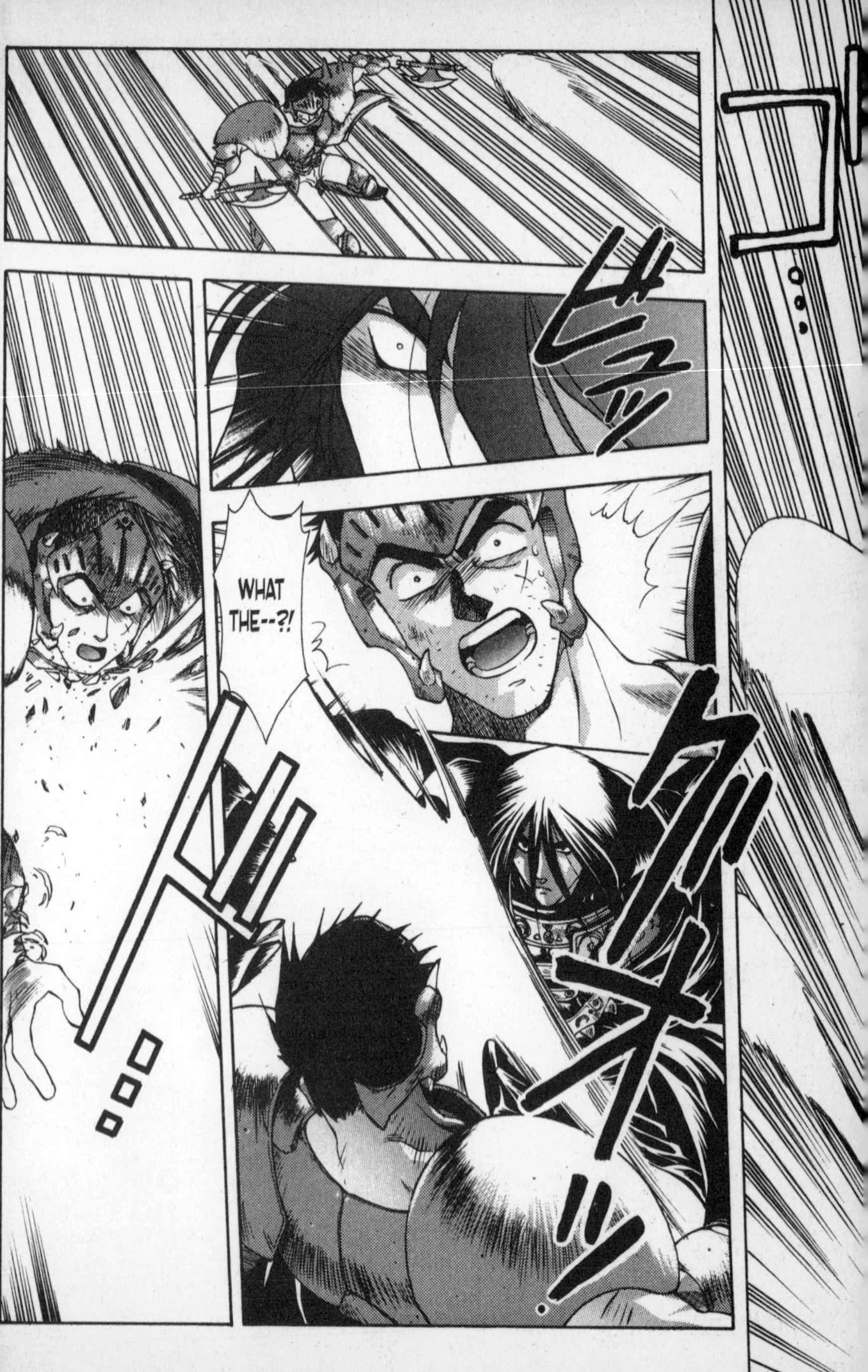
WHAT THE--?!

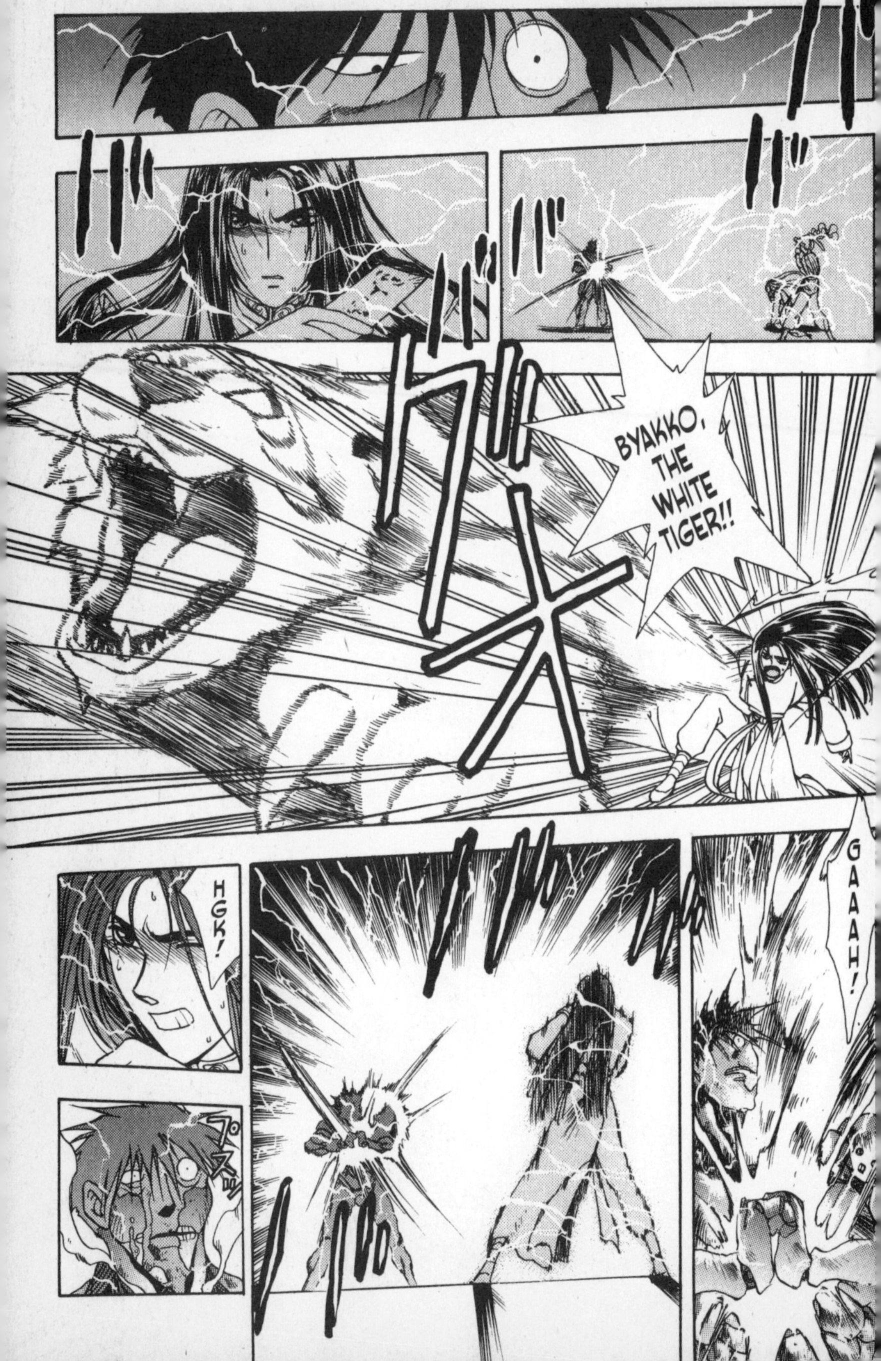
BYAKKO, THE WHITE TIGER!!
GAAAH!
HGK!

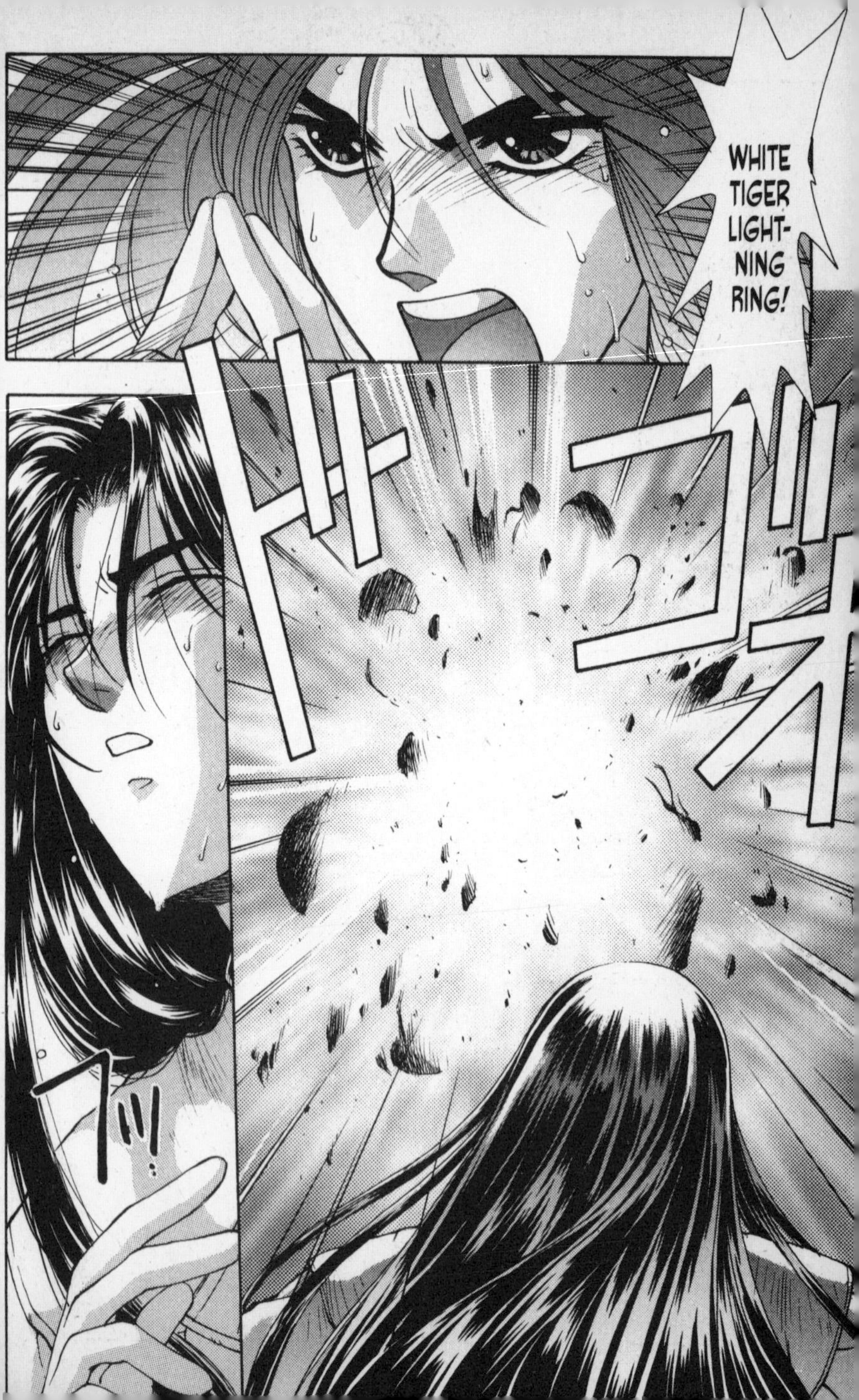
WHITE TIGER LIGHT-NING RING!

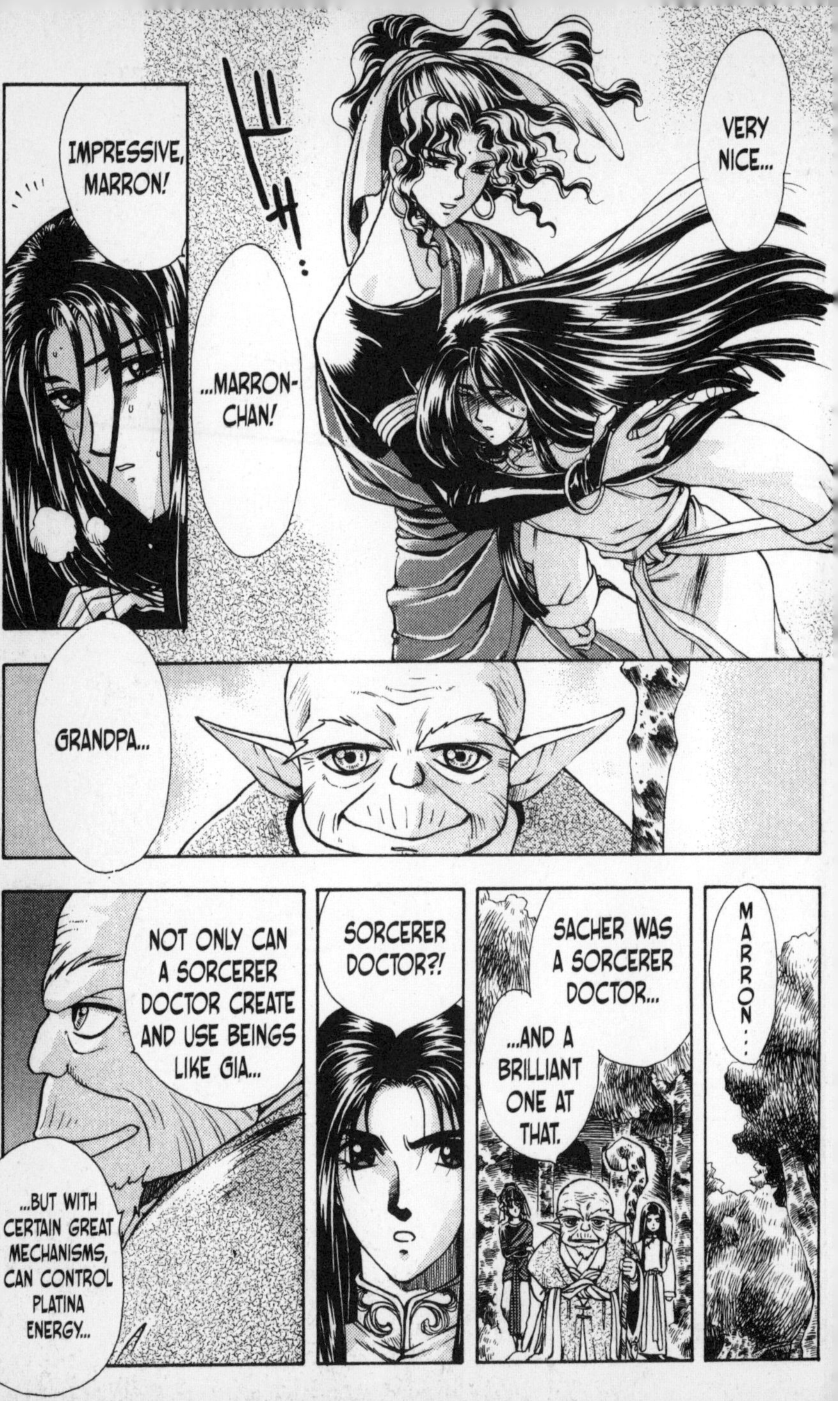
VERY NICE...
...MARRON-CHAN!
IMPRESSIVE, MARRON!
GRANDPA...
MARRON...
SACHER WAS A SORCERER DOCTOR...
...AND A BRILLIANT ONE AT THAT.
SORCERER DOCTOR?!
NOT ONLY CAN A SORCERER DOCTOR CREATE AND USE BEINGS LIKE GIA...
...BUT WITH CERTAIN GREAT MECHANISMS, CAN CONTROL PLATINA ENERGY...

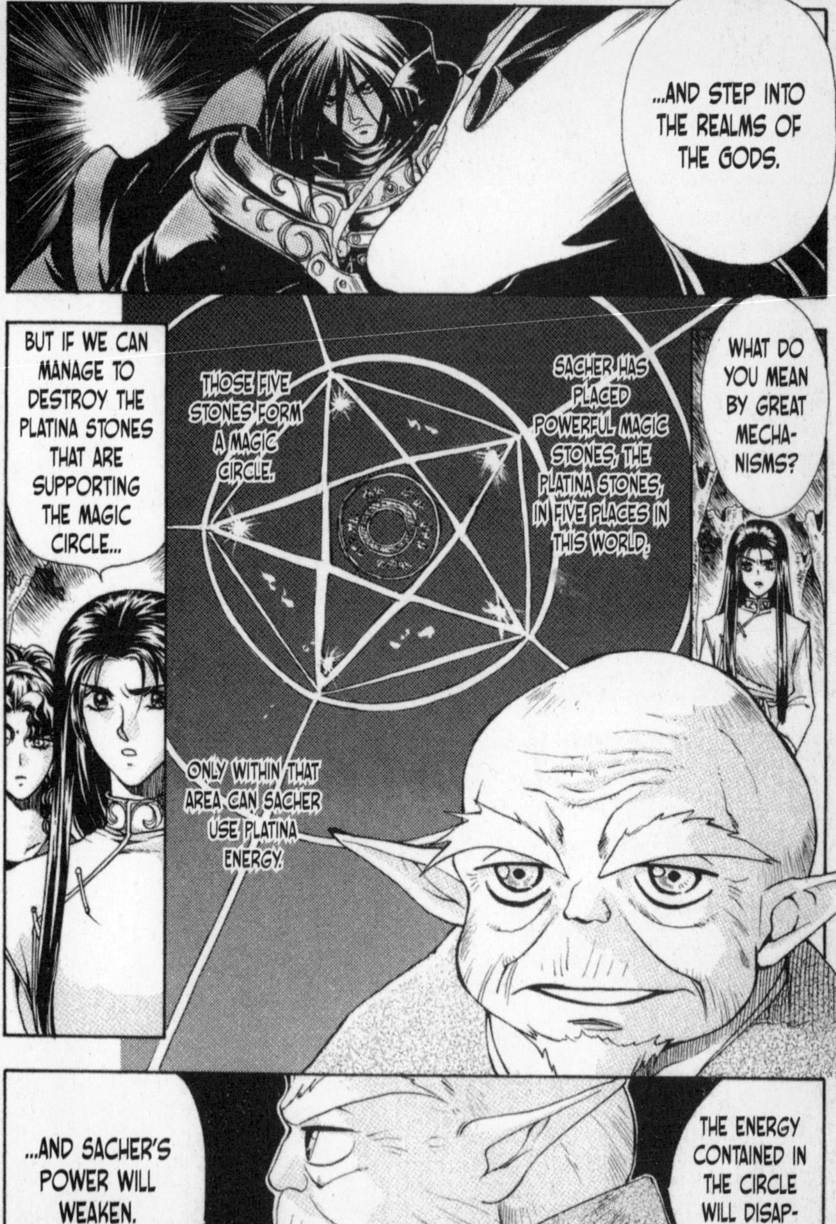
...AND STEP INTO THE REALMS OF THE GODS.
WHAT DO YOU MEAN BY GREAT MECHA-NISMS?
SACHER HAS PLACED POWERFUL MAGIC STONES, THE PLATINA STONES, IN FIVE PLACES IN THIS WORLD.
THOSE FIVE STONES FORM A MAGIC CIRCLE.
ONLY WITHIN THAT AREA CAN SACHER USE PLATINA ENERGY.
BUT IF WE CAN MANAGE TO DESTROY THE PLATINA STONES THAT ARE SUPPORTING THE MAGIC CIRCLE...
THE ENERGY CONTAINED IN THE CIRCLE WILL DISAP-PEAR...
...AND SACHER'S POWER WILL WEAKEN.

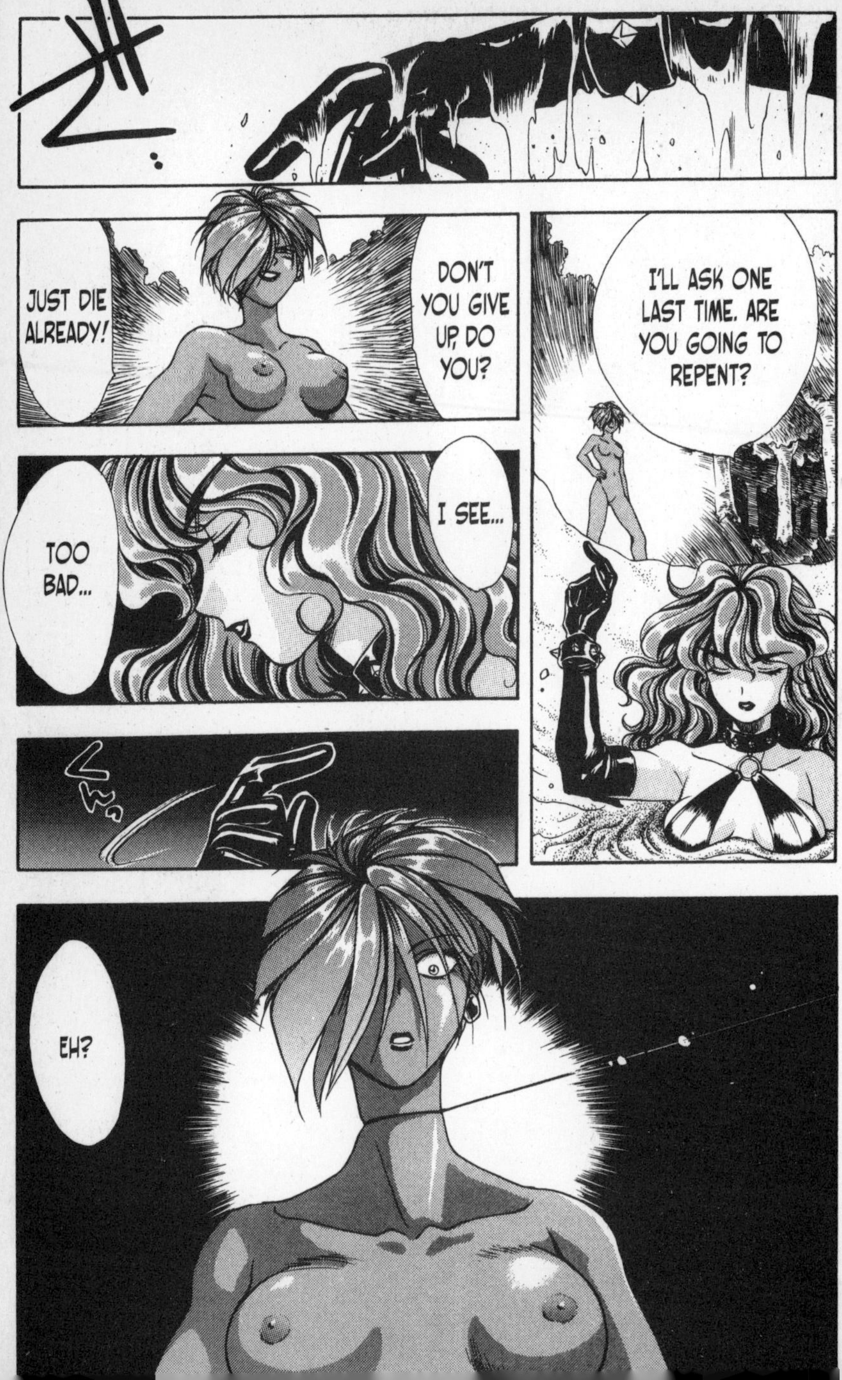
I'LL ASK ONE LAST TIME. ARE YOU GOING TO REPENT?
DON'T YOU GIVE UP, DO YOU?
JUST DIE ALREADY!
I SEE...
TOO BAD...
EH?

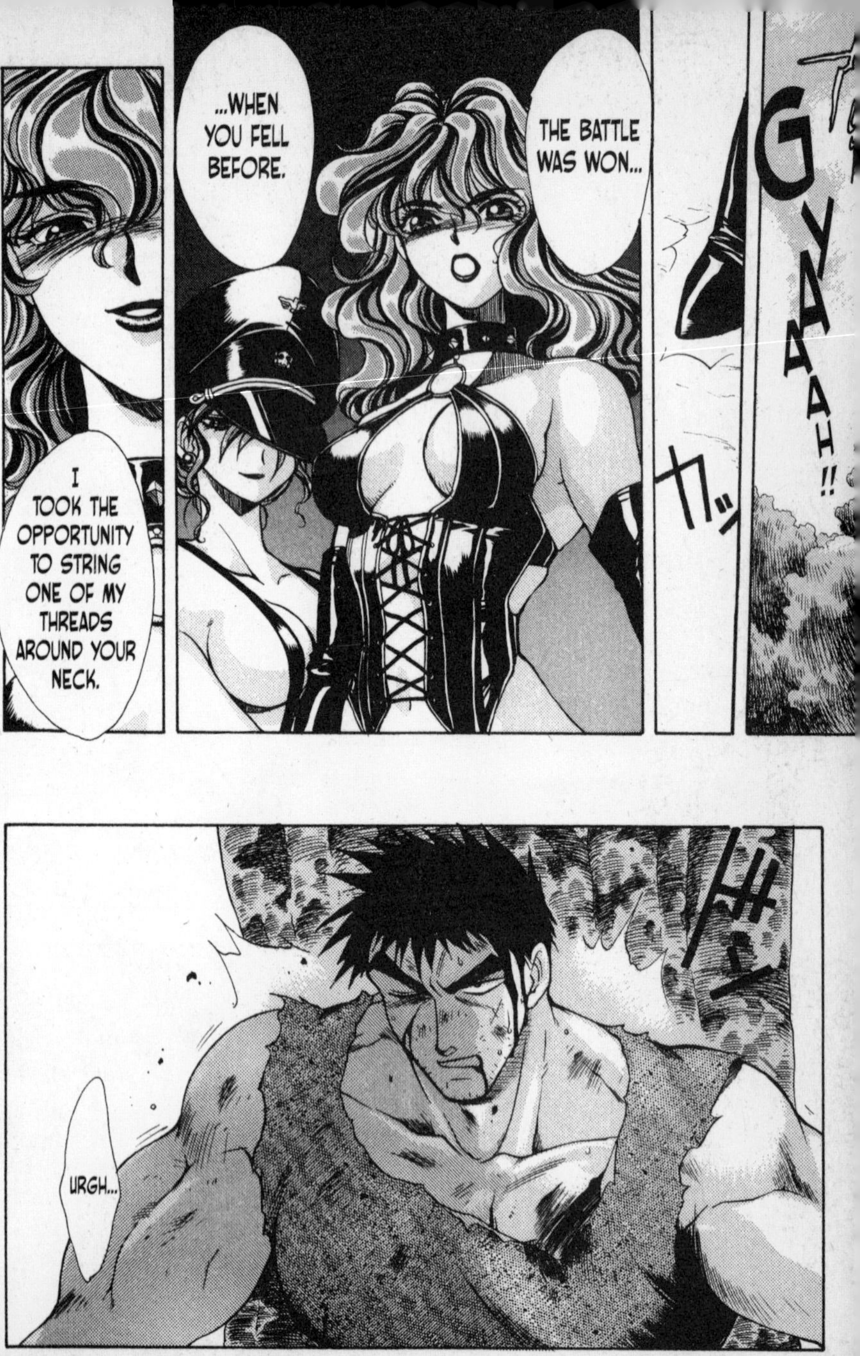
GYAAAAH!!
ガッ
THE BATTLE WAS WON...
...WHEN YOU FELL BEFORE.
I TOOK THE OPPORTUNITY TO STRING ONE OF MY THREADS AROUND YOUR NECK.
URGH...

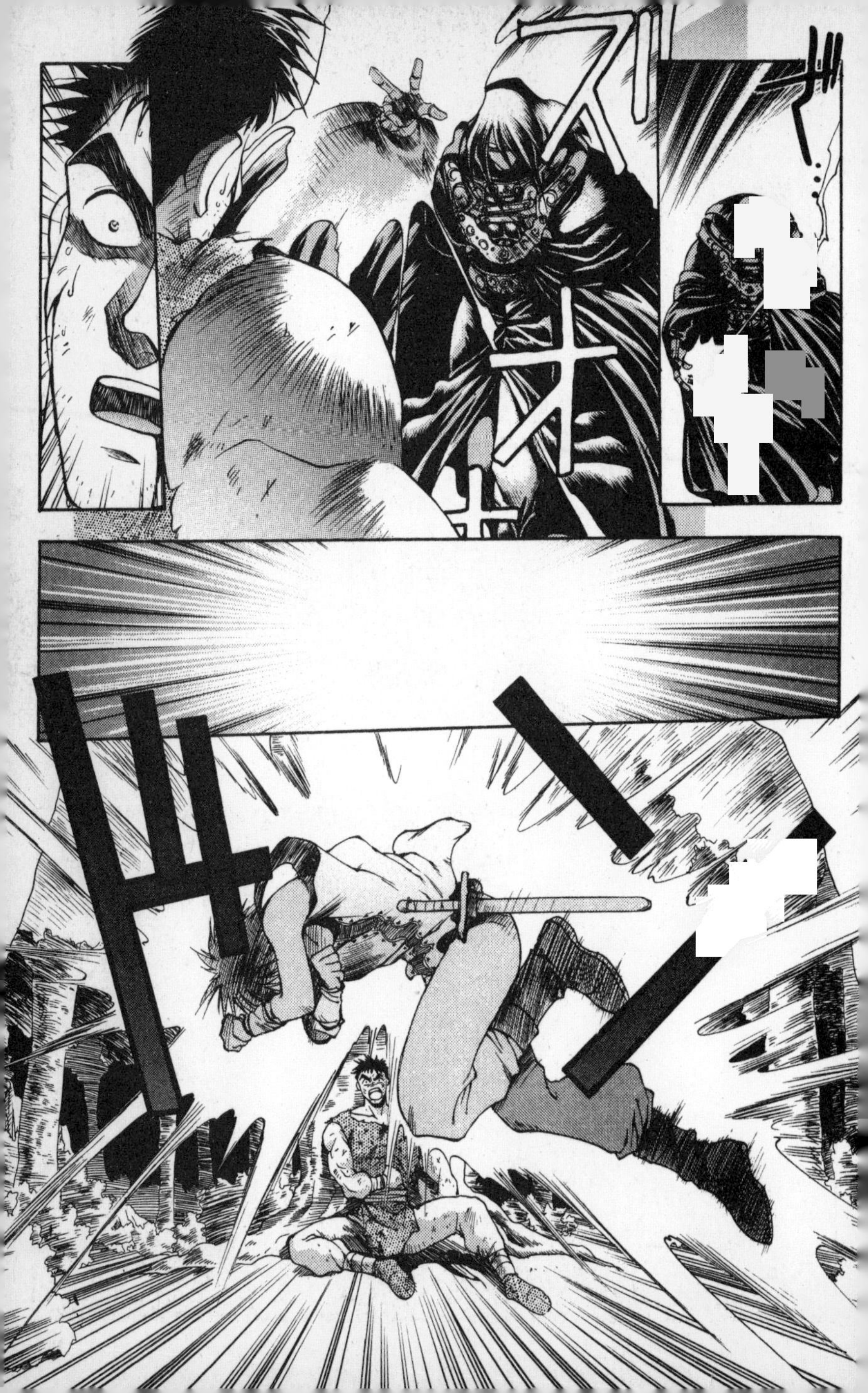

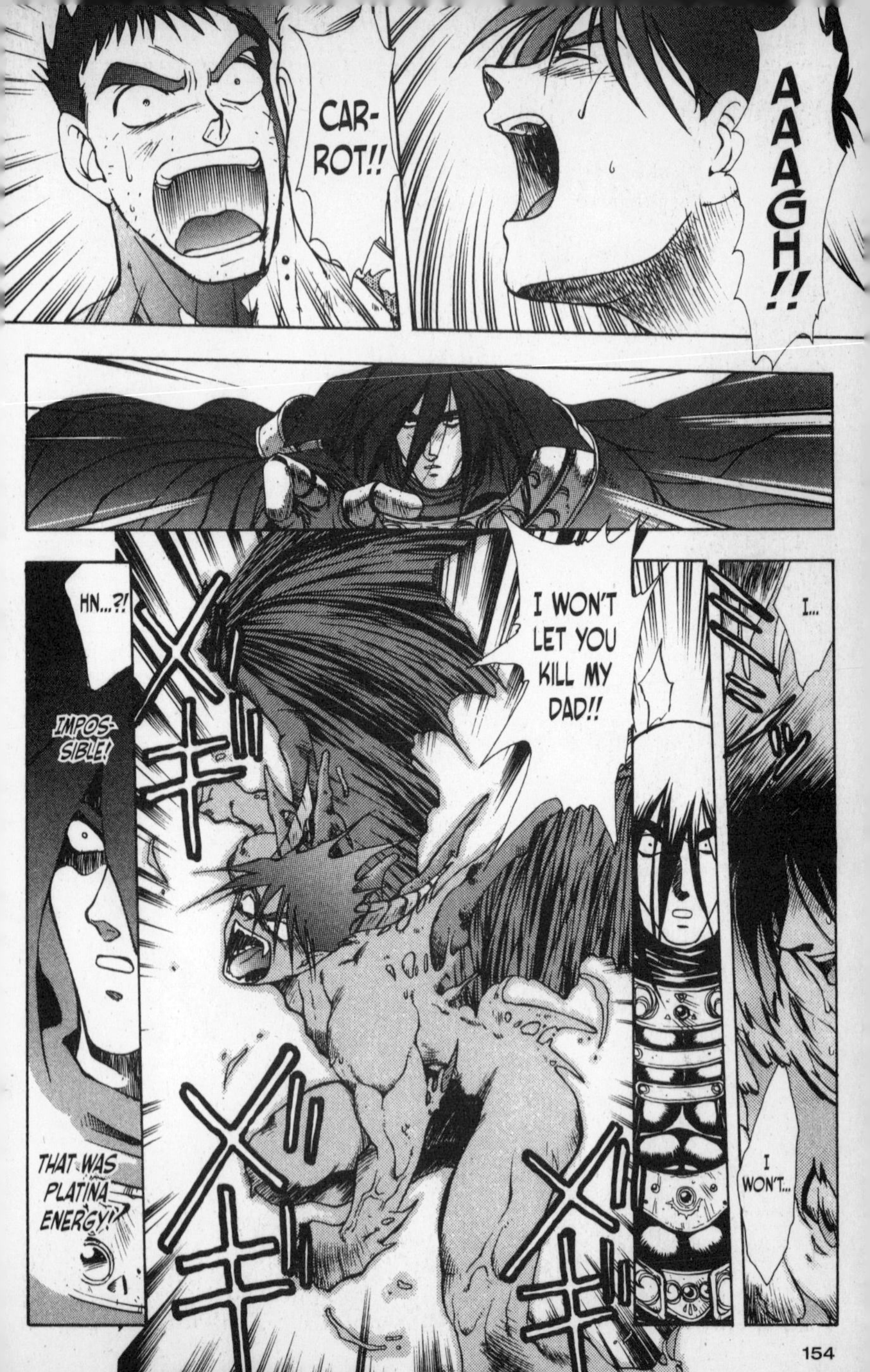
AAAGH!!
CAR-ROT!!
I...
I WON'T...
I WON'T LET YOU KILL MY DAD!!
HN...?!
IMPOS-SIBLE!
THAT WAS PLATINA ENERGY!

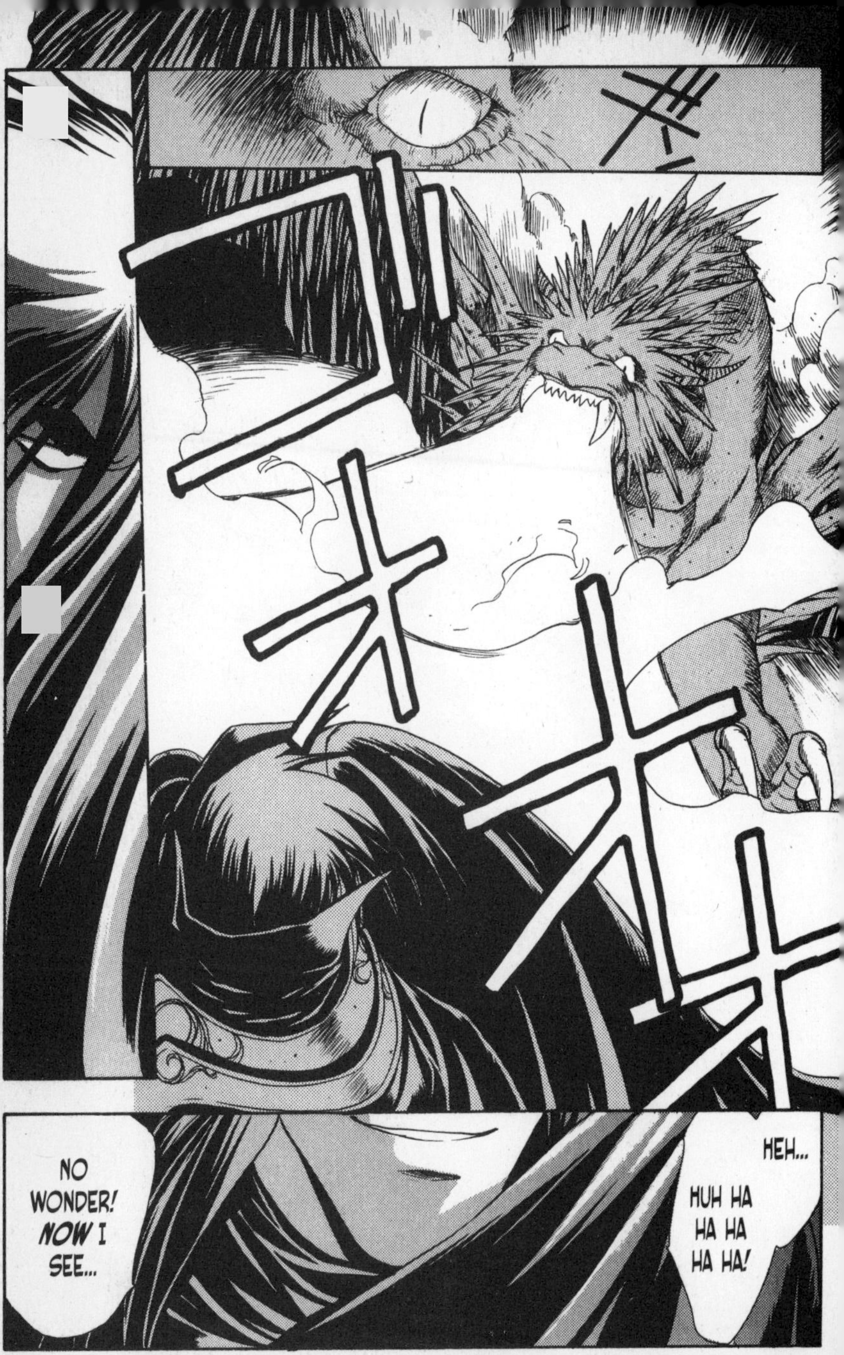
HEH... HUH HA HA HA HA HA!
NO WONDER! NOW I SEE...

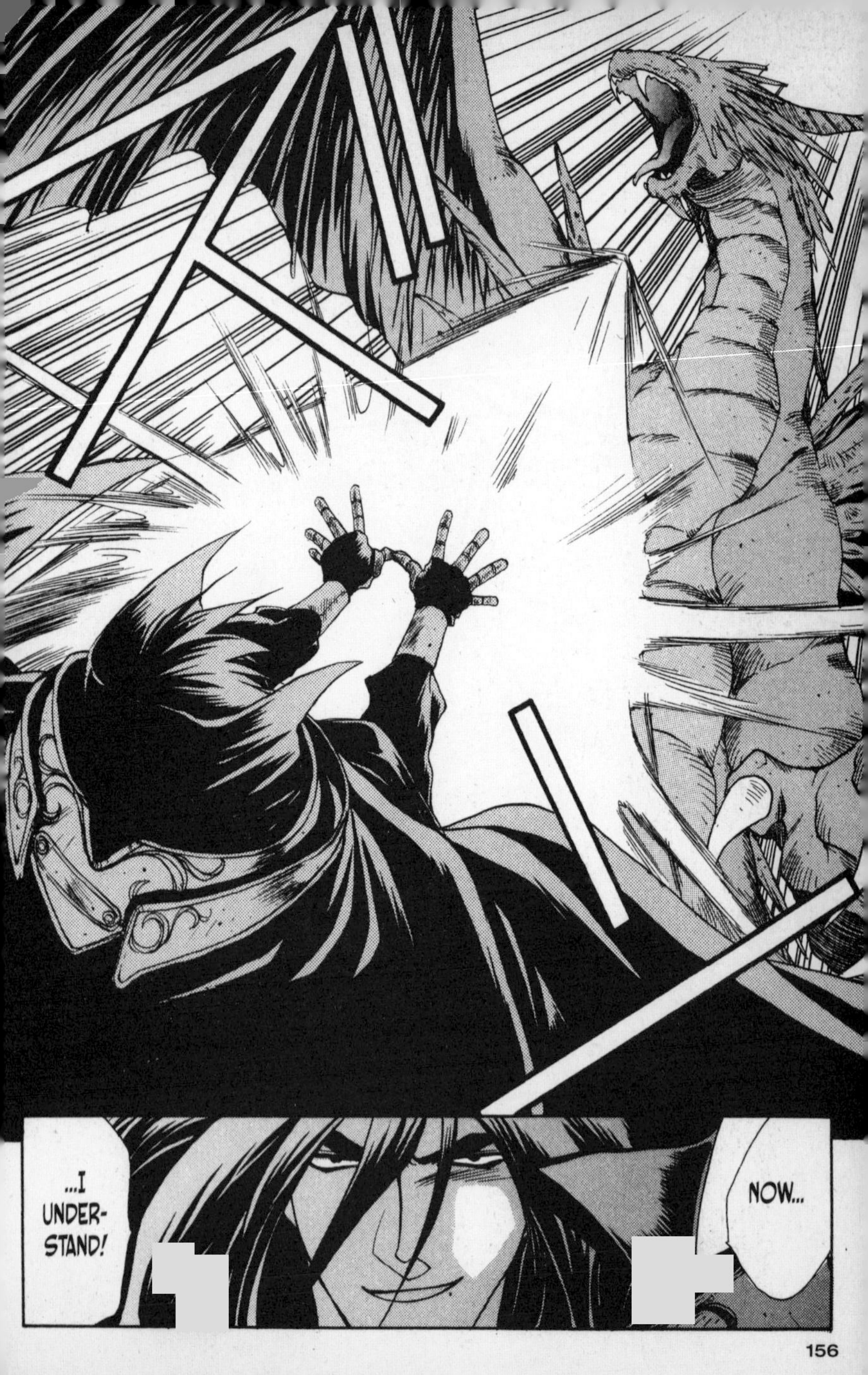
NOW...
...I UNDER-STAND!

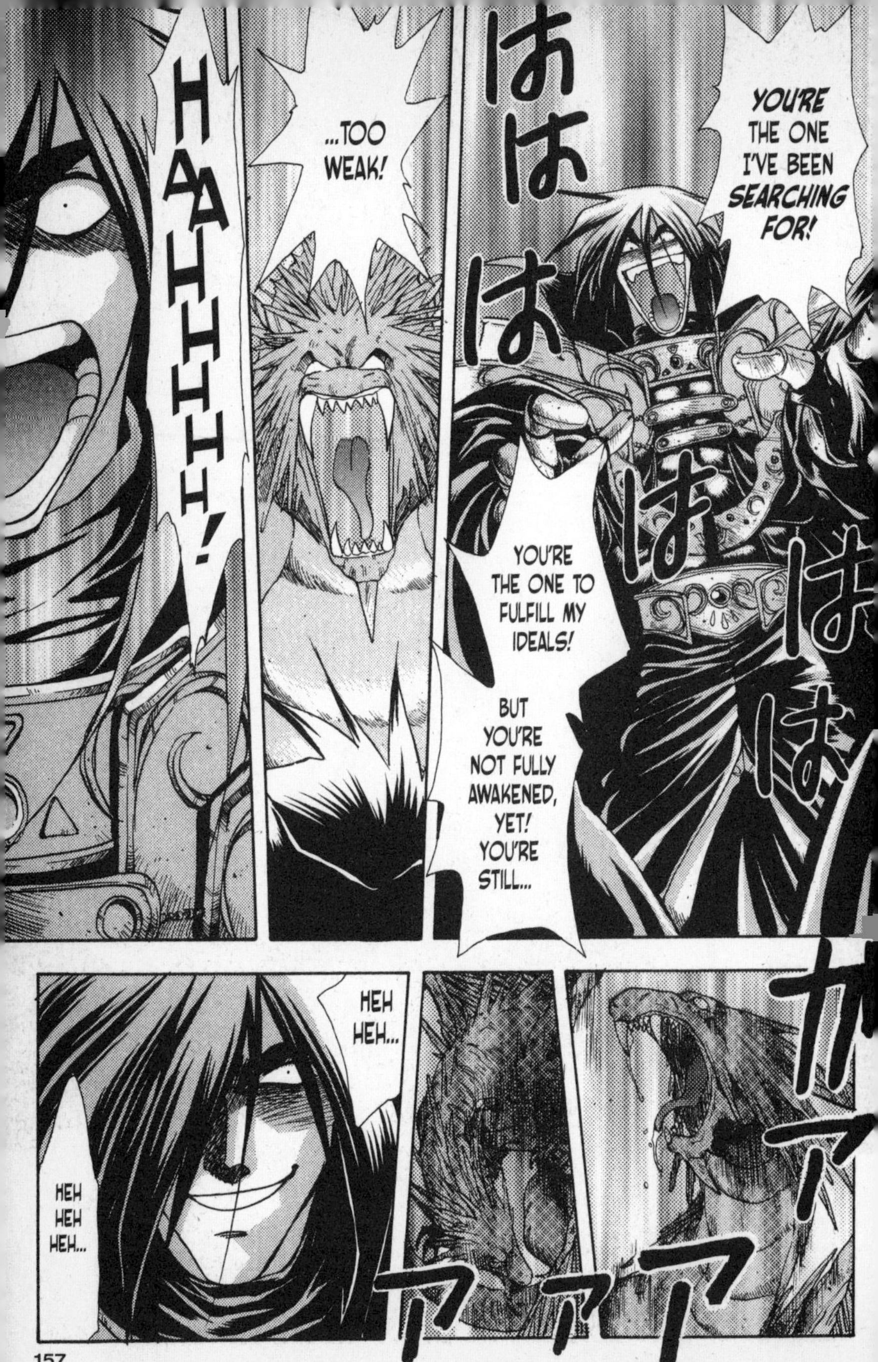
YOU'RE THE ONE I'VE BEEN SEARCHING FOR!
ははははは
YOU'RE THE ONE TO FULFILL MY IDEALS!
BUT YOU'RE NOT FULLY AWAKENED, YET! YOU'RE STILL...
...TOO WEAK!
HAAHHHHH!
ガァァァ
HEH HEH...
HEH HEH HEH...

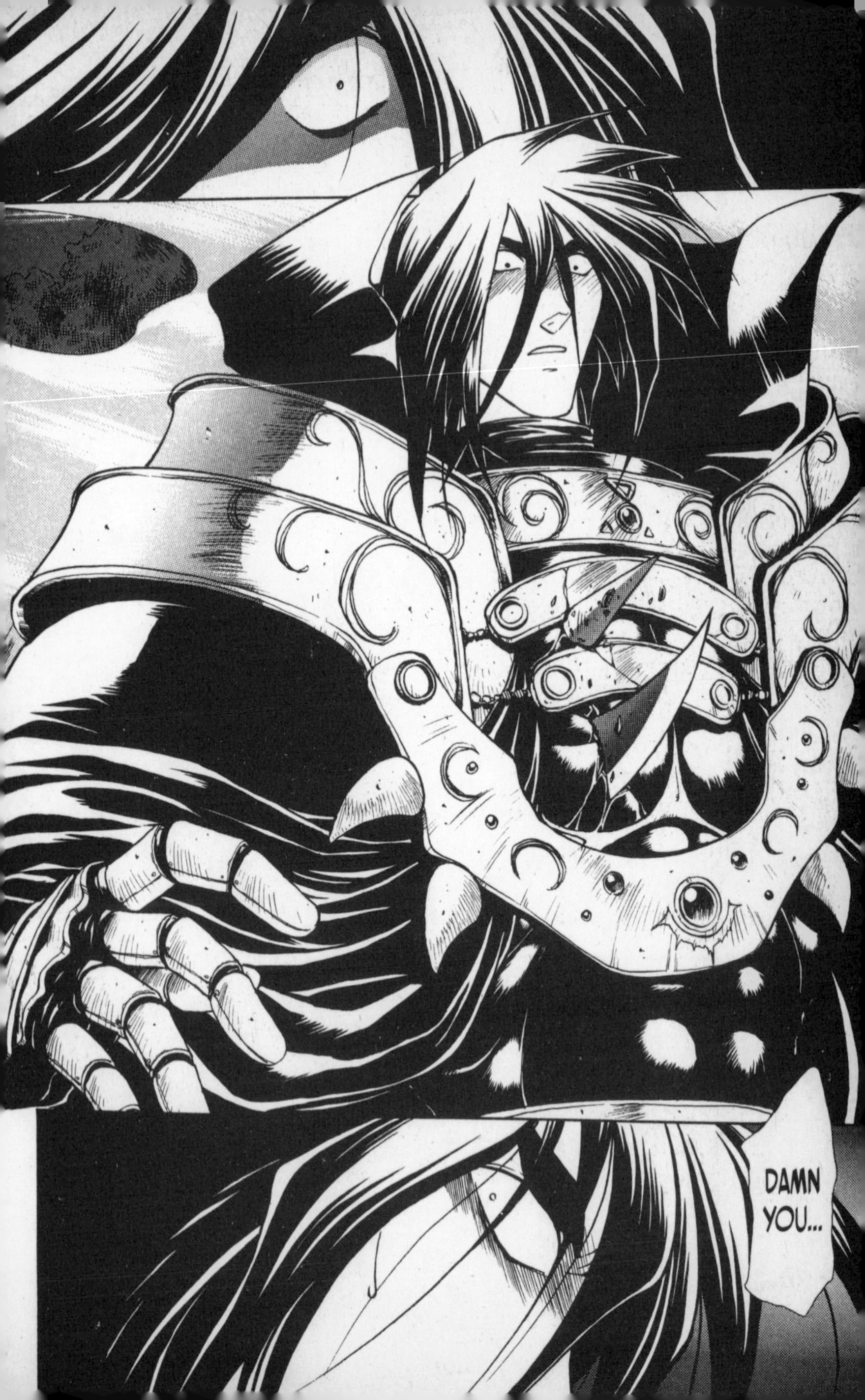
DAMN YOU...

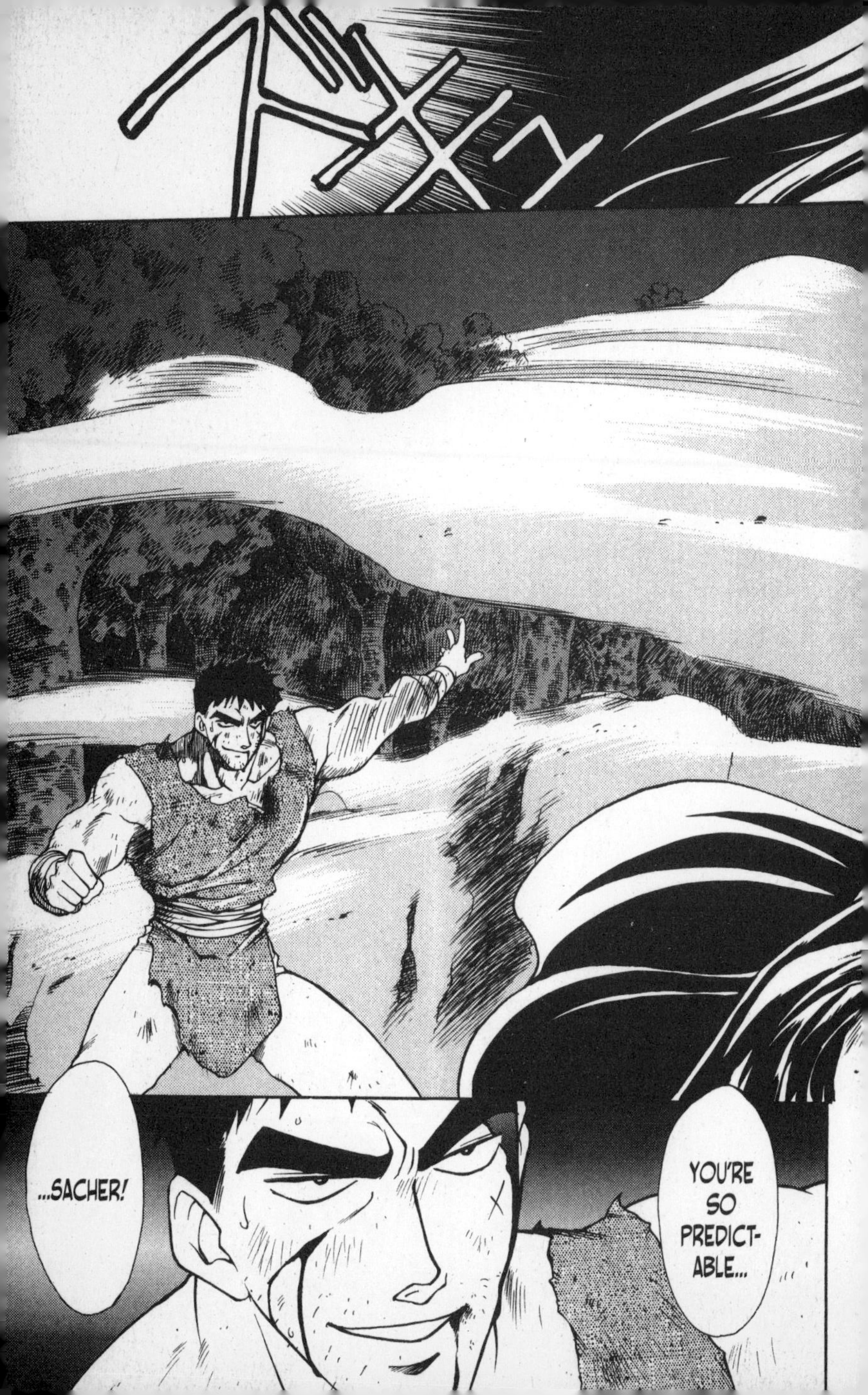
YOU'RE SO PREDICT-ABLE...
...SACHER!

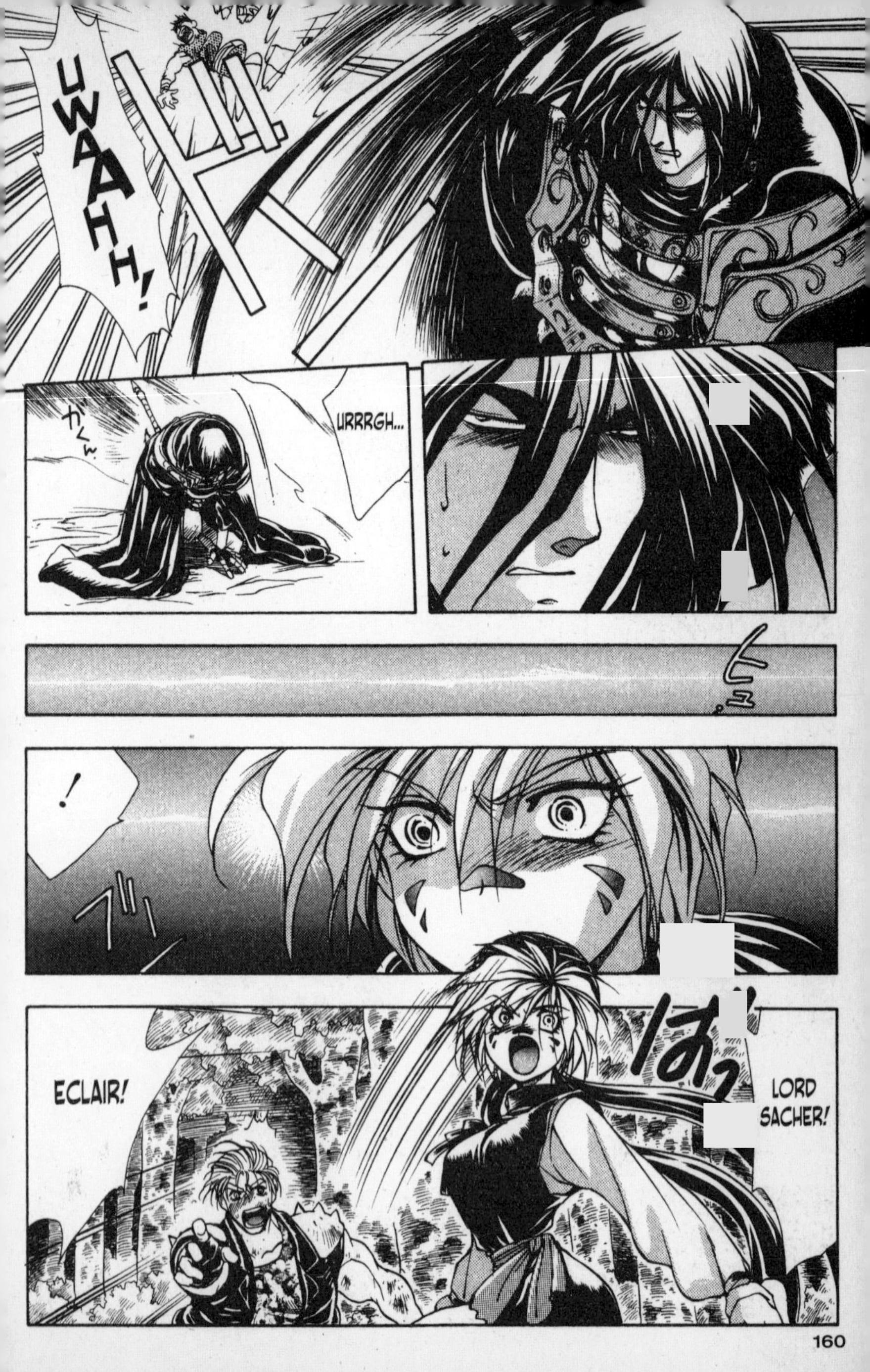
UWAAHH!
URRRGH...
!
はっ
LORD SACHER!
ECLAIR!

URK...

LORD SACHER!

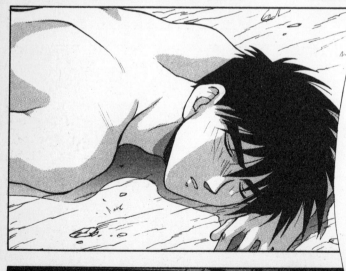

YOU WON'T GET AWAY NEXT TIME...

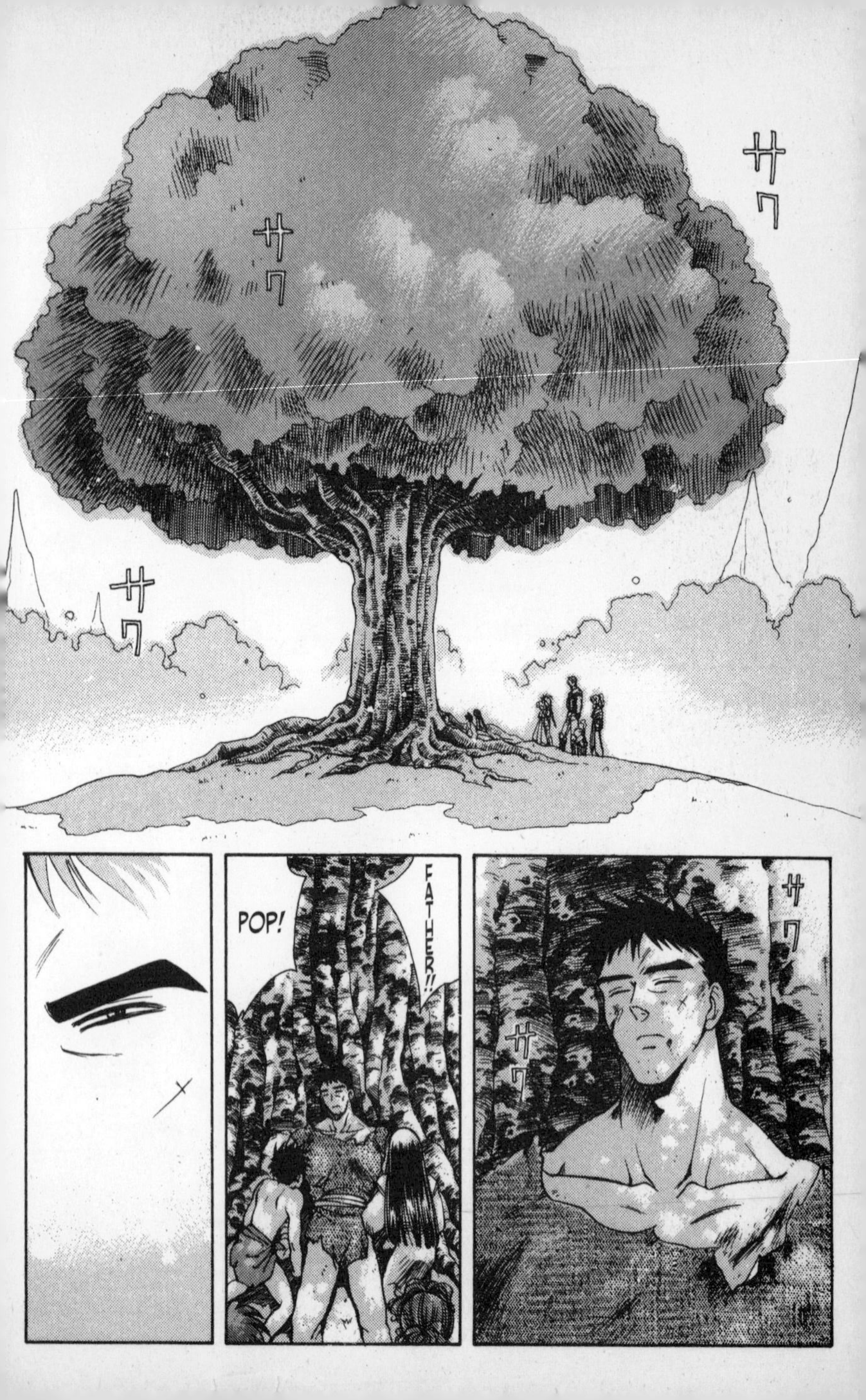
サク
サク
サク
サク
サク
FATHER!!
POP!

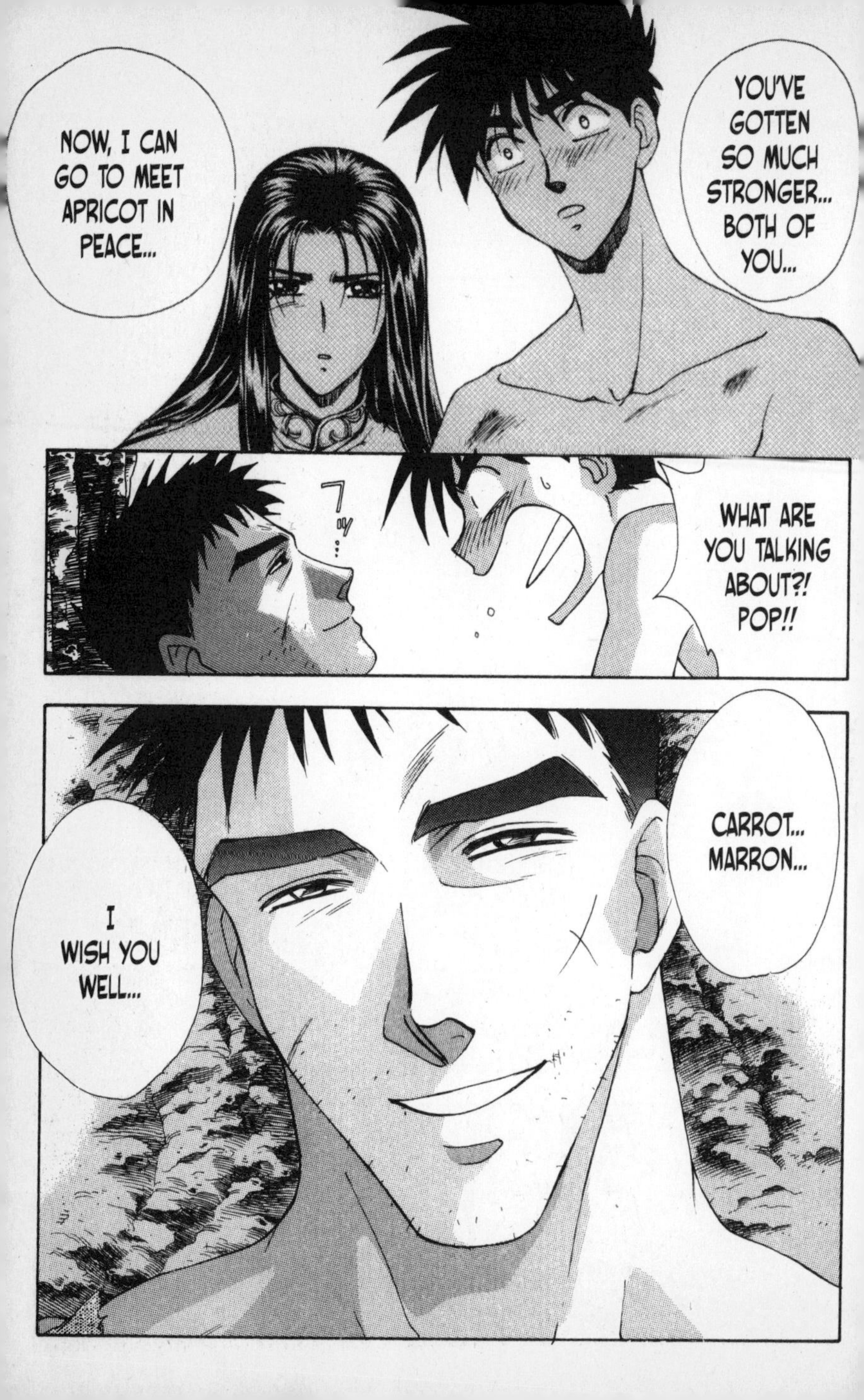
YOU'VE GOTTEN SO MUCH STRONGER... BOTH OF YOU...
NOW, I CAN GO TO MEET APRICOT IN PEACE...
WHAT ARE YOU TALKING ABOUT?! POP!!
フッ…
CARROT... MARRON...
I WISH YOU WELL...

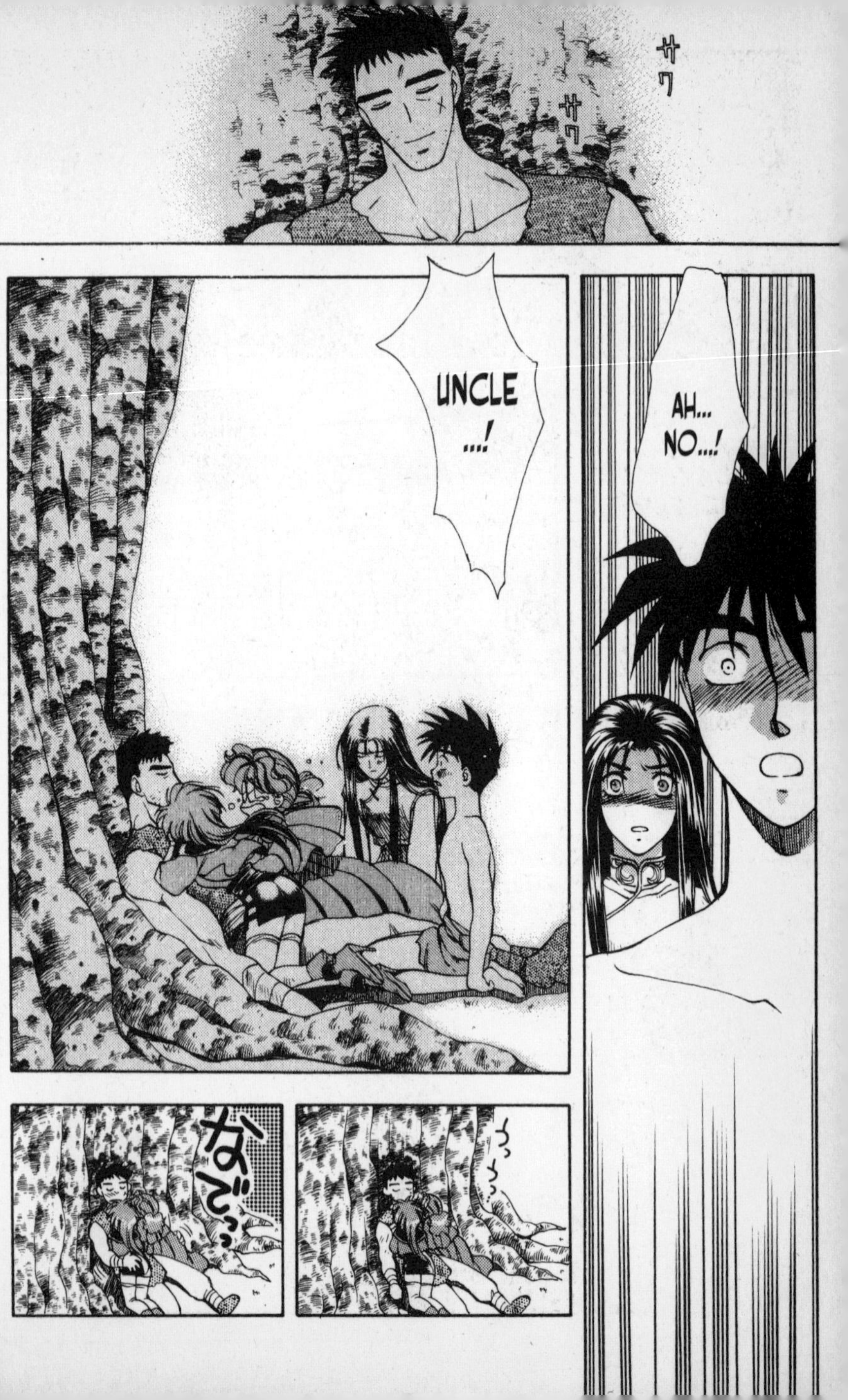
サク
サク
AH... NO...!
UNCLE ...!
うっ うっ…
なでっ

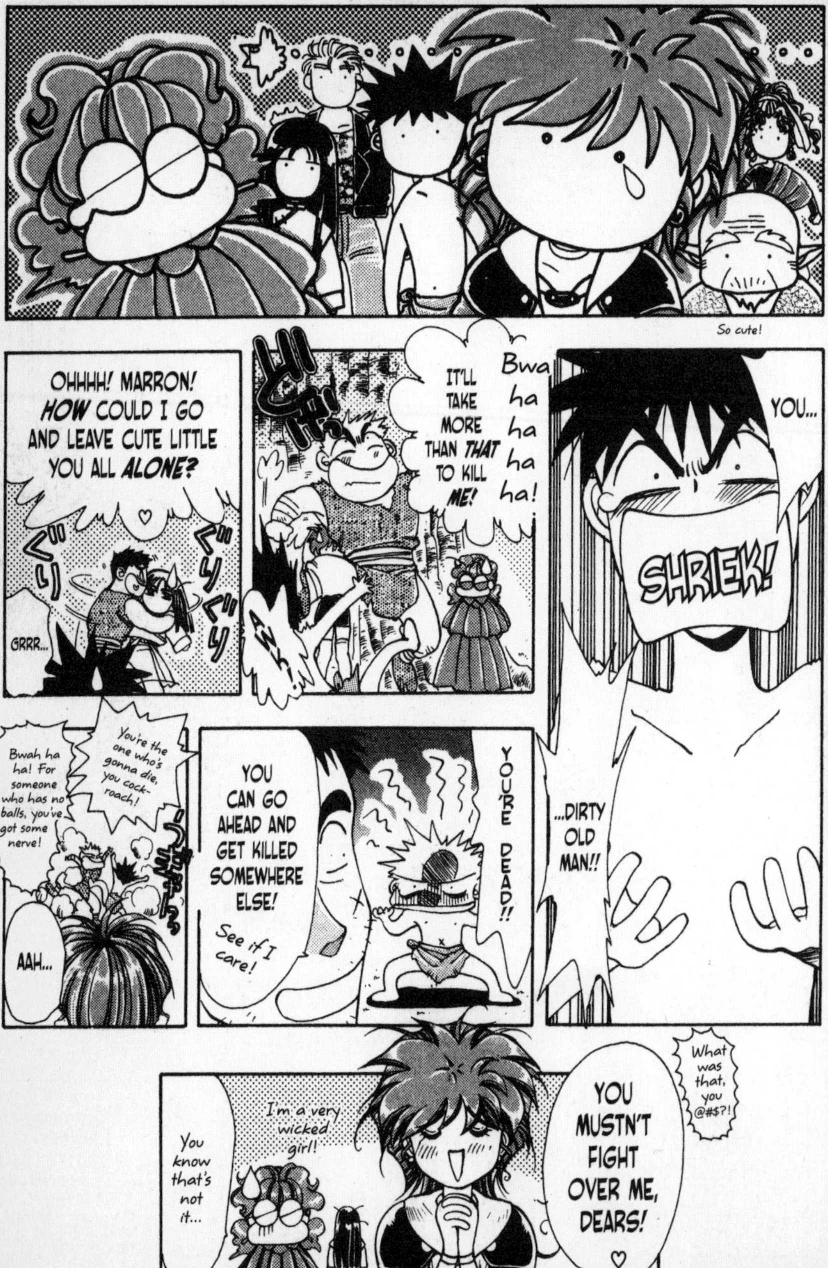
So cute!
YOU...
SHRIEK!
...DIRTY OLD MAN!!
IT'LL TAKE MORE THAN THAT TO KILL ME!
Bwa ha ha ha ha!
OHHHH! MARRON! HOW COULD I GO AND LEAVE CUTE LITTLE YOU ALL ALONE? ♡
GRRR...
YOU'RE DEAD!!
YOU CAN GO AHEAD AND GET KILLED SOMEWHERE ELSE!
See if I care!
You're the one who's gonna die, you cock-roach!
Bwah ha ha! For someone who has no balls, you've got some nerve!
AAH...
What was that, you @#$?!
YOU MUSTN'T FIGHT OVER ME, DEARS! ♡
I'm a very wicked girl!
You know that's not it...

• GATEAU (BOY VERSION) •
YOU KNOW HE CAN'T HAVE BULKED UP THAT MUCH, YET. AS I TRIED TO DRAW HIM, HE GOT YOUNGER THAN I INTENDED HIM TO BE. BUT MAYBE HE WASN'T SO TALL WHEN HE WAS YOUNG...THE PICTURE TO THE RIGHT IS HIM AT ABOUT 12 YEARS OLD. HOW WILL HE EVER BECOME MACHO?

• ECLAIR •
THIS IS ECLAIR AT ABOUT FIVE OR SIX. SHE'S AN ENERGETIC LITTLE GIRL. EVEN AT THIS AGE, SHE HAD THE POTENTIAL TO BECOME A FIGHTER TO CHALLENGE GATEAU. (BUT, THAT SAID, GATEAU WAS STILL A CHILD AT THIS AGE, TOO.) THEY'RE SCARY SIBLINGS.

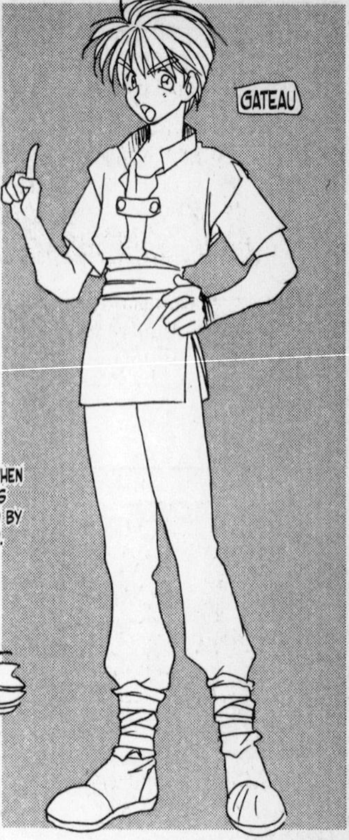
GATEAU

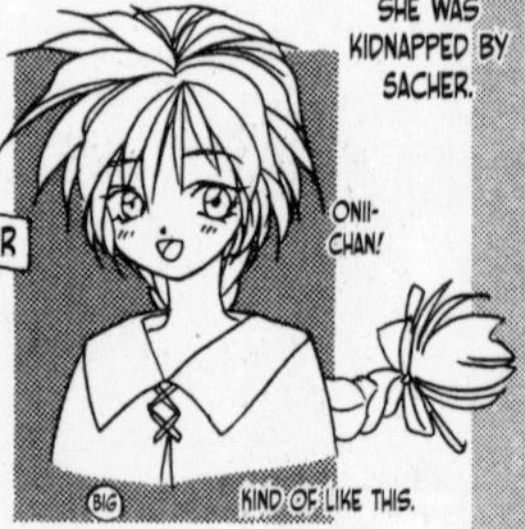
THE AGE WHEN SHE WAS KIDNAPPED BY SACHER.
ONII-CHAN!
BIG
KIND OF LIKE THIS.

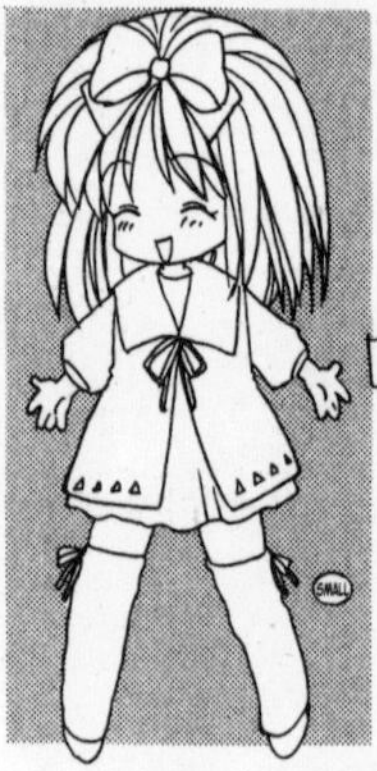
ECLAIR
SMALL

HOW TO DRESS LIKE GRANDPA

WHAT'S THAT?

I REALLY PUT A LOT OF THOUGHT INTO EVERYONE'S CLOTHES. I THOUGHT I WOULD SHOW YOU GRANDPA'S OUTFIT BECAUSE IT'S ONE OF THE MOST STRAIGHTFORWARD.

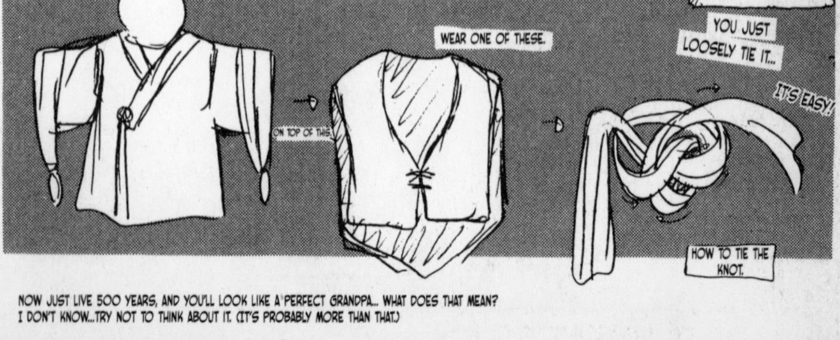
ON TOP OF THIS.
WEAR ONE OF THESE.
YOU JUST LOOSELY TIE IT...
IT'S EASY!
HOW TO TIE THE KNOT.

NOW JUST LIVE 500 YEARS, AND YOU'LL LOOK LIKE A PERFECT GRANDPA... WHAT DOES THAT MEAN? I DON'T KNOW...TRY NOT TO THINK ABOUT IT. (IT'S PROBABLY MORE THAN THAT.)

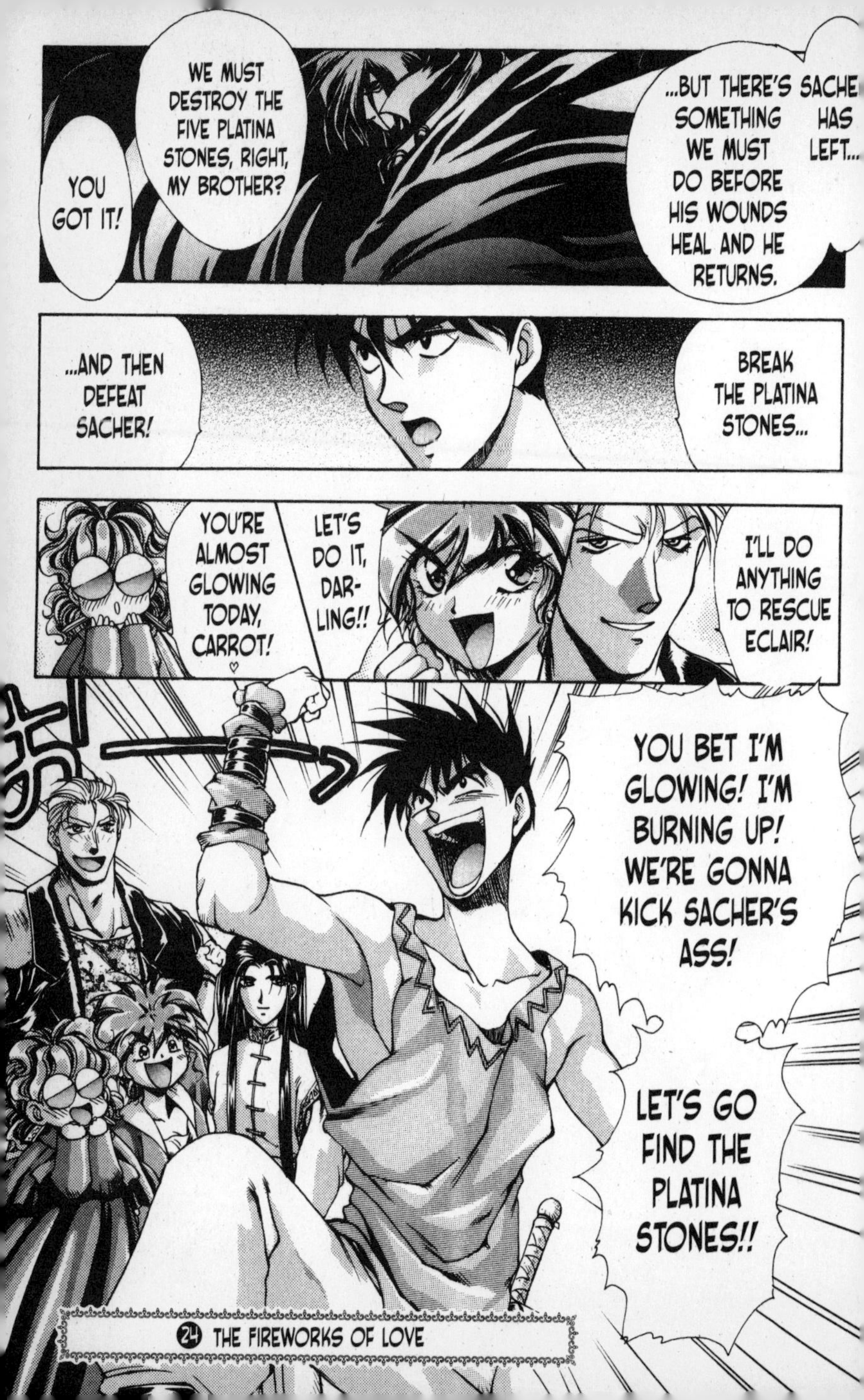
SACHE HAS LEFT...
...BUT THERE'S SOMETHING WE MUST DO BEFORE HIS WOUNDS HEAL AND HE RETURNS.
WE MUST DESTROY THE FIVE PLATINA STONES, RIGHT, MY BROTHER?
YOU GOT IT!
BREAK THE PLATINA STONES...
...AND THEN DEFEAT SACHER!
I'LL DO ANYTHING TO RESCUE ECLAIR!
LET'S DO IT, DAR-LING!!
YOU'RE ALMOST GLOWING TODAY, CARROT! ♡
YOU BET I'M GLOWING! I'M BURNING UP! WE'RE GONNA KICK SACHER'S ASS!
LET'S GO FIND THE PLATINA STONES!!
24 THE FIREWORKS OF LOVE

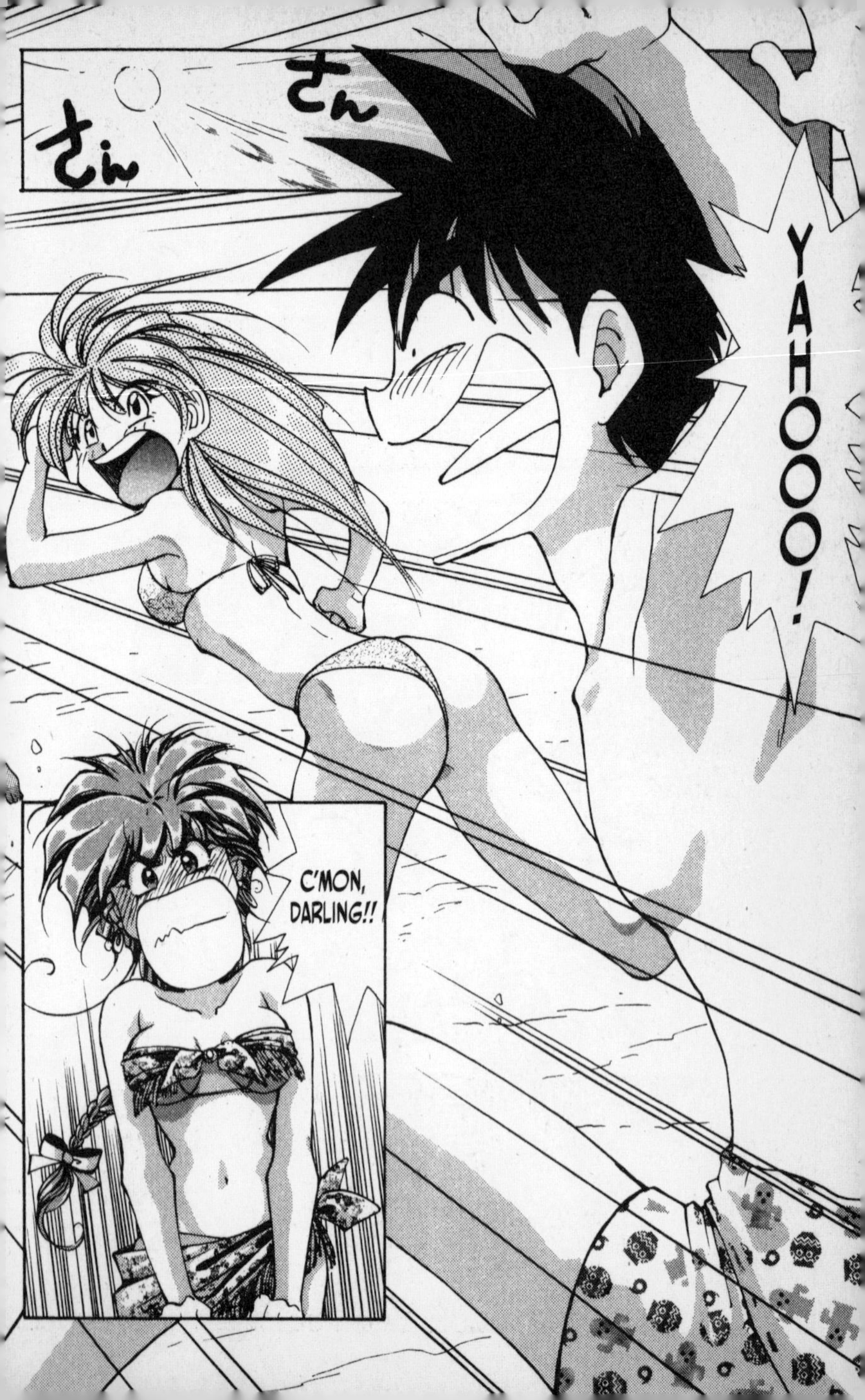
さん
さん
YAHOOO!
C'MON, DARLING!!

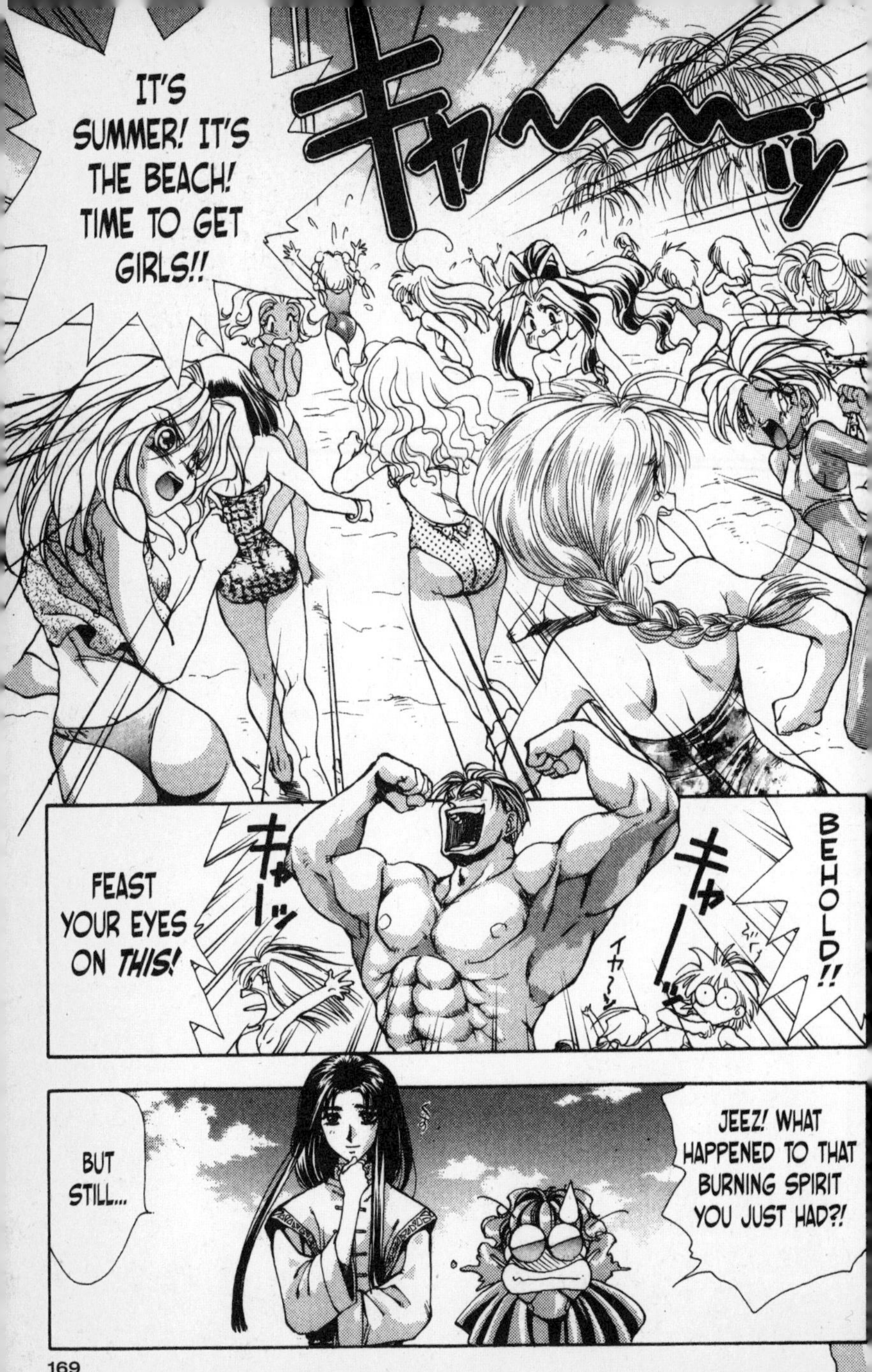
キャ〜〜〜ッ
IT'S SUMMER! IT'S THE BEACH! TIME TO GET GIRLS!!
BEHOLD!!
キャー
FEAST YOUR EYES ON *THIS!*
キャーッ
JEEZ! WHAT HAPPENED TO THAT BURNING SPIRIT YOU JUST HAD?!
BUT STILL...

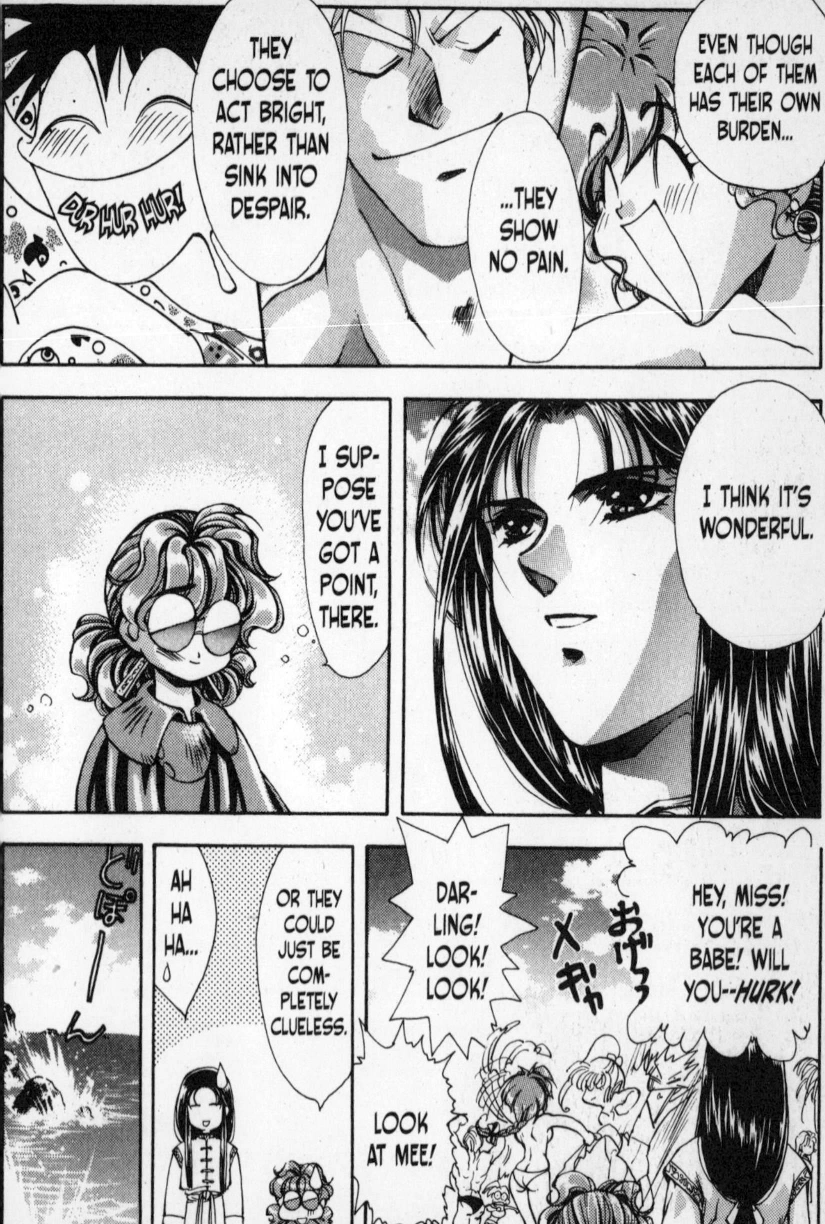
EVEN THOUGH EACH OF THEM HAS THEIR OWN BURDEN...
...THEY SHOW NO PAIN.
THEY CHOOSE TO ACT BRIGHT, RATHER THAN SINK INTO DESPAIR.
DUR HUR HUR!
I THINK IT'S WONDERFUL.
I SUP-POSE YOU'VE GOT A POINT, THERE.
HEY, MISS! YOU'RE A BABE! WILL YOU--*HURK!*
おげっ
メキャ
DAR-LING! LOOK! LOOK!
LOOK AT MEE!
OR THEY COULD JUST BE COM-PLETELY CLUELESS.
AH HA HA...
どぼーん

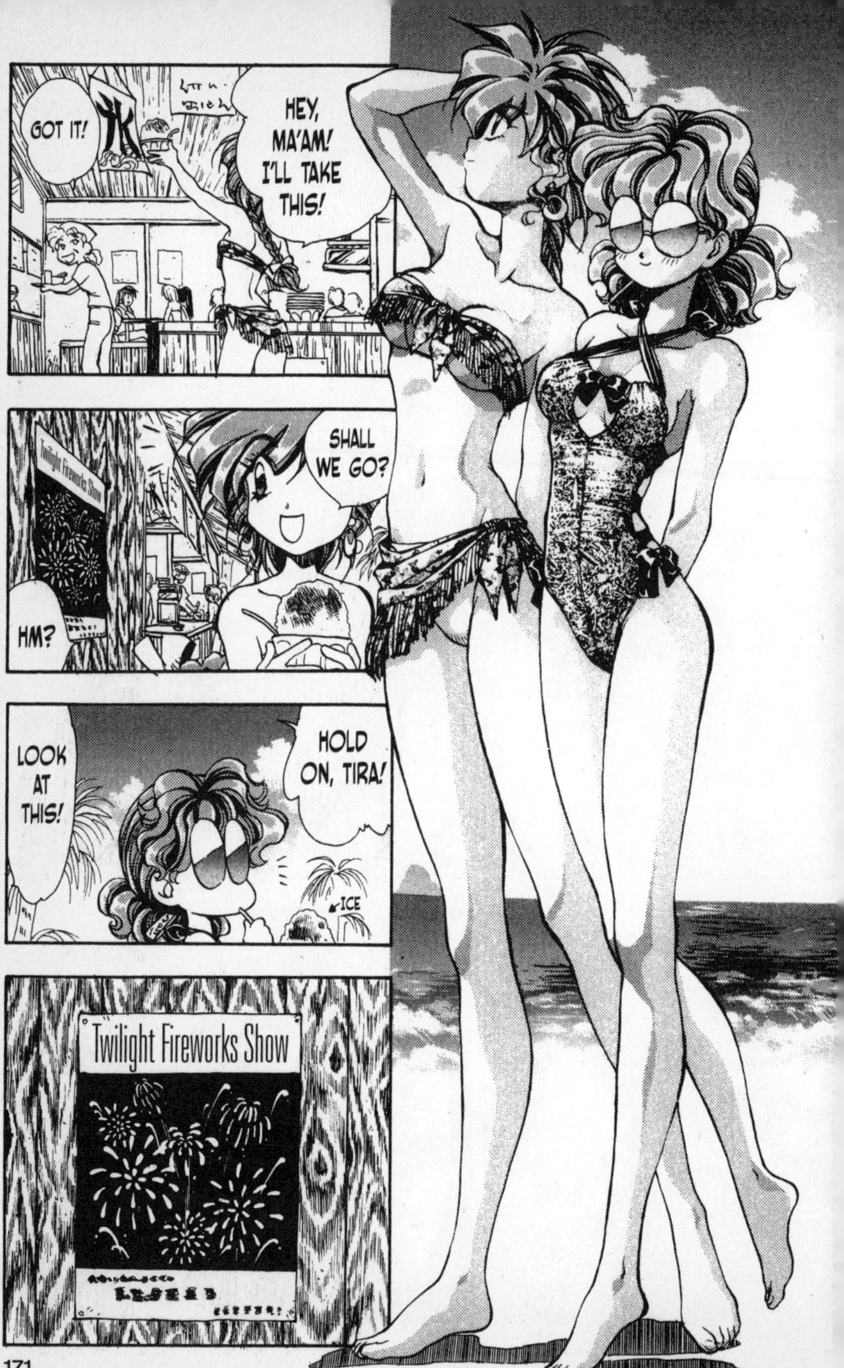
HEY, MA'AM! I'LL TAKE THIS!
GOT IT!
SHALL WE GO?
Twilight Fireworks Show
HM?
HOLD ON, TIRA!
ICE
LOOK AT THIS!
Twilight Fireworks Show

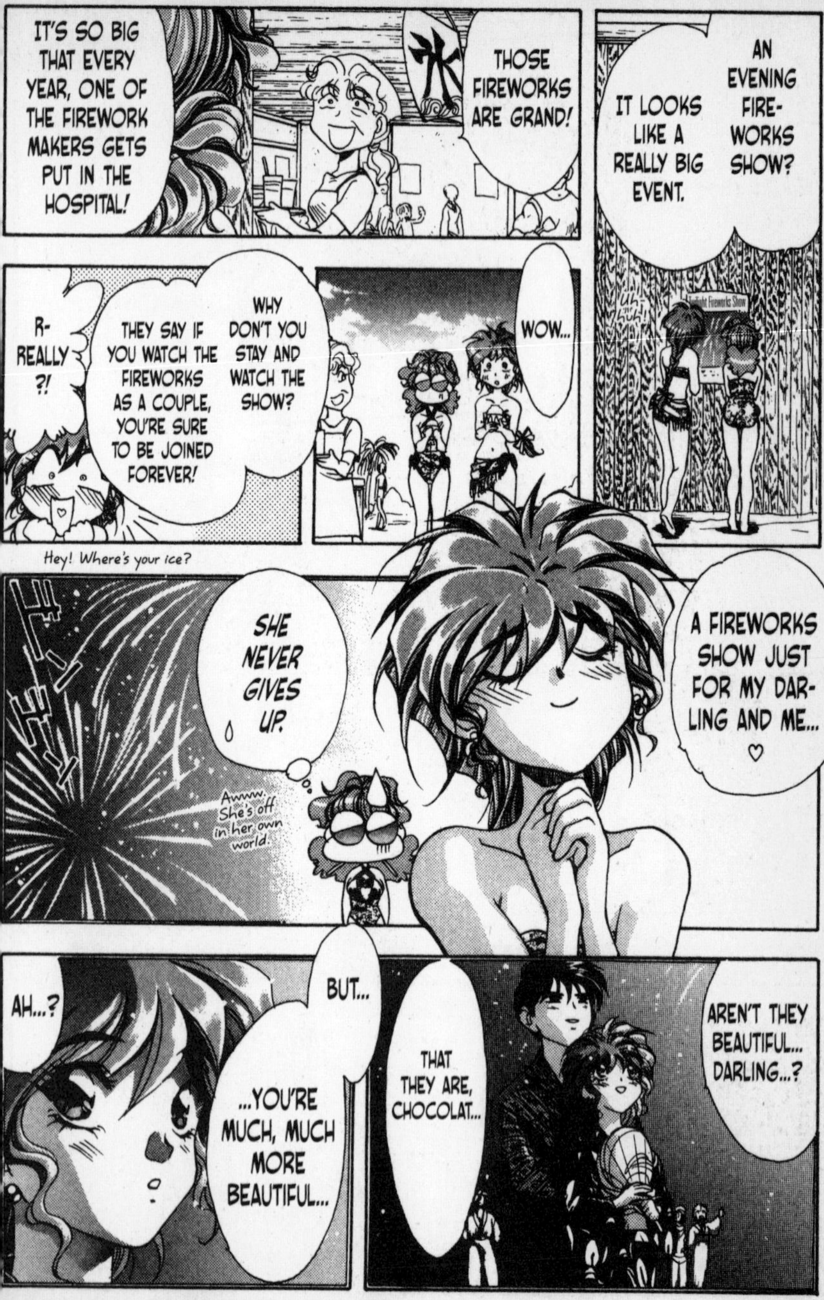
AN EVENING FIRE-WORKS SHOW?
IT LOOKS LIKE A REALLY BIG EVENT.
THOSE FIREWORKS ARE GRAND!
IT'S SO BIG THAT EVERY YEAR, ONE OF THE FIREWORK MAKERS GETS PUT IN THE HOSPITAL!
WOW...
WHY DON'T YOU STAY AND WATCH THE SHOW?
THEY SAY IF YOU WATCH THE FIREWORKS AS A COUPLE, YOU'RE SURE TO BE JOINED FOREVER!
R-REALLY?!
Hey! Where's your ice?
A FIREWORKS SHOW JUST FOR MY DARLING AND ME... ♡
SHE NEVER GIVES UP.
Awww. She's off in her own world.
AREN'T THEY BEAUTIFUL... DARLING...?
THAT THEY ARE, CHOCOLAT...
BUT...
...YOU'RE MUCH, MUCH MORE BEAUTIFUL...
AH...?

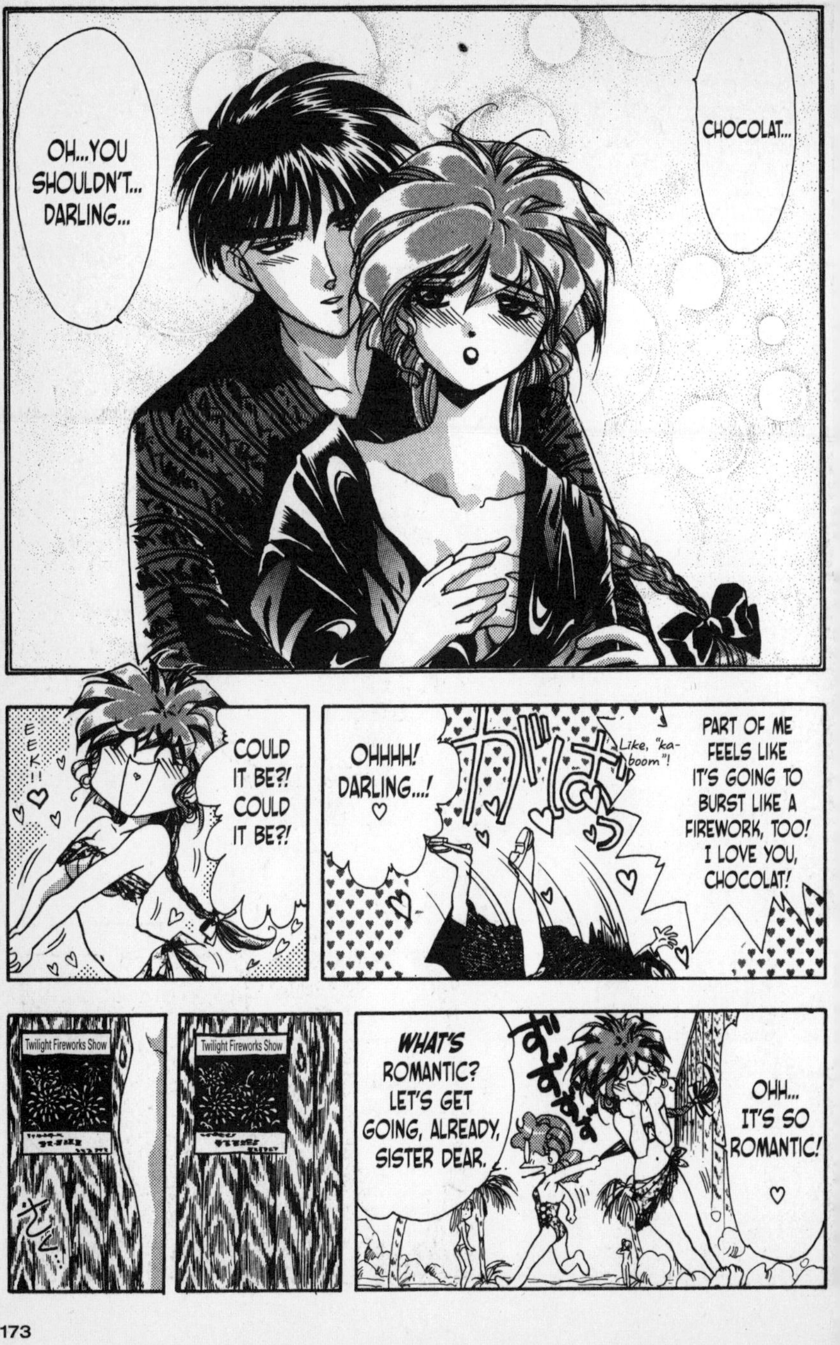
CHOCOLAT...
OH...YOU SHOULDN'T... DARLING...
PART OF ME FEELS LIKE IT'S GOING TO BURST LIKE A FIREWORK, TOO! I LOVE YOU, CHOCOLAT!
Like, "ka-boom"!
OHHHH! DARLING...!
COULD IT BE?! COULD IT BE?!
EEK!!
OHH... IT'S SO ROMANTIC!
WHAT'S ROMANTIC? LET'S GET GOING, ALREADY, SISTER DEAR.
Twilight Fireworks Show
Twilight Fireworks Show

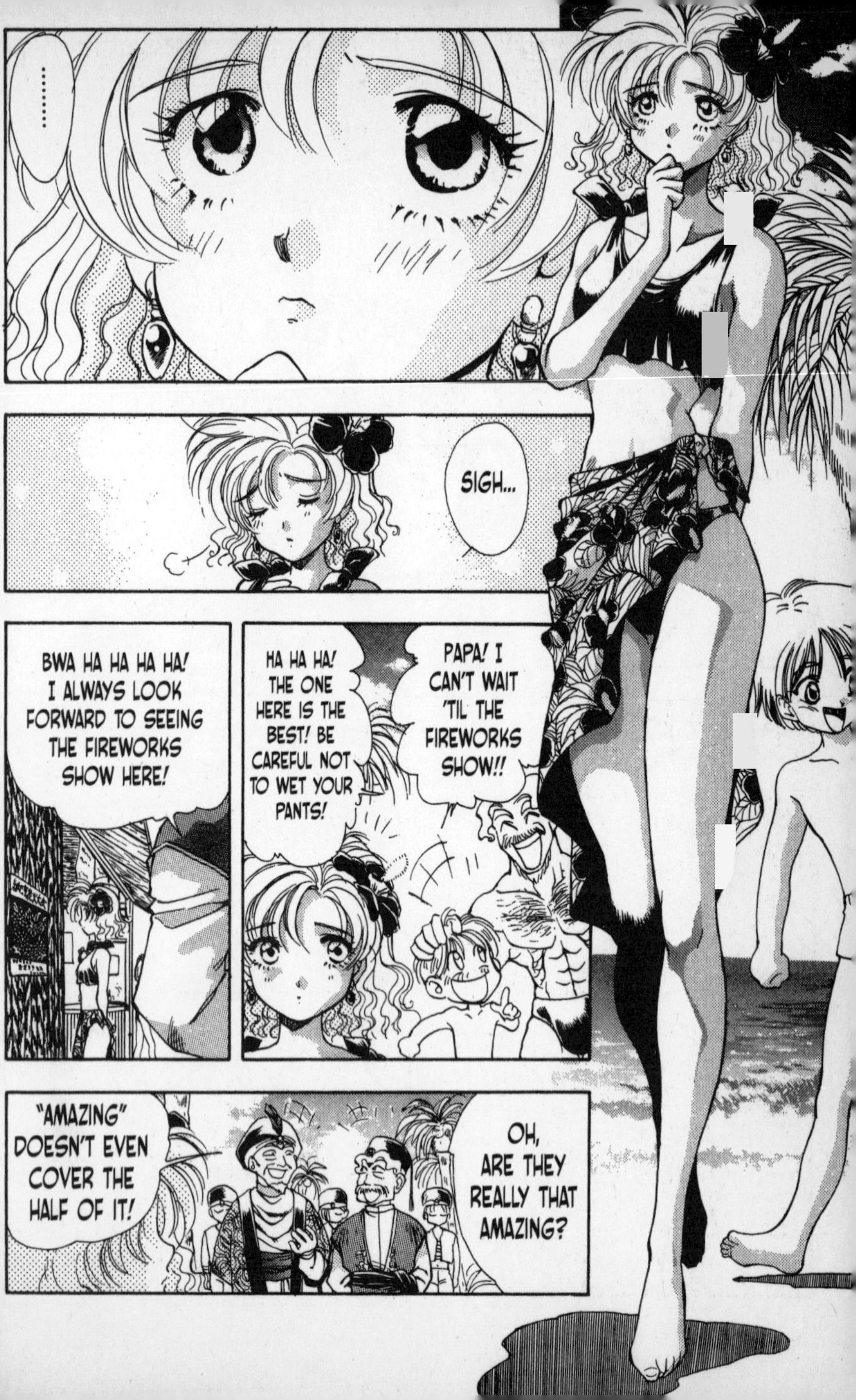
......
SIGH...
PAPA! I CAN'T WAIT 'TIL THE FIREWORKS SHOW!!
HA HA HA! THE ONE HERE IS THE BEST! BE CAREFUL NOT TO WET YOUR PANTS!
BWA HA HA HA HA! I ALWAYS LOOK FORWARD TO SEEING THE FIREWORKS SHOW HERE!
OH, ARE THEY REALLY THAT AMAZING?
"AMAZING" DOESN'T EVEN COVER THE HALF OF IT!

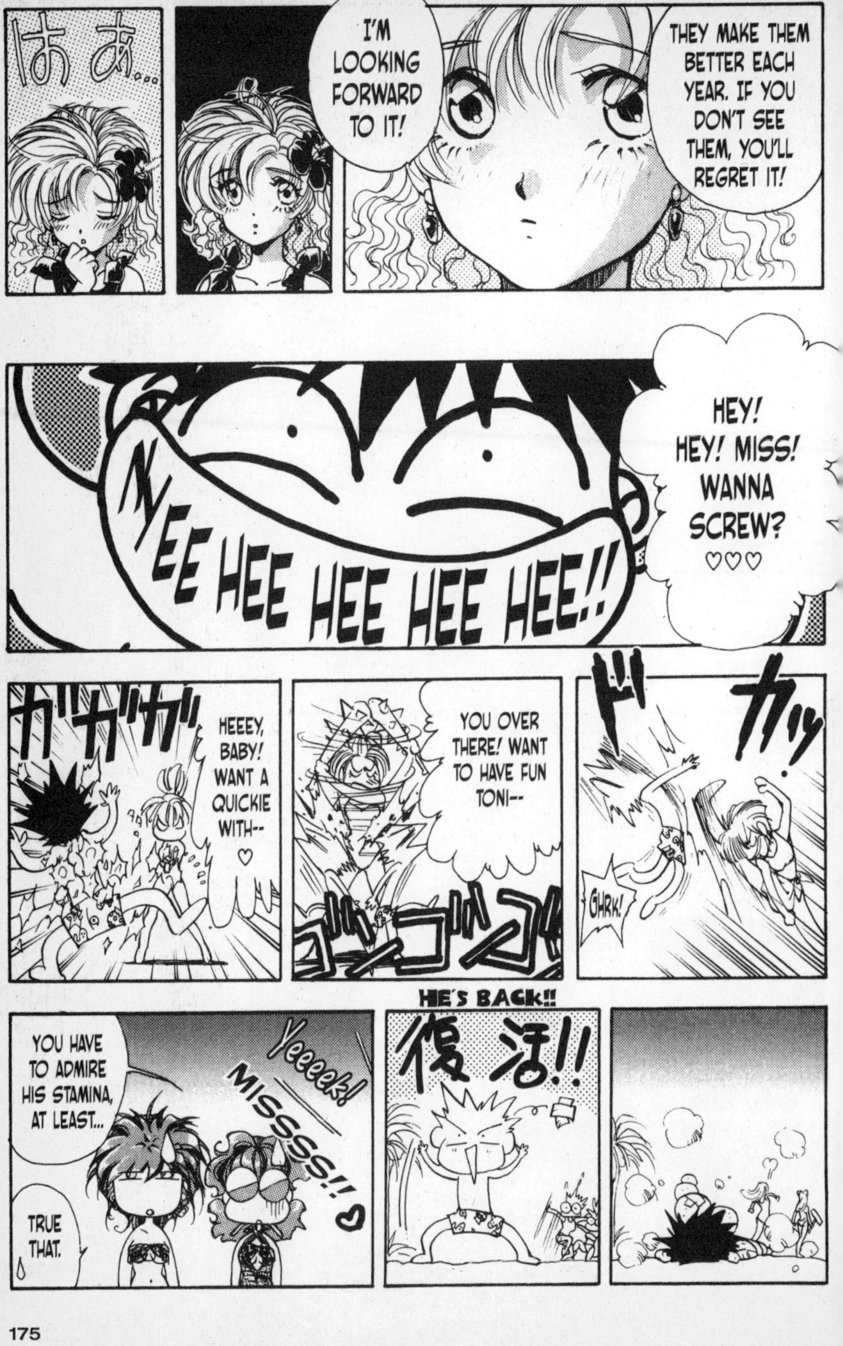
THEY MAKE THEM BETTER EACH YEAR. IF YOU DON'T SEE THEM, YOU'LL REGRET IT!
I'M LOOKING FORWARD TO IT!
はあ…
HEY! HEY! MISS! WANNA SCREW? ♡♡♡
NEE HEE HEE HEE HEE!!
ドカッ!
GHRK!
YOU OVER THERE! WANT TO HAVE FUN TONI--
HEEEY, BABY! WANT A QUICKIE WITH-- ♡
HE'S BACK!!
復活!!
Yeeeek!
MISSSS!! ♡
YOU HAVE TO ADMIRE HIS STAMINA, AT LEAST...
TRUE THAT.

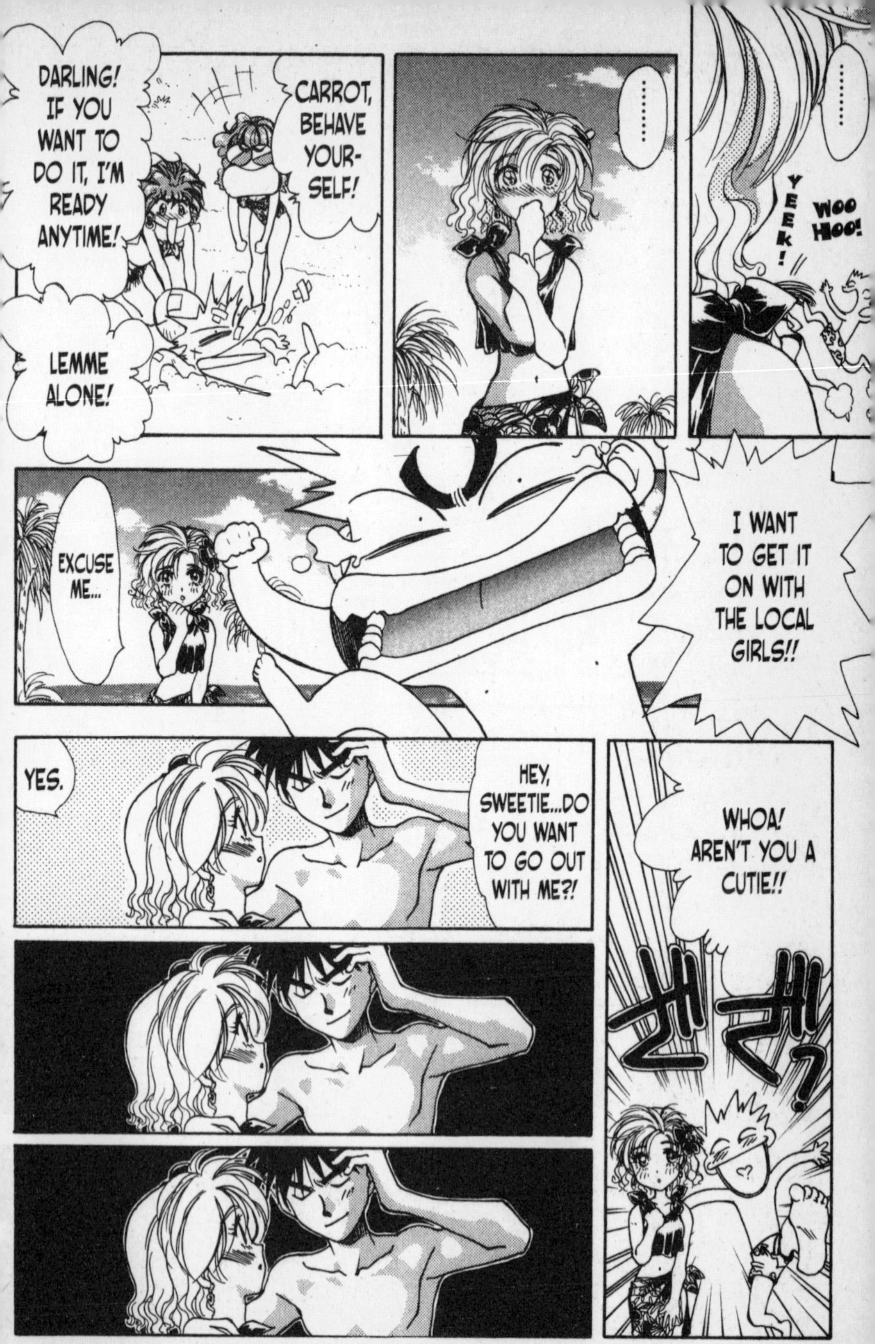
......
YEEEK!
WOO HOO!
......
CARROT, BEHAVE YOURSELF!
DARLING! IF YOU WANT TO DO IT, I'M READY ANYTIME!
LEMME ALONE!
I WANT TO GET IT ON WITH THE LOCAL GIRLS!!
EXCUSE ME...
WHOA! AREN'T YOU A CUTIE!!
HEY, SWEETIE...DO YOU WANT TO GO OUT WITH ME?!
YES.

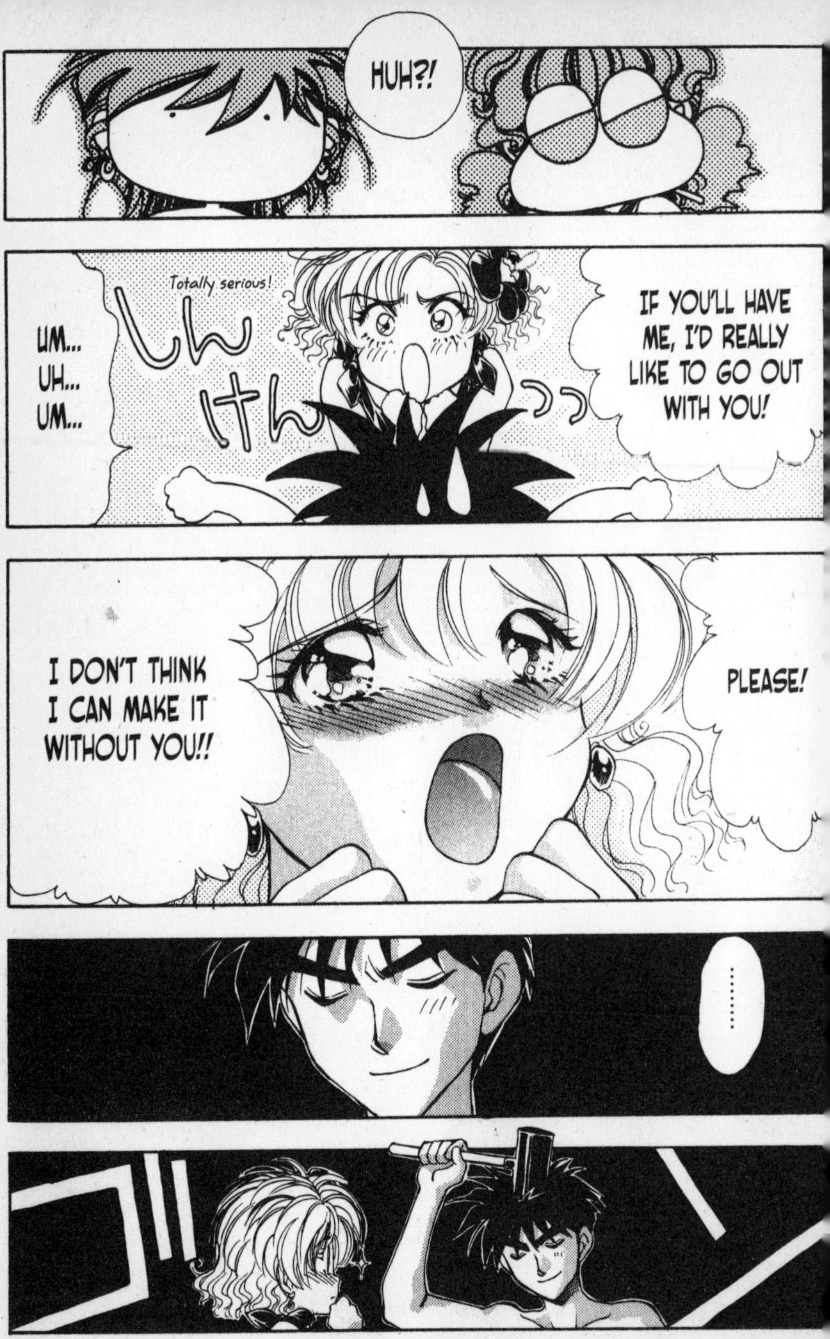
HUH?!
IF YOU'LL HAVE ME, I'D REALLY LIKE TO GO OUT WITH YOU!
Totally serious!
しんけん
UM... UH... UM...
PLEASE!
I DON'T THINK I CAN MAKE IT WITHOUT YOU!!
......

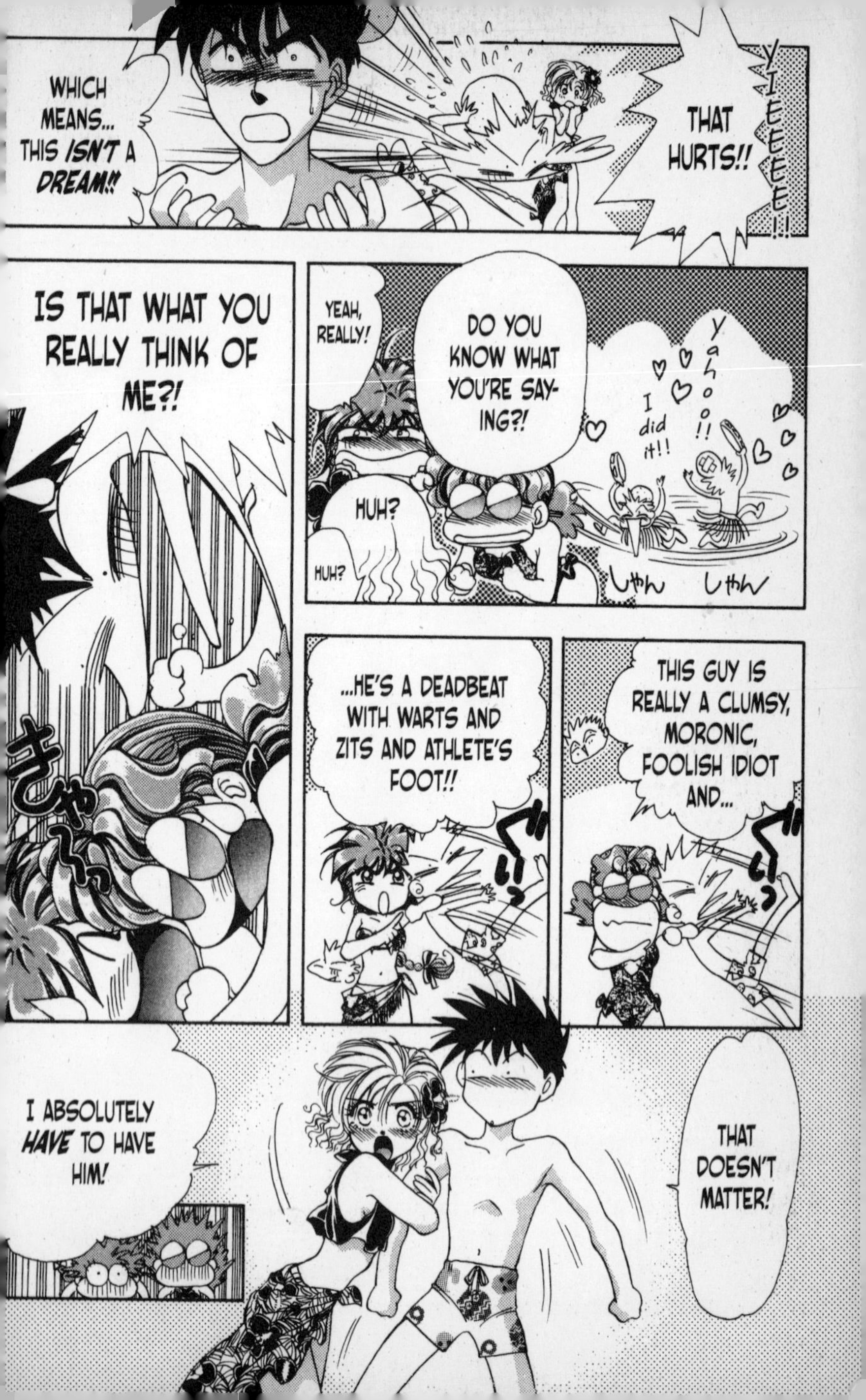
YIEEEEE!!
THAT HURTS!!
WHICH MEANS... THIS *ISN'T* A *DREAM!!*
Yahoo!!
I did it!!
DO YOU KNOW WHAT YOU'RE SAY-ING?!
YEAH, REALLY!
HUH?
HUH?
しゃん しゃん
THIS GUY IS REALLY A CLUMSY, MORONIC, FOOLISH IDIOT AND...
...HE'S A DEADBEAT WITH WARTS AND ZITS AND ATHLETE'S FOOT!!
IS THAT WHAT YOU REALLY THINK OF ME?!
きゃ〜っ
THAT DOESN'T MATTER!
I ABSOLUTELY *HAVE* TO HAVE HIM!

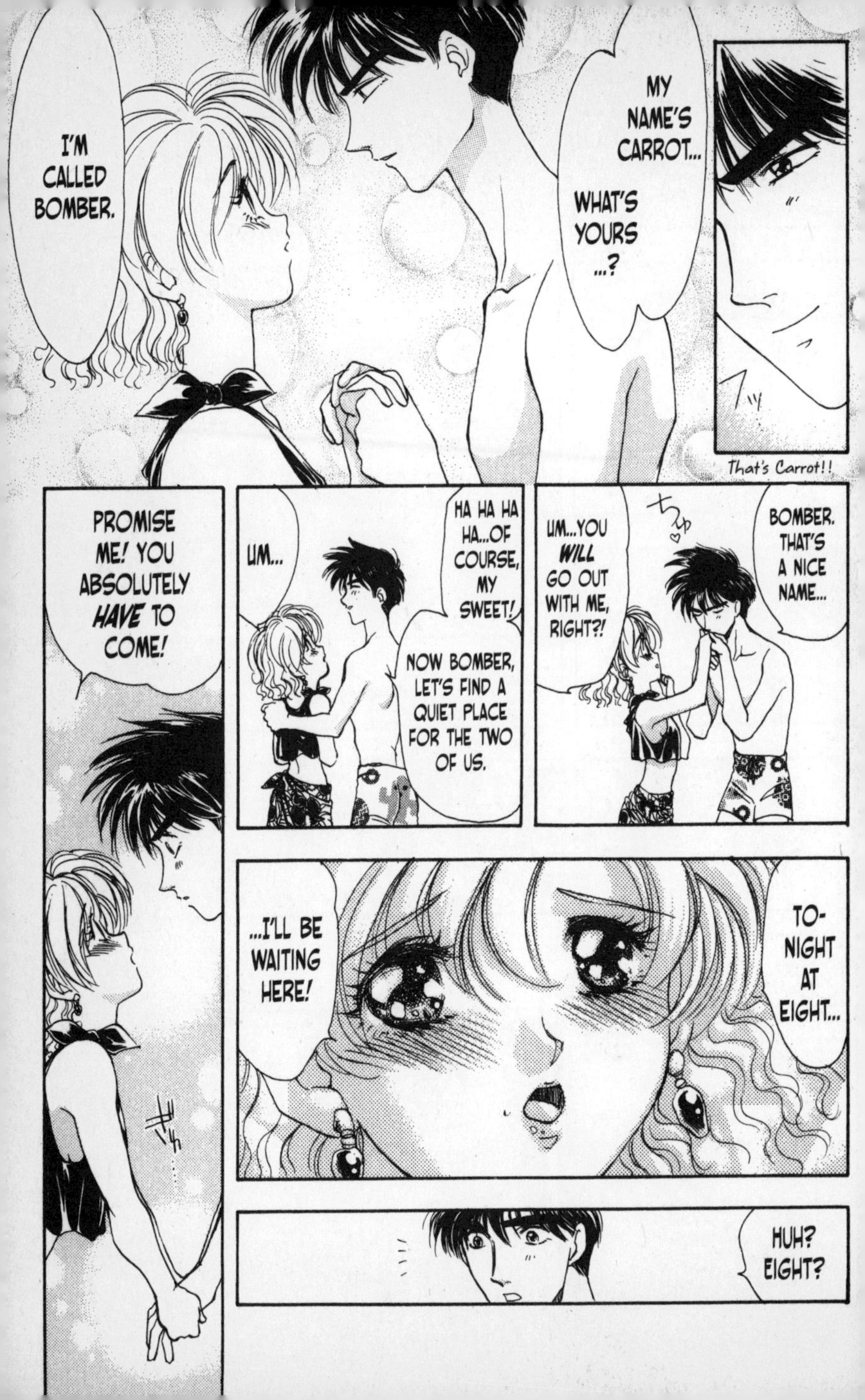
That's Carrot!!
MY NAME'S CARROT... WHAT'S YOURS ...?
I'M CALLED BOMBER.
BOMBER. THAT'S A NICE NAME...
UM...YOU **WILL** GO OUT WITH ME, RIGHT?!
HA HA HA HA...OF COURSE, MY SWEET!
UM...
NOW BOMBER, LET'S FIND A QUIET PLACE FOR THE TWO OF US.
TO-NIGHT AT EIGHT...
...I'LL BE WAITING HERE!
HUH? EIGHT?
PROMISE ME! YOU ABSOLUTELY **HAVE** TO COME!

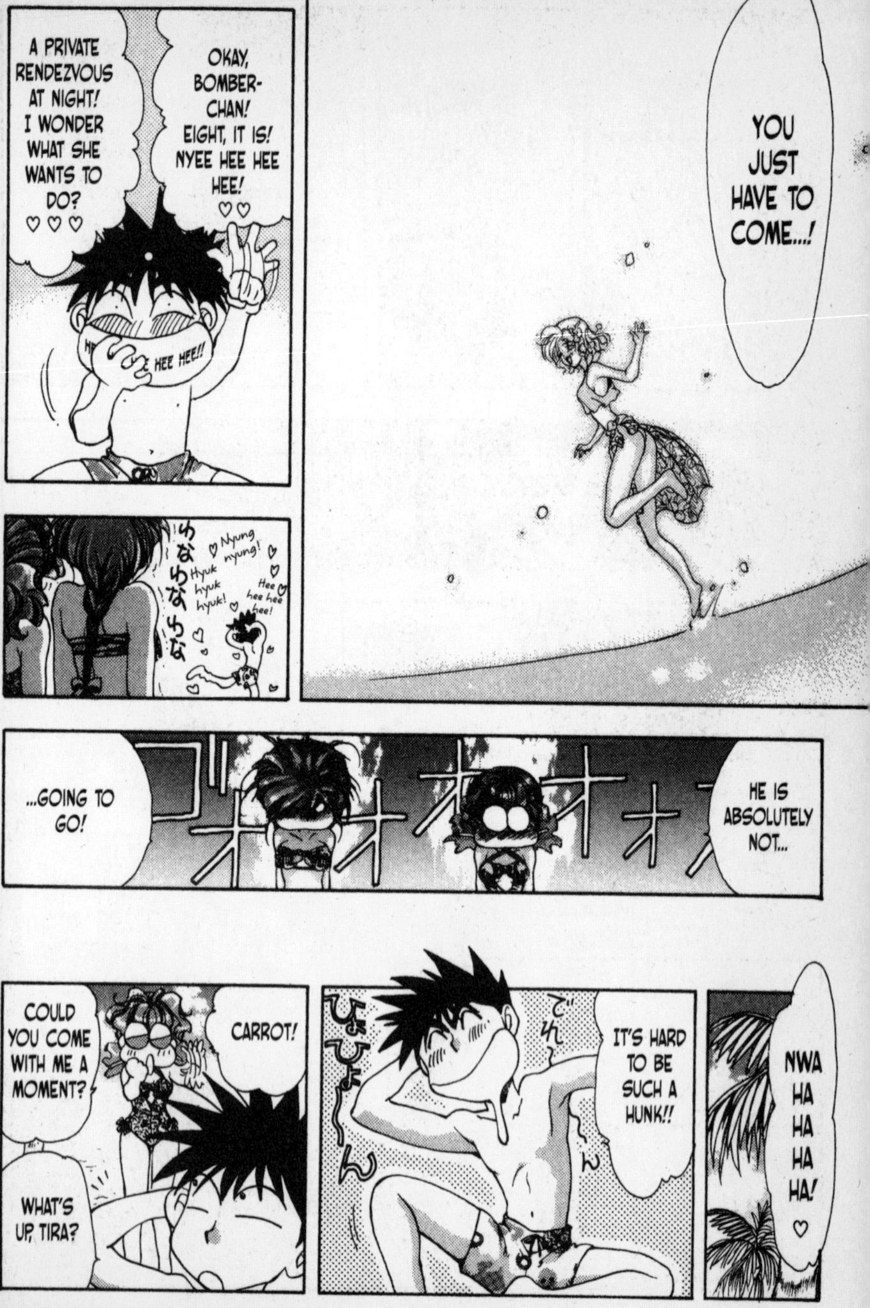
YOU JUST HAVE TO COME...!
OKAY, BOMBER-CHAN! EIGHT, IT IS! NYEE HEE HEE HEE! ♡♡
A PRIVATE RENDEZVOUS AT NIGHT! I WONDER WHAT SHE WANTS TO DO? ♡♡♡
HEE HEE!!
Nyung nyung!
Hyuk hyuk hyuk!
Hee hee hee hee!
HE IS ABSOLUTELY NOT...
...GOING TO GO!
NWA HA HA HA HA! ♡
IT'S HARD TO BE SUCH A HUNK!!
CARROT!
COULD YOU COME WITH ME A MOMENT?
WHAT'S UP, TIRA?

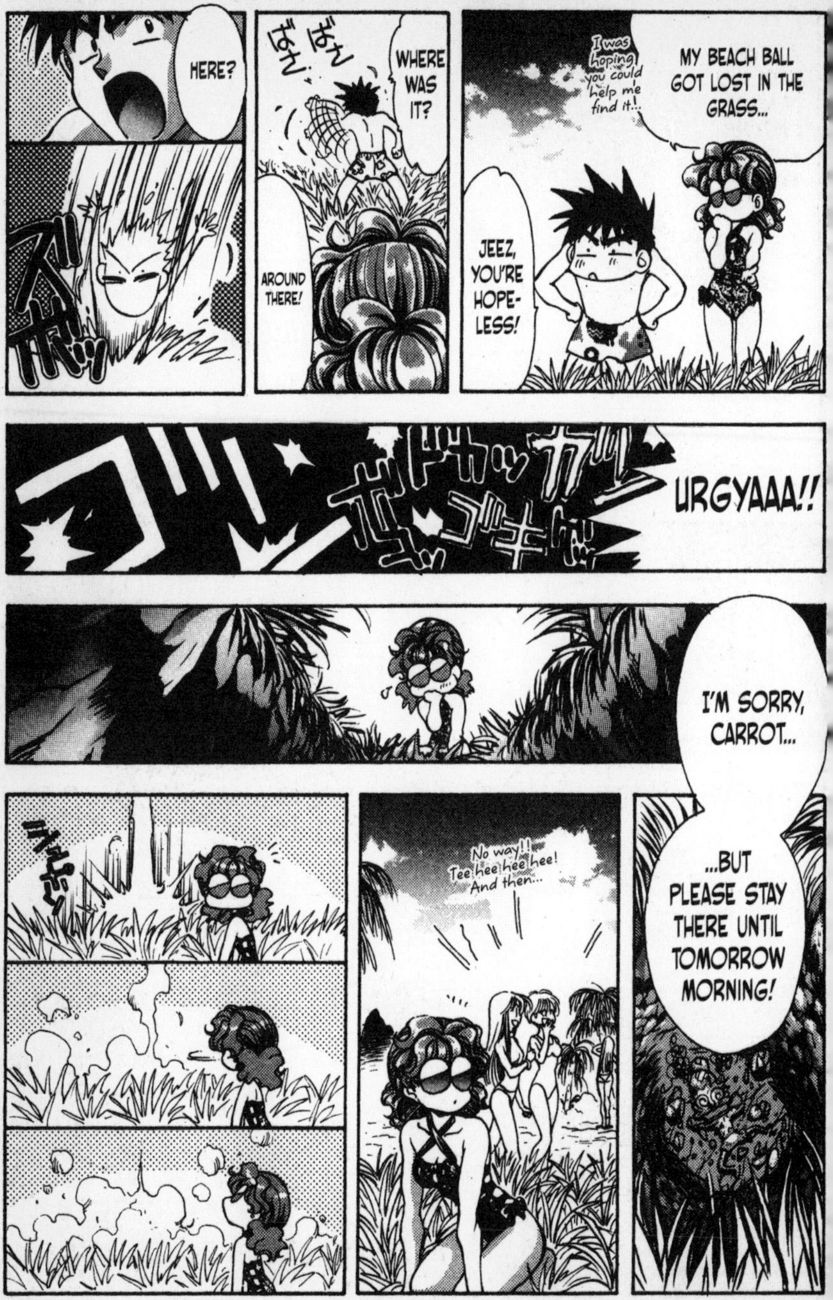
MY BEACH BALL GOT LOST IN THE GRASS...
I was hoping you could help me find it!..
JEEZ, YOU'RE HOPELESS!
ばさ ばさ
WHERE WAS IT?
AROUND THERE!
HERE?
URGYAAA!!
I'M SORRY, CARROT...
...BUT PLEASE STAY THERE UNTIL TOMORROW MORNING!
No way!! Tee hee hee hee! And then...

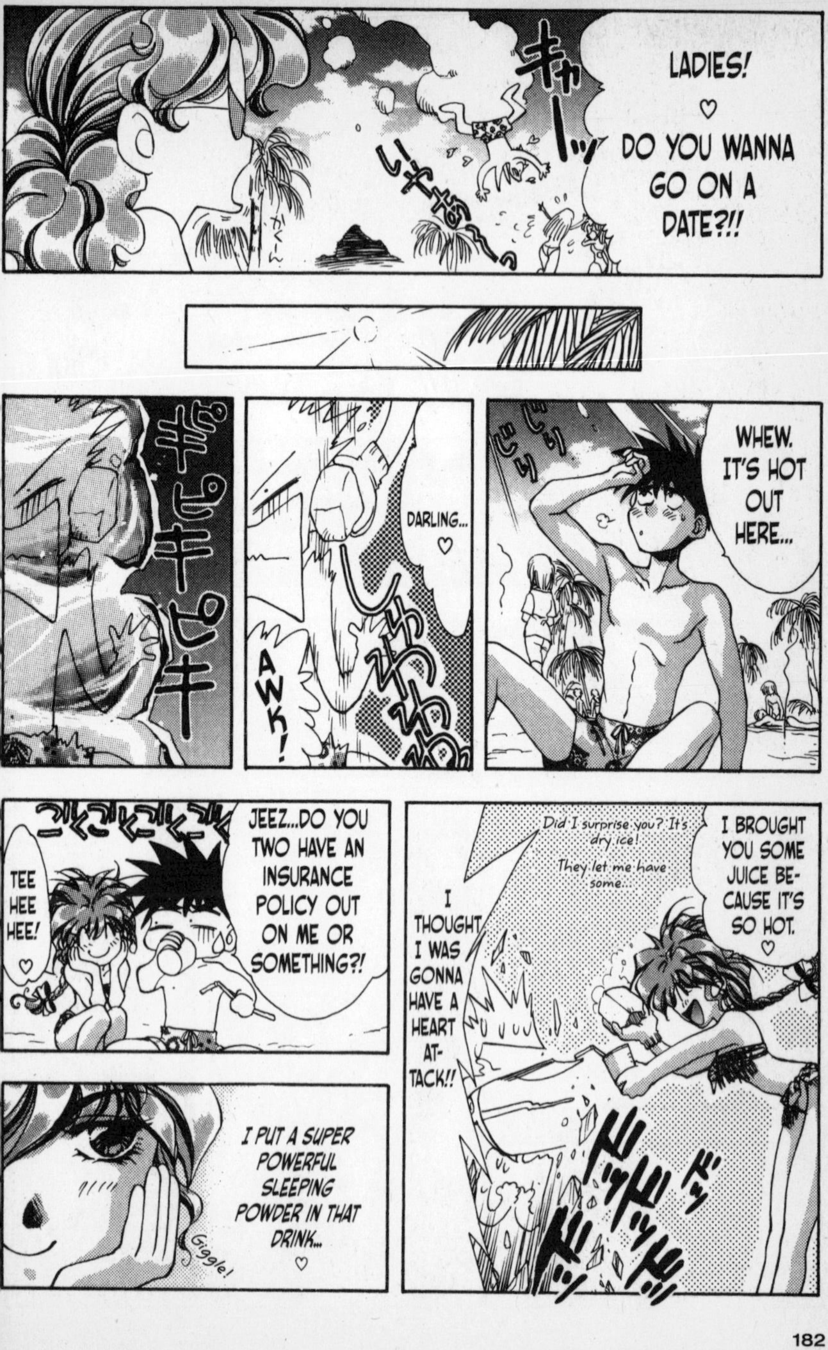
LADIES! ♡ DO YOU WANNA GO ON A DATE?!!
キャーッ
WHEW. IT'S HOT OUT HERE...
DARLING... ♡
AWK!
I BROUGHT YOU SOME JUICE BECAUSE IT'S SO HOT. ♡
Did I surprise you? It's dry ice!
They let me have some...
I THOUGHT I WAS GONNA HAVE A HEART ATTACK!!
JEEZ...DO YOU TWO HAVE AN INSURANCE POLICY OUT ON ME OR SOMETHING?!
TEE HEE HEE! ♡
I PUT A SUPER POWERFUL SLEEPING POWDER IN THAT DRINK... ♡
Giggle!

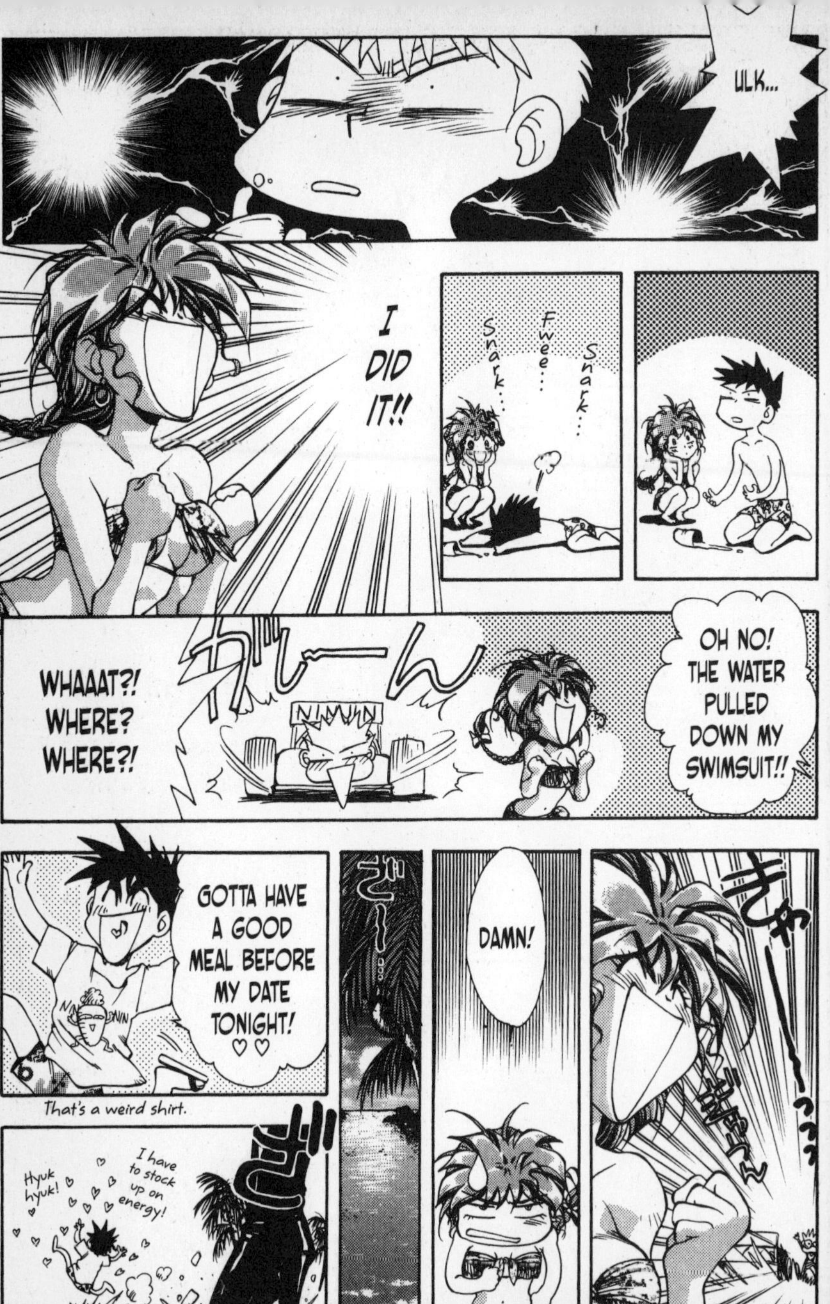
ULK...
Snark...
Fwee...
Snark...
I DID IT!!
OH NO! THE WATER PULLED DOWN MY SWIMSUIT!!
がーん
WHAAAT?! WHERE? WHERE?!
きゃーっっ
DAMN!
ざー…
GOTTA HAVE A GOOD MEAL BEFORE MY DATE TONIGHT! ♡♡
That's a weird shirt.
I have to stock up on energy!
Hyuk hyuk!

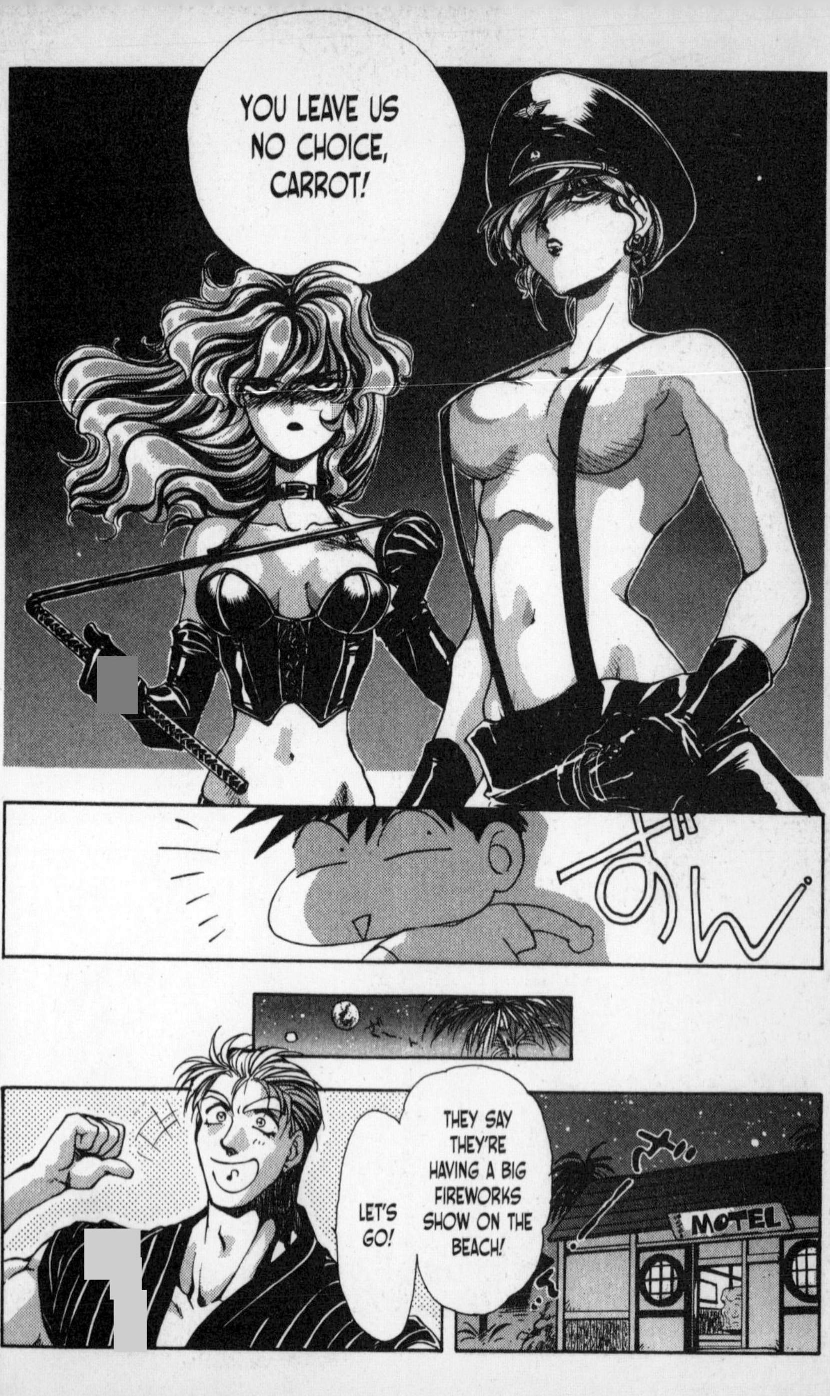
YOU LEAVE US NO CHOICE, CARROT!
MOTEL
THEY SAY THEY'RE HAVING A BIG FIREWORKS SHOW ON THE BEACH!
LET'S GO!

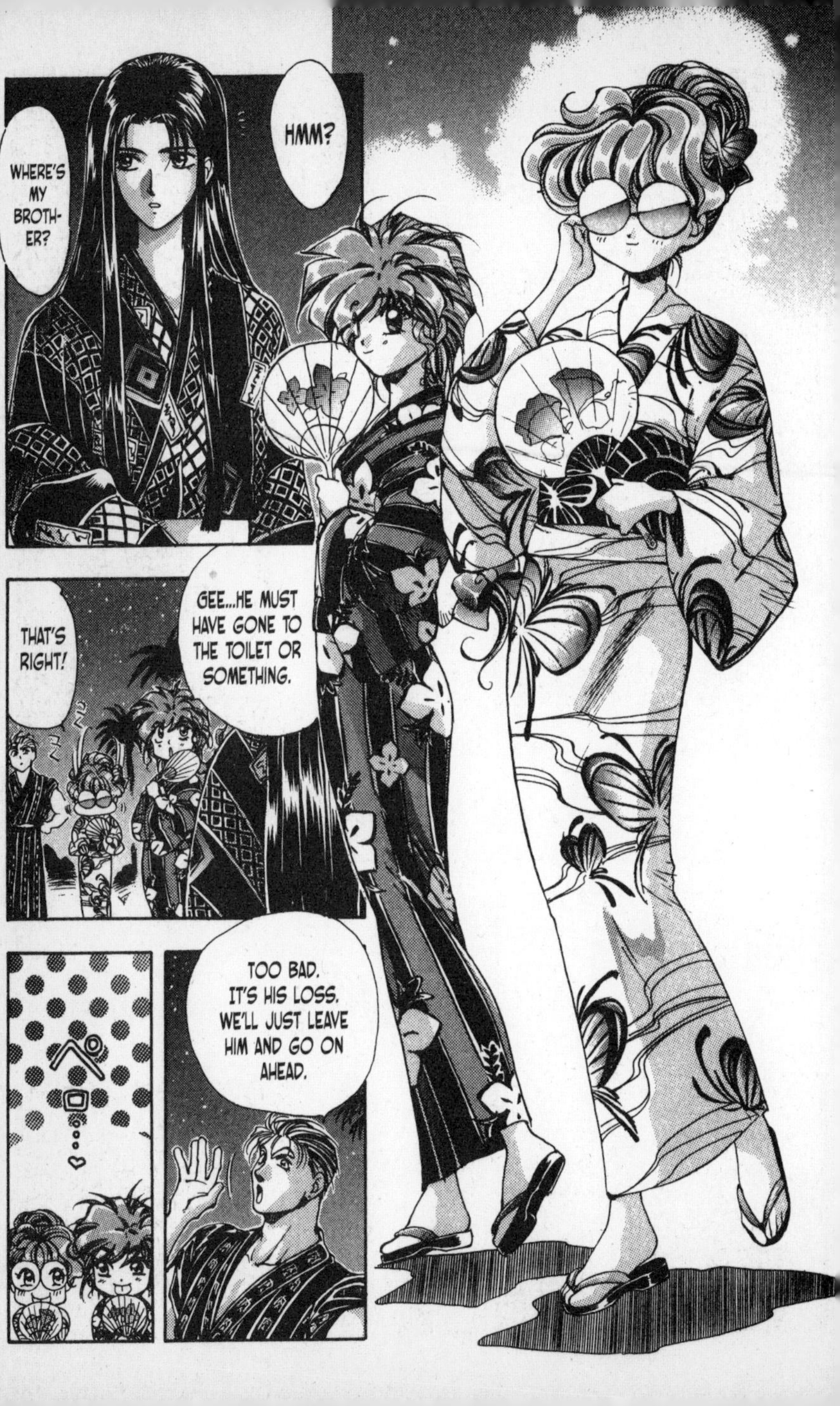
HMM?
WHERE'S MY BROTHER?
GEE...HE MUST HAVE GONE TO THE TOILET OR SOMETHING.
THAT'S RIGHT!
TOO BAD. IT'S HIS LOSS. WE'LL JUST LEAVE HIM AND GO ON AHEAD.

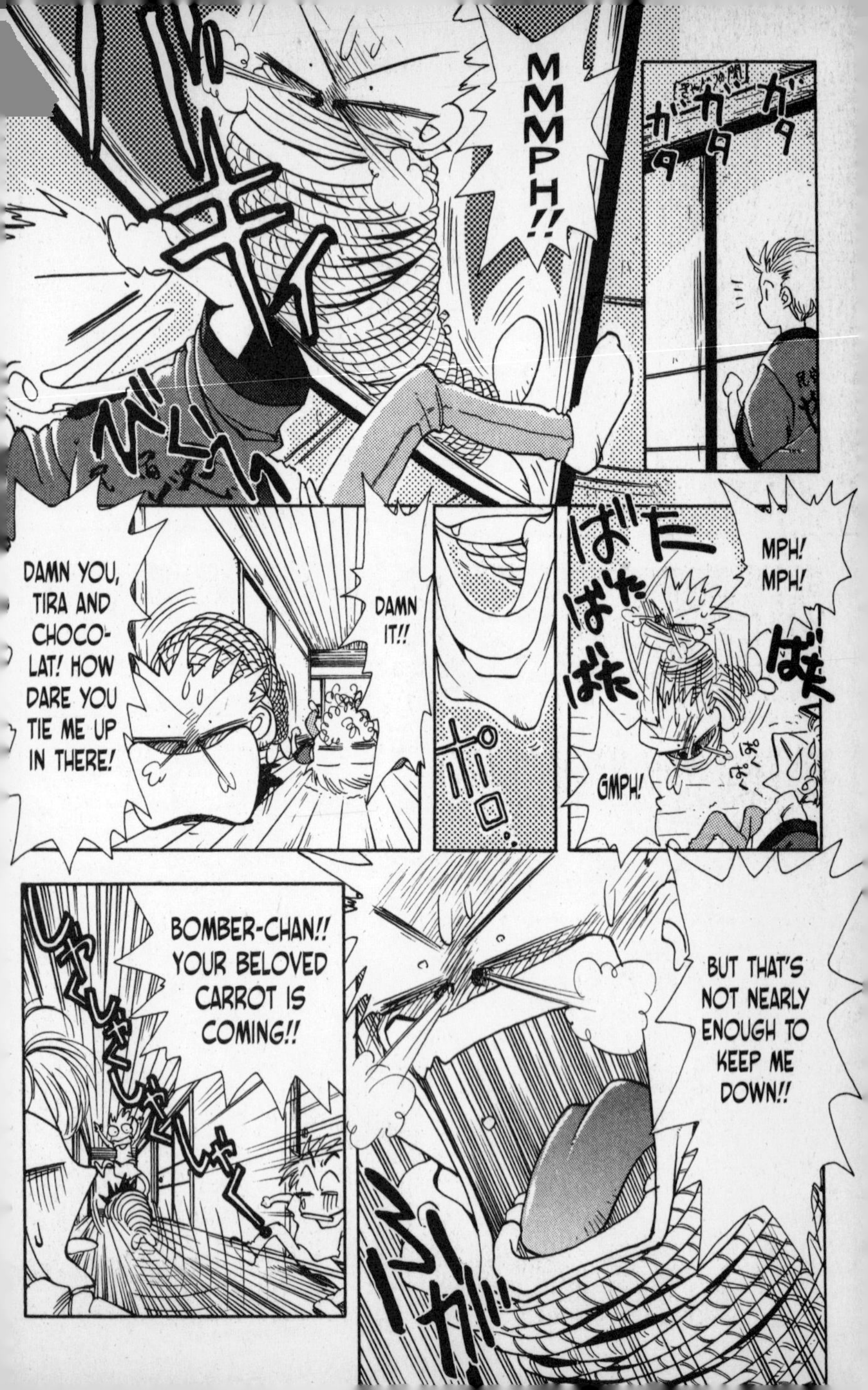
MMMPH!!
MPH! MPH!
GMPH!
DAMN IT!!
DAMN YOU, TIRA AND CHOCO-LAT! HOW DARE YOU TIE ME UP IN THERE!
BUT THAT'S NOT NEARLY ENOUGH TO KEEP ME DOWN!!
BOMBER-CHAN!! YOUR BELOVED CARROT IS COMING!!

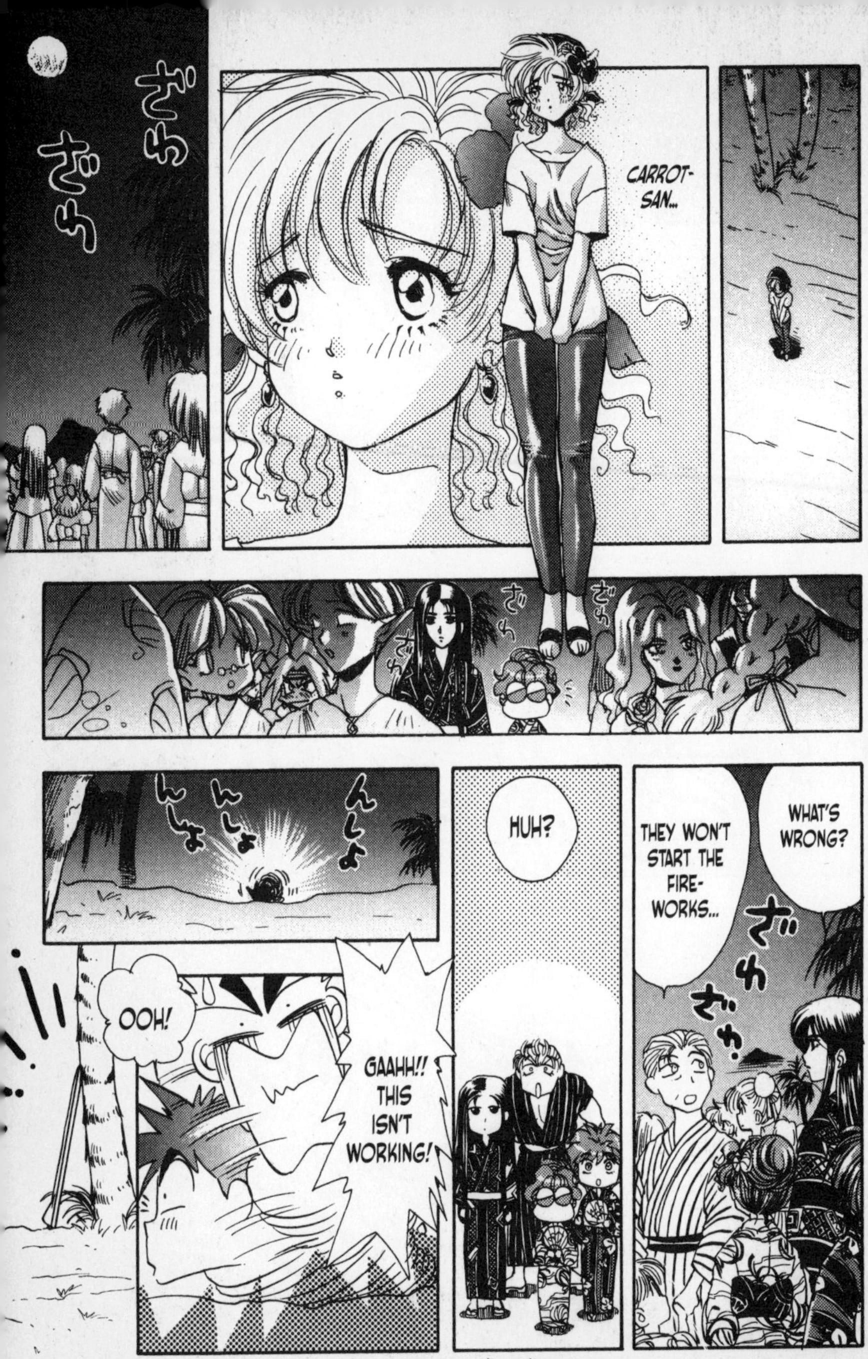
CARROT-SAN...
ざわざわ
ざわ
ざわ
ざわ
WHAT'S WRONG?
THEY WON'T START THE FIRE-WORKS...
ざわざわ
HUH?
んしょんしょんしょ
GAAHH!! THIS ISN'T WORKING!
OOH!

Tira shrunk...

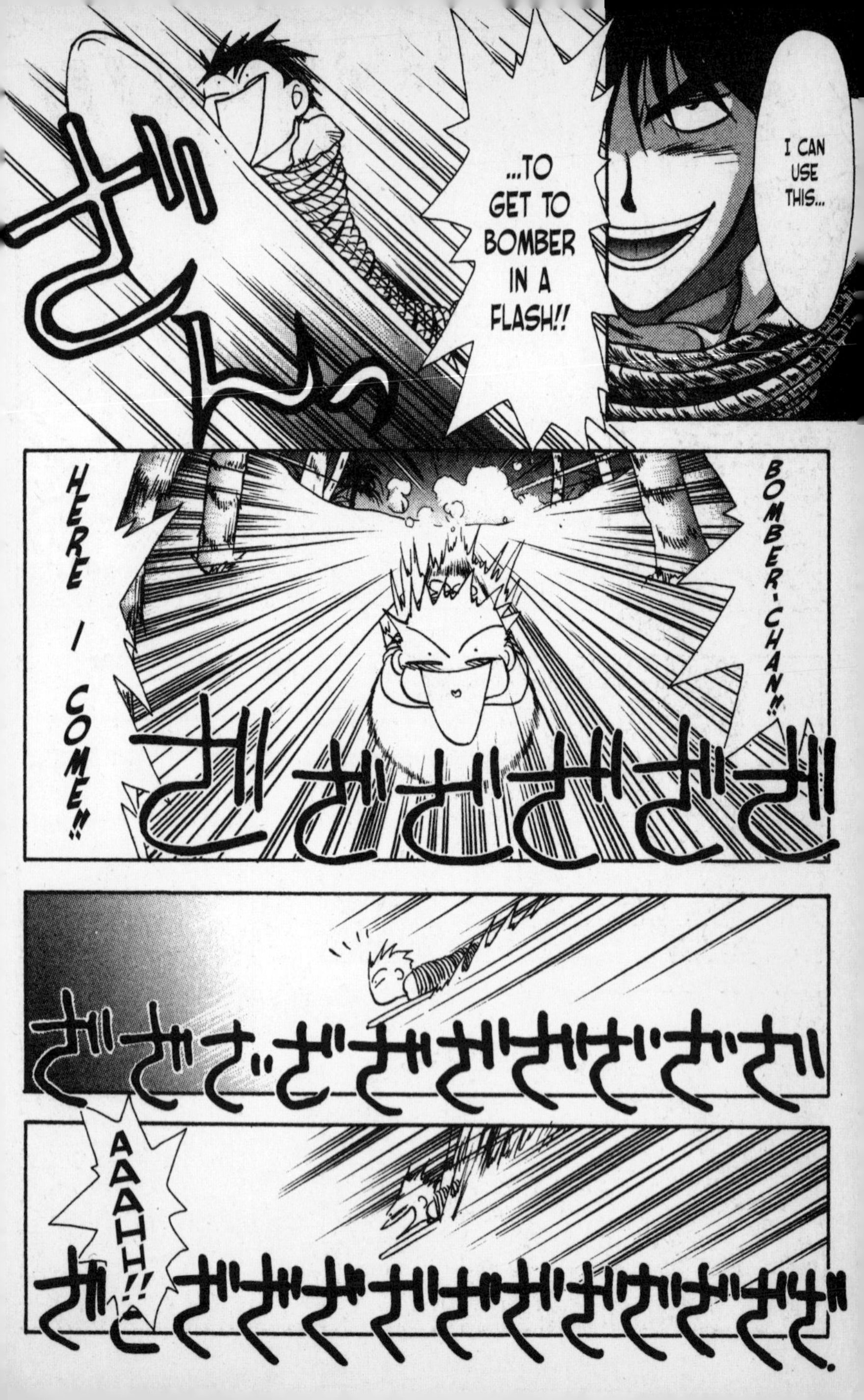
I CAN USE THIS...
...TO GET TO BOMBER IN A FLASH!!
BOMBER-CHAN!!
HERE I COME!!
AAAHH!!

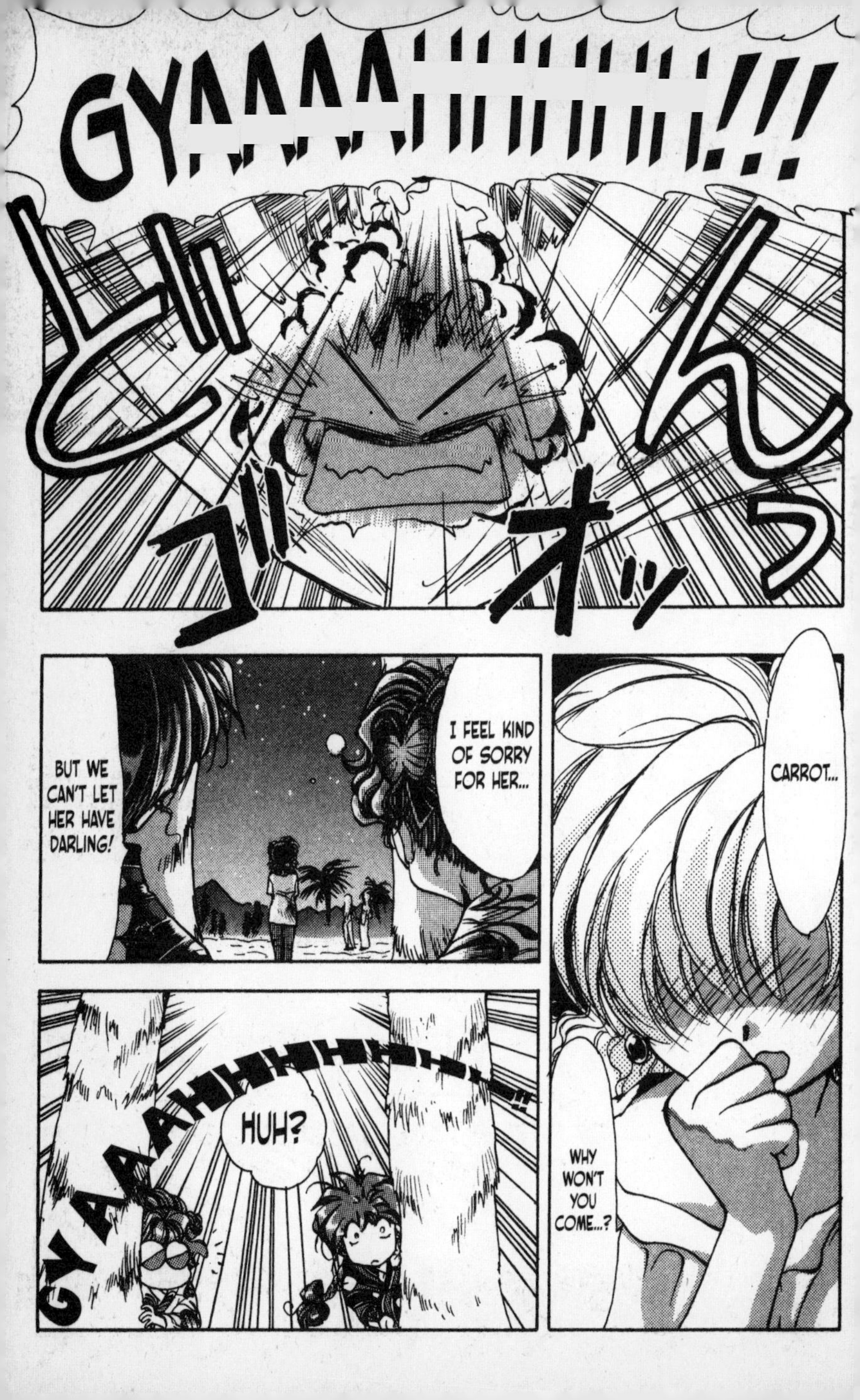
GYAAAA!!!!!!!!!!!!
どーん
ゴオッ
CARROT...
WHY WON'T YOU COME...?
I FEEL KIND OF SORRY FOR HER...
BUT WE CAN'T LET HER HAVE DARLING!
GYAAAHHHHHHHHHH!!
HUH?

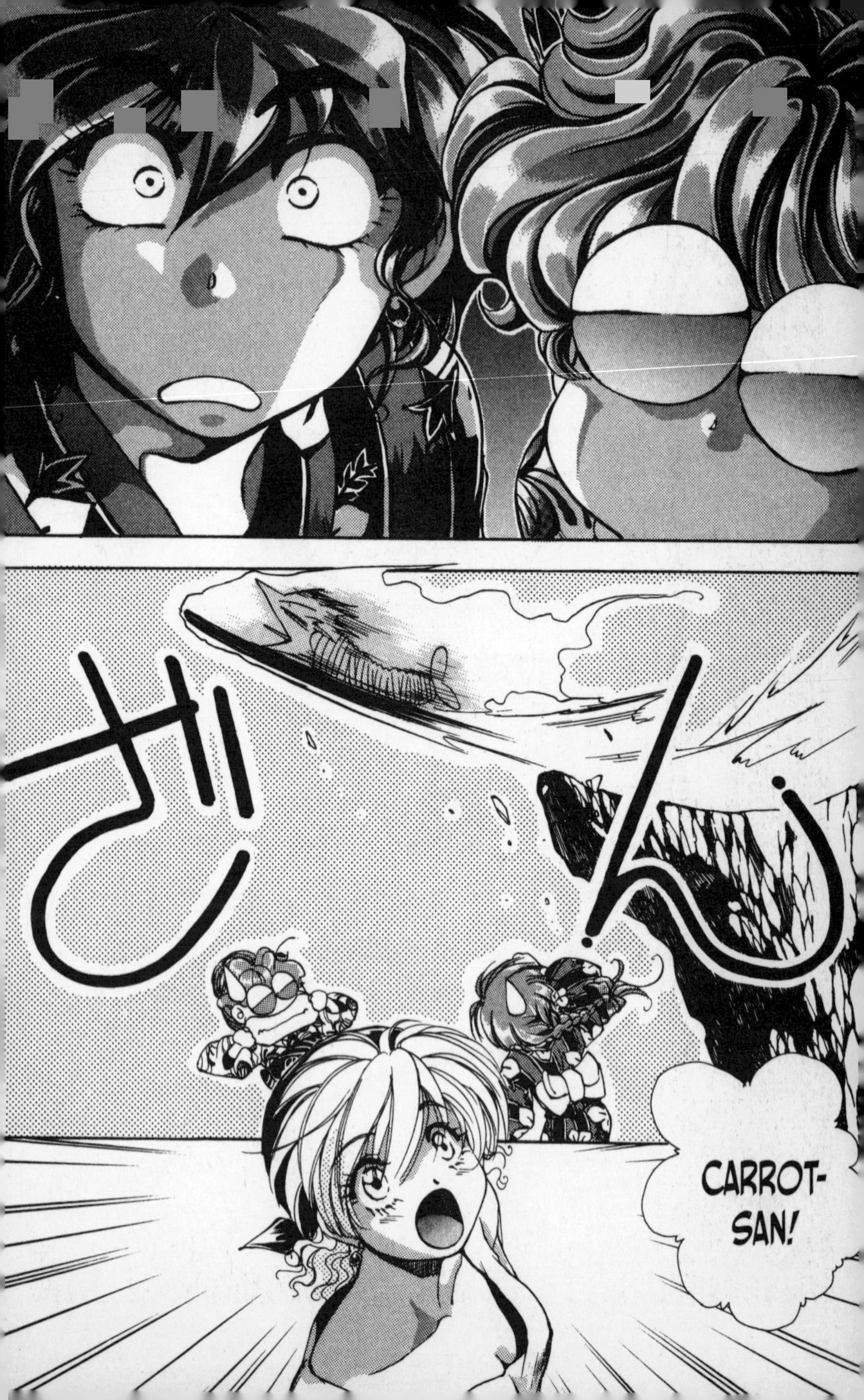
がん
CARROT-SAN!

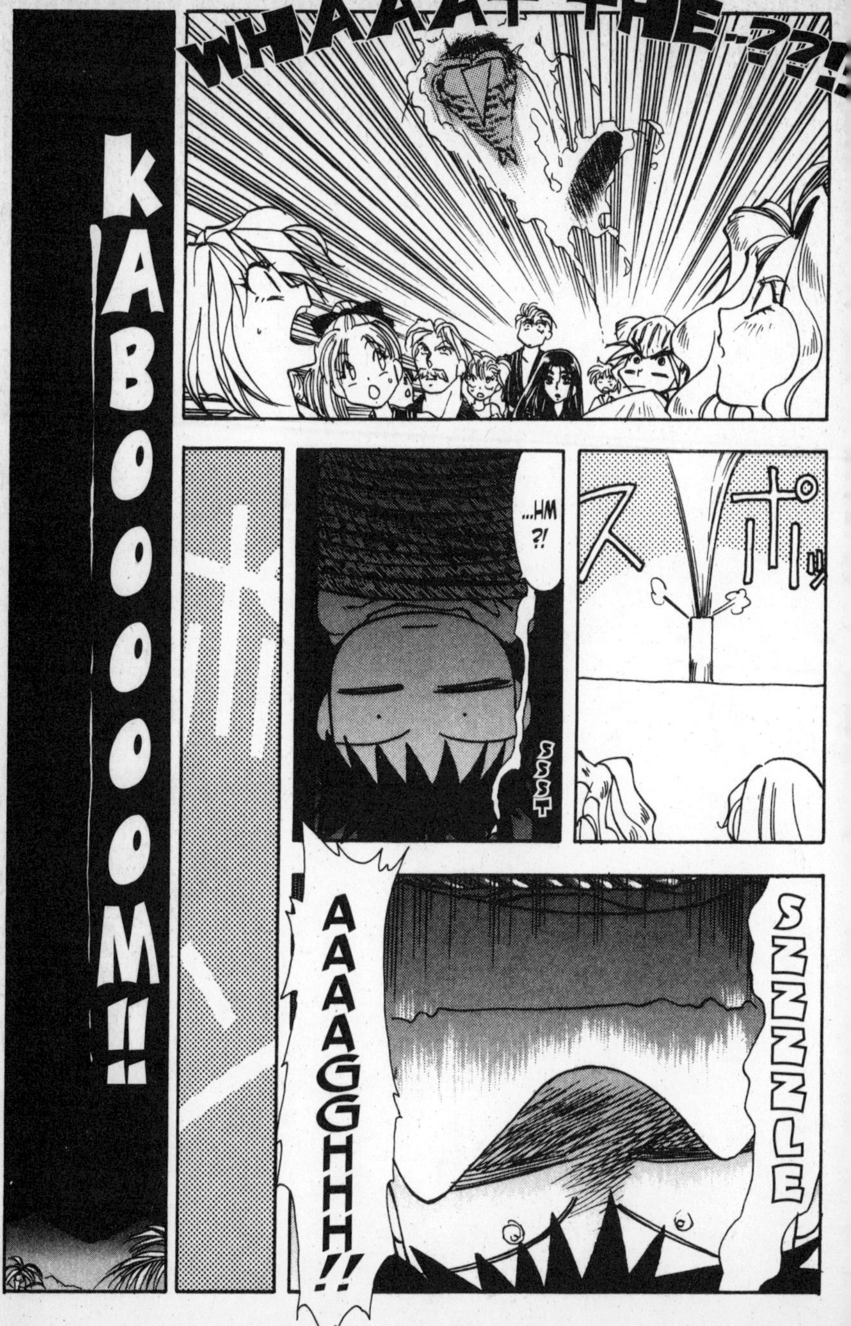
WHAAAT THE-??!!
スポッ
...HM ?!
SSST
SZZZZLE
AAAAGGHHH!!
KABOOOOOM!!

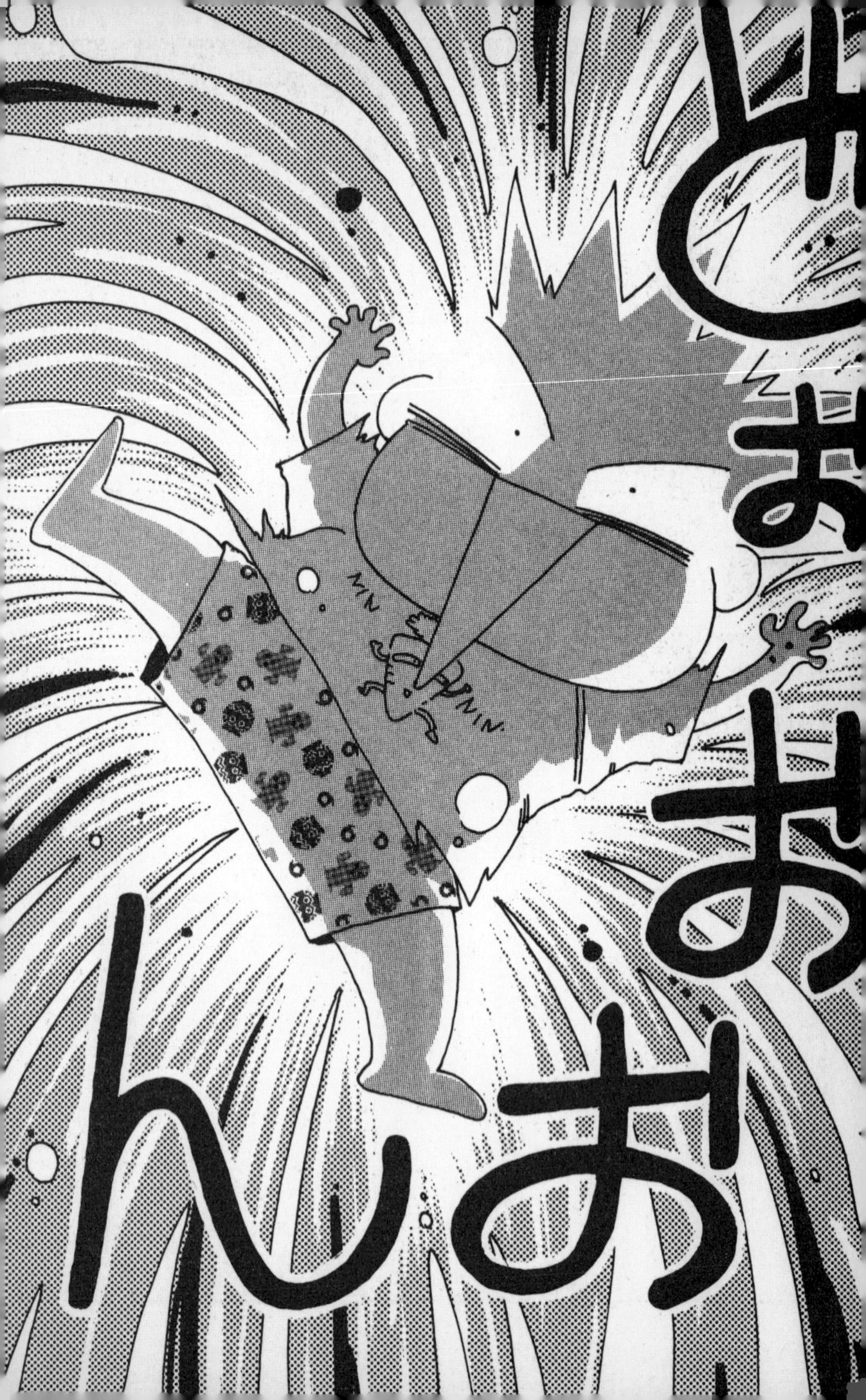
とおおおん

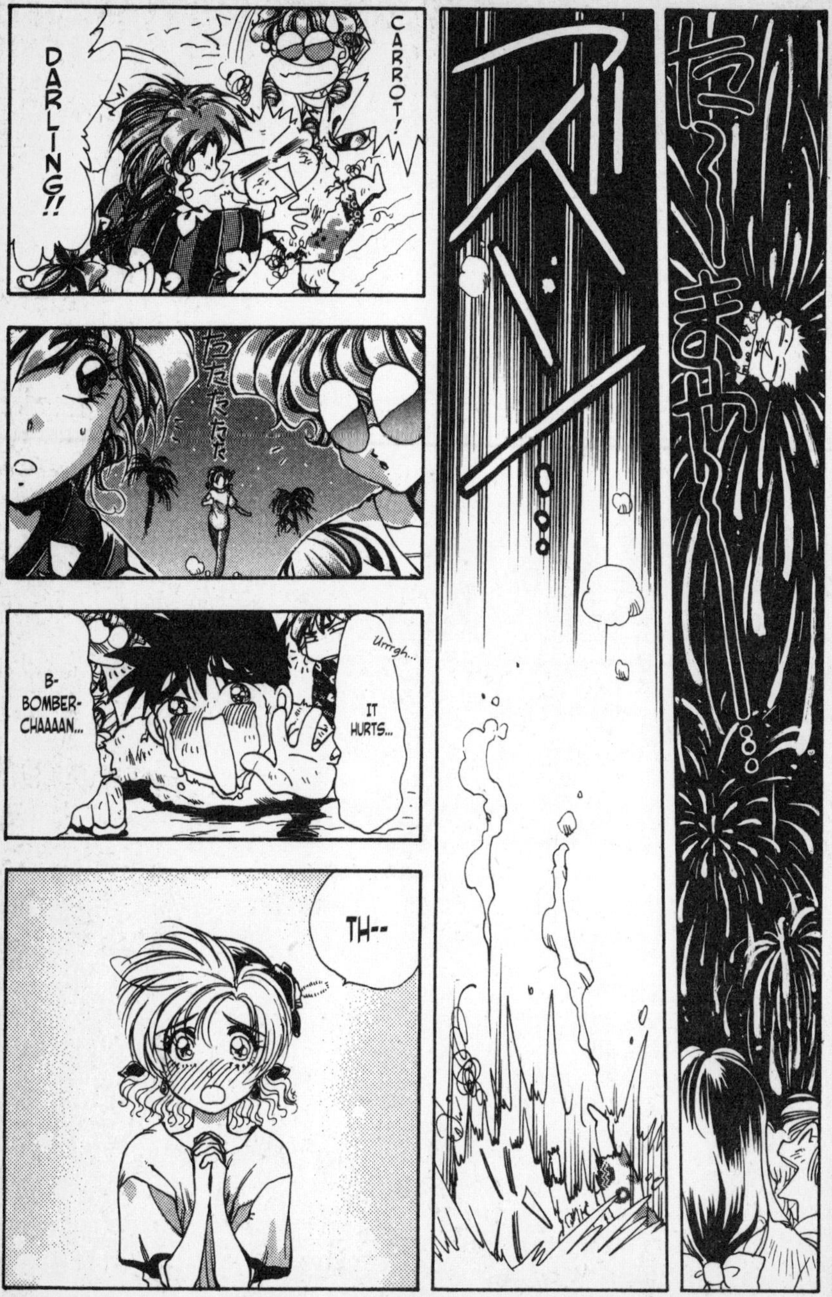
CARROT!
DARLING!!
Urrrgh...
IT HURTS...
B-BOMBER-CHAAAAN...
TH--

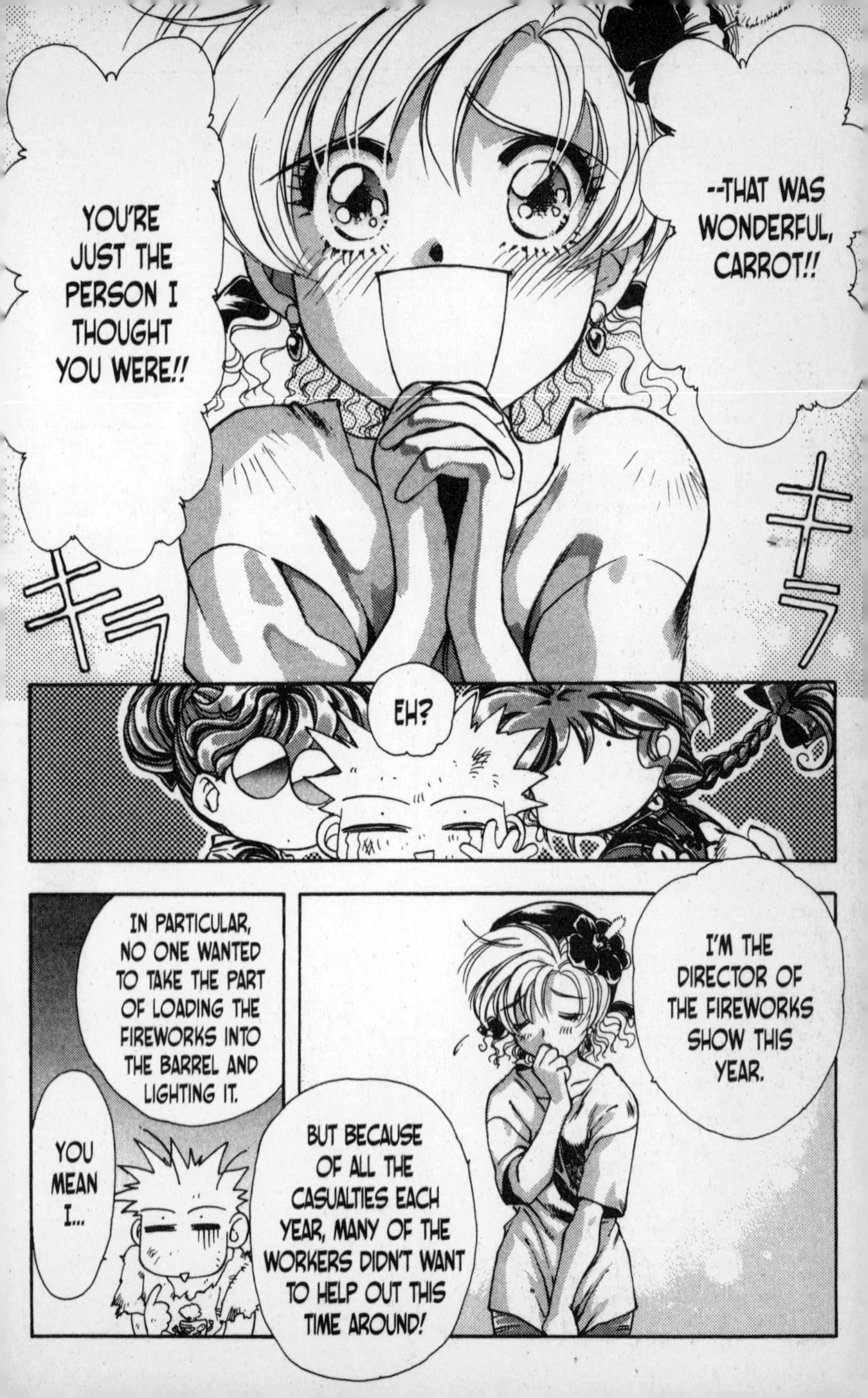
--THAT WAS WONDERFUL, CARROT!!
YOU'RE JUST THE PERSON I THOUGHT YOU WERE!!
キラ
キラ
EH?
I'M THE DIRECTOR OF THE FIREWORKS SHOW THIS YEAR.
BUT BECAUSE OF ALL THE CASUALTIES EACH YEAR, MANY OF THE WORKERS DIDN'T WANT TO HELP OUT THIS TIME AROUND!
IN PARTICULAR, NO ONE WANTED TO TAKE THE PART OF LOADING THE FIREWORKS INTO THE BARREL AND LIGHTING IT.
YOU MEAN I...

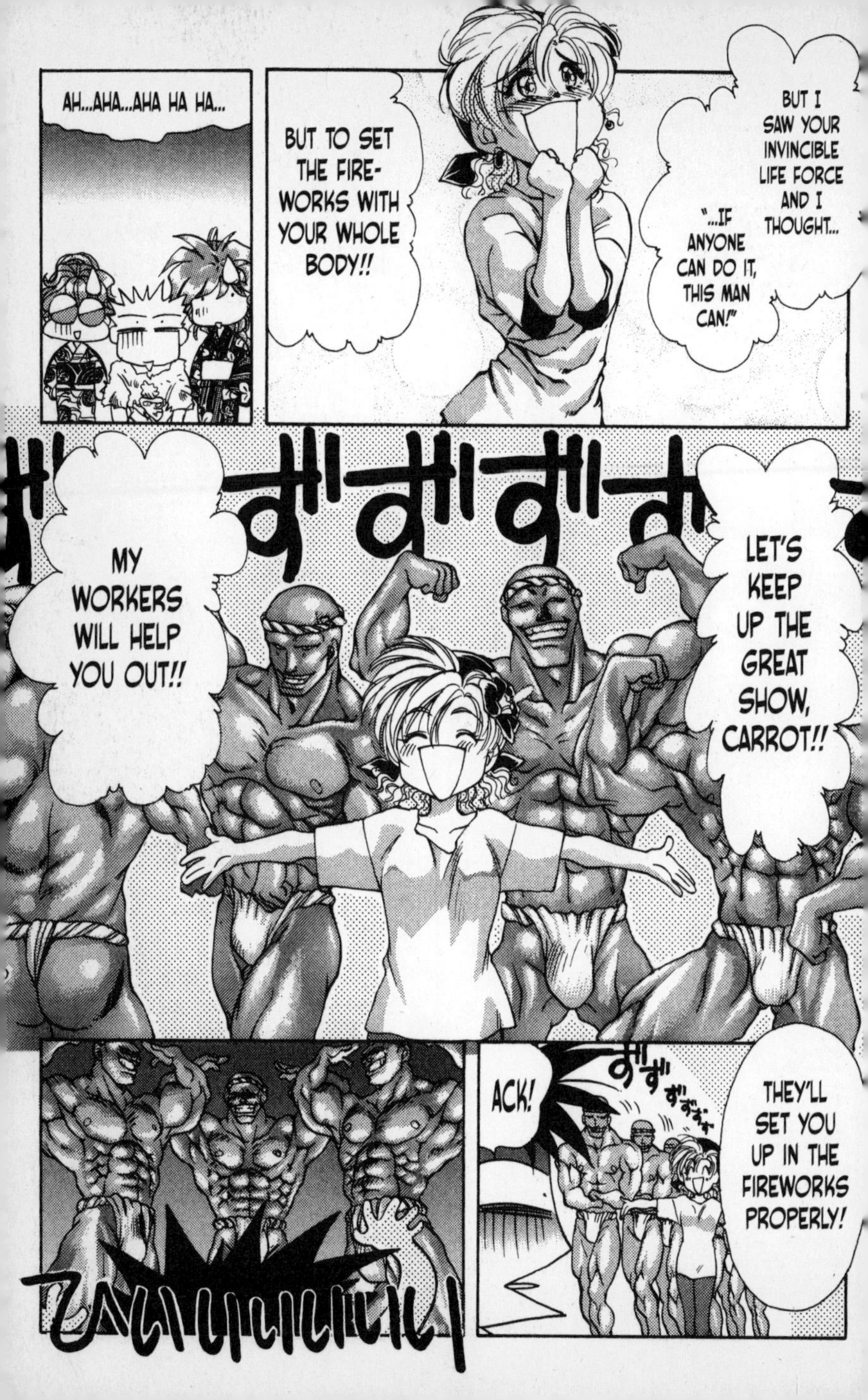
BUT I SAW YOUR INVINCIBLE LIFE FORCE AND I THOUGHT...
"...IF ANYONE CAN DO IT, THIS MAN CAN!"
BUT TO SET THE FIRE-WORKS WITH YOUR WHOLE BODY!!
AH...AHA...AHA HA HA...
LET'S KEEP UP THE GREAT SHOW, CARROT!!
MY WORKERS WILL HELP YOU OUT!!
THEY'LL SET YOU UP IN THE FIREWORKS PROPERLY!
ACK!

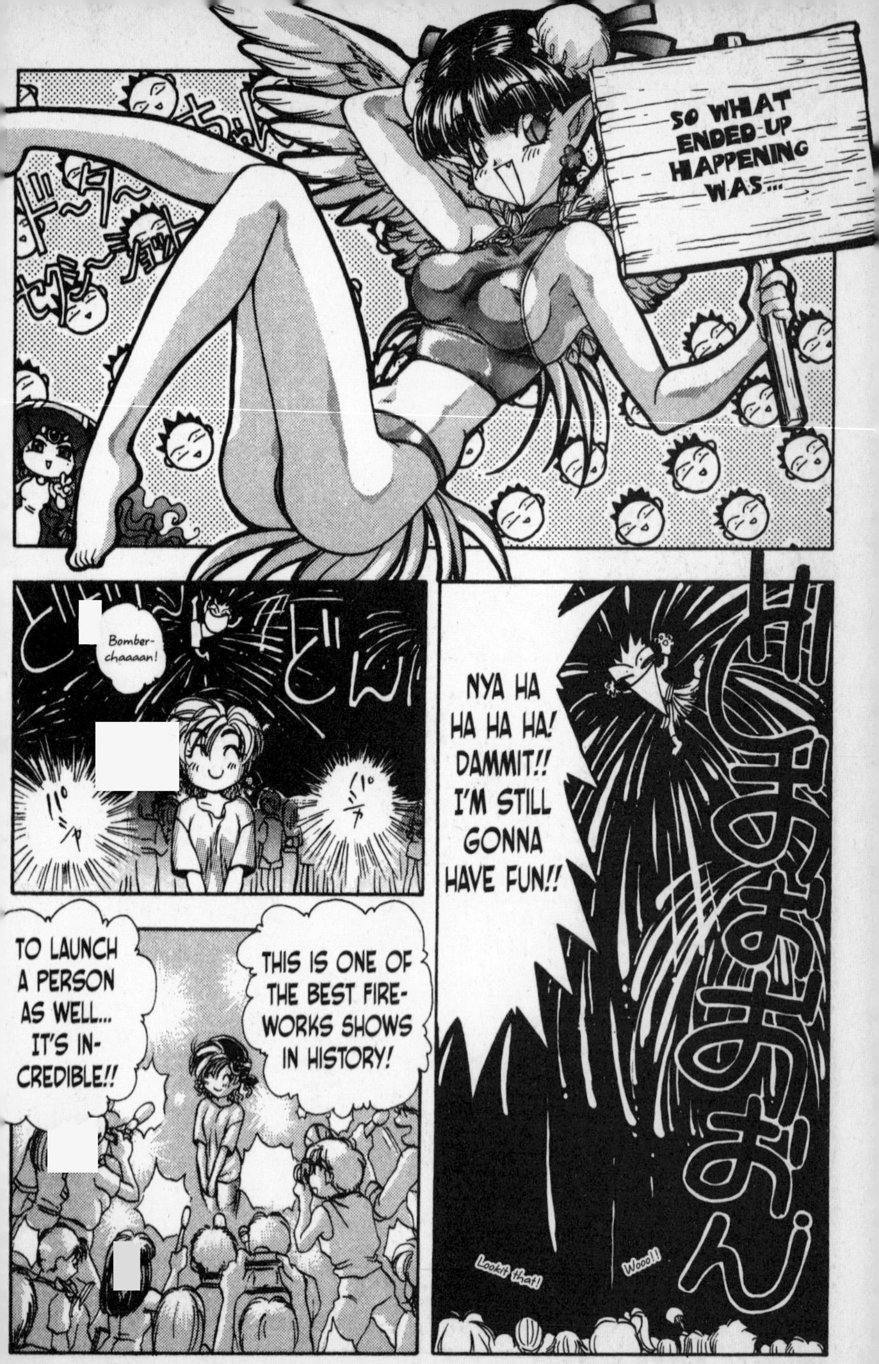
SO WHAT ENDED UP HAPPENING WAS...
NYA HA HA HA HA! DAMMIT!! I'M STILL GONNA HAVE FUN!!
Wooo!!
Lookit that!
Bomber-chaaaan!
THIS IS ONE OF THE BEST FIRE-WORKS SHOWS IN HISTORY!
TO LAUNCH A PERSON AS WELL... IT'S IN-CREDIBLE!!

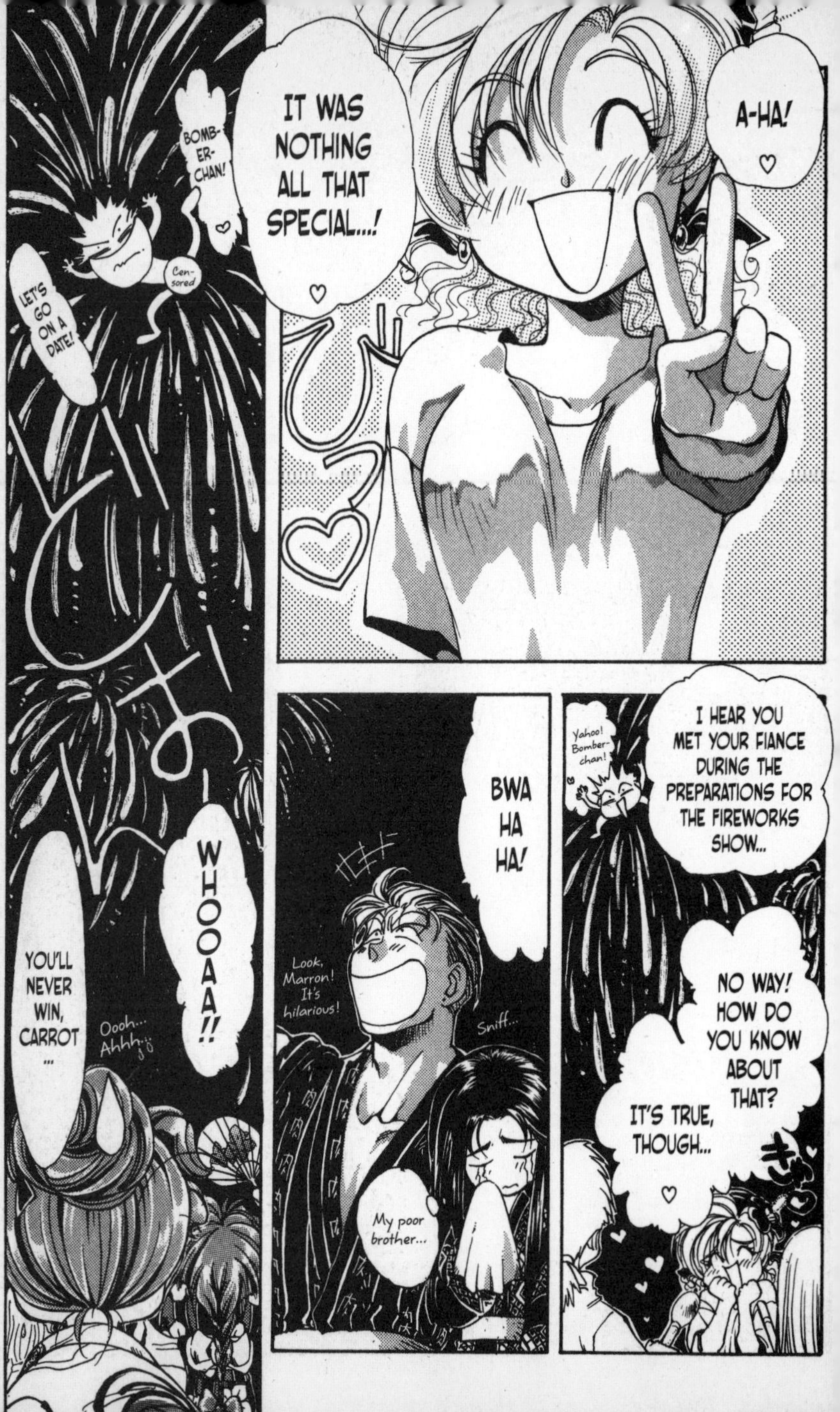
A-HA! ♥
IT WAS NOTHING ALL THAT SPECIAL...! ♥
I HEAR YOU MET YOUR FIANCE DURING THE PREPARATIONS FOR THE FIREWORKS SHOW...
Yahoo! Bomber-chan!
NO WAY! HOW DO YOU KNOW ABOUT THAT?
IT'S TRUE, THOUGH... ♥
BWA HA HA!
Look, Marron! It's hilarious!
Sniff...
My poor brother...
BOMB-ER-CHAN! ♥
Cen-sored
LET'S GO ON A DATE!
WHOOAA!!
Oooh... Ahhh...
YOU'LL NEVER WIN, CARROT ...

OMAKE

• GUESS WHO? •
WHO COULD THIS BE? IT'S CHOCOLAT!
IT'S HER FIRST DRAFT. WHY SHOULD I
LIE? THIS IS A CHOCOLAT THAT NO ONE
HAS EVER SEEN...A MYSTERY CHOCOLAT!
SHE BECAME MORE RELAXED, AND I
WANTED HER HAIRSTYLE TO HAVE A
UNIQUE STYLE--SO SHE BECAME THE
CURRENT CHOCOLAT. BUT...IT'S HARD TO
DRAW CHOCOLAT'S CURRENT HAIRSTYLE.
HER CLOTHES ARE THE SAME AS THEY
WERE IN HER FIRST APPEARANCE, AT
LEAST. BUT SHE JUST KEEPS CHANGING
HER CLOTHES. ALL OF THEM DO, REALLY...

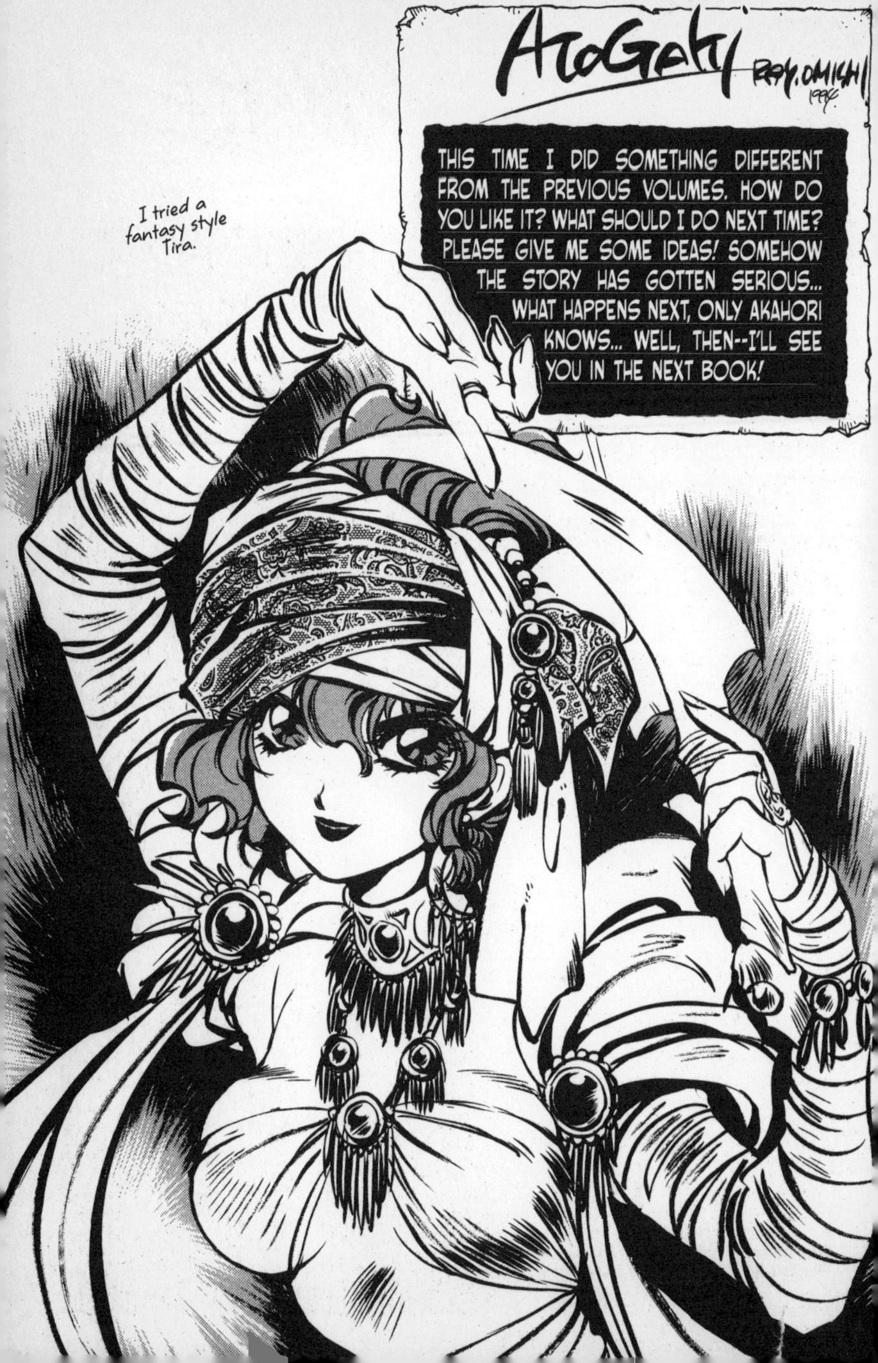
AtoGaki
RAY.OMISHI
THIS TIME I DID SOMETHING DIFFERENT FROM THE PREVIOUS VOLUMES. HOW DO YOU LIKE IT? WHAT SHOULD I DO NEXT TIME? PLEASE GIVE ME SOME IDEAS! SOMEHOW THE STORY HAS GOTTEN SERIOUS... WHAT HAPPENS NEXT, ONLY AKAHORI KNOWS... WELL, THEN--I'LL SEE YOU IN THE NEXT BOOK!
I tried a fantasy style Tira.

PREVIEW

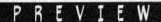

WHEN THE SORCERER HUNTERS SEEK SHELTER IN THE ZELKOVA HOUSE, THEY DISCOVER THAT THINGS MAY NOT BE AS HOSPITABLE AS THEY SEEM. CHOCOLAT, TIRA, CARROT, MARRON AND GATEAU MUST RELY ON THEIR STRENGTHS AND SKILLS IN ORDER TO SEPARATE ILLUSION FROM REALITY!

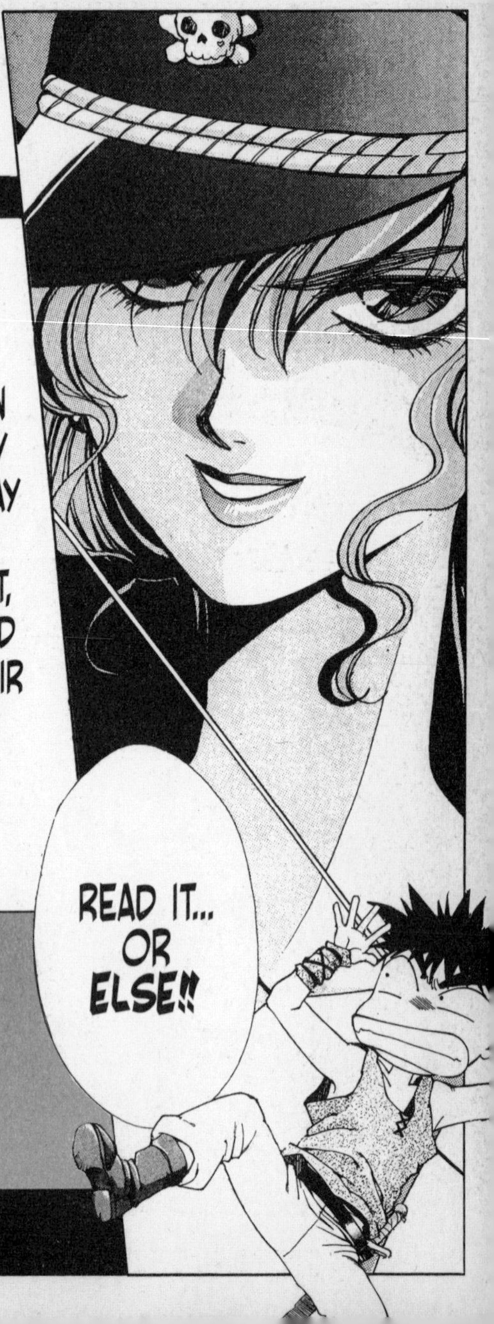
READ IT... OR ELSE!!

Ai from *Princess Ai*

TOKYOPOP® SHOP

WWW.TOKYOPOP.COM/SHOP

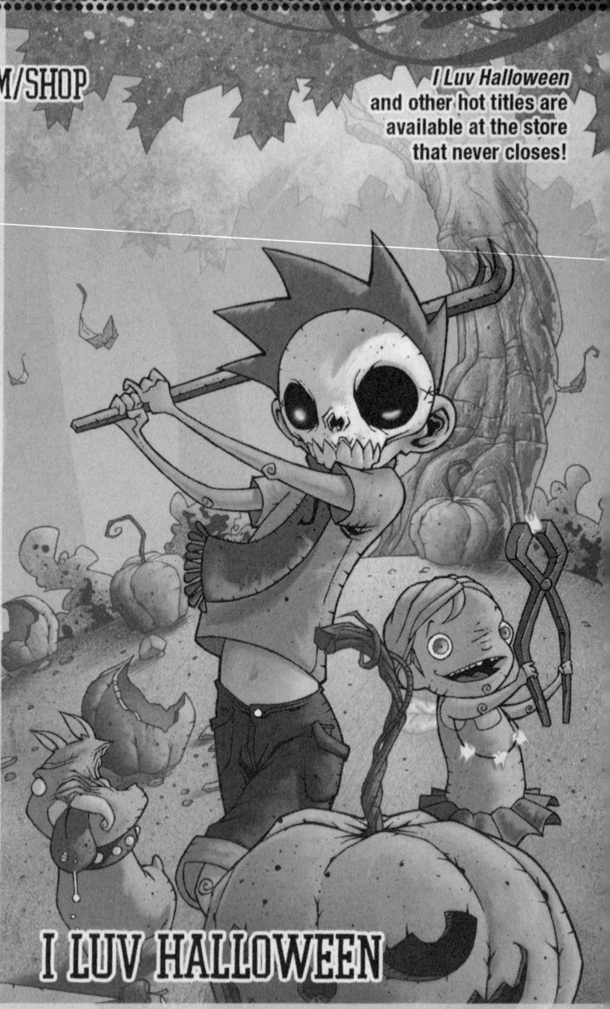

I Luv Halloween and other hot titles are available at the store that never closes!
I LUV HALLOWEEN

HOT NEWS!

Check out the TOKYOPOP SHOP! The world's best collection of manga in English is now available online in one place!

KAMICHAMA KARIN

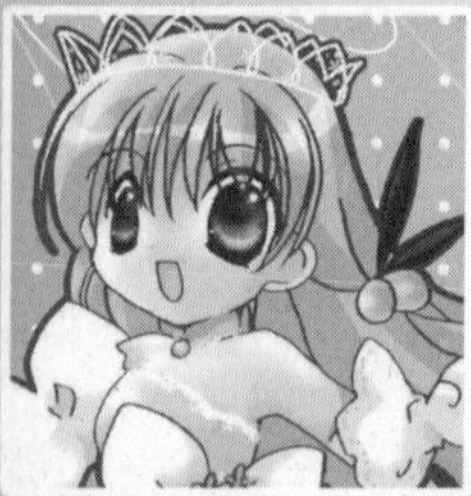

KANPAI!

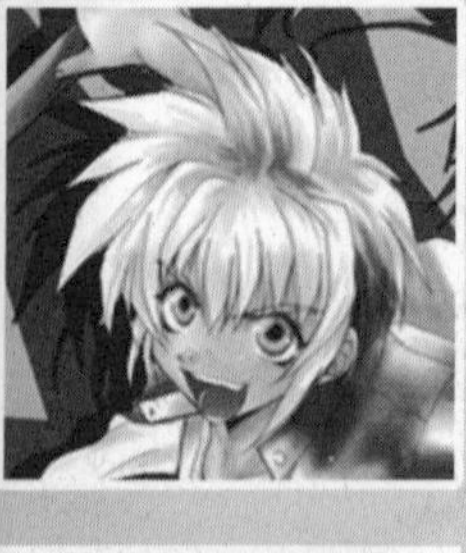

WWW.TOKYOPOP.COM/SHOP

0 00000 00000 0

- LOOK FOR SPECIAL OFFERS
- PRE-ORDER UPCOMING RELEASES
- COMPLETE YOUR COLLECTIONS

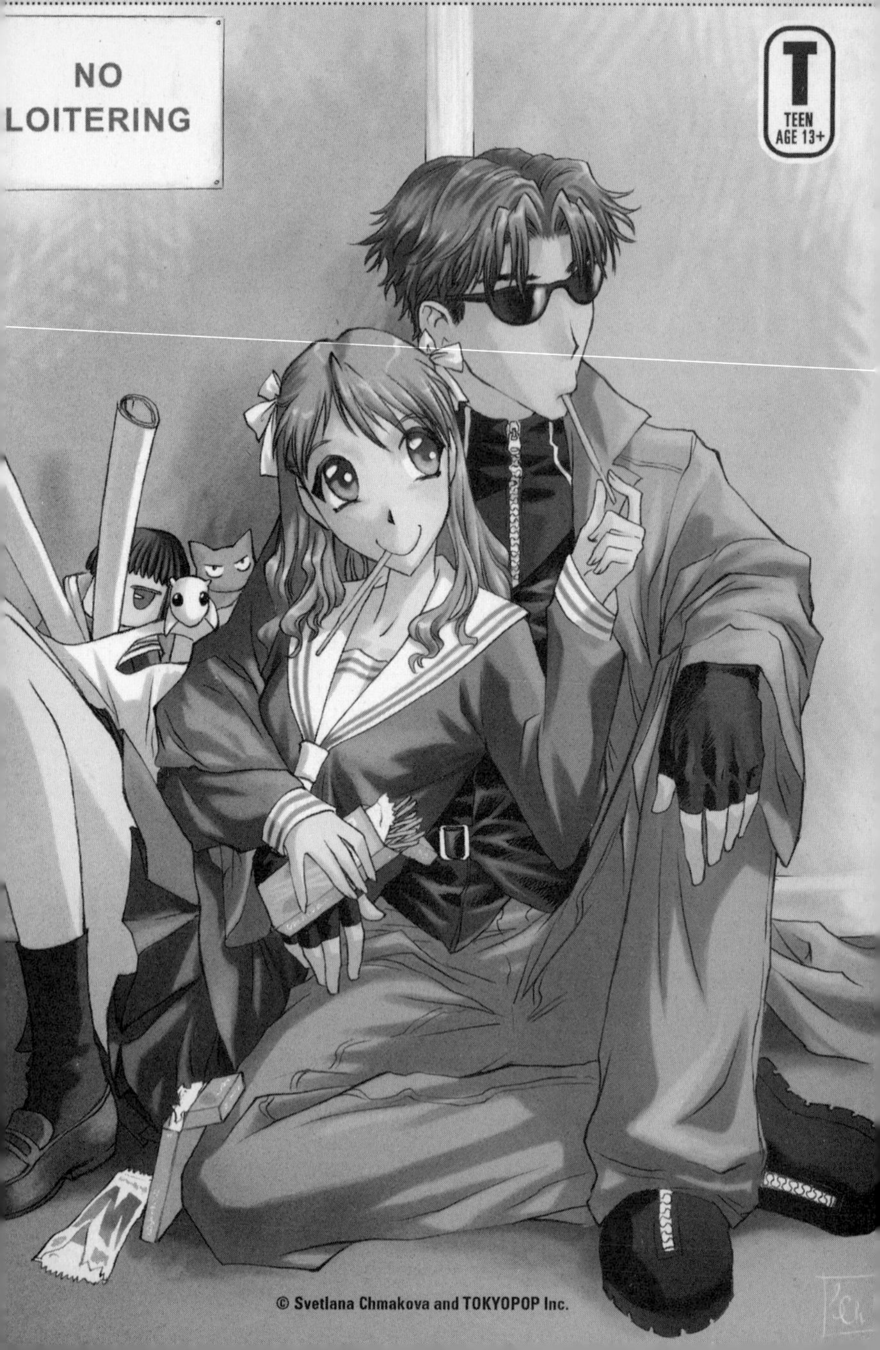
NO
LOITERING
T
TEEN
AGE 13+

DRAMACON ™

Sometimes even two's a crowd.

When Christie settles in the Artist Alley of her first-ever anime convention, she only sees it as an opportunity to promote the comic she has started with her boyfriend. But conventions are never what you expect, and soon a whirlwind of events sweeps Christie off her feet and changes her life. Who is the mysterious cosplayer that won't even take off his sunglasses indoors? What do you do when you fall in love with a guy who is going to be miles away from you in just a couple of days?

CREATED BY SVETLANA CHMAKOVA, CREATOR OF MANGA-STYLE ONLINE COMICS "CHASING RAINBOWS" AND "NIGHT SILVER"!

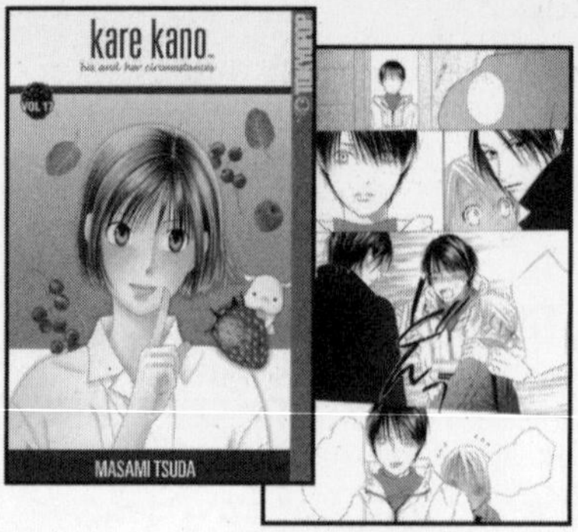
kare kano
MASAMI TSUDA

BY MASAMI TSUDA

KARE KANO

Kare Kano has a fan following for a reason: believable, well-developed characters. Of course, the art is phenomenal, ranging from sugary sweet to lightning-bolt powerful. But above all, Masami Tsuda's refreshing concept—a high school king and queen decide once and for all to be honest with each other (and more importantly, themselves)—succeeds because Tsuda-sensei allows us to know her characters as well as she does. Far from being your typical high school shojo, *Kare Kano* delves deep into the psychology of what would normally just be protagonists, antagonists and supporting cast to create a satisfying journey that is far more than the sum of its parts.

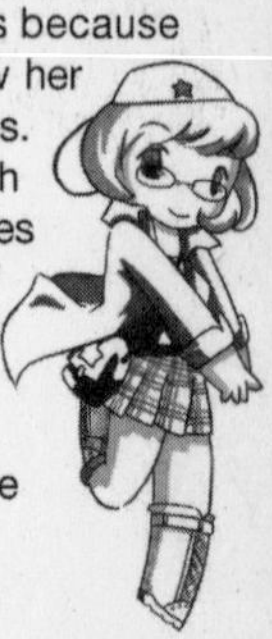

~Carol Fox, Editor

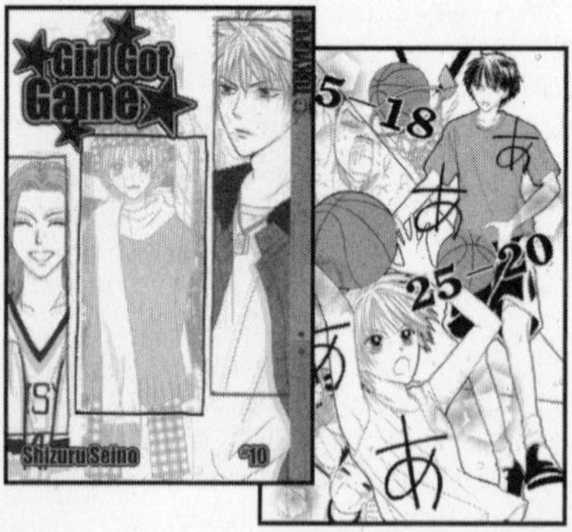
Girl Got Game
Shizuru Seino

BY SHIZURU SEINO

GIRL GOT GAME

There's a fair amount of cross-dressing shojo sports manga out there (no, really), but *Girl Got Game* really sets itself apart by having an unusually charming and very funny story. The art style is light and fun, and Kyo spazzing out always cracks me up. The author throws in a lot of great plot twists, and the great side characters help to make the story just that much more special. Sadly, we're coming up on the final volume, but I give this series credit for not letting the romance drag out unnecessarily or endlessly revisiting the same dilemmas. I'm really looking forward to seeing how the series wraps up!

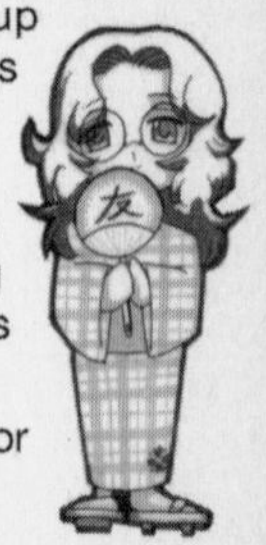

~Lillian M. Diaz-Przybyl, Jr. Editor

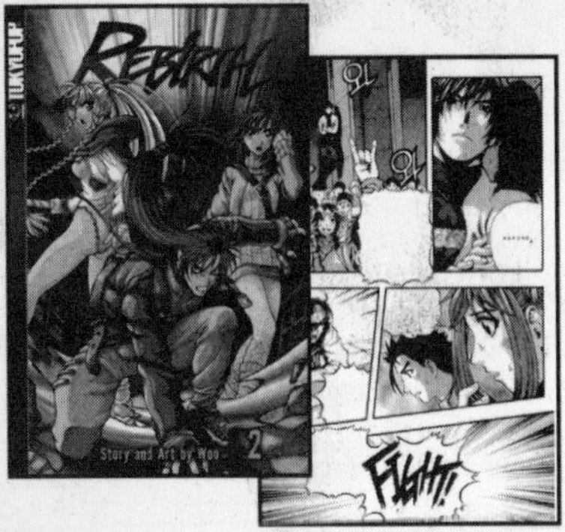
Rebirth
TOKYOPOP
Story and Art by Woo
2
FIGHT!

BY WOO

REBIRTH

Every manga fan has their "first love." For me, that book is *Rebirth.* I've worked on this series in one fashion or another since its debut, and this epic, action-packed vampire tale has never yet let me down. *Rebirth* is a book that defies expectations as well as first impressions. Yes, it's got the dark, brooding vampire antihero. And, sure, there's lots of bloodshed and tight-bodied maidens in peril. But creator Woo has interwoven an enthralling tale of revenge and redemption that, at its heart, is a truly heartbreaking tragedy. Were you a fan of TV's *Angel*? Do you read Anne Rice? Well, my friend, *Rebirth* is for you!

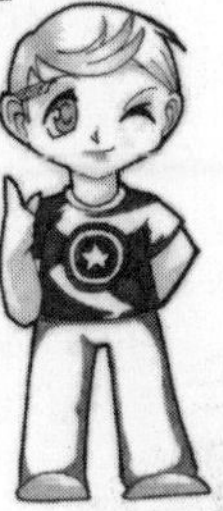

~Bryce P. Coleman, Editor

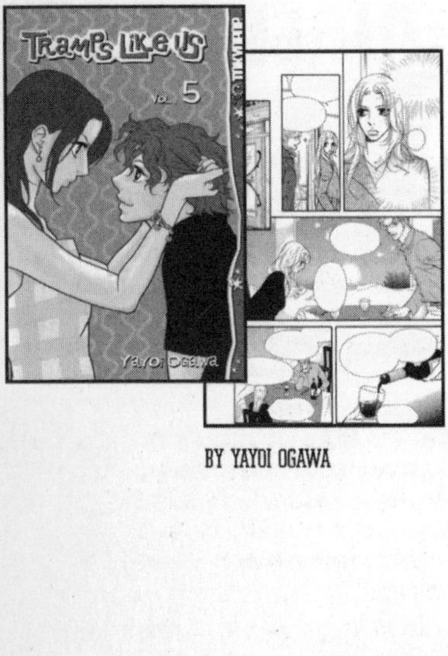
Tramps Like Us
TOKYOPOP
Vol. 5
Yayoi Ogawa

BY YAYOI OGAWA

TRAMPS LIKE US

Thrillingly erotic but relentlessly realistic, *Tramps Like Us* turns gender stereotypes on their head. Sumire Iwaya, a beautiful and busy news exec, is disappointed by the men in her life. So she takes in a gorgeous young boy and makes him her pet. As a man, am I offended? Not really. Actually, I find it really sweet. Sumire is no wide-eyed, skirted, young manga vixen. She's tall, womanly, with a wide mouth and serious, appraising eyes. Momo is cute as a puppy one minute, graceful and petite the next. But the book only indulges the fantasy aspect partway. The abnormal situation gets awkward and even burden-some. I love it. And the tone Carol Fox sets in the English adaptation is one of the best around.

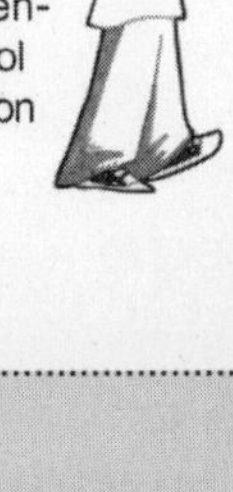

~Luis Reyes, Editor

STOP!

This is the back of the book.
You wouldn't want to spoil a great ending!

This book is printed "manga-style," in the authentic Japanese right-to-left format. Since none of the artwork has been flipped or altered, readers get to experience the story just as the creator intended. You've been asking for it, so TOKYOPOP® delivered: authentic, hot-off-the-press, and far more fun!

DIRECTIONS

If this is your first time reading manga-style, here's a quick guide to help you understand how it works.

It's easy... just start in the top right panel and follow the numbers. Have fun, and look for more 100% authentic manga from TOKYOPOP®!